Brides of Christ, Martyrs for Russia

Brides of Christ, Martyrs for Russia

Mother Catherine Abrikosova and the Eastern Rite Dominican Sisters

Irina Osipova, Compiler and General Editor

Memorial Center for Information and Education
"Repressions of Clergy and Laity, 1918-1953"
Moscow, Russia

Geraldine Kelley, Translator

Originally published as
Vozliubiv Boga i sleduia za Nim:
Goneniia na russkikh katolikov v SSSR
[Having Fallen in Love with God and Now Following Him:
Persecutions of Russian Catholics in the USSR]
Moscow: Serebrianye niti, 1999

ISBN: 978-0-578-14523-5

Photos courtesy of Irina Osipova and Dominikanki Misjonarki, Zielonka, Poland.
Maps prepared by Christopher Rice, Colorado Cartographics, Ltd.
Cover and layout design by Jonathan Gullery
Cover photo courtesy of www.catholicmartyrs.org

Printed in the United States of America

Contents

TRANSLATOR'S INTRODUCTION

IRINA Ivanovna Osipova and her colleagues at Memorial Center for Information and Education have given us a treasure trove of materials about the persecution of Catholics under the Soviet regime. The present work is the second of two on this theme. Catholics of the Latin Rite, primarily those of German, Polish, and Belorussian heritage who resided within the Russian Empire, were the subject of an earlier work, published in 1996 and translated as *Hide Me Within Thy Wounds* (Fargo, North Dakota, 2003). The present work treats the persecution of those who became members of a fledgling Russian Eastern Rite of the Catholic Church, the existence of which dates to the early twentieth century. In other words, it had barely come into being when the hammer of persecution fell upon it. Thus references herein to "Russian Catholics" will mean Catholics who belong to the Russian [Eastern] Rite of the Catholic Church, not Russians who converted to Latin Rite Catholicism.

In the few years of its relatively free existence, the Russian Catholic Church had three main centers: St. Petersburg, Moscow and Saratov. Not much is recounted about the Saratov community; the St. Petersburg community, however, was thoroughly described in a work published in 1966 about Exarch Leonid Feodorov.[1] The Moscow Russian Rite community until now has remained much less known. After referring her readers to Basil von Burman's work about the St. Petersburg community, Osipova focuses in the present work almost exclusively on the Moscow community, known by its leaders as the Abrikosov community. The exception is her inclusion of the Leningrad investigation files (in Appendix 1) and the biographies of Leningrad Russian Catholics (in Appendix 5). The biographies have not been included in this translation. They have been translated and are available online at https://biographies.library.nd.edu.

1 Deacon Vasilii von Burman, OSB, *Leonid Fëdorov: Zhizn' i deiatel'nost'* [Leonid Feodorov: Life and Work], (Rome, 1966).

The non-Russian reader may find helpful some words about topics that will provide some context to the reading. A list of recommended titles in English follows the Appendices.

Corrective labor camps. The sentencing documents consistently used this euphemism for "forced labor camps." (The Soviets denied the existence of forced labor camps.) How these began, what their economic value was, their "re-education" value, etc. – all these topics and more have been thoroughly explored in Anne Applebaum's *Gulag: A History.* We note only her words: "From Aktyubinsk to Yakutsk, there was not a single major population center that did not have its own local camp or camps, and not a single industry that did not employ prisoners." The root of the Russian word for camp – *lager'* – is usually the suffix for the camp name: thus, Bamlag (the Baikal-Amur Magistral Camp), Siblag (Siberian Camp), Sevvostoklag (Northeast Camp). There were over 30,000 camps, the larger ones with more than twenty-five thousand prisoners, and smaller ones with fewer than five thousand.

Solovetsky Special Purpose Camp deserves special mention as one of the first camps, and one that was especially designated for members of the clergy of all faiths. This dreaded camp was originally a complex of Orthodox monasteries on islands in the White Sea.

During the early years of the regime, to process the large number of "offenders" more expeditiously, local three-person boards ("troikas") were authorized to issue sentences of up to three years without having to consult with higher authorities. They readily did so – and many of the early sentences are for the three-year term. But time flies, and people sentenced to three-year terms were soon flooding back into the metropolitan areas, carrying shocking tales of woe. What to do? Some were simply resentenced to another three-year term; others were released with severe restrictions on place of residence, in many cases resulting in their continuing to live in remote areas for many years after the official completion of their original term. Over time, longer sentences became more common, and after World War II 25-year sentences were being meted out.

Internal exile. A concept that had been in use throughout several centuries in Russia, internal exile under the Communist regime resulted in the far-flung relocation of large numbers of people. In 1930 and 1931 alone,

Stalin banished close to two million peasants into internal exile.[2] Once arrived at the point of exile, the convict or "administratively exiled person" would have to find lodging (perhaps becoming a boarder in a local home) and some form of employment approved by the local security organs. In a highly unusual move, local authorities allowed at least one of the Dominican Sisters to teach while serving out her term of exile in Siberia. After 1932, internal passports were required, as well as residency permits, and thus even upon completion of a term of exile, the right to return to one's home city or village was not guaranteed.

Residence restrictions, as a sentence or as an addition to a term of exile. At first the only "off limit" cities for those returning from exile were the three capital cities (Moscow, St. Petersburg and Kiev). Gradually the list grew. Odessa, Kharkov and Rostov brought the number to six. The list grew to twelve with the addition of capital cities of other union republics. By the 1940s it had grown to 135.[3] As for the borderland regions, "border zones" were established in 1934; in most places they were 7.5 kilometers, but up to 90 kilometers deep along the Estonian border.

Rehabilitation. After Stalin's death in 1953, and especially after Khrushchev's denunciation of the excesses of the Stalin personality cult, it became possible to have one's file reviewed. The faulty evidence, the shoddy investigations, the tortured confessions – all came to light. Thus many had their terms cut short and were released. Their record could be cleared and they were considered "rehabilitated."

St. Louis des Français Church. Built in 1789 under Catherine the Great for French residents in Moscow, this church was across the street from Lubyanka Prison and thus under constant surveillance. It was under the protection of the French embassy and staffed by priests from the Assumptionist Order; after 1934 these priests were from the United States (Assumption College, Worcester, Massachusetts). Frs. Leopold Braun and Antoine Laberge figure in the stories recounted herein.[4]

Political Red Cross. An organization that existed in the tsarist period to

---

[2] Lynne Viola, *The Unknown Gulag: The Lost World of Stalin's Special Settlements* (Oxford, 2007), p. 2.

[3] Rossi, *The Gulag Handbook*, p. 235.

[4] See Leopold Braun, *In Lubianka's Shadow: The Memoirs of an American Priest in Stalin's Moscow, 1934-1945*, Ed. G.M. Hamburg (Notre Dame, Ind.: Univ. of Notre Dame, 2006), for the intriguing story of this parish and helpful background to some of the incidents recounted herein.

assist the families of persons imprisoned for political reasons. It continued in existence until 1937, and its archives have thousands of case files that provide a look at the conditions of the families of those arrested. A sample has been assembled and edited by Irina Osipova and Lia Dolzhanskaia, *Dorogaia Ekaterina Pavlovna* [Dear Catherine Pavlovna] (St. Petersburg, 2005). Catherine Pavlovna Peshkova, Maxim Gorky's wife, headed the organization and the letters are often directed to her.

Acknowledgements

IT has been a privilege to work so closely with the stories of the Dominican Sisters of the Abrikosova community and I am deeply indebted to Irina Osipova for allowing me to bring her work to English readers. My work would not have been possible without her painstaking archival work, and I wish to acknowledge the debt we have to her and all who assisted her in the original compilation of these valuable materials. She has graciously provided many of the photographs that appeared in the original work.

Sister Maria Gemma Marek, OP, of the Dominican Sisters of Mary, Mother of the Eucharist, who studied in Russia prior to entering the community, knew of the Abrikosova Dominican Sisters and has encouraged me with this project since the very beginning. She kindly prepared translations of the litanies and the poetry. In addition, she responded to inquires about Dominican customs, located remote Siberian outposts on old Soviet maps, and offered valuable suggestions with respect to the translation.

The Dominican Missionaries of Jesus and Mary, Zielonka, Poland, who befriended and assisted the surviving Abrikosova Dominicans in their later years in Vilnius, graciously shared photographs from their archives. Christopher Rice of Colorado Cartographics patiently worked with an ever-changing list of data points to create the four maps that accompany this translation. I am also grateful to Father Alexey Yandushev-Rumyantsev, Postulator for the cause of the Russian New Martyrs, for permission to use a photograph of Mother Catherine. Natasha Lyandres, Russian and East European Studies Curator and Head of Rare Books and Special Collections at the University of Notre Dame, oversaw the creation of a website that presents translations of brief biographies of almost 1,900 Catholics who were repressed in the USSR; these biographical sketches provide an important supplement to the present work and can be accessed at https://biographies.library.nd.edu. Along the way, I have been encouraged by Professor Paul Kengor of Grove City College and Professor Dennis Dunn of Texas State

University at San Marcos, whose assessment of the value of the work has been most appreciated. Reaching into the distant past, I remember fondly and acknowledge the gift given me by my Russian language teachers at Indiana University.

Finally, I owe an incalculable debt of gratitude to an unknown army of religious and lay Dominicans and family and friends who have been recruited to pray for the success of this endeavor – to the glory of God. May He be forever blessed in all His angels and in His saints!

Geraldine Kelley
August 8, 2014
Feast of St. Dominic

Editor's Introduction to Russian Edition

RUSSIAN Catholics have never fared well in their own homeland. Under the tsars, they were persecuted by State authorities and the Orthodox Church, and then the Bolshevik regime, upon seizing power in November 1917, intensified that persecution with still greater ferocity. Even the tsar's much-vaunted 1905 decree on religious toleration failed to extend that religious toleration to Russian [i.e., Eastern Rite] Catholics. Only under the Provisional Government (February-November 1917) did these Catholics enjoy a fleeting period of normalcy. We will attempt to trace briefly the stages of their struggle for the unrestricted exercise of freedom of religion.[1]

The first Catholic community in Russia dates to the 1680s with the arrival of the Jesuit mission in Moscow during the regency of Tsarevna Sophia. Sophia was overthrown in 1689 and anti-western views, inimical to Catholicism, gained ground. The Jesuits were expelled from the country and the Russian Catholic community ceased to exist.

In the eighteenth and nineteenth centuries many of Russia's leading intellectuals were sympathetic to Catholicism, and it became their spiritual footing in the internal polemics between Westernizers and Slavophiles about the best path forward for Russia. The most prominent among them were Prince Peter Kozlovsky, a distinguished diplomat; the Decembrist Michael Lunin; and the Russian philosopher, Peter Chaadayev. Sophia Svechina, from a prominent family of the nobility, also made a vivid imprint on nascent Russian Catholicism, but after becoming a Catholic she was forced to abandon the fatherland and settle in Paris.

We must also mention Prince Ivan Gagarin, a church historian and publicist, the head of the Parisian circle of Russian émigré Catholics and

---

[1] Translator's Note: The Russian resource cited for this Introduction has not been translated; an excellent English resource for background information is Dennis J. Dunn, *The Catholic Church and Russia: Popes, Patriarchs, Tsars and Commissars*. Burlington, Vt.: Ashgate, 2004

one of the best-known figures of the nineteenth century. He founded the Slavonic Library in Paris and the journal Etudes, and later became a Jesuit. Other Russian émigrés in Paris who also became Jesuits included the church historian and journalist Father Ivan Martynov and Fathers Eugene Balabin and Paul Pirling. It should be noted that all conversions to Catholicism were prosecuted by law and thus those who converted were forced either to keep their conversion secret or emigrate from Russia to avoid arrest (the rejection of the state religion – Orthodoxy – was considered a punishable crime against the state).

The real founders of the Catholic movement in Russia were two people who proposed a uniquely Russian insight that envisioned a path to unity with Rome while preserving the fullness of the Eastern Christian tradition. These were the distinguished Russian philosopher Vladimir Soloviev (1853-1900) and the church writer Princess Elizabeth Volkonskaya (1838-1897). Their writings exemplified "two facets of Russian Catholic thought, like two mutually enriching psychological approaches to one and the same truth."

By the end of the nineteenth century one could speak of the beginning of an Eastern Rite Russian Catholic Church. Its inception dates from the clandestine conversion to Catholicism of two Orthodox priests: Father Nicholay Tolstoy in 1894 and Father Alexey Zerchaninov in 1896. Their conversions coincided with a general movement toward the renewal of church life in the Eastern Rites of the Catholic Church. In Russia, however, they found themselves in difficult straits: the Latin Rite hierarchy did not accept them, and the Orthodox Church and the tsarist government persecuted them.

The April 17, 1905, promulgation of a tsarist decree on religious toleration finally brought about the long-awaited freedom of religious confession and became the legal basis for conversion, for example, from Orthodoxy to Catholicism. True, the requirement that the conversion be to a Western Rite was a serious restriction (the Eastern Rites were, as before, forbidden), but Soloviev's proposal for preserving the Russian religious and cultural tradition and harmonizing it with Catholicism continued to attract much interest even after his premature death in 1900.

In 1907, Pope Pius X verbally authorized Andrey Sheptytsky, the Byzantine Catholic Metropolitan in Lemberg [Lviv], to undertake "uniate" work in Russia. Metropolitan Sheptytsky then accepted Father Alexey Zerchaninov into his jurisdiction and sent him to Russia as his delegate with the directive that he "observe the Byzantine Slavic rite in all its purity, without deviation."[2]

The reactionary policies that the tsarist government implemented following the first Russian revolution in 1905 greatly worsened the situation of the Catholic Church in general, but the activity of a certain group in Saint Petersburg that vigorously pursued the idea of church unification particularly aroused the deep suspicions of state authorities and Orthodox hierarchs. Supported by Natalia Ushakova, a pupil of Soloviev and an ardent Catholic, these Russian Catholics followed the Orthodox Rite but confessed the teachings of the Catholic Church and recognized the Roman Pontiff as the head of the Universal Church. Furthermore, acting against tsarist restrictions on foreign confessions, their priests preached in Russian.[3]

After lengthy negotiations with the authorities, the Russian Catholics were able to open the first Eastern Rite Catholic Church in Saint Petersburg in 1909, where Father Alexey Zerchaninov became the pastor. Other priests soon came to serve in this new parish: Father Johannes Deibner, a pupil of Soloviev who had been secretly ordained by Metropolitan Sheptytsky, and Father Eustace Susalev, an Old Believer who had converted to Catholicism.

Father Leonid Feodorov, who had been ordained in Constantinople by the bishop of Eastern Rite Bulgarian Catholics and had made three visits to Saint Petersburg, managed to quell the differences that arose among the priests of this small community. Thanks to his presence, the activity of the Russian Catholic community intensified and expanded – the community by that time numbered as many as 700 members.

The first issue of *Word of Truth* [Slovo Istiny], the journal of the Russian Catholics, came out on January 7, 1913, and publicly set forth the community's "manifesto," which called for the unification of the Catholic and Orthodox Churches. The journal caused a scandal and on February 21, 1913, the authorities closed the Russian Catholic Church.

Meanwhile, a community of Russian Catholics had sprung up in

---

[2] Translator's Note: In so doing, he was following the directive of Pope Pius X, "Nec plus, nec minus, nec aliter." See "History of the Russian Catholic Church," at *www.rumkatkilise.org* .

[3] Translator's Note: Catholic Churches within the Russian Empire served foreign Catholics living in the Empire usually for business or diplomatic reasons (French, German, Italian) or Catholics who had been absorbed into the Empire during its expansion (Poles, Lithuanians). To hinder the conversion of Russians to Catholicism, priests serving in these churches were restricted to preaching in the languages of these communities, and prohibited from preaching in Russian.

Moscow in 1910. It formed itself around the Abrikosovs, Vladimir and Anna, who had, with the blessing of Pope Pius X, converted to Eastern Rite Catholicism. The attempt to open an Eastern Rite chapel in their quarters was unsuccessful; the community therefore associated itself with the parish of Saints Peter and Paul. The Abrikosovs later both joined the Third Order of Saint Dominic.

After the victory of the February 1917 Revolution, the church of the Russian Catholics in Petrograd that had been sealed by the authorities in 1913 was once again opened, and with the Easter liturgy it became their official parish church. The first Russian Catholic Council was held in Petrograd from May 29 to 31, 1917, with Metropolitan Andrey Sheptytsky presiding. He officially established the Exarchy of the Eastern Rite in Russia with jurisdiction over the whole territory of tsarist Russia, excluding Ukraine and Belorussia. The metropolitan designated Father Leonid Feodorov as his representative for all Russia with the title "Mitered Protopresbyter," which was confirmed by Pope Pius XI on March 1, 1922. In addition to Exarch Feodorov, the clergy of the Russian Catholic Exarchy included nine other priests. The Provisional Government officially recognized the Russian Catholic Church on August 8, 1917.

During this same visit, Metropolitan Sheptytsky ordained Vladimir Abrikosov a priest of the Eastern Rite and appointed him the first pastor of the Moscow parish of Russian Catholics that by then numbered approximately 100 members. From August 1917, a community of Dominican nuns began in the Abrikosovs' quarters; later a community of Dominican brothers was also founded. Mother Catherine Abrikosova became the head of the religious community, which was officially recognized by the Master General of the Dominican Order in 1923.

On the initiative of Russian Catholics and supported by representatives of the Orthodox episcopate and clergy, a broad movement toward church unity was now underway in Moscow and Petrograd. Patriarch Tikhon publicly declared his support for the reconciliation of the Churches and he gave his blessing to the open lectures and discussions of the issue. True, the very idea of rapprochement was not unanimously accepted in Russian society, inasmuch as many Orthodox clergy and laity were firmly convinced that "union" was a Polish, Jesuit, papal connivance, designed to convert the Orthodox faithful to Catholicism.

The life of the Moscow community of Russian Catholics was permeated by this idea of a rapprochement of the Churches. Catholic and Orthodox clergy and leading figures of the capital city's professoriate participated in meetings that were regularly held in the Abrikosovs' quarters, and Exarch Leonid Feodorov presented outstanding papers at more than one of these meetings. It would seem that Russian Catholics were now finally beginning to enjoy religious freedom....

The decree "On the Separation of the Church from the State," published January 23, 1918, served as the formal pretext for the beginning of Bolshevik persecutions of religion. It was followed in August 1918 by a special instruction that deprived all religious organizations of legal rights and declared their property "the common property of the people." In connection with this confiscation of property, the authorities prepared "receipts" for the pastors of Catholic parishes to sign, agreeing to the transfer of church property – which the Catholic Church categorically refused to do.

Later, decrees dated December 26, 1921, and January 3, 1922, required the advance censorship of sermons and forbade the religious instruction of children under the age of fourteen. A vigorous campaign for the seizure of church valuables to aid to those starving in the famine along the Volga served as the pretext for an all-out pogrom against the Church – widespread searches and violent confiscations of church vessels, with beatings, arrests and extra-judicial executions of clergy and laity.

The state subsequently created the appearance of legality in its on-going struggle against religion, and thus from the first group show trials of clergy and laity we see in the documents of the investigatory files all the apparent trappings of jurisprudence: decisions and orders for arrest, statements of witnesses and the accused, descriptions of the material evidence, indictments, sentences, and so forth. How the investigations were conducted, how the witnesses' statements were obtained and interpreted – that was another question altogether. Blackmail and threats, and later on physical abuse, became normal methods of investigation.

One way or another, from 1922 through 1949 the state security organs (OGPU, NKVD, MGB) conducted a series of group trials in cases against Russian Catholics – all of which were closed proceedings. The following paragraphs briefly describe these cases..

December 5, 1922 – all the Catholic churches and chapels in Petrograd were closed and sealed. On March 5 the Catholic clergy of Petrograd was summoned to appear before the Supreme Revolutionary Tribunal in Moscow. From March 25 to 27, a show trial was held in a case against a group of Catholic priests, the main target being Archbishop Jan Cieplak, but also including Father Feodorov, Exarch of the Russian Catholics. This trial, subsequently called the Cieplak-Budkiewicz Trial, was for the Catholic Church in Russia analogous to the "Trial of Patriarch Tikhon" for the Orthodox Church. The standard (at that time) accusations were leveled against the Catholic clergy: participation in a counter-revolutionary conspiracy and organizing resistance to the Soviet government. By decree of the Revolutionary Tribunal, Archbishop Cieplak and Monsignor Budkiewicz were sentenced to death by firing squad.[4] Exarch Feodorov and four priests were sentenced to ten years in prison; the remaining priests were sentenced to three years in prison.

Autumn 1923 – GPU agents in Moscow and Petrograd arrested sixty-four persons, including priests, laity, and Mother Catherine Abrikosova and several of the Dominican Sisters [most of the remaining Sisters were arrested in the spring of 1924]. They were charged with creating a monarchist organization with ties to the Vatican and sending abroad materials that disparaged the Soviet regime. This first group trial against Russian Catholics concluded in May 1924. Active members of the community were sentenced to five to ten years in labor camps or in solitary confinement prisons for political criminals ("political isolators"), and the rest were internally exiled.

January to July 1927 – Mass arrests of all the Dominican Sisters and parishioners still at liberty were carried out in Moscow and Petrograd. They were charged with the organization of aid to exiled priests and Sisters and they were sentenced to three to five years in labor camps or administratively exiled. Parishioners remaining at liberty in Moscow now gathered around Father Sergey Soloviev, and liturgical worship, clandestine conversions to Catholicism, and receptions of candidates into religious life all continued under his guidance.[5]

---

[4] Translator's Note: The Vatican and Britain strenuously objected to the sentencing and through their intervention Archbishop Cieplak's sentence was commuted to expulsion from Russia. He died in Passaic, New Jersey, while visiting the United States in 1926 to inform American Catholics about the persecution of the Church by the Bolsheviks. See Francis McCullagh, *Bolshevik Persecution of Christianity* (New York: E.P. Dutton, 1924).

[5] Translator's Note: Father Sergey Soloviev was the nephew of the previously noted philosopher, Vladimir Soloviev.

February 4, 1931 – Members of the community of Russian Catholics headed by Father Soloviev were arrested in Moscow. They were charged with the "creation of a counter-revolutionary monarchist organization," and the receipt of money from, and transmittal of espionage information to, a representative of the Vatican. In August 1931 ten of the accused were sentenced to three to five years in labor camps or administratively exiled.

Autumn 1933 – Mass arrests in Moscow, Kostroma, Krasnodar and Smolensk of the Dominican Sisters of the Abrikosova community who by that time had been released from prison or exile. The Sisters were charged with the "creation of a counter-revolutionary monarchist terrorist organization," espionage, anti-Soviet agitation, and preparation of an act of terrorism. In February 1934 sixteen persons were sentenced to five to ten years in labor camps or administratively exiled.

Autumn 1934 – Arrest in Moscow of members of the Catholic and Orthodox community of the suppressed Vysoko-Petrovsky Monastery, headed by Archbishop Bartholomew Remov. The standard charges were filed against them: creation of a "counter-revolutionary, monarchist, fascist organization," espionage, anti-Soviet agitation. In February 1935 Archbishop Remov was executed by firing squad; twenty-two others were sentenced to five to ten years in labor camps or administratively exiled.

January 1935 – Mass arrests of Catholic clergy in the Central Black Earth region; a group of Dominican Sisters of the Abrikosova community who were living out their administrative exile in Tambov were among those drawn into this group case. In November 1935 a closed judicial proceeding concluded with the acquittal of the Sisters and their release from the courtroom; the priests, however, received five – to ten-year sentences in labor camps.

1935 to 1948 – Continuing re-arrests and re-sentencing to labor camps and administrative exile of those Dominican Sisters and parishioners of the Abrikosov and Soloviev communities who had been released upon completion of earlier sentences.

November 1948 – Arrests of a group of Dominican Sisters of the Abrikosova community in Maloyaroslavets and Tambov. They were charged with "creation of a counter-revolutionary, monarchist organization, and receipt of money from, and transmittal of espionage information to, representatives of the Vatican." In August 1949 nine Sisters were sentenced to ten to fifteen years in labor camps.

The present work does not pretend to present all the documents and memoirs available on this topic. The selected materials, in the Editor's opinion, give the clearest picture of the tragic fate of the Dominican Sisters of the Abrikosova community. As to the life of the Petrograd community of Russian Catholics headed by Father Leonid Feodorov and concerning Julia Danzas and her works, one can consult Leonid Feodorov – His Life and Work.[6]

Our collection opens with the memoirs of Sophia Eismont (Sister Philomena, OP, 1900-1993), who recounts the tragic via dolorosa of the Dominican Sisters of the Abrikosova community sentenced in the group cases against Russian Catholics. She was one of the Sisters who endured the prisons, labor camps and administrative exile from 1923 through 1956.

Following her memoirs we present:

- Letters of the Dominican Sisters of the Abrikosova community to the Political and Polish Red Cross in which they describe in detail their life in the prisons, camps and exile from 1924 through 1935;
- Letters of Galina Jętkiewicz (Servant of God, Sister Rose of the Heart of Mary, OP, 1896-1944) to her relatives in Poland about her life in the Irkutsk political isolator prison, and then in exile in Kolpashevo (Narym region) and Poshekhone, outside Rybinsk, from 1923 to 1941;
- Letters of Dominican Sisters from convents in France in support of the Russian Sisters.

These letters are followed by theological writings of Anna Abrikosova (Mother Catherine, OP, 1882-1936).

We attribute special significance to two litanies presented in the next section. According to Father Georgy Friedman, OP, these could be seen as

---

[6] Deacon Vasilii von Burman, OSB, *Leonid Fëdorov: Zhizn' i deiatel'nost'* [Leonid Feodorov: Life and Work] (Rome, 1966); see also, *Simvol*, No. 37 (1998). Translator's Note: These works have not been translated, but the reader can find an excellent treatment of Exarch Feodorov in Paul Mailleux, S.J., *Exarch Leonid Feodorov: Bridgebuilder between Rome and Moscow* (New York: P.J. Kenedy & Sons, 1964).

the Sisters' "spiritual program." The Litany to Saint Dominic was one of many Western spiritual writings translated into Russian by the Sisters.

In the next section we have the recollections of the Sisters' spiritual children, recalling events of the Sisters' lives in Moscow, Saint Petersburg and Vilnius after their release from the labor camps. We include here the recollections of members of the Polish congregation of Dominican Missionaries of Jesus and Mary, founded in 1932 by the Servant of God Father Jacek Woroniecki for the purpose of evangelizing Russians living under Soviet atheism. We also place here the letters of the Abrikosova Dominican Sisters to their spiritual children from 1975 to 1977.

Appendix 1 contains the investigation files of the group cases against Russian Catholics, 1923 through 1934.

Appendix 2 is a rebuttal written by Sister Philomena, OP, to statements made about the Abrikosova Dominican community in the above-referenced book about Exarch Feodorov.

Appendix 3 presents a remembrance of Father Sergey Soloviev by Sr. Catherine of Siena (Nora Rubashova).

Appendix 4 presents poetry by Vera Gorodets (Sister Stephania, OP, 1893-1974) and Natalia Borozdina.

Appendix 5, "Confessors of the Faith – Religious and Laity Sentenced in Cases against Russia Catholics," presents brief biographies of the women who entered the Abrikosova Dominican community. These were taken from the investigatory files and include date of birth, date of entrance into religious life, arrest and sentence.[7]

Unless otherwise noted, the footnotes are those of the authors of the texts.

Work on this collection was performed as part of "Repressions of Clergy and Laity, 1918-1953," a program of the Memorial Center for Information and Education where I have worked for many years. I extend my sincere

[7] Translator's Note: The Russian edition included as well biographies of Russian Catholics arrested in the group cases presented in Appendix 1. Those additional biographies, as well as biographies of Latin Rite Catholics who appear in Sister Philomena's memoirs, are available at *https://biographies.library.nd.edu*. See "Additional Biographies" following Appendix 5.

gratitude to friends and colleagues at Memorial, especially to the director of the research program, Arseny Roginsky.

I take this opportunity to thank the following for their invaluable assistance in the preparation of this collection for publication: Father Georgy Friedman, OP, Father Bronisław Czaplicki, Anna Godiner, Ida Zaikina, Evgeny Krasheninnikov, Margarita Kurganskaya, Olga Mironova and Olga Salnit.

I would especially like to mention the constant support and encouragement of Francis Greene, without whose assistance the many years of work in the archives and the preparation of this book for publication would not have been possible.

Irina Osipova

The Dominican Sisters of the Abrikosova Community

MORE detailed biographical data about these women are presented in Appendix 5. When more than one Sister has chosen the same patron saint in religious life, her family name is added in the narrative to distinguish between them. The list was compiled by a review of biographical entries posted on www.catholic.ru.

Mother Catherine – Anna Ivanovna Abrikosova
Sister Agnes – Elena Vasilyevna Vakhevich
Sister Agnia – Tatiana Kuzminichna Tomilova
Sister Antonina – Valentina Vasilyevna Kuznetsova
Sister Catherine de Ricci – Maria Filippovna Sokolovskaya
Sister Catherine de Ricci – Tatiana Jakovlevna Galkina
Sister Catherine de Ricci – Anastasia Vasilyevna Selenkova
Sister Catherine of Siena – Aleksandra Vasilyevna Balasheva
Sister Catherine of Siena – Nora Nikolayevna Rubashova
Sister Dominica – Elizabeth Vasilyevna Vakhevich
Sister Hyacinth – Anna Ivanovna Zolkina
Sister Imelda – Anna Spiridonovna Serebriannikova
Sister Joanna – Catherine Ivanovna Gotovtseva
Sister Lucia – Anna Kirillovna Davidyuk
Sister Magdalina – Maria Grigoryevna Komarovskaya
Sister Margaret Mary – Olga Aleksandrovna Spechinskaya
Sister Margaret of Hungary – Raisa Ivanovna Krylevskaya
Sister Maria Cecilia – Olga Volokhina
Sister Maria Rosa of Lima – Vera Aleksandrovna Khmeleva
Sister Monica – Monica Antonovna Zvidrin
Sister Osanna – Nadezhda Andreevna Tsybina

Sister Philomena – Sophia Vladislavovna Eismont
Sister Rosa Maria – Nina Iosifovna Vasileni-Pozharskaya
Sister Rose of the Heart of Mary – Galina Fadeyevna Jętkiewicz
Sister Stephania – Vera Lvovna Gorodets
Sister Teresa – Nadezhda Yefimovna Tsvetkova
Sister Teresa of the Child Jesus – Minna Rakhmyelovna Kugel
Sister Veronica – Vera Yefimovna Tsvetkova

Secular Third Order Members in Moscow[1]

Sophia Aleksandrovna Ivanova
Lyudwiga Koch
Catherine Antonovna Malinovskaya
Anatolia Ivanovna Novitskaya [Nowicka]
Elena Agafonovna Plavskaya
Tamara Arkadyevna Sapozhnikova
Valentina Arkadyevna Sapozhnikova
Anna Iosifovna Tyshman

[1] Translator's Note: Status not clear. These women may have been novices or postulants (i.e., not professed) for the religious community or lay Dominicans.

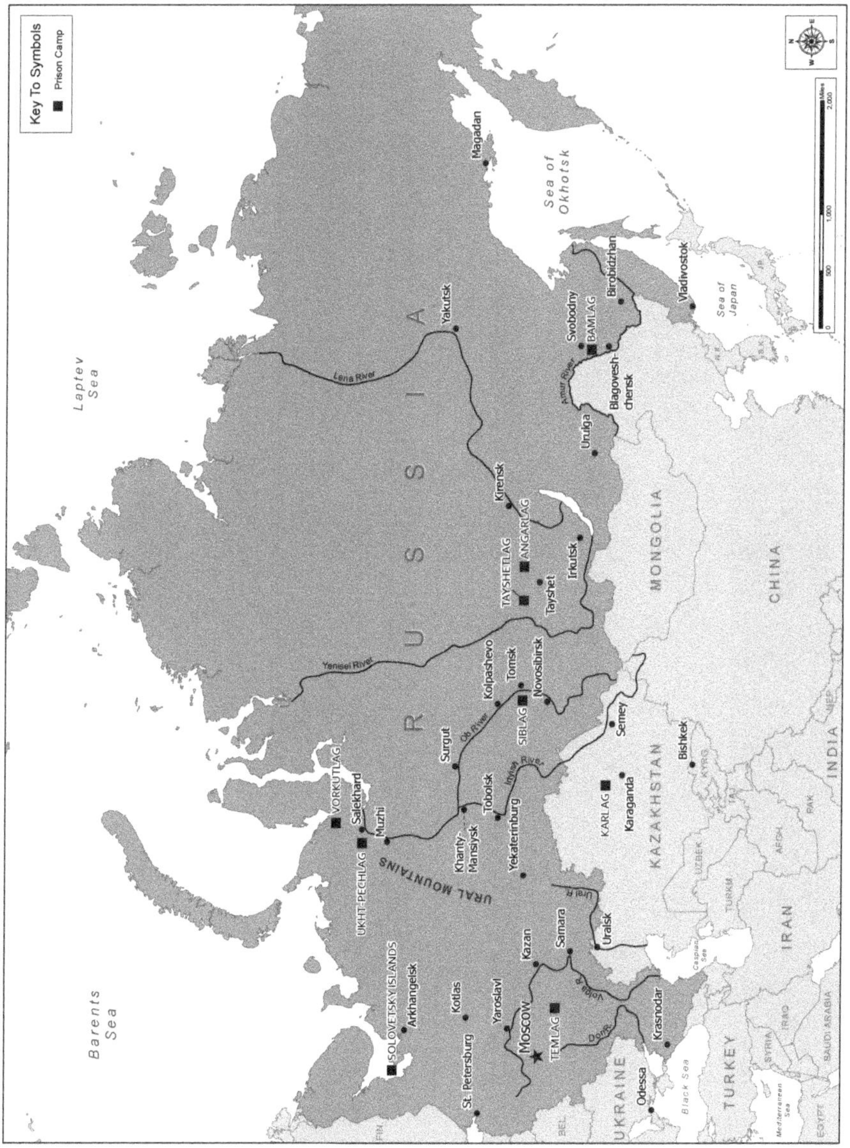

Map 1 – General Map of Russia with Present-Day Borders

Dominican Sisters of the Eastern Rite

By Sister Philomena, OP. Manuscript provided by Father Georgy Friedman, OP

IN 1721 Peter the Great established a Holy Synod to manage the affairs of the Russian Orthodox Church and appointed a secular protégé to serve as its chief procurator. From that moment the Russian Orthodox Church became, in effect, a State Church, and at the beginning of the twentieth century the Orthodox Church was completely subject to the government. Not surprisingly, some members of the clergy were essentially clerical bureaucrats, more intent on their own personal welfare and careers than on the zealous fulfillment of pastoral obligations and personal holiness.

The Russian people have always been religious and inclined toward asceticism and heroic spiritual feats. Through all the past centuries and down to the present day many highly enlightened, righteous-living Orthodox priests have led their flocks along the path of salvation. The best known of these – Saint Sergius of Radonezh, Saints Zosima and Savvati of Solovetsky, Saints Antony and Theodosius of Kiev, Saint Seraphim of Sarov – were esteemed for their radiant joy and all-embracing love.

The Russian Orthodox Church, separated from the supremacy of the Roman Pope after the separation of the Churches in 1054, preserved all the church institutions that had existed prior to that separation – the sacraments, liturgy and rituals – but it was now guided by, and drew exclusively upon, the spiritual strengths found in the holy fathers of the Church who lived prior to 1054. After 1054, the Western Catholic Church, despite huge difficulties and dangers both within and without, had ceaselessly grown, going deeper in its knowledge of the Truth.

Many prominent Russians – people who loved their country and their people – understood that salvation could only be found through a return to that unity from which they had originally fallen – not through any own fault of their own, but automatically, as it were. Such a notion was unacceptable to the tsarist government. From bygone times it had fomented a hostile attitude toward the Catholic Church and the Holy See, and it harassed those who converted to Catholicism, depriving them of State employment, confiscating their property, and persecuting them in every way, even to the point of imprisonment. The persecution of Orthodox clergy who converted to Catholicism was even more severe.

Several prominent members of the Russian intelligentsia in the nineteenth century were looking more and more to the West. For our purposes we would note, in particular, Vladimir Soloviev (1853-1900), a philosopher, writer and poet, and Princess Elizabeth Volkonskaya (1838-1897), a woman dedicated to apostolic work and possessing a theological education that was exceptional for a woman at that time[1]. Volkonskaya and Soloviev are the real progenitors of the Catholic movement in Russia during the nineteenth and early twentieth centuries. The Abrikosovs, Vladimir Vladimirovich and Anna Ivanovna, were among the intellectual champions of Catholicism in Moscow.

The Founding of the Abrikosov Community

Vladimir Vladimirovich Abrikosov was born in 1880 into the family of a wealthy factory owner. He graduated from the Historical Philology Department of Moscow University with an interest primarily in Western and ancient philosophy. In his youth he was a completely secular person with very broad interests, assimilating ideas with unusual depth and precision. The friends of his youth said of him: "Vova Abrikosov is a swell guy, but he's going to end up a monk." Endowed with a noble soul, from early on he understood the vanity and nothingness of all worldly goods; true wisdom ripened early, penetrating into the real essence of things. His strivings were always noble and lofty. At the same time, he had both an inner and outer charm – he was intelligent, kind and attentive to all around him. Basil von Burman, OSB, in a work dedicated to another leading figure among the

[1] The fruit of her persistent labors are two historico-theological works: *On the Church* (1888) and *Church Tradition and Russian Theological Literature* (1898).

Russian Catholics of the Eastern Rite, includes the following description of the young Abrikosov:

> He was completely unfamiliar with Orthodoxy and did not even attend church. His religious sympathies were toward Protestantism. He saw Catholics as "obscurantists" and "reactionaries," a view he presented in a theme on his State examination on the causes of the Reformation. There was of course nothing exceptional in this; such a frame of mind was typical in Russian "cultured circles" of that time. Abrikosov's political sympathies were on the side of the revolutionaries.[2]

Anna Ivanovna was born in 1882 into a well-known wealthy merchant family. She graduated from the First Women's Moscow Gymnasium with a gold medal, and she received her higher education at Girton College, Cambridge University, in England. Upon returning to Moscow she married her cousin Vladimir Vladimirovich. She was a person of a grand, broad intellect and a noble, kind heart. Her strivings and interests were likewise broad and lofty. She was taller than average, with penetrating, light blue eyes. Her entire demeanor reflected the imprint of intelligence and nobility. Anatolia Nowicka, a member of the Abrikosov community and later a secular Third Order Dominican, provides the following description of Anna Ivanovna:

> Now let us say a bit about Anna Ivanovna's external appearance. She was of average height; she had a well-proportioned figure, firmly built; she was a light brunette and her face was large, thin, very expressive, with a clear, high forehead, high cheek bones and an aquiline nose. Her eyes were expressive, calm and penetrating; in the shape of her lips one could sense a strength of character, but in her smile, goodness and joy of spirit. The profile of her face reminded one of the profile of the portraits of Girolamo Savanarola. She walked sedately; her movements were calm, her head slightly

---

[2] Deacon Vasilii von Burman, OSB, *Leonid Fëdorov: Zhizn' i deiatel'nost'* [Leonid Feodorov: Life and Work], (Rome, 1966), p. 171.

> elevated. She dressed simply, primly, in black and white, always with taste. In a word – she had the outer appearance of a noble matron.[3]

The couple shared a deep mutual understanding and spiritual closeness in their common aspirations and interests. After they married they went abroad, where, being interested in the spiritual life, they read much and were attracted to Catholicism. At the end of December 1908, in Paris, Anna converted to Catholicism, in the Church of the Madeleine, after serious preparation under the tutelage of the parish vicar and the Superior of the community of the Sisters of Mercy of Saint Vincent (Novitskaia, p. 63). Vladimir had not yet agreed to take this step and, to emphasize his own position, he increased his attendance at the Orthodox Church. After a short time (in 1909), he too became Catholic, but he declared that he was not setting himself any big goals and bought himself the very smallest prayerbook. But the spiritual literature they read captivated him more and more. He especially loved Saint Thomas Aquinas and Saint Dominic and the Dominican spirit of piety and service to God and others – the spirit of apostleship, repentance and prayer.

Returning to Moscow in 1910 and heartsick on account of the plight of Russia and the Russian Orthodox Church, they began their apostolic work among the intelligentsia in their former social milieu. Their prior connections in society, however, were suddenly broken off; invitations to social functions ceased and they were thus censured for their conversion and their new way of life.

Vladimir and Anna belonged to Saints Peter and Paul parish and they soon held a prominent position in the group of Russian Catholics as well as among many brilliant representatives of Muscovite society. Later Father Albert Liberse, pastor of the French parish (Saint Louis des Français), accepted the Abrikosovs into the Dominican novitiate.

The Abrikosovs were fluent in four European languages in addition to Latin and Greek, had a thorough grounding in theology and philosophy, and possessed a deep inner life. They were well cultured. Having found the Truth, they wanted to help their compatriots to find it as well. They

[3] A. Novitskaia, "Mat' Ekaterina (Abrikosova): Dominikanskaia obshchina v Moskve" [Mother Catherine Abrikosova: The Dominican Community in Moscow], *Logos* (1993), No. 48, p. 68.

dedicated their lives to this purpose and their home became the center of the dissemination of Catholic ideas in Muscovite society.

The Abrikosovs' home at that time reminded one of the old Roman patrician homes where the Christian masters welcomed everyone in the name of Christ, from slaves to patricians. In the Abrikosovs' home everyone was greeted in the name of Christ (Novitskaia, p. 67). They hosted religious and philosophical meetings and readings of excerpts from religious compositions, and together they prayed the rosary and the Stations of the Cross. While Vladimir carried on conversations on philosophical and dogmatic themes, Anna excelled in discussions of asceticism, mysticism and the history of the Church. She also instructed individuals in spiritual formation, preparing them for conversion to Catholicism and confirming them in the faith. All sorts of visitors were at these meetings: one might see a young student and a university professor, a modest young girl and a lady of high society, and both Catholic and Orthodox priests. The meetings began with the reading of a paper and concluded with heartfelt conversations over a cup of tea.

Father Leonid Feodorov wrote of this household to His Excellency Andrey Sheptytsky in February 1911:

> About this family one can say with the words of the Apostle Paul, 'I hail this domestic church!' Rarely does one meet young people in the bloom of life so devoted to the work of the Church and so religious. They spread Catholicism by all means at their disposal: through acquaintances, influence, material assistance, etc. From morning to evening the wife is busy instructing the children of Russian Catholics; she visits acquaintances and receives them in her home with the sole purpose of converting them to Catholicism. Her husband does the same. He even confided to me his wish to become a priest and asked me to recommend the required textbooks. (Von Burman, pp. 171-173)

Vladimir and Anna continued to deepen their theological knowledge and their inner spiritual lives. They studied specialized Dominican literature and they were successful in combining an understanding of the modern world with the highest spiritual principles. They possessed a great keenness of observation and psychological analysis and these character traits fostered in them the formation of accomplished spiritual guides.

The Abrikosovs spent the summer of 1913 abroad, including time in Rome where they made vows as Third Order Dominicans on November 21, 1913. They were accepted into the Order by Father Henri Desqueyrous, OP, Procurator General. The Holy Father, Pope Pius X, received them in a private audience, during which he expressed a lively interest in their work in Moscow. He presented them with his autographed portrait and imparted his blessing on their future work in Russia.

Even more ardent in their apostolic zeal, they began to gather young women, hoping to find for God souls who would be completely given to Him in service as Third Order Dominicans. These young women were mostly university students, teachers and conservatory pupils. For many of them the very fact of conversion from Orthodoxy to Catholicism caused them troubles and involved them in hostile formalities. They had to submit to the official administrative authorities a statement concerning their conversion to Catholicism, which was then followed by admonitions from the Orthodox clergy. Furthermore, their parents and relatives were often categorically opposed to their conversion to Catholicism, and thus many of the young women had to sever ties with their families. In such cases Anna always and actively rendered moral support to bolster their courage. She herself often endured troubles in this regard, what with parents making a scene, slandering her and complaining to the authorities, but she was always guided by the highest spiritual principles, for the good of the soul and the Church (Novitskaia, p. 71).

This first group became the kernel of the future community of Dominican Sisters; there were more than ten of them in 1917. Although they belonged to Saints Peter and Paul parish, these Russian Catholics attended the French church, Saint Louis des Français, because most of them knew French and it was nearby, whereas they did not know Polish, the language in which homilies were preached at Saints Peter and Paul. The pastor of Saint Louis Church was one of the Dominican Fathers, a Frenchman, and he accepted the newly entered Dominican Sisters into the community.

During Metropolitan Andrey Sheptytsky's visit to Russia in 1917, he ordained Vladimir Abrikosov to the priesthood of the Eastern Rite and entrusted him with the spiritual care of the growing parish of Russian

Catholics in Moscow. Most of the Russian Catholics belonged to the Eastern Rite and thus a new parish was formed. Both the parish and the community of Sisters grew quickly.

> After Father Vladimir's ordination these Sisters took upon themselves all the concerns associated with the organization of the parish and setting up its liturgical life: the singing, reading, care of the church, and so forth. . . . Both the community of Sisters and the parish found shelter in the Abrikosovs' quarters, sacrificially donated for the work of the Russian Catholic Church. In one room they set up a domestic chapel (without an iconostasis) that could accommodate up to fifty people. Another room was set aside for Father Vladimir as pastor of the parish and confessor of the community. Another room was designated for Anna Ivanovna and was also used for sick Sisters. When the community grew and the number of ill Sisters increased, this room at times was like an infirmary. There were two other rooms used as dormitories for the Sisters. (Von Burman, pp. 538-539)

Long before this, Vladimir and Anna had made vows of chastity and since that time had dedicated themselves entirely to apostolic endeavors – he, to the management of his small parish, and she, to the organization of a community of Third Order Regular Dominican Sisters. Father Vladimir chose Saint Thomas Aquinas as his Dominican patron. Anna took the name of Saint Catherine of Siena, and she shared many character traits with her holy patroness: the same heroic faith, humility and simplicity in her dealings with people.

> As well as I can remember, one always sensed in her a freedom and loftiness of spirit; she knew how to be faithful to God in riches and in poverty, in sickness and when suffering indignities. Her free soul soared like an eagle – from the first moments of her conscious life she labored much for God and she received much from Him. (Novitskaia, p. 67)

A domestic chapel in honor of the Nativity of the Most Holy Virgin

Mary was set up in the Abrikosovs' quarters, where daily Mass was celebrated. Community living united the Sisters even more and from this point forward they began to live the regular life of a religious community. As Anatolia Nowicka notes, "Gradually, with the deepening of their apostolic work, the externals of their way of life and the appearance of the Abrikosovs' quarters changed. Only one maid remained; all the superfluous comforts and luxuries disappeared" (Novitskaia, p. 72). The community of Sisters could have been even more numerous but the Abrikosovs' quarters could not accommodate any more; thus, some who wished to join had to remain in the world as secular Third Order Sisters. By 1922 there were already approximately twenty-five Sisters living in the community.

At that time the Sisters and the parishioners lived an intense, deep spiritual life with an ever-increasing awareness of the need of sacrifice for Russia. The Sisters led an austere life and carried out various penances, such as taking the discipline, keeping nocturnal vigils, adoration, and fasts. They slept on the floor, using books for pillows. The Mother Superior had a bed in her room which she often gave up to sick Sisters. She once took into her room a Sister who was ill with cancer and cared for her until her death. When she herself was sick, she never claimed any privileges, in food or anything else. In Anatolia Nowicka's words, "Anna's freedom of spirit was astonishing. She was the same both in abundance and in poverty. She gave generous sacrifices to God: her wealth, the bustling glitter of the world, and earthly happiness with her husband, whom she ardently and tenderly loved" (Novitskaia, pp. 72-73).

It was at that time that Mother Catherine and the Sisters made an explicit vow to sacrifice themselves for the salvation of Russia and for priests:

> To the honor of Almighty God, Father, Son and Holy Spirit, the Blessed Virgin Mary and Saint Dominic, we, the consecrated Sisters (Third Order of Preachers, Moscow Community) of Saint Dominic, hereby offer our life in sacrifice to the Holy Trinity to the last drop of blood for the salvation of Russia and for priests. May our Lord Jesus Christ, his Immaculate Mother, our Holy Father Saint Dominic and all the holy ranks of our brethren in the Order of Preachers come to our assistance. Amen. (Von Burman, p. 595)

During Lent, on Monday of Holy Week and Good Friday the Sisters ate nothing at all, and on all other Fridays during Lent they had only one meal of bread and water. Some Sisters and Father Vladimir fasted completely on the first three days of Lent, and Father Vladimir fasted completely for all of Holy Week except for Holy Thursday. For several years, whether he was well or ill, Father Vladimir never lay down to sleep – he slept sitting. Once after an operation, he celebrated Mass almost immediately, without going to bed. For the grace of conversion and the good of souls he constantly made all sorts of sacrifices. He treated the Sisters with uncommon gentleness, sympathetic tenderness, attentiveness, leniency, and a love that was manifested constantly in matters big and small.

Mother Catherine had a clear and broad intellect and was always guided by the spiritual. She had a heart that was sympathetic and sensitive, but without sentimentality. She was a good psychologist and an ingenious woman. To an outside observer, Mother Catherine could seem stern and severe. During the period of organization and the first years of the life of the community, however, this severity was absolutely necessary in order to introduce religious discipline and obedience to the Rule of the Order, the constitutions of the community and the authority of Superiors. Anatolia Nowicka recalls that one refined Muscovite poet said of Mother Catherine that "from her gently blew the chill of mountain heights". "This was," she says,

> an excellent poetic comparison. In fact, in just this way did worldly people, far from the spiritual life, perceive Anna's personality. Mother had a very integrated nature, and this was reflected in her spiritual life – in all things, consistently and to the end, she was guided by supernatural principles and intentions. And therefore she looked at life as if from a mountain height, and it was as if from her "it blew cold." (Novitskaia, pp. 76-77)

By nature Mother Catherine had a soft, tender heart and she had to force herself to be strict. The charm of her happy and noble personality attracted to her the hearts of all around her, even people not inclined toward religion or Catholicism, who trustingly felt drawn to her. She guided the souls not only of the Sisters, but of many of the parishioners as well.

As a priest, Father Vladimir constantly assisted and supported Mother Catherine's work, but he was always fair and impartial. The fact that those Catholics who drew close to them led intense and devout lives bears witness to the depth of the spiritual guidance provided by both Father Vladimir and Mother Catherine. Later, many of their parishioners would also suffer for the Faith in administrative exile and prisons, enduring all things with complete dedication to the will of God. One can say of this couple that what was characteristic for Father Vladimir was his strength in gentleness; what was characteristic for Mother Catherine was her gentleness in strength.

Despite the difficult years of the revolution and civil war, with all their consequences – famine, disease – the Sisters' spiritual life grew ever deeper. Their heroic way of life fostered this growth. Their faith, a burning zeal and spiritual unity all grew stronger. Mother Catherine endured all privations together with the Sisters. The Sisters earned some income by working in various institutions, schools and so forth. One of them, Sister Catherine de Ricci (Selenkova), was a university professor. She also served the community as novice mistress for six Dominican brothers.

In the first period after the October Revolution, while the Civil War was still going on and economic ruin was devastating the country, the government was occupied with setting the economy aright and for the time being did not touch upon the question of religion and the Church. This was a period of broad freedom of speech and conscience: there were lectures in public auditoriums on various themes, including religion and philosophy, and public debates and meetings were conducted openly. The community of Russian Catholics continued to hold its evenings of conversations, with presentations of papers and cycles of lectures on religious themes. It was mostly Sister Stephania and Sister Catherine de Ricci who led these meetings. Slowly and steadily restrictions began to be imposed on religious freedom and church activity. Lectures in public auditoriums were no longer as widely and openly permitted, and the government began to forbid certain kinds of activity within the churches themselves.

By 1922 a campaign of persecution against religion had been launched on a broad front. The government began to close churches and arrest clergy. In March 1922 an open trial was initiated against a group of Leningrad Catholic priests, the main target being Bishop Jan Cieplak. Exarch Leonid Feodorov was also joined to the case. The government of course then turned its attention to the parish of Russian Catholics and the Dominican community in Moscow.

The situation in the parish was becoming more and more tense. Because much of the activity of the community took place in Father Vladimir's quarters, he was torn in all directions at once – meetings, visits, and conversations took a lot of his time. In addition, he was still the confessor and director of the Sisters, whose number was growing without interruption. By the end of 1921 there were already thirty-six Sisters, including a group of secular Third Order Sisters who lived in their own homes. His health was noticeably deteriorating – he fell ill three times, in addition to suffering from a heart condition. During the course of the three preceding years he had been arrested twice, and after the second arrest he had been held in prison for about a month.

At dawn on August 17, 1922, when the Sisters had begun to sing Matins, Father Vladimir was again arrested. During the two previous nights a whole slew of arrests had been made in Moscow, taking in as many as seventy professors, literary figures and scholars of an idealistic tendency.[4] After a brief interrogation they sentenced Father Vladimir to "the ultimate penalty," but later commuted the death sentence to permanent expulsion from the country. The same fate was meted out to Dmitry Kuzmin-Karavayev and many other leading representatives of the intelligentsia, whose activities were considered unacceptable in a Soviet country.

Mother Catherine could have departed with Father Vladimir but she remained with her beloved family to fulfill her vow of sacrifice. On September 29, 1922, Father Vladimir left Russia. He was Mother Catherine's "soulmate," a person whom she so deeply loved. The parting was difficult but she bore it courageously. Once abroad, Father Vladimir settled at first in Rome, but later moved to Paris. Correspondence was possible in the beginning, but soon it came to an end and later nothing was known about him.[5]

Mother Catherine well understood what threatened her and her handful of Sisters; she had a premonition about the arrests and harsh punishments

---

[4] Among those arrested were Simyon Frank, Pavel Novgorodtsev, Nikolay Berdyayev, Ivan Ilyin and others. Dmitry Kuzmin-Karavayev was arrested at the same time as Father Vladimir.

[5] Translator's Note: Father Vladimir lived out his final years as a hermit in a small room in the Auteuil district of Paris. He entered eternal life in 1966, and is buried in Meudon, France (outside Paris), according to Aidan Nichols, OP, in "Ekaterina Sienskaya Abrikosova: A Dominican Uniate Foundress in the Old Russia," *New Blackfriars* (April 1991), vol. 72, no. 848, pp. 164-172.

awaiting them in the future. "As for myself," she wrote to Princess Elizabeth Volkonskaya on the eve of Father Vladimir's departure abroad,

> I am alone in the complete sense of the word, with half-naked children, with Sisters torn in all directions, with the youthful, wonderful, holy priest Father Nikolay, who himself needs support – and with bewildered parishioners. I myself expect to be arrested because during the search they took our Rule and Constitutions.... We feel like little slivers in God's hands, and where He will take us, we do not know. We have no plans, no vision into the future, nothing.... We have to live by pure acts of faith, hope and love. And meanwhile the work goes on, souls are joining us, the community of Sisters grows; instead of sixteen we have already squeezed eighteen into three rooms, and in the past week three people have joined the parish. (Cited in Von Burman, p. 547)

Despite her premonitions, she did not hesitate to accept new Sisters into the community when she recognized a true vocation. She openly spoke to these candidates about the possibility of persecution, but at the same time she knew how to instill in them her own sacrificial spirit and show them the ways and precepts of the spiritual and religious life.

After Father Vladimir's departure, Father Nikolay Aleksandrov, who was also a Third Order Dominican, became the Sisters' spiritual director and the head of the parish. His Dominican patron was Saint Peter of Verona, Martyr. Deacon Von Burman offers the following description of Father Nikolay:

> From among the number of laymen close to him, Father Vladimir chose and prepared the engineer Nikolay Aleksandrov for the priesthood. Upon the representation of Father Leonid, Bishop Cieplak ordained him at the beginning of 1922. Father Vladimir's choice was very appropriate, and Father Leonid was soon able to inform His Excellency Andrey Sheptytsky that Father Nikolay had become an "excellent priest." This became particularly clear after Father Vladimir's exile, when he "became Father Vladimir's replacement and led the Moscow parish no worse than Father Vladimir would have led it." Father Leonid attested that "the parish not only did not

> fall apart, it became stronger and grew with every passing day."... "Despite Father Vladimir's absence," he wrote, "the work has not at all collapsed, conversions have not ceased." (Von Burman, p. 540)

The Sisters were busy with a school the community had illegally organized for the parishioners' children. Mother Catherine loved children; they always had access to her room and simply adored her. "At times the sound of children's laughter and merriment came from her room. Mother knew how to devise clever, fun diversions for the children. They idolized her" (Novitskaia, p. 77). In addition to her daily prayers and other obligations, Mother Catherine still found time to translate spiritual texts – masterpieces of ascetic literature – into Russian for those Sisters who did not know foreign languages. She herself also wrote some meditations based on the liturgical year and Dominican feast days.

The Sisters in the community so deeply revered and respected Mother Catherine that none of them kept any secrets from her; their hearts, their souls, their thoughts were all open to her. Many, deeply trusting her, gave her their own "spiritual journals" and even their examinations of conscience. She was like a conscience for the Sisters. From a letter of Anna to Father Vladimir, in Rome, dated November 11, 1922, we read:

> Christ now wants in Russia only individual victims who are walking toward complete slaughter, like the Sisters. So it seems to me that now is not a time for any [precautionary] measures, but only a time for chivalry and holiness, for sacrifice and humility. Obedience to death on the cross and humility – these are the two virtues that I preach to the Sisters. Mass and the rosary – these are the two means of victory, nothing else is needed. An ardent spiritual life, a pure faith, and an iron will – i.e., a love that demands nothing but hands over everything. (Von Burman, pp. 588-589)

Mother Catherine was truly the guide of their spiritual and intellectual lives, which under her influence developed abundantly. They said about them that "the Sisters are in a hurry to live." Again, Von Burman describes that life:

> In fact the Sisters, day after day . . . were working, torn in all directions. One of them tutored parish children in order to free them from attending Soviet schools. In the library, the Sisters read hand-written books together with the parishioners who, under the living conditions prevailing at that time in "Red" Moscow, either had no rooms of their own or whose rooms were so cold that reading there was impossible. Almost all the translations of Catholic authors and the copying out of multiple copies were done by the Sisters themselves. In the community's kitchen they fed up to ten literally starving elderly people every day and also gave dinners to homeless Catholics, whose plight in Moscow at that time was very difficult. The Sisters also took upon themselves the care of ill parishioners. To all this must still be added that they supported their own community by their own labor and approximately ten children, including several orphans, were completely under their care. (Von Burman, p. 547)

They all, as it were, had a premonition that trials would soon come, when they would be deprived of this blessed common life and the Holy Sacraments. They prayed day and night, taking turns in adoration of Jesus in the Most Holy Sacrament of the Eucharist.

The moment of the beginning of their long via dolorosa was drawing near....

The Beginning of Their *Via Dolorosa*, 1923-1927

On November 11, 1923, after 10 o'clock in the evening, GPU agents arrived and began a search that lasted until morning. They gathered all the Sisters in one room – some read, others prayed. They were all completely calm, and Sister Lucia even lay down under a desk, fell asleep, and slept almost till morning. Mother Catherine and half the Sisters were arrested. During the same night they arrested Father Nikolay and many parishioners.

The orphaned Sisters who were left behind, no longer having Mass in their own chapel, began to attend daily Mass at the Cathedral of the Immaculate Conception on Malaya Gruzinskaya Street, where Father Michael Tsakul was the pastor at that time. The Sisters' lives went along according to the same schedule as before, under the leadership of one of the remaining professed Sisters, Sister Margaret of Hungary.

On March 9, 1924, a second search was conducted and the rest of the Sisters still at liberty were arrested, with the exception of the seriously ill Sister Catherine de Ricci (Galkina) and two Sisters who were allowed to remain at liberty to care for her, Sister Catherine of Siena (Balasheva) and Sister Hyacinth. Several parishioners were also arrested. At that point they were all held at Butyrka Prison (although some had earlier been at Lefortovo Prison), and Mother Catherine was held in the inner prison at Butyrka in the GPU section. Von Burman provides a description of these prisons:

> Lubyanka Prison differed from the other prisons in its severity and the strict isolation of its prisoners from the outside world. No walks in the yard, no visits, no correspondence, no reading were permitted here; it was forbidden to have paper, a writing utensil – even a simple pencil – or thread or needles. No kind of manual work was permitted. Prisoners were to be kept in complete inactivity. A deathly quiet and grave-like silence reigned in the prison. Windows with iron grates were further fortified with iron screens so that the prisoners could see nothing – neither the courtyard nor even a bit of sky. A blinding electric light burned all night in all the cells. Nocturnal interrogations in the investigator's office were arranged with particular secretiveness. . . . For a believer, the interrogations were a real trial. The investigators were interested in the details of the past life of not only the prisoner himself, but of his relatives, friends and acquaintances as well. To speak the truth about oneself was not so difficult, but speaking of others, even without wanting to do so, could always harm them – just mentioning someone's name could lead to that person's arrest. At the same time, refusing to name names or talk about others would result in an increased sentence. (Von Burman, pp. 592-593)

At first Mother Catherine was confined in a solitary cell in Butyrka, but to make her imprisonment more difficult, she was transferred to a cell with criminals serving sentences for theft, prostitution, robbery and other more serious crimes. The cell was constantly full of noise, shouting, arguments and fights.

Once they brought a woman into the cell after the weather had already turned cold. She was half-dressed in dirty rags and she had nothing else. The others would not allow her to lie down near them. She lay down next to Mother Catherine, who covered her with her own blanket. The other women warned her: "Don't do that! She's infected, she's got syphilis." Mother Catherine responded, "And so? If I get an infection, I'll get it treated."

Mother was simple, friendly and tender with compassionate love for all the women in the cell. And these women, who had absolutely gone to ruin, who were amoral and mired in crime – women who had an attitude of contempt and even hatred toward all non-criminals, especially those arrested under the political statutes (Article 58 of the Criminal Code) – these women fell in love with Mother Catherine and became attached to her. Gradually their cell was transformed. The shouting, the fights, the obscenities all ceased. After Mother Catherine was transferred to another cell, when the women went to work [at their prison jobs] and the cell was no longer locked, if they knew that the guards were escorting Mother Catherine along their corridor, they would dart out of the cell at the risk of punishment to kiss her shoulder strap or just to look at her. As Anatolia Nowicka tells us in her recollections about Mother Catherine,

> The charm of Mother Catherine's personality was involuntarily acknowledged even by the investigators. One of them, interrogating a Sister who was one of Mother's assistants, said: "What an interesting and charming personality your Mother has – it's just a shame she's not a Communist." This of course did not keep them from holding this "charming personality" under a strict regimen and giving her a ten-year prison sentence.
>
> The investigators more than once struck up conversations with Mother on themes of a theoretical nature: on religious and materialistic worldviews and on the advantages of the latter. We see here, on the one hand, the investigators' desire to study the person under investigation and decide how dangerous his influence might be in Soviet society and then to give him the appropriate degree of

> isolation from society (closed prison, solitary confinement, a labor camp or administrative exile) – and on the other hand we see the investigators' subconscious interest in people of that world – and that worldview. Mother Catherine laid out her views for them fearlessly, clearly and interestingly. It was a unique Christian witness given in the secret chambers of the investigators of the Soviet GPU. (Novitskaia, pp. 79-80)

The Sisters and parishioners were placed either in common cells with up to twenty-five people arrested on a variety of charges (often criminal charges), or in single cells that, because of the overcrowding in the prison, often held three, four or five people. As a rule, they were summoned for interrogations during the night.

Sister Agnia was in the prison hospital with pulmonary tuberculosis (which subsequently subsided). Everyone in the hospital loved Sister Agnia and she helped many of the patients as much as she could. Out of sympathy for her, one of the nurses secretly brought her a copy of the Gospels that later on was useful to the other Sisters as well.

Sister Catherine de Ricci (Selenkova) was also found to have tuberculosis and consequently also landed in the prison hospital. Both Sisters were later transferred to the common cell where Mother Catherine and other Sisters were being held. Sisters Osanna, Antonina, Joanna and I were also transferred from solitary cells to this common cell.

At this time a protest-strike broke out in the prison. Working prisoners (those serving out their sentences within the prison) agreed among themselves not to eat or work. On the day it began, the prisoners crowded around the open windows of their cells and let out a desperate cry "A-a-a!" Butyrka Prison, built as a huge fortress in the eighteenth century during the time of Catherine the Great, is located relatively close to the center of Moscow. And now this fortress, this beehive, buzzed and rumbled with a desperate cry that continued from noon until six in the evening.

After several hours, an armed group of prison workers and the head of the prison came into the central yard of the prison where most of the prison buildings stood. He announced that the prison was under martial law. From the window grates the prisoners yelled out their demands, including demands that they be able to write and receive letters more often, that they not be fed spoiled meat and rotten cabbage, and so forth.

All the other women in the cells with the Sisters were also under investigation (i.e., not working in the prison) and therefore had no connection to these events. But watching from the windows of their cells what was going on and caught up by the wave of excitement and outrage, they also began to shout with the strikers. The Sisters tried every means to stop them because they believed that no one would later escape punishment.

In fact that very night, when they had barely lain down to sleep, the head of the prison appeared in the cell with a group of armed soldiers and shouted abruptly and harshly: "I declare that the prison is under martial law – whoever speaks a word gets a bullet in the head! Get your things and your beds and be ready to leave the cell in five minutes." In a short time they all came in again, ordered everyone to go by two's out into the corridor and place all their things on the floor and then re-enter the completely empty cell, now turned into a special punishment cell.

Those whom they considered the instigators were led out into the corridor and forced to stand face to the wall before being sent to the cold special punishment cell, where many spent the night on the cement floor – some spent several days there. The remaining strikers sat for three days in their empty cells and had only bread and water. Their things all the while were lying on the floor in the corridor.

Lent was coming to an end. Passion Week began. Many of the prisoners received holiday packages from relatives. We Sisters also received packages through the Political Red Cross.[6] Easter was coming.... On Holy Saturday, the mood of the women prisoners was very heavy – taken unexpectedly from their families, their nerves overwrought on account of the interrogations, completely in the dark as to their immediate future, almost without hope for anything good – some of them had come to despair. We supported them in whatever ways we could, reassuring them, strengthening their courage. We ourselves prayed quite a bit. We were calm and full of faith and a deep trust in God.

Mother Catherine and all of us Sisters were confident that the Lord had accepted our vow of sacrifice for Russia, and we accepted our arrest,

---

[6] Headed at this time by Catherine Pavlovna Peshkova, the wife of Maxim Gorky.

imprisonment and all that lay ahead in the future as His response to our vow. We viewed our circumstances as an expression of the mercy of God, who would give us the happiness of uniting ourselves to His Cross of redemptive sufferings, and therefore we were joyfully inspired by these events and courageously and calmly ready for all that lay ahead.

On Holy Saturday we prepared for the holy day: we covered the long prison table with sheets and set out the painted eggs and Easter cakes we had received in our packages. Standing before the large open window praying, we waited for the first peal of the bells. And when at midnight we heard the din of the Easter bells ringing from the nearby churches, announcing the beginning of the liturgy, we began to sing Easter Matins.

Gone were the iron-shackled doors with their peepholes, the gloomy cell and the window grates. Light, joyful and free, our souls soared upward toward the stars shining in the sliver of dark sky visible in the cell, blending together with the exultant hymn of peace, hymning and praising the Risen Christ.

Here and there in the cell could be heard the sounds of sniffling and sobbing; having finished singing and praying, we hastened to reassure those who were crying, calming and comforting them as best we could. We had to postpone the shared holiday meal until morning.

Early in the morning the cell doors were opened and the guards began to call out the family names of several Sisters – Sister Osanna, Sister Antonina, Sister Joanna and me. They also summoned a Leningrader in the cell – Sister Lucia Chekhovskaya. They ordered us to get our belongings ready for a transfer. The other women were grief-stricken and exclaimed, "How will we get along without you?!"

The guards led us to the next cell and, when we went in, we saw behind a long prison table, also covered with a sheet and festively decorated, almost all the Sisters and Mother Catherine at the head of the table – all dressed for the holy day in their white blouses and black skirts! It is difficult to describe the joy of this meeting after several months of separation – on this first day of Easter, within prison walls that had, as it were, ceased to exist.

After a prayer we all sat down and suddenly the door of the cell flew open and a group of prison bosses, apparently making the rounds of the cells, entered the cell. We immediately stood up, in accordance with prison rules. The bosses wordlessly looked at everyone and at the holiday decorations on the table and suddenly, absolutely unexpectedly, said "Happy holiday!" This was like an unexpected gift because in those times no one could expect anything good.

This incident fostered an ever better and merrier mood. In addition to Mother Catherine and us Sisters, there were also several parishioners in the cell – there were only three outsiders. Mother Catherine conversed much with all and with each individually, and everyone prayed quite a bit. Later on there would be more than twenty-five people in the cell, and for lack of free space two Sisters slept on narrow benches. Anatolia Nowicka gives this additional information about this time in the cell:

> Several Latin Rite Catholics in the same cell also joined them. Among them was Sister Lucia Chekhovskaya, now the main Superior of the Sisters of the Holy Family in Ratov, Poland. According to her words, all the women in the cell, regardless of their nationality or religious denomination, were captivated by the beautiful spiritual character of Anna Ivanovna and the Sisters. They all called her "Mother". (Novitskaia, p. 81)

It was wonderful to be in such a cell. We observed silence, having recreation only during mealtime. Everyone was occupied in prayer, spiritual conversations or spiritual reading. (In the prison library we had found a Bible that somehow had not been discarded and a copy of the lives of the saints.) Sister Catherine de Ricci (Selenkova) taught an expanded catechism, the epistles of Saint Paul and the Gospels. The Sisters (mainly Sister Stephania) talked about the lives of the saints, particularly those whose names the Sisters had taken in religious life. We prayed the rosary together and on Saturday evening we sang Vespers. Crosses and rosaries had been taken from all of us when we were arrested, but we made new ones out of white bread, painted with indelible pencil – nice and even pretty. In addition, some Sisters studied French and English.

Before the feast of Saint Catherine of Siena (April 30), each Sister made a retreat guided by Mother Catherine and on the feast day itself the professed Sisters renewed their vows. "Many Sisters wanted to make perpetual vows but Mother would only allow them to make temporary vows" (Novitskaia, p. 82). Three Sisters made first vows, having finished their novitiate in prison.

It was an unusual and thrilling triumph within the prison walls. The Sisters also renewed their vow of sacrifice for Russia.

Von Burman describes the culmination of the spiritual growth that was occurring during this time in prison, with these words spoken just before their departure on the convoy:

> "Most likely, each of you, having fallen in love with God and now following Him, has more than once in your soul asked Christ to give you the opportunity to share in His sufferings. Well, now this moment has arrived. Now your desire to suffer for Christ's sake is being realized."
>
> If Anna Ivanovna's words have been correctly handed on to us, there is no reason to doubt that she expressed in these words what she herself carried in her heart during months of solitary confinement. Those months had to have been, even for her, a time of strong spiritual enlightenment. Calling the Sisters to follow her on the Way of the Cross, which they had begun with their imprisonment, Anna Ivanovna shared with them that ardent desire to be united to Christ's sufferings, a desire that had ripened in her during her solitary confinement in Lubyanka. (Von Burman, pp. 594-595)

The Sentences and Departure by Convoy

The sentences of the Collegium of the GPU were read out in the cell at the beginning of July 1924, and they were more severe than could have been expected. Mother Catherine was sentenced to ten years of strict prison isolation; Sister Catherine de Ricci (Selenkova), to ten years in prison; Sister Rose of the Heart of Mary and Sister Agnes, to five years in prison; Sister Imelda, to eight years in a concentration camp (and sent to Solovetsky); and Sister Dominica, to five years in prison. They sentenced Father Nikolay Aleksandrov to ten years in a concentration camp and sent him to Solovetsky. All the rest of the Sisters got three years' administrative exile to Siberia. In addition to the Sisters, parishioners who had actively participated in the spiritual life of the parish were also sentenced to various terms in the concentration camp at Solovetsky or administrative exile.

We signed the sentences [as required], accepting them with joy as being a clear expression of God's will, showing His acceptance of the readiness of each of us to suffer for Russia in union with the suffering of Christ. We then broke into a hymn of thanksgiving, "Te Deum Laudamus!" Each of us Sisters then spoke individually with Mother Catherine who gave us instructions and advice, preparing us for our new life, possibly in isolation, as it in fact soon turned out to be the case.

After two or three days they summoned Sister Imelda with her belongings. At that point it was still not known where they were taking her. This parting was the hardest because it was the first. Mother Catherine, although she was courageous and calm, was obviously suffering as she yielded up the first victim, sending one of the older Sisters off to distant imprisonment. Many of us cried as we bid farewell. Sister Imelda was leaving without a penny for, as we later learned, the Solovetsky Special Purpose Camp. Two days later they summoned Sister Catherine de Ricci (Selenkova), who had open tuberculosis sores on her neck – she subsequently lay for months in the prison hospital. After her they summoned Sister Dominica and sent her to Orel Prison.

They called all the rest of us and took us to the room for exiled prisoners – a huge hall full of convicts waiting to be taken to board a rail car for departure by convoy. Seeing the group of Sisters enter the hall, several exclaimed, "Where are they taking this kindergarten class?!" Most of us were from nineteen to twenty-five years old and looked very young. We were all buoyant, animated and even cheerful.

Some Leningraders were joined to our group on the convoy: Father Epifanius Akulov, an Eastern Rite Catholic priest, and Sisters Justina Danzas and Lucia Chekhovskaya. Together with Mother Catherine and Sisters Maria Rosa, Margarita, Magdalina, Teresa, Veronica, Joanna and me, they all rode in the same train car to the transit point in Sverdlovsk [Yekaterinburg].

Upon arrival in Sverdlovsk we went on foot to the transit prison, located in a large courtyard surrounded by a high wall. We arrived in the evening, after dusk had fallen. When we entered the building and began to go up to the second floor where we were supposed to stay, we caught sight of a strange, incomprehensible scene. Lying and sitting on the steps were the contorted bodies of sleeping women. We thought that the cell must be so overcrowded that the women were forced to huddle together on the staircase, but upon opening the door we saw with amazement that the cell was completely empty, with wooden boards for sleeping all along the wall. We were all very tired – the prison was a long way from the train station – and so everyone began to settle in right away, the sooner to get to bed. Then, just as soon as we had lain down and begun to fall asleep, we understood why the cell had been completely empty.

A countless multitude of bedbugs began to mercilessly bite us from all sides. They rained down through the cracks of beams charred from a long-ago fire. We had never seen such big bedbugs – a centimeter and more in length and fat! More like beetles than bedbugs. What came to mind were those "bedbug cells" where they threw people as a punishment back in the time of serfdom. It was impossible to endure for long – impossible to rest or sleep because one's whole body was burning, as if on fire. It was torture! Mother Catherine continued to lie there, and when the two Sisters next to her began to brush the bedbugs from her, she forbade them from doing so.

Being able to spend almost the whole day outdoors in the courtyard, together with prisoners from the other cells, we came into contact with women criminals for the first time. Once an old woman with a gloomy expression on her face sat down on a bench where two young Sisters were sitting. One of the Sisters asked, "And why are you here?" The answer came: "I hacked my old man to death." Astounded by the response, they stopped saying or asking anything. We heard of other frightful and bloody reasons for prison sentences.

We spent two weeks at the Sverdlovsk transit prison. Mother Catherine and Sister Lucia Chekhovskaya remained at the Sverdlovsk transit prison and the rest of us were transported by train to Tyumen, where we spent two weeks under more normal conditions in the Tyumen transit prison. In every city we always walked from the train station to the transit prison in file, down the middle of the road, together with the other convicts, most of whom were criminals, surrounded by an armed convoy with bayonets tilted forward, accompanied by police dogs – which presented a plaintive and curious spectacle for city residents. In Tyumen our group of Sisters was combined with a group of Leningraders that included eight Kronstadt sailors, a grey-haired Orthodox priest, formerly the pastor in a leper colony in Hamburg, and ten so-called "former people" – i.e., people with titles who had a privileged social status prior to the revolution.

At the wharf they loaded everyone into the hold of a steamship and we set off down the Tobol River for Tobolsk. The hold was basically filled with criminals naked to the waist because it was so hot and stuffy. Their bodies were heavily tattooed with all sorts of drawings and inscriptions. There was little air in the hold – it was saturated with the acrid odor of fuel oil, petroleum, fish and human sweat. Many felt nauseous because of the lack of air and the heat. The young and energetic sailors demanded of the head of the convoy and steamship administration that a telegram be sent immediately to the Political Red Cross with a protest against the unbearable conditions. They managed to get all the women and elderly transferred from the hold to a large cabin that was freed up for them. Thus the convoy arrived in Tobolsk.

We spent a few days in the prison. We of course had to sign a "collective responsibility" agreement, meaning that each of the exiles separately answers for any violation of the signed conditions, thus vouching with his own head for each one in the group. The convoy then gave everyone the right to go independently to his or her place of exile, which would be assigned by the local GPU. In the morning they released us onto a large square. One had to find a place to spend the night until departing for one's assigned place of exile. There was very little money – and one had to pay for the overnight lodging, buy a ticket for the steamship, and somehow manage to eat.

Northern Tobolsk Exile – 1924-1927

The GPU made the exile assignments: some Sisters were sent to villages south of Tobolsk, others to the north, along the Irtysh River and the Ob River; all would be placed alone except for the blood sisters, Sisters Teresa and Veronica, who were allowed to live together in the village of Chernoye. When the Sisters heard that I – the youngest one – was being exiled to Obdorsk, a settlement on the Arctic Circle, the older Sisters, interrupting one another, began to ask that one of them be sent there instead of me. But the GPU wouldn't listen to them and everything remained unchanged.

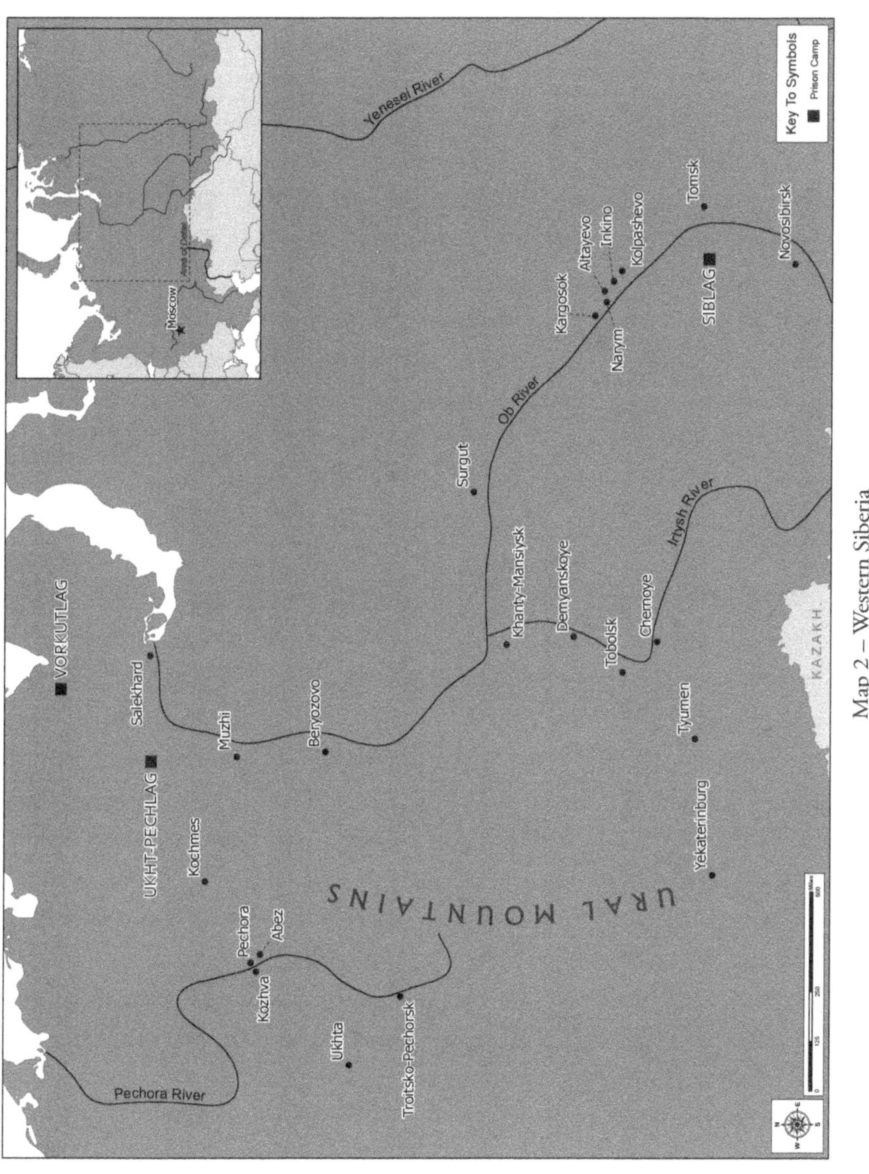

Map 2 – Western Siberia

We spent several days in Tobolsk awaiting a steamship down the Irtysh, then further north on the Ob. Steamers to the Far North plied the river very rarely, only three or four times in a navigation season. The first ice breaker would arrive around June 20, and the last, at the beginning of September. At that time there was no other way of travel other than by river. Sisters Maria

Rosa, Magdalina and I were going north; Sisters Lucia and Joanna were temporarily remaining in Tobolsk. At the village of Samarovo [now Khanty-Mansiysk], at the confluence of the Irtysh and the Ob, 240 miles north of Tobolsk, two Sisters had to change ships – Sister Maria Rosa, the mistress of postulants and novices, and I, the youngest, who had been the next to last to enter the community. We still had a long way to go down the Ob.

Our steamer traveled through the taiga. When it stopped to take on a supply of wood from the bank, passengers, most of whom were also exiles, would go ashore and into the surrounding forest. The sailors would shout after them, “Don't go far or you'll meet up with Mikhail Ivanovich!” (That was the nickname for a bear.) One had the impression that no human foot had ever stepped here. Woodland animals scurried by – rabbits, chipmunks, squirrels. There were a lot of fallen trees and when you stepped on one you fell right through because everything was rotten under the bark. How many years had they lain there untouched?

The further north we went, the broader and higher the river became. The forest was thinning out, becoming sparse as it steadily changed into tundra. The air became colder even though it was the middle of summer and the sun shone brightly. There was almost no night. Everyone on the steamer wore warm clothing. We had long passed Beryozovo, where the forest ended and the tundra began. In the village of Muzhi (660 miles from Tobolsk), Sister Maria Rosa had to debark. It was hard for her to leave me, the youngest Sister, all alone. Our parting was touching.

Further on, the Ob was so wide that you could barely see its banks. There was only water, sky, God – and the surging of the soul toward Him. There was no disturbance – only a complete isolation from everything and everyone. Awareness of the nearness of God and union with Him penetrated my soul more deeply than ever before.

The steamer arrived in Obdorsk (780 miles from Tobolsk) early in the morning. The steamer's arrival was always a big event and holiday for the local population, who had impatiently been awaiting the mail and food supplies being delivered for the whole year – until the next navigation season. Ice on the river breaks up around the third week of June and the river freezes up again at the beginning of September. An ice breaker moves through at the beginning and the end of the navigation season. In July and August an icy wind can unexpectedly blow in from the north and leave a thick layer of snow that lasts several days. There were times when there was not enough food and everyone went hungry. So when the ice breaker appeared, dragging barges with food, some of the locals, risking their lives, would go out in boats to meet the caravan, maneuvering between huge ice floes, in order to bring food to their starving families more quickly.

Obdorsk (renamed Salekhard in the 1930s) is situated on a high point on the right bank of the Ob, almost at its confluence with a small tributary, the Poluya. The bank goes down to the river like an amphitheater. Those who had come to meet the steamer, most of whom were exiles, were spread out along the ledges. Fragments of their words in French and English reached us. The sky was blue, the sun shone brightly, but it was so cold that both exiles and local residents were all in warm fur clothing – reindeer skins and high fur boots. And this was mid-July.

The tundra, covered with moss, ledum (commonly known as Labrador Tea), and cowberries, stretched out around Obdorsk and further toward the Arctic Ocean. There wasn't a single normal tree, just a few misshapen, bush-like birches stunted by permafrost. In the summer there were two months of warmth, when the tundra melted a bit. The sun never set and we had round-the-clock daylight. In the winter the temperatures dropped down to minus 60 degrees Celsius (minus 76 degrees Fahrenheit) and there was a grayish night instead of day. From time to time we saw the aurora borealis. People got around by light sleighs drawn by three or four pairs of reindeer. Contact with other populated points was only by the river – in summer, on the infrequent steamers, and in winter, on sleighs drawn on the ice by reindeer and horses. (At least that's how it was back then.)

It was hard to find a place to live in Obdorsk because many other exiles had already arrived. An elderly Komi woman helped me find a place to live, and this woman remained a friend to the end of my exile. The population of Obdorsk comprised Komis and Russians. Ostyaki and Nentsy (Samoyeds) led a nomadic life with herds of reindeer on the tundra and they came in to Obdorsk only to trade furs, cod-liver oil and reindeer meat for bread and other foods and also for the trade fair.

The local residents of Obdorsk were fishermen and hunters – basically good and religious people. At least, that's how it was in those day. One could come to believe that the further one went from the large cities and the so-called cultural centers, the better the people were – honest, kind-hearted, good, and spiritually more simple. Their relationships with one another were full of trust and good will, and their universal honesty was such that nothing was ever locked – not the sheds, their warehouse with a year's supply of food, nor their own homes, even when the owners and their whole family would go on a fishing trip for a couple of weeks. I expressed surprise, but they told me, "Why lock up? No one will take anything." I attributed this to the salutary influence of missionaries who had come to Obdorsk and labored there and in the tundra among the nomadic Ostyaki and Nentsy.

The other exiles tried, under all kinds of attractive pretexts, to draw me into their company, but understanding the danger in this, I firmly declined their efforts. At the beginning of my first year of exile, I received a telegram from the Political Red Cross to the effect that I could be included on a list for an exchange [of prisoners] with Poland and that I should telegraph my agreement to Moscow. I rejected the offer – which I had to do two more times. For me, leaving Russia would be a rejection of those difficulties and trials now facing me, which I, like all the Sisters, considered the Lord's response to our desire to sacrifice ourselves for Russia, and thus to undergo suffering was a great honor. In my understanding, agreeing to the exchange would simply be a desertion. At this same time, Sister Rose of the Heart of Mary, serving a five-year sentence in the Irkutsk prison, received a similar telegram and gave the same refusal even though all her relatives lived in Poland. We wanted to be faithful to our vows to the end.

In the summer of the second year of our exile, Sister Maria Rosa unexpectedly came from Muzhi for several days. She wanted to visit me, and for me this was a great joy. During the past year Sister Maria Rosa had sent me several letters, always solicitous, containing valuable advice, and serving as a support and a theme for spiritual reflection.

In that same year, the main church of the two that were in Obdorsk was closed; the church had a large missionary library. The church elder, meeting me one day on the street, told me that since they hadn't yet removed the books from the church, I was welcome to take whatever I wanted for myself. I chose a volume from the collected works of Saint John Chrysostom, several books of Saint Gregory the Theologian, a book of Saint Theodore the Studite, a volume of patristics, and a volume of Lives of the Saints. Great was my joy when I leafed through these books, as if meeting my very dearest and closest friends after a long separation! This spiritual support greatly strengthened me.

In the spring of 1925 I was living with a Russian family that had four children, little girls ranging in age from two to eight years old. The mother, Catherine Benediktovna, was an intelligent and strong-willed woman who had taken an interest in me; we had become acquainted and she posed many questions concerning faith and the Church. Once settled in with this family, I began catechizing the mother and children and told them about many things.

That summer the local GPU re-assigned me to a place even further north, the village of Khe, located in Ob Bay in the Gulf of the Arctic Ocean and comprising a few little houses. This further exile was apparently a punishment for my categorical refusal to cooperate with the GPU (for which I had been promised immediate release from exile and well-paid employment for the rest of my life). But the captain of the small commercial steamer going there refused to take me because he had no passengers and did not want to take the responsibility upon himself.

Instead of the re-assignment, a great joy came to pass. In His ineffable mercy, God turned everything to the good. Sisters Magdalina and Lucia came to Obdorsk. Wanting to talk without eavesdroppers, to pray and thank God for the favor this meeting, we went out into a large open space where there was a pile of logs. We found a place among the logs that was the most hidden from view and had just begun to pray the rosary when suddenly a local woman appeared and, giving us several large fish, she bowed and said, "Take these, servants of God!" By our outward appearance we looked nothing like nuns – we were very young and wore secular clothing, but rumor about the fact that we were Catholic Sisters followed us everywhere.

Sisters Magdalina and Lucia settled in together with me and from that moment we began to live in accordance with our community rules. There was only one wooden trestle bed in the room for sleeping. Sister Magdalina wanted Sister Lucia or me to sleep on it – but we persuaded her to let us sleep on the floor, as in the community. So the bed stood there like a "decoration," used only if one of us fell ill. Sister Lucia and I continued our novitiate under the guidance of Sister Magdalina, who instructed us as well as Catherine Benediktovna and her children.

Sister Magdalina, one of the eldest sisters (she was fourth in order of profession), was very well educated, spiritually mature, truly full of repentance, faithful to the three religious vows, self-disciplined and selfless. Always bright and cheerful, she worked a lot, taking upon herself always the most difficult and unpleasant work – and for food and clothing, always the worst. She would say, "Everything that is not from us is from God." In order to somehow earn some money to live on, Sister Magdalina had more than once washed the dirty laundry of the sailors of the ocean steamers passing through [Tobolsk] on their way to Obdorsk, even though she had never in the past had any experience with that kind of work. I worked as a typist in each of the few establishments in Obdorsk, but only for two months at each because that was all the GPU would permit. Sister Lucia drew pictures – the Most Holy Virgin Mary of the Immaculate Conception, Christ with a crown of thorns, and others. God's blessing was evident in all things.

We spent the Great Fast (Lent) with the family of Catherine Benediktovna, and we spent it well. We had solitude. The children (the older ones were nine, seven and five years old) also actively participated in everything. They would run to their lessons with joy, with bright eyes hungrily listening to the conversations of the Sisters with their mother. They absorbed everything well and diligently copied out short stories of the saints' lives with their large children's letters.

Easter came. The father of the family went to Matins at the church. We Sisters, dressed in our holy day finest, and Catherine Benediktovna woke the children around midnight, just as they had begged us to do. We dressed the little girls in their best dresses. In our room we had set up a beautifully adorned little altar. A lamp burned near the icon and candles and little lanterns were burning on little shelves that Sister Lucia had arranged on both sides of the little altar. With faith and a great uplifting of the spirit, we began to read and sing the Liturgy.

Suddenly both the little shelves on either side of the altar jumped up, as if shaken from below by someone, and the little lanterns went out. Calmly, without a word, we put everything back in place and began to sing Easter Matins. Almost immediately a deafening crash resounded, as if from an exploding bomb. It seemed as though the roof was crashing down and that the ceiling over the stove and the large Russian oven, which served as a partition, were all tumbling down. For an instant everyone stood still – deafened, pale, and the children with fright on their faces. The Sisters and Catherine

Benediktovna, calmly, without a word, took the lamp and went outside expecting to see the destruction. But there was nothing. The ceiling and the stove were fine. Everything was in its proper place and right order.

This phenomenon could not be explained by natural causes. It was obvious that "Someone" was blatantly displeased by the shared exaltation, faith and joy, and apparently his goal was to bring chaos and impede the common prayer praising God and the Risen Christ; but no such chaos occurred. We reacted to everything calmly and in complete silence, and without any hindrance we finished singing Matins. This event in no way spoiled everyone's festive mood – on the contrary, it made even more tangible the nearness of God and the joy of our common safety in Him. Thus did our life blessedly pass....

At the same time, something sorrowful and difficult happened. Someone coming from Muzhi informed us that Sister Maria Rosa, who lived there, had married one of the exiles. This news struck us like a thunderbolt and wounded our hearts. How could it be?! Sister Maria Rosa, the eldest of the Sisters, intelligent, soft-spoken, so spiritual, the one who knew so much, who had guided not only the novices but many parishioners as well – she had married? How could this have happened? We were inconsolable. Sister Magdalina took it especially hard; by nature a bright blond woman with a fresh, attractive face, she literally grew dark – even her lips became parched and cracked, as sometimes happens when a person has a high fever.

But then, how did this happen? Sister Maria Rosa, upon arriving in Muzhi, helped her landlords with their work and also gave private lessons to several local residents. She wrote Mother Catherine (in Tobolsk prison) short and always inspiring letters, and several times she had sent me letters with admonitions and instructions. When the wife of one of the exiles fell ill, Sister Maria Rosa often visited her and selflessly looked after her. Here, at the bedside of the sick woman, she was also in contact with her husband. The woman died. The husband was grief-stricken, and Sister Maria Rosa, of course, considered it her Christian duty to give him moral support. And thus what began in the spirit ended in the flesh. Such happenings, alas, are not uncommon in every age.

How easily and unnoticeably does a person, having begun with the purest, loftiest spiritual intentions, in the absence of vigilance, slide onto a purely material level, and here his natural inclinations, his passions and instincts gain the upper hand, gradually blinding him. In such situations, the feeling of natural pity is especially dangerous. The person's psychology, understanding, and attitude toward everything change completely. How incessantly must one keep watch over one's soul, over one's thoughts and feelings!

Around the same time another incomprehensible event happened. A family of postal workers lived in Obdorsk. The parents were Communists, the sons were in the Pioneers. In the summer they were going on vacation for a month to Tobolsk and they asked us to live in their house for that time. Prior to this they had turned to us several times, asking us to pray for their needs. We settled into the first room of the house, firmly closing the doors to the other rooms. As always, we lived the regular life, in accordance with all the rules of the community. And thus once after evening prayer, while we were making our examination of conscience, we were sitting in the dimmed light of the lamp such that the room was in semi-darkness.

Suddenly, in the opposite corner of the room, a loud noise sounded from above, as if the ceiling were collapsing; it was as if from this heap something alive and light-weight had fallen on the little table standing in the corner. Sister Magdalina and I looked around and, turning up the light in the lamp, without saying a word went to the corner to see what had happened. But everything was in order – nothing was out of place. Sister Lucia hadn't heard or noticed anything and looked at us with surprise. After finishing our prayers, thinking that perhaps someone's cat had crawled into the room, we again carefully inspected the room – which was practically empty and tightly closed off – but we found nothing. Again, it was impossible to explain this by natural causes.

We joyfully lived together for a year. Then in the summer of 1926 the GPU sent Sisters Magdalina and Lucia from Obdorsk to separate villages further to the south. I once again remained alone and lived as before in the friendly, cordial household of Catherine Benediktovna, instructing her and her children. At that time two other women began to visit me for conversations: an elderly local woman and a young Orthodox nun who had also been exiled to Obdorsk and had rather poor religious formation.

The nun would come, bow low, and call me "mother." She often cried, so touched was she by our conversation. She brought me letters that she had received from Orthodox laity asking her advice in difficult situations, mostly concerning questions of faith and religion; this kind nun did not understand them and did not know how to answer. These people didn't know which of the two pastors serving them they should believe as they preached and taught in contradiction to each other. I managed to sort out their difficulties and answer their letters. In doing so, I thought sadly, "Truly, a flock without a shepherd." These poor people want to find the true way and guidance, and they do not find them. "The harvest is great but the laborers are few!" This young nun eventually stopped coming to see me; apparently the Orthodox bishop, newly arrived to his place of exile, forbade her these visits.

At the beginning of 1927 a young local woman began to visit me for conversations. Zoya Mikhailovna was the same age as I (twenty-seven) but she already had four children, the youngest of whom was only six months old. It was hard for her to get away from the house because her husband and the grandmothers were against it and followed her. Secretly slipping behind the houses, she ran to my place. I was joyful and amazed at how correctly and ardently Zoya Mikhailovna absorbed everything, and how deeply she was touched by everything. Later on, both Catherine Benediktovna and Zoya Mikhailovna with their children became Catholic, which they officially formalized two years later in Tobolsk, where Father Alexey Zerchaninov, a very elderly Eastern Rite Catholic priest, was serving out his exile.

The head of the family – Samuel Afanasyevich, a good and kind man – kept himself aloof. Many years later, after the death of his wife Catherine in the 1950s, he also became a Catholic, having come to Moscow. Of their children, the second (Lyubov) and fourth (Nadezhda) are faithful Catholics to this day and occasionally travel with their children from Siberia in order to fulfill their Christian obligations. Zoya Mikhailovna, who many years ago became a secular Third Order Dominican, every year comes to visit the Sisters in Vilnius from the Crimea where she lives with her daughter.

In August 1927, after finishing my third year of exile, I was allowed to leave Obdorsk. Catherine Benediktovna was inconsolable. She loved me so much and had become very attached to me. On the eve of my departure, she cried so hard that her eyes and face were all swollen – and because she had just recently given birth to their second son,[7] she wasn't able to go with her husband and their three daughters to accompany me to the wharf. As

[7] The first son had been born a year and a half earlier.

the steamer made its way further and further from the wharf, where all those bidding farewell were standing and waving their handkerchiefs, I burst into tears even though until this moment I had bravely held myself together. In the more than two years of living with this family I had come to love them all so much and now, departing, I left with them a part of my heart.

Eastern Tobolsk Exile – 1924-1930

Sisters Stephania and Rosa Maria were assigned to places east of Tobolsk. Once settled into the wooded village, they began to live regular religious observance, as they had earlier in the community, and they prayed much in contemplation and silence. Sister Stephania worked with the landlord's children and did general work around the house, and Sister Rosa Maria earned money sewing; they lived on this money, without any outside help. Sister Rosa Maria fell ill with pulmonary tuberculosis, but kind people supported them, bringing them milk and eggs, and the forest's pine air was good for her health. Thus did they peacefully and quietly spend their three years of exile.

Sister Magdalina, living in the village of Samarovo further down on the Irtysh River (near its confluence with the Ob), fell ill and the authorities allowed her to go back to Tobolsk for treatment. Sister Margaret of Hungary also ended up in a wooded village east of Tobolsk. Once she got permission from the local authorities to go mushroom-gathering with the peasants. The forest stretched out over huge expanses. They all agreed not to lose sight of each other and to call out back and forth. Sister Margaret became engrossed in gathering mushrooms but then realized that she no longer heard any response to her calls. She had become separated from the group of peasants. She had lost her bearings and, frightened, she turned now in one direction, then another. She wandered through the woods for a long time and became tired. They had come to the forest in early afternoon and now dusk was already falling. It was clear that she wouldn't be able to find her way out of the woods on her own. And both wolves and bears were on the prowl.

Sister Margaret sat under a bush to rest and pray, entrusting herself entirely to God's help. Thus she sat for some time and suddenly she caught the sound of a faraway gun shot, and then it became louder and louder. Filled with hope, she jumped up and went toward the sound of the gun shots that kept getting louder. She began to cry out and after a short time the peasants surrounded her. They were glad they had found her, but they cursed her out roundly for having caused them so much trouble.

There was no work to be had in the village except for working in the fields. Digging potatoes, Sister Margaret caught a cold, and on account of the cold and her nerves, she completely lost her voice; she was therefore allowed to go to Tobolsk for treatment. In Tobolsk, together with Sister Magdalina who had come from Samarovo, they began to take packages to Mother Catherine, who had also recently been brought to Tobolsk [Prison]. Sisters Lucia and Joanna, who had been left temporarily in Tobolsk, had found work: Sister Lucia found a position as a kindergarten teacher where she was universally respected, distinguishing herself as a capable teacher. Sister Joanna also worked as a school teacher, despite the fact that such positions were not usually open to administrative exiles.

The Sisters, now joined by Sister Margaret and Sister Magdalina, were happy that they could attend Mass each day at the local church, celebrated by the well-versed and devout Father Alexey Zerchaninov. He knew by heart the lives of all the saints of the year, and after Mass in the sacristy he would narrate the life of the saint for the day. At the end of the year, the authorities summoned Sister Lucia to the GPU and after questioning forbade her from attending church – to which she responded: "I will be going to church." After this, in the second year of her exile, they sent her and Sister Magdalina to Obdorsk [Salekhard] on the Arctic Circle, and Sister Joanna was assigned to the village of Demyanskoye.

Sisters Teresa and Veronica, being related by blood, were sent together to the village of Chernoye [south of Tobolsk by more than 60 miles]. Because they hadn't enough money, they had to walk to Chernoye, with their things then brought by cart. Along the way, all their belongings were stolen and they were left without beds and warm clothing. This caused serious problems for them until the Sisters still back in Moscow were able to send them the basic necessities. The Sisters earned their way by working in the fields and gardens and by sewing, but mostly by making children's toys. After serving out their three-year exile, Sister Veronica (the younger of the two and still a novice) managed to return to Moscow and enrolled in the Economics Institute. Sister Teresa (who had already made vows) went back to her parents' and soon thereafter married.

Narym Exile, 1924-1927

Another group of Sisters and parishioners sentenced to administrative exile was transported from the Moscow prison eastward, to the city of Tomsk, in the Narym region, and then on to the regional center, the village of Kolpashevo. The Sisters in this group were Sisters Osanna, Agnia, Antonina and Margaret Mary; the parishioners were Boris Ivanovich Feodorov, Elena Vasilyevna Feodorova, and Catherine Vladimirovna Pozen. From Kolpashevo the Sisters were split up and assigned to villages along the Ob River. They each went alone. At first they all set out together on the steamship, but gradually along the way they had to part from one another.

The first to go ashore was Sister Margaret Mary. There were no buildings whatsoever on the river bank; the settlement was a ways in from the river, which flooded in the spring. There was only one other peasant who left the ship with Sister Margaret Mary. They set off together along the road to the settlement and the Sisters aboard the ship for a long time watched the departing figure of Sister Margaret Mary with a rucksack on her shoulders.

The next to leave their company was Sister Antonina, at the village of Inkino. There was something like a wharf and four little houses on the bank – the village was further, about two miles. As the steamer approached the wharf, exiles gathered around, as this day was always a holiday for them. The steamer brought the mail that everyone impatiently awaited. There was a medical clinic at Inkino and the following year, when Sister Margaret Mary was in need of treatment, she got permission to move to Inkino.

This was a great joy and a relief for them. Sisters Antonina and Margaret Mary could now once again live the regular life in accordance with the rules of the community and the three vows of religion – even the vow of obedience. Sister Antonina, who had entered the community half a year before Sister Margaret Mary, became the Superior.[8] They lived in harmony and good cheer despite frequent difficulties. Sister Catherine of Siena (Balasheva) sent them money from Moscow – not much, of course, because she had to be concerned about the many Sisters who were in prisons, labor camps and exile. Soon after the death of Sister Catherine de Ricci (Galkina), Sister

---

[8] Mother Catherine, in preparing to send the Sisters off into their exile, gave them this wise directive: when living with another Sister, always be obedient to the Sister who first entered the community. Thus the regular life of the community would be continued under any conditions, which would help to preserve their vocation and the practice of religious life.

Catherine of Siena and Sister Hyacinth, who had been allowed to remain in Moscow to care for her, were also arrested and exiled.

The Narym region was terribly desolate – sparsely populated, with very difficult living conditions. Sister Agnia got a position alone as a nurse at the hospital in Inkino. Working all day, from morning until late at night, she still prayed the Divine Office at the appointed hours for community prayer, as she had in the past. Sister Antonina worked with the children of the owner of the house. Nothing disturbed the Sisters – in all things they saw the will of God and they tried to observe all the rules of the community, especially silence. During Lent they decided to keep silence every day of the week except Sunday. This brought them great joy – and when Sunday came, words seemed so significant that there was no desire to say anything superfluous.

Village residents treated the Sisters with great respect, and when the Sisters walked through the village on the great feasts during the summer, wearing their best white dresses, the villagers said among themselves, "There go our white swans." They had just finished their postulancy and did not know what they were to do next – and the older Sisters had been sent further north. So they needed to visit an older Sister, but it wasn't possible to travel by steamer without the permission of the president of the village soviet. So Sister Antonina decided to take the risk and travel during the winter by sleigh. At that time they were living not in Inkino itself, but about two miles from the village. The president of the village soviet was responsible for exiles there as well. He was going to the village of Altayevo, where Sister Osanna was, and he agreed to take Sister Antonina with him. Thanks to this meeting the Sisters were able to clarify some questions with a professed Sister; however, they were only able to do this once.

Like all exiles, the Sisters had to go twice a week to register, and thus they became acquainted with several exiles. Among them was a family of Masons: a performing artist with his wife and little girl and their friend, a painter. Once they all came to visit the Sisters and the painter became interested in the icon hanging in the corner of the room. It had no particular value as a work of art, but he asked permission to hold it for a short time. Soon he returned it and the Sisters again hung it in the corner.

That same evening (it was before a holy day), the Sisters were praying before bedtime. Suddenly they heard some kind of noise in the kitchen: bottles knocked against each other in the cupboard and the wooden washstand jangled. They looked at one another with bewilderment, but they did not interrupt their prayers. When they finished praying they went to look in the kitchen. Everything was in its place, except water was spilled near the washstand. They returned to their room and went to bed, but something seemed somehow unpleasant, not right – and they couldn't sleep.

They didn't turn out the lamps, but just lowered the flame. Sister Antonina began to pray the rosary. Suddenly the door squeaked and opened slightly. Sister Antonina saw a white chicken come into the room and head for the trestle bed on which she was lying. She thought it was funny – here it was just the chickens that were kept in a cage in the kitchen and had gotten out of the cage and made all the noise. She got up quickly to lead the chicken back to its place, but it was nowhere to be found, and the chickens in the kitchen were calmly sleeping in their places in the cage. There was not a white chicken among them.

The Sisters remembered that they had some holy water brought from Tomsk, where there was still a church and a priest at that time. They prayed and sprinkled the holy water throughout the whole room. It was quiet in the house, but a noise arose outdoors. It sounded like horses with wagons rushing around the house on a stone pavement. But there was no stone pavement – the house was surrounded by grass. They did not sleep the whole night after this adventure. They could not explain these phenomena by natural causes – they were undoubtedly connected with the Masons' visit and with the icon taken by the artist. The older Mason, the performing artist, whenever he would encounter Sister Antonina, would say something nasty to her and he mockingly called her "Mother Superior."

In the second year of their exile, in 1926, a nine-year-old boy named Vova came to live with them. He was the son of parishioner Catherine Pozen, a young widow [and the sister of Sister Margaret Mary] who had been arrested at the same time with the Sisters and was serving out her exile not far from Kolpashevo. Catherine had married an exile and her son soon thereafter announced that this new husband interfered with his "spiritual perfection"; thus he asked to go to live with his Aunt Olga, Sister Margaret Mary. They put him on a steamship, entrusting him to an exile who was going in the same direction, and the little fellow came to live with the Sisters "for his perfection." And thus the Sisters took on another task – dealing with a young boy. In addition they were also studying English with Sister

Margaret Mary, who knew it well. (Her brother sent her the necessary books from Moscow.) The days passed without notice, quickly, in prayer, studies and housework.

In the third year of their exile the Sisters had a very distressing experience. They found out that Sister Agnia, who had been working at the hospital as a nurse and was much respected and in good standing, was engaged in an intimate relationship with a doctor. After the end of her three-year exile, without even stopping to see the Sisters, she left for the Crimea with this man. Sister Osanna also eventually married. One of the Sisters later ran in to her – by then she already had two sons. With great bitterness she said, "I traded gold for dirt!"

Mother Catherine, 1924-1933

After the departure of the Sisters from the Sverdlovsk transit prison, Mother Catherine and the Leningrader Lucia Chekhovskaya remained there among the women convicts, most of whom were criminals. Mother Catherine disliked listening to their conversations about various crimes, which they did not at all regret; in fact they even seemed to take pleasure in recalling them and bragging about them. It was difficult to see the boundless degradation of human nature.

The food was awful – pea soup with spoiled meat for dinner and wheat kasha for supper. There was very little money and it had to be saved for the rest of the trip. The bedbugs wouldn't let one sleep at night and to protect themselves from them, they slept without undressing and struggled all night with bedbugs. The window panes were broken, so it was cold and the beds were wet from the wind and rain. They slept on solid bed planks, lying on one half of a blanket and covering up with the other half.

At the end of August the authorities sent them to Tobolsk along with the criminals, most of whom were men. En route they spent two weeks at the transit prison in Tyumen. On September 7, 1924, they arrived by steamer in Tobolsk. They had to walk a long way from the wharf to the prison, through thick mud that was so deep that it was hard to lift one's feet. Mother Catherine and Lucia were glad when they saw Sister Lucia and Sister Rosa Maria walking along the sidewalk. They, along with Sister Joanna, had been in Tobolsk since July. Sister Magdalina was also temporarily in Tobolsk at that time.

At the prison Mother Catherine and Sister Lucia were put in a common cell with criminals, but in the morning they were moved to a small cell, which they considered a blessing. They tried to use the silence and solitude for prayer and spiritual reflection. At the end of October they were moved back into the common cell with the criminals where they again slept on solid bed planks, without mattresses; fortunately, there were not so many bedbugs.

The Sisters who were living in Tobolsk brought packages to the prison twice a week. Sister Magdalina, having declared that she was the adopted daughter of Mother Catherine, was granted permission to visit her twice a month. Mother Catherine often received letters from the Sisters and she immediately answered them. (There were no restrictions on correspondence in the Tobolsk prison.) Over the course of two years Mother Catherine carried on a lively correspondence with the Sisters, for whom her letters were a great consolation. She was later forbidden the right of correspondence, except for three or four letters a year, and those could only convey her material needs. Life in prison seriously affected her health; she began to suffer from boils on her legs due to bodily exhaustion.

Finding herself among criminals, Mother Catherine maintained her own personal dignity and she related to them cordially and straight-forwardly, always sharing with them everything she received. She established such good relations with them that they respected her, came to love her, and were even concerned about her, not allowing her to engage in physical labor – they washed the floors for her, tidied up, and washed her laundry. If some sort of brawl arose among the criminals and the prison guards were unable to out-shout the women, the supervisor would say, "We need to call Abrikosova – that'll settle it." If the women began to quarrel and use foul language, seeing her walking by their cells they would say, "Hush, Anna Ivanovna is walking by!" Mother Catherine was for them a very dear person and they were ready to do anything for her. Once they even planned to beat up one of the guards on her account, but Anna Ivanovna talked them out of it.

Much later – in 1928 or 1929 – when Zoya Mikhailovna came to Tobolsk from Obdorsk with her children to officially complete her entrance into the Catholic Church with Father Alexey Zerchaninov, she became acquainted with a certain Barbara Yakovlevna who was living in the building where Zoya was staying. Barbara worked in the prison as a medical assistant, and she spoke glowingly of Mother Catherine. As a result of such popularity, the prison officials isolated her, transferring her to a solitary cell.[9] From this time forward Mother Catherine spent all of her years in prison in solitary confinement – which was fine with her. It was possible to read secular books in prison, but there were no religious books. They were forbidden.

The women prisoners with whom she had previously been confined retained their fondness for her and tried to do kind things for her, sending her flowers and various plants which she loved a lot. The women were able to pick them while working in the prison gardens. The solitary cell in which Mother Catherine had been placed had an unusual appearance: it was always clean and tidy, with a little table covered with white cloth, and over the table and the bunk hung fresh or dried flowers.

Mother Catherine, as always, was calm, bright and in a somewhat festive mood. When representatives of the investigatory organs and the prosecutor came out from Moscow for an inspection of the prison, they made the rounds of the convicts' cells, including Mother Catherine's cell. They were amazed not only by the unusual appearance of the cell, but also by the dignified appearance of the convict. One of them, going into the next cell, remarked about her, "Things apparently aren't all that bad for convicts in Tobolsk Prison – she looks more like a lady of the court than a convict."

After five years they transferred Mother Catherine from Tobolsk Prison to the Yaroslavl Political Isolator, which was known for its strict regimen and isolation, not only from the outside but from other convicts as well. Von Burman provides interesting information about this period of strict isolation:

> In the Yaroslavl isolator correspondence was particularly restricted. Prisoners were allowed to write two or three times a year to one of their closest relatives, but even for this they needed special permission from the central GPU. The prisoner would submit a request and the Moscow GPU would make inquiries regarding the person, and based on that information either granted or denied the request.

---

9 By this time Lucia Chekhovskaya was no longer in the prison. She had been selected as part of an exchange with Poland and departed for Poland in the autumn of 1932.

> And furthermore, not just anyone could render assistance to convicts in the form of money, food parcels or clothing. Only someone from among one's closest relatives could submit a petition for such permission. Food parcels sent to the Yaroslavl isolator without prior permission would fall into the "common pot" or would be returned to the sender.
>
> Anna Ivanovna wrote to no one during her whole time in Yaroslavl. On the one hand, this was prudent, as it avoided subjecting others to danger; on the other hand, she had no need to write because she had the benefit of regular assistance through the wife of Maxim Gorky, Catherine Pavlovna Peshkova, head of the Political Red Cross. Mme. Peshkova assumed the role of go-between for rendering assistance to any convict from any person who wanted to send something. As a result, the assistance lost any personal nature and came from the institution that she headed. On the other hand, Mme. Peshkova could remain well-informed about the fate of convicts. She was thus able to inform benefactors that Anna Ivanovna was alive, that she was still in Yaroslavl, and that packages were reaching her. (Von Burman, p. 691)

Convicts were taken from their solitary cells out to the yard for their exercise walk at the same time; this gave them the opportunity to become acquainted and speak with each other. Von Burman also notes, however, that "[A]nother Sister from her own community was simultaneously incarcerated at Yaroslavl, yet despite the fact they both very much wanted to be together, the authorities would in no way permit it. In the course of the six years during which they were both in the same prison, they did not once meet up with each other even on these walks in the yard" (Von Burman, p. 691).

Mother Catherine gave great moral support to many with whom she came into contact during these infrequent walks. For example, talking several times with a young man in a very depressed spiritual state and thinking of ending his life in suicide, Mother Catherine had such a beneficial influence on him, inspiring him with hope and courage, that his spiritual state changed completely. When he later was free, he recalled her help with great gratitude and her unforgettable, bright appearance.

During these walks she could have the good fortune of confession, meeting up and talking with priests who were also in the political isolator. She was unable, however, to receive Holy Communion the whole time of her imprisonment. Father Teofil Skalski, with whom she walked in the same group, became her confessor. Included on a list for exchange with Poland, he passed through Moscow after his release in 1932 and spoke there of Mother Catherine. Later, in 1932, he wrote a letter from Poland to Father Vladimir Abrikosov containing the following lines:

> She prayed a lot in her cell – she had Sacred Scripture and some liturgical booklets. She especially loved the penitential canon and the practice of spiritual Communion. I copied out several prayers from my breviary for her, which she liked. She prayed them every day.... She subscribed to the Soviet newspaper and was interested in the politics and life of her unfortunate fatherland.
>
> ... When she told me she had a lump in her breast, I insisted that she go to the doctor. He somehow guessed that it was cancer and sent her to the prison infirmary in Moscow. She had time to prepare herself before her departure, and her first priority was to attend to her soul. She asked me to hear a general confession of her whole life.

And in a letter written in 1937, he stated:

> I can attest that this worthy witness of the Catholic faith, always steadfast and even-tempered under trials, by the grace of God enjoyed perfect possession of spirit; she was reconciled to her bitter fate, and was an example to others, even to us priests. I do not remember her ever grumbling.[10]

Second Exile – Romny, Ukraine, 1927-1930

After they had completed their three-year exile, the Sisters were informed by the GPU that their terms had been extended another three years, but under less severe conditions: they could choose their own place of residence,

---

[10] Two letters of Father Teofil Skalski are reproduced *in toto* in a later section of this book.

excluding the six off-limit cities.[11] In reality, it turned out that there were many more than just six such cities.

Sisters Magdalina, Stephania, Lucia and Rosa Maria left Tobolsk and went to Romny, Ukraine, to serve out their new three-year terms. Sister Magdalina was the Superior of the community. She took care of children and gave private lessons; Sister Stephania took care of the landlady's son; and Sister Rosa Maria went from house to house, earning money as a seamstress.

Sister Magdalina shared all that she could with the needy who surrounded them. In particular, she shared her dinner with a certain poor woman who was ill with a serious disease. This poor woman, wanting to pay Sister something for her help, began to put the discarded scraps of food that she collected in her tureen, and Sister Magdalina, not wanting to offend her, shared this "repast" with her. Having observed this meal several times, Sister Stephania later received "permission" from the poor woman and, suppressing her repugnance, also joined her.

The government had not closed the church in Romny, but it lacked its own priest. Once every two months Father Peter Baranovsky came from Nezhin for services. Every Sunday – and every day in May and October – many of the faithful gathered in the church to pray and sing hymns, and Sister Lucia played the reed organ for these gatherings.

At the end of their second year of exile, Father Baranovsky was arrested, sentenced to ten years in "corrective" labor camps and sent to the Solovetsky Special Purpose Camp, where he died.[12]

The authorities decreed the church closed, but by the efforts of Sister Stephania the people managed to hold on to it. In response, the authorities ordered Sisters Magdalina and Stephania to leave Romny immediately. Sister Magdalina went to Smolensk and Sister Stephania went to join the Sisters in Kostroma.

---

[11] In other words, they had a "minus 6" on their papers. They were not allowed to live in Moscow, Leningrad or the capitals of the republics of the European parts of the USSR [Kiev, Odessa, Rostov, Kharkov]. Translator's Note: The list kept growing – by the 1940s it was up to 135.

[12] Editor's Note: Peter Avgustovich Baranovsky was arrested in the autumn of 1937 in Kemi; on October 9, 1937, by order of a Special Troika of the Directorate of the NKVD for the Leningrad Region, he was sentenced to the supreme penalty. On November 3, 1937, he was shot.

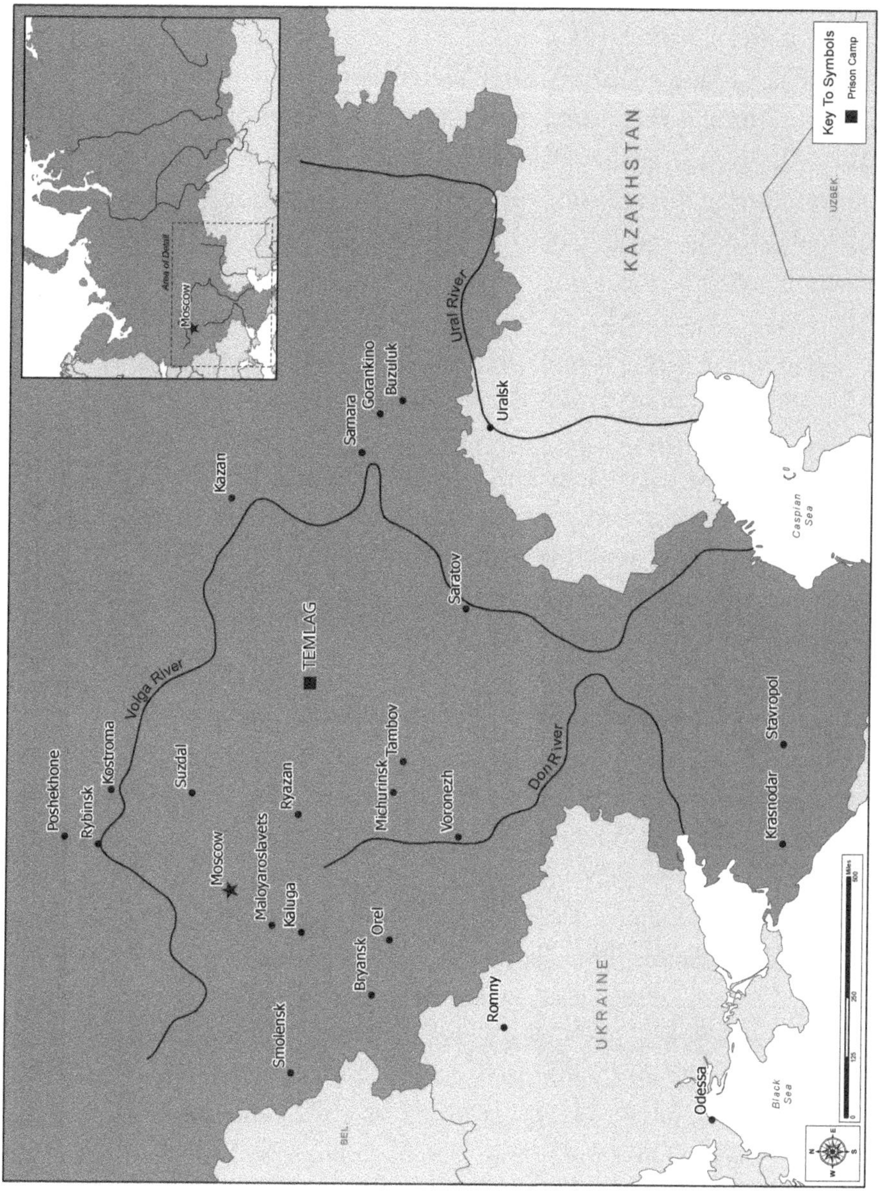

Map 3 – Western Russia

Second Exile – Kostroma, Odessa, 1927-1932

Sisters Antonina and Margaret Mary, after their Siberian exile, went to Kostroma, on the Volga River, where they settled into the house of a Jewish family, the Kugels, good and decent people, faithful to all the precepts of the Jewish religion. The family included a daughter, Minna, a good fifteen-year-old girl who was in school in Yaroslavl where she lived with relatives. When she finished school in 1929, she returned home and here she became more closely acquainted with the Sisters. Having grown up with the atheistic teachings of her school education, Minna had no notion of Christianity, and in her first conversations with the Sisters never thought that she would ever become a Christian.

At that time the church in Kostroma had still not been closed, but it lacked its own priest. Father Josiukas came from Yaroslavl from time to time and then the Sisters were able to fulfill their Christian obligations, receiving the sacraments of Confession and Holy Communion. At the end of 1930 Sister Stephania came from Romny. When the local authorities decided to close the church, the Sisters, including Sister Stephania, did all they could to keep it open – and this caused major difficulties for them.

In 1930, after completing their second three-year term of exile, the Sisters were again informed that they were not being released and that their terms were again extended. There was no legal basis for this, and Sister Stephania, without permission to do so, risked traveling to Moscow, to the Political Red Cross, to seek assistance. The head of the organization, Catherine Peshkova, still had considerable influence and consequently the new term of exile was cancelled and the three Sisters were able to leave Kostroma.

They went south, to Odessa, where there were two functioning churches at that time. They settled on the outskirts of the city in a tiny little cottage with an earthen floor and a lot of mice. They lived the regular life there in extreme poverty, but harmoniously, in accordance with all the rules of the community, under the strict and loving leadership of Sister Stephania. She helped them grow spiritually and, as she was very knowledgeable, gave them themes for meditation and retreat. Sister Antonina, who worked at a macaroni factory, and Sister Margaret Mary were remarkable for their agreeable nature, inclined to merriment, but it often happened that they would be in tears after Sister Stephania's strict reprimands.

Second Exile – Krasnodar, 1927-1930

In Tobolsk the Sister Superior told Sister Joanna and me that we were to go together. We chose Krasnodar in the Northern Caucasus. One of the other exiles gave us an address where we would be able to stay, if only for a couple nights. Sister Joanna was older than I by almost twenty years. She had graduated from the Physics and Mathematics Department of Moscow University and finished four years of the Medical Institute, whereas I had only a high school education and had studied in the piano class at Moscow Conservatory. Yet because I had entered the community a month earlier than Sister Joanna, I was to be the Superior in accordance with Mother Catherine's directive on precedence.

We could not find a place in the city, but after several days we found a small room in a village five miles from the city and connected with the city by bus. There was still a functioning church in Krasnodar. The pastor at that time was Father Pietro Alagiagian, a Jesuit priest of the Armenian rite; there was also another priest, of the Syro-Chaldean rite, and two or three times a year Father Jacob Wolf, a Roman Catholic priest, came from Novorossiisk.

We were boundlessly happy: after the harsh climate of northernmost Siberia, the wonderful, warm – and in the summer, hot – climate of the Northern Caucasus seemed like paradise. Soon we managed to find a small room with an earthen floor and a large stove in a shed in the outskirts of Krasnodar. The only furniture was a broken stool, an empty trunk with a sagging lid that Sister Joanna slept on, and a small three-legged table that I slept on, putting bricks and my suitcase in place of the missing leg. Sometimes there were "mishaps" during the night – Sister Joanna, who was short, quick, and thin, with lively black eyes, would suddenly fall into the trunk. Or, when the bricks would move apart because of any sudden movement, I would fall from the table onto the ground. These adventures in no way diminished our cheerful disposition and merriment.

We were unable to find work because no one wanted to give work to exiles. We had no means of existence and we lived not just in poverty, but extreme destitution. Nothing, however, could darken the bright and joyful state of our souls. The Lord, as always, preserved and strengthened us.

We walked each day to the church, which was a long way off. Autumn set in and the rains began. The unpaved sidewalks and roads turned into complete mush and the mud was up to your ankles.

Soon a tiny little room in one of the little houses rented by the church and located next to it became available; it was only big enough, however, for one bed and a small table. With the joint permission of the church council, the priest solemnly entrusted us with the key to this room. There was no limit to our joy! One could enter this little room only by passing through another room in which a family of three was living. In order not to disturb them, we sealed up the common doorway and began to crawl into our room through a small window that faced out onto a glassed-in veranda. There were some comical moments – for example, when friends of Sister Joanna – very solid and respectable people and no longer young – wanted to visit Sister. Not without some difficulty they also crawled into the room through the little window, saying, "If you can do it, so can we!" This only added to our merriment.

After a while I had two pupils for private music lessons and Sister Joanna found temporary work calculating statistical tables, which she was able to do at home. We lived together in such an amicable and joyful manner, united totally in mind and heart, that parishioners commented: "The two of you have one soul: Sister Philomena begins to speak, and Sister Joanna completes the thought. As soon as Sister Joanna forms a thought, Sister Philomena is already speaking it." Neighbors often remarked how well and joyfully we lived together.

In the second year of exile in Krasnodar I acquired three additional music pupils, and Sister Joanna gave three lessons in general subjects. One of the pupils was a young Jew, a pianist who had finished the conservatory and now was continuing his studies in mathematics and physics. He was a fine, modest young man with a tender and good heart. A year later he was baptized and Sister Joanna was his godmother. Our neighbor came often to visit us – a young woman along with her mother and two other women. We read the Bible with them and had religious conversations. This time of life in Krasnodar was wonderful and blessed.

On July 22, 1929, the feast of Saint Mary Magdalene, Father Pietro Alagiagian, SJ, received our vows. In the autumn of 1930, toward the end of our second three-year exile, in connection with an event in the church, the GPU expelled Father Pietro from the country, and many parishioners, including Sister Joanna and I, were summoned for interrogation.[13]

They held me at the GPU for two days; then, after releasing me, they summoned me again three days later, and then again another two or three days later. Each time over the course of two or three hours there would be absurd and strange conversations. First the investigator tried in every way to humiliate me, calling me "rotten intelligentsia" and other such things of this sort, then going in reverse, he would begin praising me for non-existent qualities, noting that I could be a necessary and useful person. Thus it continued for two weeks.

Understanding where all this was leading, and having lost my patience, I wanted to cut short this game of cat and mouse, so I exclaimed "What are you thinking? That you'll make me a spy?! That will never happen!" So the investigator shouted, "Fine! I don't have to put up with you! You have twenty-four hours to get out of Krasnodar!" I was sorry to leave Sister Joanna, but nothing could be done. I had to leave. We parted in tears.

Before returning to Moscow, where my mother was living all alone, I decided to go to Odessa where Sisters Stephania, Antonina and Margaret Mary were living. It was a great joy to see them after our six years of separation. We had a lot to talk about. The Sisters here were living in extreme poverty, on the edge of the city, in a ramshackle cottage with an earthen floor. I slept on the floor – and in the morning a few mice always jumped out from under the warm blanket. The main joy for the Sisters was the fact that there was a functioning church in Odessa and they could go to Mass and receive the sacraments of Confession and Holy Communion.

Smolensk and Moscow, 1930-1932

After visiting the Sisters in Odessa, I set off for Smolensk where Sister Magdalina was living at that time, having moved there from Romny. Sister Magdalina was living with a certain Third Order Franciscan, Antonina Barkowska, in a small room with a few other people. The cramped conditions

[13] Translator's Note: Born in 1894 in present-day Turkey, Pietro Alagiagian began his classical studies in Italy in 1908 and remained to become an Italian citizen and a Jesuit priest of the Armenian Rite. His first term of missionary service in the Soviet Union (1919-1930) ended with his expulsion in 1930; his second term of service, as a chaplain to the Italian forces in southern Russia, ended in his captivity and a 12-year confinement in Soviet prison camps. See Peter Alagiagian SJ, My Prisons in *Soviet Paradise.*

were awful. Sister Magdalina arranged for me to sleep on her trestle bed while she herself slept on a board placed on two chairs. None of my requests to be allowed to sleep on the board made any difference. Sister Magdalina lived here under very difficult conditions, but despite these, she actively participated in the life of the church.

I stayed two months with Sister Magdalina, then left for Moscow. Later I learned that mass arrests began in Smolensk at the beginning of 1931, and everyone lived in constant fear, even though absolutely not guilty of anything. Among those first arrested were Father Ivan Pavlovich and some of the parishioners, including Sister Magdalina.[14] They sent her to Moscow for investigation and put her in Butyrka Prison, where she fell seriously ill and almost died. Later, after she recovered, she was exiled for three years to Saratov. There she soon submitted an application with a request to be transferred to Krasnodar, where Sister Joanna was living and there was a functioning church. The request was granted and she left for Krasnodar.

Elizabeth Vasilyevna Vakhevich, a secular Third Order Dominican and the mother of Sister Dominica and Sister Agnes, was living in Moscow. She had breast cancer, but she refused to undergo surgery and lay motionless in her bed. Two women, complete strangers, lived in the same room with her. They left each morning for work and the sick woman was left all by herself until evening.

Now that I was back in Moscow, and since I had not yet gone to work, I began to take care of the sick woman, staying by her bedside all day. She was rather tall and heavy, so it was difficult for me to turn her over to make up the bed. Sometimes Sister Hyacinth, who was physically stronger, came and helped. Elizabeth Vasilyevna died after two months. Her daughters were at that time living in a far-away and difficult exile on the Lena River in Eastern Siberia,[15] so we Sisters buried their mother.

After Elizabeth Vasilyevna's death, I went to work as a typist at the State Bank. At that time Sister Veronica, who had returned from exile, was also living in Moscow, working and studying at the Economics Institute. We

[14] Editor's Note: Sister Magdalina was arrested April 10, 1931, and drawn into the investigation in the case against the Soloviev community of Russian Catholics in Moscow. On October 28, by decree of the Collegium of the OGPU, she was sentenced to three years' exile.

[15] 440 miles north of Irkutsk, much further north of Kirensk. The daughters had each already served their first five-year sentences, Sister Agnes in the Irkutsk prison and Sister Dominica in Solovetsky.

attended Mass each morning at Saint Louis Church, where Bishop Pius Neveu was the pastor, then went to work. We often got together and sometimes spent our days off together.

In the summer of 1931, Sister Imelda, one of the older Sisters, returned to Moscow from the Solovetsky Camp where she had served out an eight-year prison term. She temporarily stayed with her own sister; and she invited Sister Veronica and me to visit so that she could talk with us freely. But soon Sister Imelda had to leave because she did not have permission to live in Moscow. We never met up with her again, and nothing is known of her fate thereafter.

At the beginning of the summer of 1932, arriving as always at Saint Louis Church before going to work, to my indescribable joy, I saw Mother Catherine, who had been released the evening before from the Butyrka Prison hospital after surgery on a cancerous tumor. Mother Catherine stayed three days with me, since my family had gone on vacation and had given me their room in an apartment. I was living in a tiny little room with a friend.

During those days in Moscow Mother Catherine went every morning to the church of Saint Louis. She was totally radiant with an unearthly light and spiritual strength. She stayed another week with one of her acquaintances in Moscow (where she was not permitted to live). Then she left for Kostroma.

In the same year, one rainy autumn morning I saw Sister Catherine de Ricci (Selenkova) at Saint Louis. She was passing through Moscow, having been released after ten years in the Yaroslavl political isolator, which was known for its strict regime. We had absolutely nowhere to go to talk, so we sat on a bench on the boulevard, and under a fine autumn drizzle we talked for several hours, and got thoroughly soaked.

Sister Catherine had fallen ill with tuberculosis during the original imprisonment in Butyrka (1923) and over the years the disease had progressed and become more acute. She had been hospitalized more than once during her years of strict isolation in Yaroslavl. They dealt very cruelly with her – they would even come to the hospital and shout and spit at her and insult her while she lay there in bed. They apparently had directives for such treatment from higher authorities.

Sister Catherine had a great, well-rounded mind; she had been a university professor. At the beginning of the 1920s she had given lectures in the

Abrikosov community [of Russian Catholics] and she had conducted a full cycle of discussions on theological and religious-philosophical themes. Many people attended these presentations, not just parishioners. In addition, she had also directed a group of six men who were Dominican novices. It was apparently this last activity that had especially embittered the GPU. I never encountered Sister Catherine again, but one of the Sisters saw her at one of the camp transit points. We heard rumors that she died during the war at Akmolinsk camp.

Sister Teresa – Kostroma, 1931-1932

At the beginning of May 1931, Bishop Neveu sent me to visit the Sisters in Odessa and Kostroma. There I became acquainted with Minna Kugel, who at that time was nineteen years old. Her baptism came about in a most miraculous way. In 1930, already suffering from pulmonary tuberculosis, Minna went to her uncle's in Yaroslavl. There, out of curiosity, she went into a church where Father Josif Josiukas was serving at that time. It was a feast day and they were celebrating a solemn Mass with exposition of the Blessed Sacrament. Seating herself on a bench, as though she were at a theater, Minna began to look at the Sacred Host in the Monstrance. And at that moment her soul was suddenly filled with light and with a feeling she had never felt before. She was instantly penetrated by the realization that "this is God." Tears poured from her eyes; her soul was completely converted. She walked out of the church a completely different person.

Soon thereafter she wanted to be baptized, so she went to Moscow where she had relatives. Father Sergey Soloviev, a Catholic priest of the Eastern Rite, baptized her. Her baptismal name was Teresa, in honor of Saint Thérèse of the Child Jesus. Her godmother was Sister Catherine of Siena (Rubashova), a twenty-two year old who had become a secular Third Order Dominican at age seventeen. Teresa at that time was unusually touching – she was so elated, overflowing with such faith and enthusiasm – she looked at me with glistening eyes, like an angel descended from heaven.

Teresa Kugel's illness quickly progressed and the doctors considered her case hopeless. Her mother was inconsolable and spent what little means she had for Teresa's treatment. Then Bishop Neveu, pastor of the French church, Saint Louis, gave Teresa a flask of water from Lourdes. And the Lord worked a miracle – she was cured of the disease. The doctors could not understand how this happened.

Mother Catherine, 1932-1936

Bishop Neveu knew of Mother Catherine's arrival at the Butyrka Prison Hospital in Moscow in May 1932, but all his efforts to visit her before her surgery were in vain. The operation was successful. They removed her left breast and part of the muscles of her back and side, but she was left unable to use her left arm and thereafter remained disabled.

For the first time during the whole time of her imprisonment Mother Catherine submitted a request to the prison administration, asking not for her release, but that they return her to her solitary cell in Yaroslavl. On August 13 they surprised her with the news that she could go free. They of course gave her a "minus twelve" (i.e., she could not reside in the twelve off-limit cities), but they allowed her to remain ten days in Moscow to arrange her affairs before departing. Her release had been obtained through the petition of Catherine Peshkova, on the basis of her serious illness and the fact that she had nearly completed her ten-year prison term.[16]

On the morning of August 14, Mother Catherine, walking out of the prison, went directly to Saint Louis des Français Church. Bishop Neveu had never met her before this morning, but after this first meeting with Mother Catherine he wrote to Father Vladimir: "This genuine confessor of the Faith is very courageous; before such a well-tempered soul one feels small. She still looks ill. She uses only her right arm; she no longer has the use of her left arm."

After Mass Mother Catherine saw me – I was so happy for this unexpected encounter! Mother Catherine spent several days with me. From my place, Mother Catherine went to see Catherine Peshkova at the Political Red Cross; Mme. Peshkova contacted one of Mother Catherine's acquaintances, who took her in. During this time Mother Catherine was able to attend Holy Mass at Saint Louis a few more times.

One day in August 1932, Sister Teresa was on her knees praying in Saint Louis Church after confession. Coming out of the confessional, the Bishop

[16] Translator's Note: The Russian word translated here as "petition" [khlopatat'] means much, much more. It involves a dogged, unrelenting effort, going from office to office, to get the right person to give the right answer.

approached her, took her by the hand, and led her to a woman she did not know, to whom he said, "Here is one more daughter for you." It was Mother Catherine, who gave her a kiss without saying a word because Holy Mass was just about to begin.

After Mass they both left the church at the same time and Mother Catherine said to Teresa with a smile, "Well, now let's get acquainted!" She asked Teresa where she was from and requested her address, in case she would not be able to go to one of the Sisters. Teresa gave her the address of a secular Third Order Dominican who was living with two other Franciscans who had been expelled from Leningrad.

Mother Catherine was not permitted to go to Rybinsk, where Sister Rose of the Heart of Mary was serving out her exile (after having served out a five-year term in the Irkutsk isolator, and three more years in Kolpashevo as an exile). Mother Catherine therefore went to Kostroma, where Teresa lived with her parents, and took up residence in a small room on the edge of the city with Sister Margaret, who was boundlessly devoted to her. Someone who saw Mother Catherine at that time described her spiritual state with these words: "She is the very picture of strength – but at the same time, the picture of meekness."

Teresa loved Mother and was happy that she could see her every day, dropping by to visit after work. Mother always greeted her with an affectionate smile, bright and clear. She was always very modestly dressed: a black skirt and a modest white blouse with black stripes. Despite her modest attire, Mother Catherine always looked stately. Her conversation was always amiable and sweet. Her whole appearance exuded an extraordinary charm.

Her whole room was permeated with some kind of fragrance even though she wore no perfume, and the door of her room was always open to the garden, day and night. Sister Margaret worried over Mother, but Mother just smiled at this. In all her conversations one could sense her great love for the person with whom she was speaking and that person's soul, and when she spoke of God, of the Gifts of the Holy Spirit, so earnestly and with such ardor, it was clear that she herself was deeply filled with all these gifts.

Sister Margaret once said that it was very dangerous to see Teresa every day. Mother responded, as always, with a smile: "For the good and salvation of even just a single soul, I am ready to go to prison again." And then she added – "and to save the soul of this little Teresa, I am ready for another ten-year term."

Once, during one of Teresa's visits, Mother Catherine was kindly making jokes, as lively and friendly as always. Accompanying Teresa to the door, Sister Margaret whispered in her ear: "Mother has a fever of 103 degrees. The cancer has come back – she didn't sleep the whole night, tossing and turning from the pain. She asked me not to tell anyone about it." Teresa was astonished by Mother's extraordinary composure and self-control. Not even a trace of her discomfort was visible on her face. She was enduring severe pain in such a way that one would never even begin to think that she was seriously ill and suffering.

Mother Catherine maintained in her heart a deep love for the Sisters. She often dictated letters to Teresa for the Sisters, full of concern and thoughtful advice. Of Teresa herself Mother Catherine foretold, as it were, that she would be very devoted to her own spiritual family. This was later proven true. Over the course of many years Teresa deeply loved all the Sisters, her own spiritual family. Selflessly forgetting herself, she helped every Sister as much as she could, and thus it was from 1932 right up until her death.[17]

During the year she lived in Kostroma (1932-1933), Mother Catherine went to Moscow twice for medical consultations. Vera Khmeleva (the former Sister Maria Rosa) was living in Moscow at that time, with her little two-and-a-half-year-old daughter, Verochka. Her husband had died two years earlier as the result of a tragic accident – he had fallen under a tram. Vera, who loved the Sisters and now realized what she had lost, very much wanted to re-enter the community. She asked to be re-admitted, and her request was sent for consideration to the highest authority, but it was refused.

In 1932 there were several Sisters in Moscow, either temporarily residing there or just passing through; they all wanted a chance to visit with Mother Catherine. And so the following Sisters gathered at Vera's for a visit: Sisters Margaret, Imelda, Dominica, Agnes, Veronica, Hyacinth and I.

It is difficult to convey the feelings that overwhelmed the hearts of all us Sisters – feelings of joy, happiness and grief at the sight of our Mother, so deeply revered, so seriously and hopelessly ill, and yet so bright, calm and animated. From her whole appearance emanated a supernatural, unearthly

[17] She died November 2, 1977, in Vilnius after a very serious surgery at the age of sixty-five.

light. We were boundlessly happy to be together. We had gone through so much, we had so much to tell, and so much about which to seek advice. These few hours spent together remained unforgettably etched in each one's memory.

On one of her visits to Moscow, someone from Saint Louis Church introduced Mother Catherine to Camilla Kruczelnicka,[18] who had heard a lot about Mother and very much wanted to make her acquaintance. Camilla invited Mother to come visit her in the evening. She invited others as well: her niece Vera, four close acquaintances, and a student – Anechka, a sweet, fine girl [Anna Brilliantova]. She also invited me. I was not very pleased with such an evening gathering because I knew very well that everyone who had served terms in the prisons, camps and exile was under surveillance – especially Mother Catherine. Although Camilla did not consult with me – I of course would not have agreed to it – it was not possible to cancel the gathering. Anechka came not alone, but with her friend Nina, also a student, who had persuaded Anechka to bring her. Nina gave the impression of being a serious and modest girl who spoke little. The evening was very lively; we all spoke rather freely of many fine things.[19]

On August 5, 1933, Mother Catherine was arrested in Kostroma and brought to Moscow for investigation.[20] She was not put in the cell with the others, and the Sisters never saw her again. They later learned that by a decree issued in absentia by a Special Board of the NKVD, Mother Catherine was once again sentenced to ten years in prison.[21] Much later it became known that she died of cancer in Butyrka Prison, on July 23, 1936. Her body was cremated.

> The details of her last days and death remain unknown to this time. She died at age fifty-four. It is doubtful that she had the opportunity

---

[18] She was a friend of my older sister, who was at that time living with her family in Paris.

[19] Editor's Note: According to investigatory file documents, Anna Ivanovna met several times with students at Camilla's apartment.

[20] Editor's Note: The Sisters of the Abrikosova community in Moscow and other cities, along with students who had participated in meetings with Anna Ivanovna in Camilla Kruczelnicka's apartment, were drawn into an investigation in a group case against a "counter-revolutionary terrorist organization that was preparing an attempted assassination of Stalin."

[21] Editor's Note: On February 19, 1934, Anna Ivanovna Abrikosova was sentenced to eight years in prison and sent to the political isolator in Yaroslavl.

> for confession and Holy Communion before her death because this would have been infeasible in Soviet prisons. In the hospital at Butyrka Prison, men and women were in strictly isolated sections, and thus it would have been impossible to meet with a priest, even by chance, under such conditions. (Novitskaia, p. 83)

In August 1936, when it became known that Mother Catherine had died, Bishop Neveu appointed Sister Stephania as the Superior of the Dominican community.

Krasnodar, *1931-1933*

No one at Teresa's house knew that she had become a Christian and had been baptized, but her sister once noticed her wearing a cross on her neck and told her mother. A grand brawl broke out, with shouts and curses. The mother left the house and Teresa, taking almost nothing with her, headed for the train station, intending to leave her home forever. The mother soon returned and, hearing what had happened, took off for the train station where she found Teresa already seated in a train that was about to depart. Her mother begged her to return, but Teresa was adamant in her decision and left for Moscow. Once there, she sought advice from Bishop Neveu, who sent her to the Sisters in Krasnodar.

When she arrived in Krasnodar she found Sisters Joanna and Magdalina. The latter had moved here from Saratov six months earlier to serve out her term of exile. Sister Teresa settled in with them. There was no furniture in the room other than a night table and a wooden trestle bed. A little altar had been arranged on the night table, and the bed stood uncovered. They slept on the floor and ate in the landlady's kitchen.

Sister Magdalina, who was mortified in all things, strict in the fulfillment of the Rule and Constitutions of the community, was a woman of extraordinary goodness and warmth. When her relatives wanted to help her, they had to send two or three times as many things because she shared everything with needy Sisters, while she herself went about dressed in whatever could be found. She slept on a little mat so she would not soil her clothes, and put a block of wood under her head (the other Sisters used books for pillows). She did everything very well, quickly and deftly. Once when Sister Teresa fretted over her own clumsiness, Sister Magdalina said that all these external things were unimportant; that even she, when she entered the community, did not know how to boil kasha. Being the Superior, she had to feed the Sisters and take care of everything, so therefore she had to know how to do everything. She was always bright and cheerful and she worked hard, taking upon herself the hardest and most unpleasant tasks.

Parishioners often came to her with their woes and seeking advice. She always greeted them with friendliness and affection. Once an elderly woman came to see her, all in tears: her daughter, who used to attend church and sang in the choir, had been married in a civil service, and her child was not baptized. Despite the fact that Sister Magdalina worked in some establishment and had very little free time, she began to visit this family until the daughter and her husband were married in the church, and then they had the child baptized and, renewed in soul, they began to go to church on Sundays and holy days.

Another mother asked her for help in her grief: her acrobat son had fallen from the trapeze at the circus and was badly hurt. He was in serious condition and the doctors said his condition was hopeless. He had not gone to confession for many years, nor did he did go to church. Sister Magdalina began to visit him and he, being reconciled with God, made his confession, received Holy Communion and died like a saint.

Sister Joanna, very thin and strict in appearance, had a heart that was tender, self-sacrificing and kind. Once she said to Sister Teresa, "Let's go see Sister Magdalina at work." The Sisters wanted so much to see her, as though their hearts felt that soon they would be separated for a long time, until they would meet in heaven. While they were walking along, they were talking about how they would most likely get a scolding from Sister Magdalina because they were going to see her for no reason at all. When they arrived, contrary to their expectation, Sister Magdalina did not reprimand them; rather, taking a free minute from her work, she embraced both Sisters with a smile and firmly clasped them to her heart as though she too had a presentiment of their imminent separation.

Arrest and Investigation – 1933-1934

In March 1933 there was a purge in Moscow of the "unreliable element," in particular, those previously arrested who had already served out their terms. As part of this purge, I was ordered out of Moscow for three years. My mother took this very hard – she was inconsolable. I went to Ryazan, not far from Moscow, where I had the address of the brother of a close acquaintance. He was living there with his family. I found work as a bookkeeper at an establishment and worked there a few months.

On July 18, 1933, I was arrested and sent to Moscow where I was interned in the inner isolation unit of the OGPU at Bolshaya Lubyanka. Simultaneously with my arrest, Mother Catherine and Sisters Margaret, Dominica and Agnes were also arrested. In addition to the Sisters in Moscow, those parishioners who had been seen with Mother Catherine at Saint Louis Church were arrested, as were all the young people present at Camilla Kruczelnicka's evening gathering – except for Nina, the student who had come with Anna Brilliantova. Because the investigator knew certain phrases spoken at that gathering by Mother Catherine and others, it became obvious that Nina was an NKVD informant and had been sent on assignment by them.

When the investigation was concluded,[22] they transferred everyone from the inner isolation unit to the "special purpose" section of Butyrka Prison. They put me in a single cell with Sister Agnes. Being there together was wonderful. I was very glad that I came to know closely such a remarkable person. Sister Agnes was a friend of Mother Catherine from their high school days. By training she was a teacher. She had a meek, child-like, trusting nature, a lofty spirituality and a self-sacrificing, courageous and pure heart. The bright figure of Sister Agnes was impressed upon me for the rest of my life.

We passed our days in strict order: in prayer and studies. Sister Agnes was quite proficient in English, so she gave me English lessons. We were able to get an unlimited number of books from the prison library. Once the administration put a student in our cell who was obviously a "plant"; she stayed two weeks with us. We spent a few months in this cell awaiting our sentencing. We both got eight years in the camps; after sentencing we were immediately transferred to a common cell where there were twenty-five inmates being held under ordinary prison regimen.

---

[22] Editor's Note: In the indictment, all those arrested are referred to as members of a "counter-revolutionary espionage terrorist organization."

Here we met up with other Sisters. Sisters Magdalina and Joanna had been arrested in Krasnodar on October 5, 1933. Sister Teresa was arrested the following day when she came to the prison with a package for the Sisters.[23] Sister Teresa was wearing just a light dress when she was arrested. Sister Magdalina, as her Superior, made her take her own coat and dress, saying with a marvelous smile, "Don't worry, my mother will look out for me." She distributed all her belongings among the Sisters and was left with just one dress. Sister Magdalina was a true Sister of Penance. She had a grand spirit of poverty.

It had taken two and a half days to travel to Moscow from Krasnodar, and the guards gave them nothing to eat along the way, not even bread. Sister Magdalina had a little money and she asked the convoy escort to buy them some bread – they brought them a small piece. Sister Magdalina kept a tiny little piece for herself and gave the rest to Sisters Joanna and Teresa, even though these two begged that it be shared equally.

When they arrived at the Moscow prison, they were not taken to a cell right away. Sister Magdalina told Sister Teresa, who had never been arrested prior to this time, what kinds of questions the investigators would ask, how to answer them, how to behave during interrogations and in general gave her a lot of very valuable advice. With deep grief, the Sisters later learned that Sister Magdalina, right after being placed in a solitary cell, died in the prison hospital on January 27, 1934. Thus she went to heaven possessing nothing but the dress she was wearing.

After some time in the common cell, when it was already spring and time for the convoy to depart, the administration gave all the convicts post-cards to inform their relatives that they could bring a parcel for the departing convicts without having to stand in line. My mother, upon receiving such a card, brought things to the prison the following day, but they informed her that her daughter had already been taken away, that the post card had apparently gotten hung up somewhere. For my mother, this was such a blow that she was paralyzed and an ambulance had to take her to the hospital. We had no other relatives in Moscow or anywhere else in Russia – all the family's friends were far away. Thus the sick woman suffered more than four years under very difficult conditions.

---

[23] Editor's Note: They were all drawn into the investigation in the case against Anna Ivanovna Abrikosova and other Russian Catholics.

Stavropol, Tambov – 1932-1935

Sister Margaret Mary was unexpectedly arrested in Odessa in 1932 and sent to the camps for three years. Sisters Stephania and Antonina were ordered to leave Odessa and went to Krasnodar, where there was a functioning church. Sister Antonina found work in an artist's shop painting statuettes. They did not stay long in Krasnodar. They soon moved to Stavropol, but it was even harder to find work in Stavropol and in 1934 they had to move to Tambov. Sister Rose of the Heart of Mary also soon moved to Tambov, having served out the remaining time on her exile in Rybinsk. At that time a priest from Moscow, Father Michael Tsakul, was serving out his exile in Tambov.

Sister Antonina worked in the military hospital, first in the laundry, then as a janitress. Finally she began to teach French in the high school. But she managed to work there only one school year – when she arrived at the school after the summer break her name was not on the roster of teachers, nor was her subject on the class schedule.

In February 1935 all the Sisters were arrested on account of their "connection with Catholic priests" who were in prison.[24] The authorities transported them for further investigation and trial to the prison in Voronezh, where they were placed in solitary cells. The interrogation and simultaneous questioning of priests and witnesses went on for nine months. At the trial [November 16-19, 1935], after a brilliant speech by Sister Stephania that captivated all those present at the trial, even the armed escorts, the Dominican Sisters were fully acquitted and set free.[25] But none of the eight accused priests was released.[26]

The Sisters returned to Tambov, but their apartment was already occupied and all their things had disappeared. Their former landlady was struck by the

---

[24] Editor's Note: The main charge for the arrested Sisters and priests: "connection with a representative of the Vatican, Bishop Pius Neveu, receipt of money from him, and giving him information that disparaged the Soviet regime."

[25] Editor's Note: Sister Stephania proved that the money received from Bishop Neveu had been given "for saying Masses," and that this was a completely legitimate action in the inter-relationships among a bishop, priest and the faithful in the Catholic Church.

[26] Editor's Note: They were sentenced to eight to ten years in corrective labor camps or internal exile, since they had signed all the charges during the interrogation. And even though the priests categorically retracted their statements during the trial, attributing them to the pressure of the investigator, they were convicted.

Sisters' calm attitude toward all that had happened. Since they had to start all over, they left Tambov and settled in the small town of Maloyaroslavets, 75 miles south of Moscow. From here it was possible, although not often, to go to Moscow, attend Mass and receive the sacraments of confession and Holy Communion.

Novosibirsk, Orel, Karlag – 1930-1939

Sisters Lucia and Rosa Maria, who were still in Romny, were soon re-arrested and sent for three years to a Siberian camp. At first they were sent to work in a brick factory where they had to spend the whole day turning over a thousand dried bricks and then stacking them. After some time they were transferred to work as dishwashers in the camp bosses' dining hall. They no longer lived in the camp, but at liberty in an apartment. The Sisters were well treated and when their term was finished they were given all new clothing and bedding as a reward for their good work and good behavior.

In 1932, after their exile, they settled in Orel, south of Moscow. At first they could find no work and they were starving. In their weakened state it was even hard to go to church. Then they found jobs as embroiderers at Rospistkan ["Painted Fabric"] and began to earn good money. Sister Lucia's brother, once he found out her address, began to send dollars from America, which was a great help. Later Sister Lucia went to work as a nurse in a tuberculosis hospital-dispensary and began courses to become a doctor.

The Sisters' life in Orel went along smoothly. Sister Lucia had to give up playing the organ at church, however, because the elderly priest, Father Alexander Kuczynski, who often visited the Sisters, feared it could lead to their re-arrest.

At that time the church needed a repair and there was no money for it, so Sister Lucia wrote to Bishop Neveu in Moscow to ask his help. The authorities found out and in 1935 the Sisters were arrested on charges of "contacts with the international bourgeoisie" [i.e., with a representative of the Vatican, Bishop Neveu]. As before, by order of a Troika of the NKVD issued in absentia, the Sisters were sentenced to three years of camps and sent to the Karaganda camp (Karlag) in Kazakhstan.

Sister Rosa Maria was sent to a distant outpost at the camp where there were a lot of criminals. She worked in a tailor shop. Living conditions were difficult: they gave them 400 grams of bread and fed them frozen cabbage and worm-eaten fish. Her bread was often stolen and she went hungry. Her tuberculosis began to become more acute and she was more than once hospitalized. When she returned to the barracks she had to sleep on the floor.

Because Sister Lucia had been studying medicine in Orel and had only nine months left to finish her diploma, they put her in the central camp station in Dolinka, as head of the medical station. She had to see patients every day and also traveled out to the distant camp stations where convicts were working. Thus she found out about Sister Rosa Maria's difficult situation. Sister Lucia got her food in the form of a "dry ration," and with the flour she baked small cakes and sent them to her friend so that she would not die of hunger. There was a lot of work at the medical point especially during sowing and harvesting. For these trips they gave Sister Lucia a horse, sometimes without a saddle. Once they gave her a balky horse that tried to throw her, but she managed, although with difficulty, to handle him. True, when she was returning home she nearly cracked her head open when the horse flew galloping into the stable. Thus Sister Lucia worked off her three-year term and even received an award for good work and proper order in her sectors. (On her watch, the convicts at these stations had no lice.)

Upon their release from camp in 1939, Sisters Lucia and Rosa Maria went to Maloyaroslavets. Six Sisters were already living in a small apartment with only two tiny rooms, so Sisters Lucia and Rosa Maria found another place in town.

BAMlag, 1934-1935

Before the convoy set off from Moscow with those sentenced in the second case against Mother Catherine and others, two more nineteen-year-old girls were added to the Sisters' group: Katia Aleksandrova, the daughter of the Russian Catholic priest, Father Nikolay Aleksandrov; and Verochka Kruczelnicka, Camilla's niece, who had seldom visited her aunt and who did not know Mother Catherine or the Sisters at all.

They crammed all the convicts into freight cars with double-decker bunks along the walls, and thus, with women criminals – bandits, thieves and prostitutes – we traveled by a long convoy to the Far East. On the way we were fed greasy soup with black bread. Twice along the way the guards took us to the bathhouses in towns we were passing through. As usual, they led us in rows down the middle of the street, surrounded by the escort with bayonets tilted forward and police dogs on all sides. In the bathhouse we had to undress completely and then walk by the armed escort that stood by each door. All the clothing was gathered up to be disinfected and treated for lice.

Thus we reached Urulga Station in the Far East, where there was a transit camp and distribution point for BAMlag (Baikal-Amur Magistral Camp), from where they dispatched convicts further by separate convoys.[27] The transit camp was situated on a very large area that included several rather high hills overgrown with young oaks, grass and yellow leaves – "little locusts."

It was the feast day of Saint Catherine of Siena – April 30, the day when the Sisters made their vows for the first time or renewed them. At this transit camp only two Sisters remained among those who had arrived by convoy: Sister Teresa and I. We climbed up one of the hills so that here, under the open sky and the sun's rays, inspired by faith and zeal, we could affirm to God our faith and our readiness for anything. I renewed my vows; Sister Teresa, although still a novice, made her vows before me. It was an unforgettable moment.

Soon they transported us to the town of Svobodny, which is on the shore of the Zeya River, a tributary of the Amur, approximately eighty miles from Blagoveshchensk. When we walked into the camp we immediately saw among those who had come out to meet the convict convoy the tall figure of Sister Margaret Mary, who had been arrested in Odessa in 1932. In a few months she would be released, since they had given her so-called credits of work days for good work (i.e., a reduction of the term of sentence, which could sometimes be as much as half the term). Sister Joanna was also here – how glad we were to see one another!

The administrative offices of Bamlag were located in Svobodny. It employed mostly civilians but there were many convicts working there as well. They assigned me to work as a senior typist in one of the administrative departments and gave me an around-the-clock pass for the camp and outside its perimeters. Sisters Joanna and Teresa at first worked in the camp

---

[27] Translator's Note: Urulga Station was located at the 6,350 km post on the Trans-Siberian Railroad, approximately 730 miles east of Irkutsk (95 miles east of Chita). The Baikal-Amur Magistral was a strategic alternate route, running approximately 400 to 450 miles north of and parallel to the TSRR, which runs close to the Chinese border. The BAM begins at Tayshet and ends at the Pacific port of Sovetskaya Gavan.

doing hard labor, but they were later transferred to work in the hospital. We all lived in one barrack that was divided into parts with double-decker bunk beds, housing thirty to fifty people. The conditions in the camp were basically not bad. Once the camp administration even held a festive gathering, at which they presented me and a few others with a certificate for good work and good conduct and a small monetary award.

It seemed that everything was fine. Then one day in December 1934, returning to the camp from work, I heard the news on the radio that Sergey Kirov had been killed – and that a counter-revolutionary organization had been uncovered, the arrested members of which had been sentenced to death, and that those death sentences had already been carried out. They read off long lists of the family names of those who had already been shot in various cities – Moscow, Leningrad, Kiev and others. On the list of family names for Moscow I heard my own family name – Eismont (Konstantin Nikolayevich). I understood quite well how easily the authorities ascribed all sorts of misdeeds to people who were guilty of absolutely nothing, without making any effort to sort things out. The thought crossed my mind that troubles would not pass me by.[28]

I was not mistaken. At the end of December they summoned me to the camp operations sector and asked me how I was related to this K.N. Eismont. I answered that I had never known anything about him or even heard of him – he was just a person with the same last name. The investigator said, "We have information that this is your cousin." I responded that this was not true and asked him to clear up the problem. He said they would clear everything up, but for the meantime I was to be in isolation. The following day they sent me to work in the laundry. Thus more than a month passed.

Ukht Pechlag, 1935-1942

On February 2, 1935, when the Sisters were together celebrating the feast of the Purification of the Blessed Virgin with a cup of tea, the camp guards came for me, ordered me to gather up my belonings and took me to the camp prison. When they led me into the cell I saw Verochka

[28] It was later determined that this K.N. Eismont was the son of Nicholas Boleslavovich Eismont, Deputy People's Commissar for Heavy Industry, arrested in the 1930s as an opportunist and sent to Ukht-Pechlag as the chief of supplies for the camp. He died in a plane crash in 1934.

Kruczelnicka – just as had happened with me, someone in Kiev with the same last name as hers had been shot. The two of us sat there for two weeks until three freight cars rolled into the camp. They put us and two other women whom we didn't know into the one empty car. Another car was for the armed escort, and the third was apparently filled with men.They transported us all by lengthy convoy across the whole Soviet Union – from the Far East to the Arkhangelsk region. They brought us to Kotlas and put us into a transit prison, then a week later they sent about a hundred convicts on foot under armed escort to the North. We had to walk 375 miles because there was no other connection, by rail or by water.

There were only ten women on this convoy; there were criminals, but fortunately only fifteen of them. Along the way two men who were no longer young constantly looked out for Verochka and me – the engineer-geologist Pobedonostsev and the astronomer Kozlovksy – for whom Verochka and I were very grateful. They took us to a camp sector not far from the town of Chibyu (now Ukhta) where there was a plant dealing with the radioactive waters of Ukht-Pechlag, which was considered a penalty camp. The convoy was assigned to six months of heavy labor.

At first they put the women at the "sieve," where you had to gather stones with large scooping shovels and throw them onto nets, sifting out the smaller ones. This work was of course completely beyond our strength – we women could not even fulfill twenty percent of the quota. After some time they transferred us to work in a swamp covered with peat moss. The whole day we had to stand in water much higher than our ankles and cut metric squares of moss with axes and then tear them out with hooks. The work was very hard and the water was ice cold.

After several months they sent me and one other educated woman from Moscow to work in the carpentry shop; the master carpenter, an Orthodox deacon, was organizing a shop of musical instruments – balalaikas, guitars, mandolins. He was gathering pupils for this work – which was sheer happiness for me even though working with an axe, saw and plane was also hard. We ourselves had to fetch from the forest all the material needed for the work. At the end of the day my hands would hurt so bad that it was hard to fall asleep. But at the same time the work was interesting and – most important – it was indoors and warm.

It was also friendly. Sometimes during a respite from the work we sang together – soprano, alto and tenor. It sounded good and it provided us some relaxation and comfort. After several months, when the assigned six months of general labor was coming to an end, they transferred me to work as a draftsman in the planning office where five people worked – engineers, architects and one draftsman. Life was beginning to return to normal.

Suddenly, at the end of winter, they put me in a sleigh and took me under escort to the transit camp. It turned out that an order had come from the Center (i.e., Moscow) to send me immediately to Vorkuta, even though in the spring the medical commission in Kotlas had determined that I could not be sent to Vorkuta on account of my health. From the transit camp they sent me by general convoy to the Pechora River and then further, by barge steamer, to Kedrovy camp sector (approximately 30 miles up the Pechora River from Pechora).

Here on the river bank there was just a radio station, an air landing strip, the administrative office and a hospital – while all around there was a wonderful, huge forest. Convicts worked at a collective farm three miles away. I was put to work in the office as a bookkeeper. The hospital and office workers lived in small rooms in a house. I shared a room with two other women – an economist and a telephone operator. In the summer one could get permission to go into the forest to pick berries and mushrooms. Everything was fine – but at the end of winter they again put me in a sleigh and took me under escort to the transit point on the Usa River (a tributary of the Pechora). The Center had inquired as to my whereabouts and had ordered me sent immediately to Vorkuta.

The medical commission in the spring again cancelled my departure to Vorkuta on account of my health, so I ended up at the Kochmes Collective Farm on the Arctic Circle, where I was assigned to work in a group of weaker convicts. Despite this, the tasks here were in the forest with an axe, in the field, in the water – and in the winter the temperatures dropped to 40 degrees below zero. Not being accustomed to such tasks, and already completely losing my strength, I was in no way able to fulfill my quota.

At the Kochmes Collective Farm the convicts at first lived in the former stable – a huge space with mangers and triple-decker bunks that were hard to crawl up into. More than a hundred women – criminals and politicals – shared this space. Apparently the horses had not long before been transferred from the stable, and by habit they came in through the wide doors that were sometimes left open in the summer. And so it would happen that you would hear the sound of hooves and then suddenly appeared two or three horses that looked at the women with bewilderment, seeing their quarters occupied. These amusing incidents gave everyone a reason to laugh.

By winter, when it became cold and the stable was needed for the horses, they resettled the women in tents, despite the severe cold – minus 50 degrees and colder. In warm weather gnats ruined the convicts' lives – mosquito netting was useless against them. The gnats crawled into everything, especially biting the most tender parts of the body, and their poisonous bites left bloody, pea-sized spots that burned and itched. These bites would result in a fever, and your face would become so swollen and distorted that no one would recognize you; your eyes would water so much that you couldn't see and, of course, in such a condition you couldn't work either. The doctors excused us from work and treated the bites.

Aside from these troubles there was also something good – and this, as always, was to be found in Nature. Nature in the North is absolutely unique. Here, on the Arctic Circle, there are no nights during the summer. The bright colors of the south are not to be found here at all – the greenery and the whole landscape are in soft pastel tones. The air is of a special crystalline purity. The sky often has a richness and variety of colors and hues that are impossible to see in the south or in the temperate zone. Working a few days near the wharf guarding sacks of provisions unloaded from the steamship for the camp, I watched the doubled beauty of the sky as reflected in the water of the river. Praying came easy here, in the silence and the solitude.

In 1937 and 1938 a heavy atmosphere came over the entire camp and the collective farm as well. The mass arrests and summary executions throughout the whole country in those years reverberated in the camp. They began arresting convicts who were serving out their sentences in the camp and sending them to the political isolator in Vorkuta. Convoys with many people passed through the collective farm, en route to Vorkuta. They sentenced many to death; the lists of those who had been shot were read out in each barrack, which brought on much grief and sobbing because the wives and sisters of those who had been shot were among the women convicts in the barracks.

At the end of 1938 healthy and strong convicts were sent from the collective farm to Vorkuta; the sick were sent to a camp sector for invalids in Abez. I was among the latter, as my health had been severely compromised. My hands were cramped from rheumatism and I could neither straighten them out nor bend them. On account of heart disease, I had a fever that went to 102 degrees and higher for more than a year. I was unable to work for seven months.

In Abez we were usually fed herring broth without anything in it instead of soup; the main course consisted of a piece of very salty codfish, rust-colored herring or a couple spoonfuls of greasy kasha made from rancid oats. The men suffered the most from these privations. I myself developed scurvy and lost almost all my teeth from the poor food and complete lack of vegetables.

At that time the camps were mixed: men and women, criminals and politicals were at the same camp sector. Many were seriously ill, mostly coming from the Vorkuta mines: convicts blind from blasting in the mine-shafts, serious tubercular patients, cardiac patients, and epileptics with serious bronchial and cardiac asthma. Because there was no railway, they transported convicts in the summer by steamship on barges on the river; but after the end of the navigation season, they drove convoys of poorly or barely dressed people on foot, regardless of the weather – and then doctors had to amputate no small number of fingers and toes. The last six months I worked as a nurse in an outpatient clinic and it was not easy to look upon the suffering of people who were so seriously ill.

It was here in 1938 that I suddenly received a letter from abroad, from my mother. She wrote me that she had passed through Warsaw and Berlin en route to Paris where she was now living with her other daughter, Galina, and her family. Galina had petitioned for permission for Mother to leave the Soviet Union. This joyful news was like a miracle!

Release – Troitsko-Pechorsk, 1942

After the declaration of war on June 22, 1941, the release of "political" convicts who had completed their term was put on hold. Only the criminal convicts were released, and they were sent straightaway to the Front. I was to have been released in 1941, having completed my eight-year camp sentence, but I had to spend one more year in the camp. In this I was fortunate because many at that time had to stay much longer, some even until the end of the war.

I was released in June 1942 along with ten sick, half-blind and deaf elderly people. From the village for invalids they sent us to the transit camp sector of Kozhva on the Pechora River, where the railroad began, and here they issued our documents. I spent a week and a half at this camp sector processing the documents for my release. There was a large tent with bunk beds near the camp where we could spend the night and take cover from the rain.

When I walked into the tent with the elderly people, I saw about six beefy bandit-type guys seated on the upper bunks. We had to spend the night in this tent, and in the morning we were to receive money for our travel. I had temporarily left my belongings in the camp, but the elderly men had brought their sacks and little suitcases, which contained nothing but zwieback, a change of underwear and some old jerseys.

In the morning I left the tent to wash up and suddenly I heard sobbing coming from the tent. Going back inside, I saw two old men crying. It turned out that during the night the bandits, working from the outside of the tent, had cut through the canvas and the old men's sacks that they had placed under their heads or close by – the bandits had taken the only things they had, wretched, miserable old clothes. Upset and outraged, I began to shout at the bandits, calling them unscrupulous and lacking any humanity, and they, seated up above like huge monkeys in cages, looked at me in surprise, "What are you shouting at us?!" From agitation and outrage I lost my voice and developed a fever. Later these criminals even stole the money given to the old men by the camp for their travel. Whatever became of these poor old men, helpless as children?!

I understood quite well that now I could not leave by train because the bandits, who would stop at nothing, would not leave me in peace. In addition, I learned that the train cars were not lit at night and since I had lost my voice, I would not be able to scream or call for help. To save myself from the bandits, I decided not to go by train – instead I decided to go down to the wharf and remain temporarily in the North, taking the steamer to Troitsko-Pechorsk, which was on the upper reaches of the Pechora River.

In the small area of the wharf, to which a staircase descended from above, there were so many people that it was impossible to pass through

– everyone was seated on the ground, crowded up against one another. I noticed that two bandits had come through the doorway on the staircase and they were obviously looking for someone. I immediately ducked down, hiding myself behind someone's back and prayed that the bandits would not see me. Everything turned out all right.

Arriving in Troitsko-Pechorsk, I found work in some sort of establishment. Three or four days later they mobilized all the employees, including me, to help at the local collective farm. All the work was heavy: first we dug potatoes, then following the mower we had to bind sheaves from ears of rye.

After this about twenty people were sent on horseback almost a hundred miles to get the seed grain for sowing the winter rye. And no matter how much I assured them that I'd never in my life had anything to do with horses and didn't even know how to harness one, it was of no avail – I had to go by horse with a small wagon. Along the way it happened that another local woman and I fell behind the rest of the group. She was riding in a large wagon with two horses. We had to go all by ourselves through a huge, thick, beautiful forest with huge birch trees that were like pines. The road in the forest was nearly impassable, with steep climbs and falls, with ruts and half-rotted branches where any minute one could get stuck. It looked like the road was rarely used.

My companion, a woman who was no longer young, was obviously accustomed to hard peasant labor from childhood and she treated me with deepest contempt because I did not know how to harness or properly manage a horse. And the horse undoubtedly completely shared this contempt, as it paid no attention to my shouts. It heeded only the voice of the other woman shouting at her horses.

Along the road from time to time we came to little wintering huts, where we could rest a bit and give the horses a reprieve. For the trip we had been given a few salted fish and bread, but almost all of mine had been stolen at one of the stops. Thus I rode hungry most of the way. Twice we had to spend the night in the forest by a campfire. And here at one of these stops after our rest we had to bring back our horses that had gone far into the forest. My companion had already gotten her horses and was riding on one of them, but my horse was running behind them, not stopping. There was no time to think – I had to throw myself quickly from a tree stump onto the horse's back as it galloped by, grabbing its mane, because it had no bridle. Not being a sportswoman, even in the best of health I could never have performed such a circus trick. How it all happened was absolutely incomprehensible. Only the miraculous help of angelic friends and the kindness of God! Otherwise I would have been left completely alone in the forest, halfway from our destination, because my travelling companion would not have been at all inclined to help or wait up for me.

The return trip with the seed was not without its adventures. There were puddles in the road from the rains of previous days. At one point several 180-pound sacks fell from my companion's wagon and we had to lift them back onto the wagon. The woman was very upset and swore at me with all sorts of unprintable words, accusing me of being of no help to her, even though I was drawing on my last strength to help in some way.

Then we came to a bridge that was slippery from the rain. There was a gap between the bridge and the road, and one of her horses slipped and fell onto its back and its back legs went into the space under the bridge. Bloody foam came from its mouth, and again we had to work together to help the horse get up. Finally the poor beast got up, trembling all over from fear and pain. Only after some time were we able to continue. The woman was happy that the horse was unharmed because otherwise she could have had major difficulties – she could even have been brought to court. As we were approaching Troitsko-Pechorsk she unexpectedly said, "Sonya, it's good that you were with me, otherwise I would have been in serious trouble."

There had been no rain for a long time and the river near Troitsko-Pechorsk had become quite shallow, such that the steamer could not make it to the city. Now, after the rains that had just fallen, the water in the river had risen and a steamer unexpectedly arrived – and it would be the last one of the season. I had to leave on it, no matter what, otherwise I would be stranded here another eight months or so, until the following navigation season in June. The steamer was stopping less than twenty-four hours, and so in one day I had to do everything: get permission from the NKVD, redeem my ration cards from the collective farm for provisions, and then at dawn be on the steamer – which was standing in the river quite a way from the city, and there were no means of transportation and absolutely no one to help me.

But God's help was miraculous! That day someone's unseen power carried me everywhere. It was as if I had sprouted wings on my shoulders, and everything that needed to be done got done. Nevertheless I was almost late for the steamer because there was no way I could quickly go the long distance with three bags that were way too heavy for me. I would drag a couple things a short way, leave them and go back for the others – and thus I slowly made some progress, but I had completely lost my strength and felt a heart attack coming on.

The steamer gave the third, final whistle and I was still a long way off. Suddenly, absolutely unexpectedly, the captain appeared on the ship's ladder, came down from the ship and headed for the wharf, which was some distance away. He had apparently forgotten something. I now knew that I was saved and could catch my breath, pull myself together and without anxiety make it to the ship.

Kuibyshev (Samara) – Uralsk, 1942-1947

During the war travel within the country was severely restricted, and relocating from one place to another was possible only for those on certified assignments or with special permission. Those coming out of the camps could go only to places noted on their release documents. I went to a village in Kuibyshev region where one of my friends from childhood had been evacuated from Moscow. It was an exhausting trip: on account of the overcrowding of the railways with military personnel and freight, I had eight train changes instead of one, and it took ten days instead of two. Once arrived in the village of Gerankino, which was about thirteen miles from the station, I found myself in the midst of Evangelicals. My friend had been a Lutheran, but in recent years she had become an Evangelical. They received me warmly.

Life in this village, however, was very hard. They had already had three years of drought and crop failures and people were starving, especially the evacuees. On their ration cards, instead of bread, they were given flour ground from rye harvested in a field where rye grew mixed in with sagebrush. The flour was so bitter that you couldn't eat the bread baked with it. To make it more palatable, you had to soak the flour several times in water, pouring off the water and again soaking it in fresh water, which removed the bitterness somewhat. But even after this, the bread was still very bitter. We earned enough for some potatoes and milk by knitting jackets and sweaters for the peasants. Thus we managed to live from summer until spring. In the spring there was no work at all and we had to eat grasses and nettle.

Uralsk, the regional center of Western Kazakhstan, was a little more than 125 miles to the south. It was surrounded by the steppe, all sown in wheat and other grains. From spring through autumn they were always in dire need of field help, which they paid in grain. Because of the crop failure, the authorities began to give peasants on the collective farm permission to go to Uralsk for work. Whoever had a horse was going there and bringing back their earnings in grain.

The peasants advised me to get permission from the collective farm to go to Uralsk to somehow earn something and thus provide bread for myself until the following year. I took their advice – but for me things were much more difficult and complicated. I had to walk to the train station, which was a long way off, and then by illegally hiding on the platform of some freight train, get to the city of Buzuluk, and then from the motor transport depot there catch a ride on a truck going to Uralsk. So that is what I did.

I left my things in the village and took only a knapsack with a change of clothes and a small pot filled with grassy mush so as to have something to eat for at least a couple days, and I set off. The summer was hot and the sun was scorching. The steppe surrounded me on all sides, without a single tree or bush. I walked along toward an unknown city, not having an address or knowing there a single person whom I could ask for advice. The peasants had told me, "In Uralsk, go to the market. Everyone comes to the market from all the collective farms and state farms. There you'll find out where workers are needed and you'll find work."

I walked through the steppe completely alone, absolutely calm, having entrusted myself and all that lay ahead into the hands of God, saying: "Lord! You see that I am completely alone, that I am very weak and defenseless, lead me and defend me. The whole world is yours! You are concerned about the least blade of grass – do not abandon me. Everyone has a place to live and work, but I have no one and nothing. Grant that I will have bread and a little milk."

Thus I walked along, praying and singing hymns. A couple times clouds unexpectedly gathered and a storm broke out. There wasn't a hut or even a tree where I could take shelter, but once I caught sight of a haystack and I ran and crawled into the hay – under the sound of thunder, exhausted, I peacefully fell asleep. When I opened my eyes and saw that the storm had passed and that the sun was again shining, I climbed out of the haystack and continued on my way. Villages were few and far between. At the end of the day I went to a house and asked if I could stay the night. It often happened that people sheltered not just one, but several travelers. They spread something on the floor, and at dawn everyone continued on their way, each by his own road.

The food I had taken with me barely lasted two days and I had to knock on doors asking for a piece of bread. During the war, there was nothing surprising about this among the evacuees, many of whom fell on hard times. It happened that some people not only allowed one to spend the night, but they also shared what they had to eat. There were many good, kind-hearted people; because of all the woes and grief of wartime, people had sympathy for one another. And the good, kind-hearted people were the poorest people, who were ready to share their last piece of bread. I came to know that among such people, you won't die.

Thus I made it to the railroad station and on the platform of a freight car, although not without complications, I made it to Buzuluk, and from the motor transport depot there, where I waited a whole day, I made it nearly to Uralsk by truck without any incidents. I had not much money, but I did have some tobacco that had been issued to me on my ration cards back in Troitsko-Pechorsk and it came to my rescue.

During my ten-day trip I found out that they had stopped paying wages in grain – so now I needed to find a permanent job because there was nothing back in the village. In Uralsk, in the mobilization department of the Regional Executive Committee one could only get an assignment to work in the central part of Western Kazakhstan, a long way from the railroad. Furthermore, the people out there were exclusively Kazakhs, and to go such a long way without knowing the Kazakh language was absolutely impossible.

I decided to look in the area around the city. I stayed about three days in one of the little settlements, substituting for a caretaker at an evacuated orphanage who had gone away on business. The Village Council sent me to stay with the head of a vegetable plantation, a gray-haired old man whose son was at the Front. Living at his home were his daughter-in-law and her year-old child, as well as his wife, a thin old woman suffering from migraines.

They were Old Believers and very religious – they recited lengthy prayers from large old books. They treated me cordially. When I would come home on a break, they would call me to dinner, and when I declined, saying I had already had dinner at the orphanage, they answered, "We know how they feed you there – with water! Come eat with us. We will not sit down to eat without you."

When I had to leave after three days, the wife, despite her severe headache, got up at dawn to see me off. She fed me and gave me a cup of millet, a piece of lard and bread, saying "Who knows when someone else will feed you, so maybe somehow you can cook these for yourself." I was touched to the depth of my soul by the truly Christian goodness of these people, and leaving the village, with tears in my eyes, I gave thanks to God that He so disposes the hearts of men.

Back in Uralsk, I was once again unable to find any work. Then I obtained the address of some establishment in Uralsk itself and right away set off, looking for the street. Along the way, walking parallel with me was a man whom I asked for directions, and he asked why I needed to know. When he found out I was looking for work, he asked, "Have you been to the agricultural seed station? I worked there last summer and the pay wasn't bad. Go there." I found out that the seed station was about four miles from Uralsk, and after getting directions, I headed out there.

The workers' settlement for the seed station was on the Derkula River, a tributary of the Ural River. Arriving there, I found out at the office that the director had gone to town and that he wouldn't be back until late evening, that I would have to return the following morning and that I could get back to town with someone going that way. In the stable I met one of the workers and when I explained that I wanted to work there, he said, "Write out an application right now. I need a record-keeper for field work on the sector I manage – it's about twenty miles from here. I will give your application to the director today."

I spent the night at the train station in the city and on returning in the morning found several people in the director's office. When they all left, he asked me, "Why do you want to work out on that sector? Do you have relatives or acquaintances out there?" I told him that I had no one out there and he then proposed, "If I offered you a job here as my secretary, would you take it?" I asked only one question: "How much bread do you pay your secretary?" When he told me 400 grams, I said I would be better off going to work out on the sector because the record-keeper out there would get 500 grams. I told him I came from a famine-stricken village. Smiling, he responded, "I feed almost half the town – somehow I will feed my secretary." I was at that time as thin as a rail and black as a jackdaw from walking in the scorching sun.

Thus my sixteen-day trip finally ended happily. Working as a record-keeper out on the steppe, spending entire days under the scorching sun, would have been very difficult, and on account of my heart condition and hypertonia doctors had in general prohibited me from working in the sun. So I had gotten the best of what was possible at that time: work that suited my strength in a place that was favorably located during the war. God's paternal, loving care and kindness were clearly evident!

The seed station, in addition to experimental fields sown in grain, had a large subsidiary operation: plantations of vegetables and melons in addition to livestock that had been evacuated from western areas and were kept in a pigsty and in cattle and horse barns. There was also a flock of sheep on the sector, as well as camels that were ridden for work. The seed station had two directors – a research director and an administrative director – and about twenty research workers who had graduated from the Timiryazev Agricultural Academy, eight of whom had academic degrees.

I was glad because it was easier to communicate with them than with the kind but uneducated people in the village. There was a lot to do: by five in the morning one had to be on the square, ready to depart to the various experimental sectors to gather information about work accomplished during the day and then telegraph to the various central institutions the daily data on the fulfillment of work for the seed station. Taking an hour break for dinner, they often had to work until late evening.

From early spring until the end of late autumn the field workers had to work especially hard and even without days off. They went out to the steppe to work at five in the morning and it was often after ten at night when they returned. Once home, they then had to set about their domestic chores: they prepared food for the family for the following day; washed clothes, sewed, put the house in order, took care of the children, and put away the livestock for the night. Sometimes they only slept two or three hours but even so they maintained a cheerful and courageous spirit. I looked upon these simple women with deep respect and admiration. Here, deep in the rear, there was a second Front where women, the elderly and adolescents were working heroically.

The director treated me well, despite the fact that he knew I had been released from a camp only a year earlier. Once when he returned from some kind of meeting in the city he said, "They gave me a hard time on account of you at the Regional Committee today. They said, 'Who do you have working for you? Who is it that you are trusting?' And I answered, 'I need workers. I fire those who show up with recommendations but don't work. I reward those who come from prison when they do good work.'" The director could behave so boldly and independently because during the war the city's central agencies had an interest in his help with foodstuffs, such as meat, dairy, vegetables and melons.

Thus I worked there without difficulties until the end of the war. In the summer of 1946, for the first time after all the war years, they gave the workers and office staff their overdue vacation leave. What had been such a big support for me during all those twelve years of spiritual solitude and complete isolation from my religious community was the awareness that not far from Moscow there was a bright spot, a kind hearth, where there were people completely dedicated to God, serving Him – my dear Sisters. And now I was on my way to them...

When I arrived in Moscow I immediately went to Saint Louis Church and went to confession for all those difficult years. It was hard to speak over my tears. Then I set off for Maloyaroslavets where I found Sisters Antonina, Monica and Teresa living in one house, and Sisters Lucia and Rosa Maria in another. It is hard to express the mutual joy of this long-awaited encounter. My week's vacation passed like lightening.

At that time I learned from Sister Antonina that during the past years it had become necessary to choose another Superior. From 1935 Sister Stephania had been the Superior in Maloyaroslavets; she was now in exile. During all the years of the community's life in Kostroma, Odessa, Stavropol, Tambov and finally, Maloyaroslavets, from 1930 until 1941, with Sister Stephania as Superior, it had seemed to Sister Antonina that the life of the community was not going along as it ought. Once a book from the church library about religious life had fallen into her hands, and she had read there how the relations between the Superior and the Sisters ought to be. Apparently Sister Stephania did not know these things, which is not surprising. She had been one of the first to enter the community, and then for external and internal reasons she had twice left the community, not having made vows, and then returned, starting again from the beginning. Thus at the time of her first arrest in March 1924, she was still in her novitiate.

Despite beautiful outward traits – Sister Stephania was clever, talented, highly educated and eloquent – she nevertheless had very little practical knowledge of spiritual life in general and religious life in particular. She had a hard time getting her bearings in complicated and difficult living conditions, which was brought about by her being somewhat cut off from life around her as a result of her deafness, a progressive sclerosis going back to her early years. Many elements of religious life that were necessary and good with respect to the relationships of Sisters and Superiors during the years of the community's normal life were absolutely not obligatory under the changed conditions. Sister Stephania did not take this into account; perhaps she simply did not know this. For all these reasons the Sisters who were working in secular establishments had more than once fallen into unpleasant and difficult situations that complicated their lives.

Sister Stephania was soon to return from exile. Sister Antonina had spoken with the Sisters' spiritual director, Father Antoine Laberge, the pastor of Saint Louis Church, about the complicated situation in the community and the desire to select a new Superior; she also gave him a letter signed by the other Sisters and me, in which the resolution of the question was submitted for his judgment. It would have seemed appropriate to await Sister Stephania's return in order to resolve the question with her present, but knowing her imperious and easily angered character, the Sisters feared that with her return all would continue as before, that she would brook no changes, and she would take the election of anyone else as a rebellion and a personal, undeserved offense. She was so well-spoken that it was hard for the Sisters to speak with her. Father Laberge decided on his own: because Sister Stephania had been in the position of Superior for a long time, by his own authority he was appointing Sister Antonina to replace her. This was an outcome that Sister Antonina did not want at all and against which she strongly protested.

When I returned to the seed station, I let them know that I would only work until spring and would then leave. Many advised me not to leave this job, explaining that after the war it would be very difficult to get food and that perhaps I would again go hungry – whereas in Uralsk I would more easily survive hard times. But for me, spiritual questions came first and in March 1947 I left Uralsk.

BAMlag, 1935-1937

When Verochka Kruczelnicka and I were transferred from Bamlag to Ukht Pechlag in February 1935, Sisters Joanna and Teresa remained at Bamlag. Sister Teresa soon began to work in a hospital, and Sister Joanna was sent after some time to another camp sector where she also began to work in a hospital. In this and the following section, Sister Teresa provides her recollections of what occurred after my departure.

Once a convict-doctor came from the camp sector in Birobidzhan (Jewish Autonomous Region) and in talking about his work and his patients, he spoke with great admiration about a remarkable nurse in his hospital. Always friendly and smiling, and despite her age and her health, she worked self-sacrificingly and did for the convicts what even a younger and healthier nurse could not do. With swollen feet, she would climb all day along ramps without handrails from one freight car to another (for lack of a normal place, patients were bedded down in freight cars), looking after them in self-forgetfulness.

I was very interested in this nurse, as it occurred to me right away that it was most likely one of our Dominican Sisters. Since the doctor did not know the nurse's family name, I asked him to find out. He promised to do so and on his next visit he told me. My intuition was right – this "remarkable nurse" was Sister Agnes.

I was consumed with the desire to visit her and I asked the hospital's head doctor (who was a priest) if he could somehow help me. It was almost impossible, but God, in His great goodness and endless mercy, fulfilled my wish. True, I couldn't go by passenger train because I had so little time. Instead I rode on a freight train loaded with coal. On this section of the route there were many hairpin curves and I thought I would tumble down from the pile of coal and be smashed to death. Although there was absolutely nothing to hold on to, by some miracle I kept from falling and everything turned out fine.

Sister Agnes was very glad for my visit. We talked all through the night because I had to leave in the morning and she had to go to work. This meeting was important and joyful for us – it strengthened our cheerfulness and courage. Later I learned from the same doctor that Sister Agnes was seriously ill with typhoid, pneumonia and a fever.

With great difficulty I again managed to visit Sister Agnes, who greeted me, as always, with a meek, sweet smile. Seeing that she was lying under just a sheet and shivering from the cold, I went to the head of the hospital to get at least a blanket for the sick woman. It turned out that all the blankets had been taken to the disinfection unit and there was no other supply. With great difficulty I nevertheless managed to get a blanket, when the head doctor stated that he loved and highly valued this nurse.

It was a barrack-like hospital. Sister Agnes's room was very cold, with an icy wind blowing in from everywhere. Sick with typhoid and lying in a cold room, without even a blanket, she had developed pneumonia. She was receiving very poor care. In fact, it seemed to me that she had no care at all. Later I was able to visit her again and she was then in a general ward. The patients in beds next to hers said that Sister Agnes was an angel of God, she was so peaceful and meek that they completely forgot about her – there was not even anyone to give her a glass of water. As one patient explained, "We can still shout at the top of our lungs so they still do things for us – but no one looks after her."

Sister Agnes already had bedsores on her back. She was lying on them and no one even thought to turn her so that she wouldn't be lying on her open sores. When I began to turn her, I did it so clumsily that I caused her great pain. She groaned slightly, but then right away said "Forgive me, Sister, for groaning." These words made a deep impression on me – what meekness, what patience, what humility!

When Sister Agnes learned that I would soon be released, she asked that no matter where else I would go afterward, I first go to Moscow and there in Saint Louis Church fulfill all that was necessary for my soul. Finding Sister Agnes in such a serious condition, I wanted to remain in the camp after my release, registering for work at the hospital as a free employee so that I would be able to look after her, to ease her sufferings, and to bury her.

But Sister Agnes would not hear of it. She ordered that I quickly leave the camp upon my release. She refused my services. Being already on the threshold of death, she talked not of herself, but recalled Mother Catherine and the Sisters with great love, asking me more than once whether I knew anything about any of them. Meek, clear and bright – this is how I remembered our Sister Agnes, who died without any care, on a hard hospital bed in a camp hospital in the Far East.

On the eve of my release, I received a small parcel from home and decided to go to Sister Joanna's to visit her. I convinced the guard to let me into the camp. Sister Joanna was on duty that night at the hospital, and we talked until dawn. I wanted to share the food in my parcel with her but Sister Joanna would not take anything.

In the morning, after her night duty, Sister Joanna asked permission to go outside the camp zone to see me off. She walked a long way with me, then she stopped and followed me with her eyes. I had known before that Sister Joanna was always a calm, self-possessed, exemplary Sister with a good and ardent heart, but during that night-time conversation I really came to understand the kind of loving heart she had and I felt her great love for God, for people and for the Sisters…

Bryansk, 1934-1937

Sister Margaret Mary was released from Bamlag in October 1934. She went to Moscow, where Bishop Neveu suggested that she go to Bryansk and find a young Catholic woman named Monica Zvidrin. We need to say a few words about Monica. She had previously lived in Leningrad and actively participated in the life of the community of Russian Catholics. In 1926 she was arrested and sent to Belomorstroi [White Sea Canal Construction Camp] on charges that she and others had collected things and sent parcels to the Exarch of the Russian Catholics, Leonid Feodorov, who was interned at Solovetsky Special Purpose Camp. When she was released from Belomorstroi she was restricted from living in the six largest cities. She settled in Bryansk, approximately 230 miles southwest of Moscow.

Sister Margaret Mary went to the church in Bryansk at a time when there were few people there, and she asked a thin woman of medium height, "Would you happen to know a woman named Monica." The response was, "I am Monica!" Thus they met and became friends, although they were not able to live together.

After bidding farewell to Sister Joanna in December 1935, I left Bamlag and went to Moscow. There I went to Saint Louis Church, met with Bishop Neveu and following his advice I also went to Bryansk. I arrived on Christmas Eve, December 24, 1935. I did not find Sister Margaret Mary at home, so I set off for church. The liturgy had not yet begun – when we saw each other, Sister Margaret Mary and I stepped outside and joyfully embraced each other.

I moved in with Sister Margaret Mary who was living in a tiny little room that was so narrow that two people could not pass each other. There was a small iron bed and a trunk that belonged to the landlady, as Sister Margaret Mary had no furniture at all. She made me sleep on the bed while she herself slept on the landlady's trunk. Given her height and the size of the trunk, it is totally incomprehensible how she managed to fit on it.

Soon we moved to another apartment, into a little room that was just as tiny. There were two boards in this room, from one wall to the other, and Sister Margaret Mary made me sleep on these boards while she herself slept on a small table without any bed linen. And how could she sleep? So she slept on the floor on thin sheets of wallpaper, with books under her head, as was the custom among the Sisters. We had no pillows or mattresses. The landlady allowed us to fix only one dish – either soup, or kasha or potatoes. We never had meat or fish. Sister Margaret Mary had a small basin for washing clothes. It was dented and old, and we also used it for washing ourselves. More than once I asked to be allowed to buy some kind of a washtub for washing clothes and a broom for cleaning the floor, and after several such requests Sister Margaret Mary laughed and jokingly said, "This will be a beautiful sight – Sister Teresa sitting in purgatory, in one hand she has a washtub and in the other, a broom!" And thus nothing was bought.

Sister Margaret Mary was gifted with a spirit of poverty and mortification. Perhaps it is not out of place to say that she grew up in the privileged circumstances of an aristocratic family, and the fact that she had been imbued with a love for such a life speaks of her great zeal and spiritual maturity. She was always sweet, friendly, merry and full of a joie de vivre – you could think she was living under wonderful conditions. Under her favorable influence Monica later became a Dominican.

Filled with a great love for God and zeal for the salvation of others, she took no account of her weak strength and ruined health. Somehow she found out that there was a couple in the city that had not sanctified their marriage in the church, nor had their three children been baptized – and this, when the wife's own brother was a priest who lived far away. Sister Margaret Mary began to visit this family, to talk with the parents and constantly pray for them. She had no rest until the couple was married in the church, the children were baptized, and the family began to attend Mass on Sundays and the major feast days.

People who needed spiritual support and guidance regularly came to see us and Sister Margaret Mary, no matter how tired she was, always willingly received them. Laughing, she would say, "Today I have a day off – I am closed for business!" She worked as a hospital nurse. After night duty she would come home tired, with swollen feet, and no sooner did I somehow persuade her to rest just a little bit, she would lie down, and someone would show up. Sister Margaret Mary would immediately get up as though it was nothing, and ever sweet, friendly and cheerful, she was ready to receive the visitor without even a trace of displeasure or tiredness on her face.

Sister Margaret Mary had a good musical education and a beautiful soprano voice. She directed the church choir and had evening rehearsals after liturgy. She was very devoted to the Sacred Heart of Jesus and had chosen in religious life the name of Saint Margaret Mary Alacoque. And although we lived in poverty – even destitution – this was nothing to her, and she longed for even greater sufferings. She often repeated that for the good and salvation of souls she would again go to prison – to which I replied, "I would rather wait." And thus it turned out.

We lived together in Bryansk, often meeting up with Monica, until 1937, when mass arrests began in the city. Monica immediately left for Maloyaroslavets in order to enter the community and she stayed there. Soon after her departure I set off one morning for Mass but on the way I met one of the parishioners who warned me not to go to the church because it had been cordoned off and was under surveillance. I returned home and there found a notice for my appearance before the NKVD. Sister Margaret Mary advised that I go immediately to Maloyaroslavets instead of the NKVD. It was practically impossible to purchase a ticket at the train station before the train's departure, but here, as always in desperate situations, the Lord came to my aid. Almost at the last minute a woman decided not to go and she gave me her ticket.

Right after my departure, Sister Margaret Mary was arrested at work.

She sent the Sisters only one letter from the road, and other than that there was not a piece of news from her, and to this day the Sisters know nothing of what became of her. She so loved her spiritual family that if she would have had even the slightest opportunity she would surely have let us know. It is possible that she died on the convoy or in a camp because prior to her arrest her feet had become terribly swollen and she was apparently having heart problems. But she never complained and she endured all things staunchly and joyfully. The blessed memory of this Sister who was perfected, mortified, heroically self-sacrificing and holy is preserved in the hearts of all who knew her.

Maloyaroslavets – Kazakhstan, 1935-1948

In 1935[29] Sisters Stephania, Rose of the Heart of Mary and Antonina moved from Tambov to Maloyaroslavets where they again established normal community life. In the summer of 1937 they were joined by Sister Catherine of Siena (Rubashova) who came from Michurinsk; prior to this time she had been living as a secular Third Order Dominican. She was born Nora Nikolayevna Rubashova in Moscow in March 1909 and baptized in April 1926 by Father Sergey Soloviev, an Eastern Rite Catholic priest. In 1925 Father Sergey had united around himself the few Sisters who were still at liberty and parishioners of the Abrikosov community, as well as his own parishioners who had secretly become Catholic and entered religious life. Nora's godmother was Valentina Sapozhnikova, a parishioner of the Abrikosov community of Russian Catholics. At the end of 1926 Nora became a secular Third Order Dominican, taking Saint Catherine of Siena as her patroness. After finishing high school she enrolled in the Historical Philology Department of the Second Moscow State University. In 1928 she spent two days at Christmas visiting Sisters Antonina and Margaret Mary in Kostroma. Later, she often met with two other Sisters in Moscow at that time – Sister Catherine of Siena Balasheva[30] and Sister Hyacinth – as well as parishioners who still remained at liberty.

Sister Catherine regularly attended Mass celebrated by Father Sergey at

---

[29] Translator's Note: Sister Philomena resumes as narrator.

[30] Editor's Note: In 1929 she was arrested in Moscow on charges of "contact with Father Leonid Feodorov, Exarch of the Russian Catholics," and sending him money and parcels. She was sent to the Solovetskii Special Purpose Camp for five years.

the Cathedral of the Immaculate Conception on Malaya Gruzinskaya Street, where the pastor, Father Michael Tsakul, had given the Russian [Eastern Rite] Catholics one of the side altars. In the summer of 1930 she became acquainted there with Minna Kugel and was her godmother when Minna was baptized by Father Sergey. Thus time passed until 1931 when, on one single day – February 15, 1931 – Sisters Hyacinth and Catherine, Father Sergey, and a group of his parishioners were all arrested. Sister Catherine was sentenced in absentia to five years in the camps and sent to the Mariinskie camps. Here at one of the camp sectors she ran into Sister Margaret Mary, who was arrested in Odessa in 1932 and sent to the camps for three years.

Sister Margaret Mary told Sister Catherine that at one of the camp sectors she had met three Catholic priests who, not long before their arrest, had been in Rome and had received from the Holy Father, Pius XI, the assignment of conveying, upon their return to the Soviet Union, His Papal Blessing to Olga Aleksandrovna Spechinskaya-Veliaminova – that is, to her, Sister Margaret Mary. Having been soon arrested, they were unable to fulfill the Pope's assignment until now, in the camps.

Once during relocation from one camp to another the convicts had to wade across a river. Sister Margaret Mary was tall and was one of the first to get across. When she turned around she saw that one of the convicts, little Lyuba, was standing on the opposite shore, afraid to go in the water, and the convoy guards were roughly pushing her into the river. Sister Margaret Mary asked permission, then returned to the other side, sat Lyuba on her shoulders and carried her across the river. Thus began their long friendship which eventually led Lyuba to God and to the Church.

After finishing her five-year camp term in 1936, Sister Catherine lived six months in Michurinsk. Here she met the Orthodox priest Father Georgy Smirnov, who in his day had studied at Moscow State University. On December 7, 1937, at Saint Louis Church in Moscow, under the tutelage of Father Leopold Braun, he too became a member of the Catholic Church.

In the summer of 1937 Sister Catherine moved to Maloyaroslavets and entered the Dominican community. Soon thereafter, in September 1937, Sister Monica arrived in Maloyaroslavets from Bryansk, where arrests had begun – and she was soon followed by Sister Teresa. The Sisters' life in Maloyaroslavets was organized in accordance with all the rules of a religious community: regular, harmonious, in complete unity and mutual love.

In 1939 Sisters Rosa Maria and Lucia came to Maloyaroslavets after their release from the camps. Because of the tight quarters, they had to find another place to live. Sisters Rose of the Heart of Mary, Antonina and Catherine worked in a school, teaching German. Soon Sister Catherine transferred to a school for adults. On the major feast days the Sisters did not work and despite the possibility of trouble at work, by God's mercy, everything went along peacefully.

After some time the Sisters at the school were placed on a list of agitators who were to disseminate anti-religious propaganda, not suspecting that the Sisters would dare to protest. When Sisters Rose of the Heart of Mary and Antonina categorically refused, there was a discussion of their religious convictions at a general meeting – and they were fired. Sister Antonina then found work in a photo lab retouching negatives and Sister Rose, as a typist. Sister Teresa continued to work in the hospital.

From 1936 to 1941 the Sisters' lives went along peacefully. Sisters Rose of the Heart of Mary and Teresa took care of the heavier household tasks, such as carrying water from the well, doing the laundry, etc. The other Sisters supported the faithful, held discussions with them, and prepared children for First Communion – it was primarily Sister Monica who worked with the children.

Once Sister Teresa saw a golden wreath and halo over Sister Rose's head and she understood by this that Sister Rose would be the first of them to die, even though there were Sisters with weaker health. When Sister Teresa told the Sisters this, they all laughed and Sister Rose declared that she was as healthy as a horse. But this presentiment later proved true.

Sister Rose of the Heart of Mary was a disciplined and exemplary religious, always sweet and friendly; she capably translated foreign literature into Russian; she did all things quickly and in the very best way. Her constant motto was "To be all things for all," and she lived this out in her daily life. She was bright, clear, self-sacrificing and humble!

The Sisters took turns going to Saint Louis Church in Moscow once or twice a month. The pastor from 1934 to 1945 was Father Leopold Braun, and he became the community's spiritual director.[31] Through him – and

[31] Bishop Neveu had been forced to leave the country in 1936 but he continued to support the Sisters materially and morally, first through Father Braun and then Father Laberge. Translator's Note: Both were American members of the Assumptionist Order.

then after his expulsion from the country, through his successor Father Antoine Laberge – the community maintained contact with the Holy See and Dominican leadership. Father Michel Florent, pastor of Saint Catherine's Church in Leningrad, came to Moscow to visit several times, until he was expelled from the country in 1941. From 1937 through 1941 Sisters Hyacinth and Veronica periodically traveled to Maloyaroslavets to visit with everyone.

Before long Sister Lucia got a job right in Moscow, in a shop that dealt in exports. She was an excellent embroiderer and Sister Rosa Maria helped her; they began to make good money.[32] Sisters Lucia and Antonina often went to Moscow – Sister Lucia for her work, and Sister Antonina to turn in reports for her correspondence courses at the Institute of Foreign Languages. Travel to Moscow at that time was restricted – one had to have special permission stamped on one's internal passport, and neither of these two had such permission. So they would present the cashier with the passport of another Sister who had such permission – or else their own passports, always praying that the cashier would issue a ticket. And it was amazing that, after looking at the passport, he would nevertheless issue a ticket, even though it seemed impossible that he would not have noticed the absence of the required stamp.

Despite their on-going material difficulties, the Sisters of the community continued to help as much as they could those Sisters who were in prison. When it was forbidden to mail parcels from Moscow or the Moscow region, they traveled more than sixty miles from the capital, carrying more than thirty-five pounds with them; they mailed food parcels from towns so small that they often had no place to spend the night. That the religious life of the community could exist almost in full view of those surrounding it (there were, after all, eight of them), preserved by God's Providence, was, for that time and under those conditions, a real miracle. All the years of the Sisters' life in Maloyaroslavets were golden years for the blossoming of the Dominican family and the formation of the three youngest sisters: Teresa, Catherine of Siena, and Monica.

With the completion of her camp term, the experienced and elderly Sister Catherine of Siena (Balasheva, b. 1878), "Aunt Shura," was to have come

---

[32] Unfortunately, it soon came to light that they were beginning to feel displeased that part of their earnings was taken for necessary expenses for the whole community. This contradicted the principles of religious life and unavoidably led later on to division in the community.

to the community; she had forwarded her belongings to Maloyaroslavets in advance of her release. However, Sister Stephania, the Superior, sent Sister Catherine's belongings back to the camp, refusing to receive her in the community. This rejection of an elderly Sister was very troubling to the other Sisters.

At the beginning of the war, June 21, 1941, Sister Dominica arrived in Maloyaroslavets, hoping to stay in the community. Sister Stephania, however, turned her away, sending her instead to Bryansk, to join Sister Hyacinth who was working there in an orphanage. Sister Dominica left in tears, and the rest of the Sisters were distressed and greatly sympathized with her. This decision on Sister Stephania's part, made without consulting with anyone, was a big mistake. It turned out that she had unwittingly sent Sister Dominica to the Front; while Sister Hyacinth had been evacuated with the orphanage to Siberia, Sister Dominica ended up in Bryansk, at the Front. Nothing was ever heard of her thereafter.

When the military units of the Red Army abandoned Maloyaroslavets, the Sisters dug a bomb shelter in a cliff in the garden and hid there during bombing raids. They had a small supply of potatoes and managed to get a little bread as well, since bread from the stores had been distributed to the populace before the arrival of the Germans. Maloyaroslavets was occupied in the autumn of 1941. The situation in the community changed immediately: there was no income whatsoever and the Sisters were going hungry. Sister Rosa Maria's younger brother supported her and Sister Lucia a little, bringing them a loaf of bread or a piece of horsemeat from time to time. Fortunately for the community, which included Sisters from Jewish families, there were no SS among the occupiers.

The owner of the house in which they lived went to the countryside and her half of the house was left empty. When the Germans arrived they occupied this vacant half. The occupying soldiers were part of the kitchen crew, with a kitchen vehicle that stood outside the house and a supply of bread in the corridor. Noticing that the Sisters did not steal the bread, the Germans sometimes gave them a loaf. This military unit was from Austria and they had a chaplain priest with them who said Mass for them. At the end of the occupation, taking advantage of the Germans' hasty departure, the Sisters took from them a sack of oats – which was a big help.

After the Germans left Maloyaroslavets, Sister Lucia was sent to work at a hospital twenty-five miles from the city, and Sister Rosa Maria walked there to help. Things there were just as difficult, although the food situation was not quite as bad. Later they continued to earn their living basically by sewing. Then Sister Lucia was assigned to work at Petrovsk Hospital outside Moscow. They treated her very well and working there was good for her.

In 1942, after the Germans had left, Sister Teresa was arrested on charges of collaboration with the Germans. After all, she was from a Jewish family, she had worked at a hospital and had not suffered at the hands of the Germans – she was still alive. They sentenced her to five years' imprisonment and sent her to Temnikov camp [Temlag]. During the war and in the post-war period, convicts in the camps were treated cruelly. The work for the most part was physical – and very heavy. Sister Teresa's health was weak and she was hospitalized twice in the camp hospital.

Once a prison guard tried to overpower her, but despite her weakness, Sister Teresa so powerfully pushed him off, nearly knocking him over, that he left her alone. He didn't dare complain to the boss, and she had no further difficulties in this respect. Another time she interceded on behalf of a woman because of a supervisor's cruel and offensive injustice toward her. For this intervention they put her in a dark, cold punishment cell with a stone floor, then brought her out barefoot on the snow. As a result her feet were frostbitten and, having now fallen ill, she had a fever for a long time.

Sister Stephania was the next to be arrested. They sentenced her to a five-year exile in Kazakhstan and sent her to the village of Novo-Shulba in the Semipalatinsk region of eastern Kazakhstan. During the war the railroad was clogged with special military trains, so the convoy to Kazakhstan took three weeks under difficult conditions. The convicts rode in train cars sitting on narrow planks without any support for the body. Along the way they starved and froze, and then with the outbreak of a dysentery epidemic many fell ill and did not reach their assigned destination.

On arrival in Kazakhstan they were all sent to the prison in Frunze and then from there to their place of exile. Novo-Shulba is sixty miles from Semipalatinsk and Sister Stephania arrived there completely ill. In 1942, knowing the Sister Superior's weak health, Sister Rose of the Heart of Mary went out to Novo-Shulba to help her out, and thus shared her difficult conditions of exile.

The populace in Novo-Shulba was mainly Kazakh. The food situation was very difficult. The Sisters furthermore had no income – they were going hungry and growing very weak. Sister Rose, as the younger and stronger of the two, took all difficulties and cares upon herself. When they were both sick in bed with pneumonia, Sister Rose, as though less afflicted, got up to look after Sister Stephania. Her heart could not take it – and she died on January 11, 1944.

They put Sister Stephania in a military hospital for the wounded, but she was still not fully recovered from her serious illness when they sent her back to her hut, where she discovered that all her belongings – her undergarments, her coat and other things – had all been stolen. Thus she was completely alone, still weak from her illness, without her things and without any money. The Sisters in Maloyaroslavets found out what had happened and in May 1944 they sent Sister Catherine Rubashova out to help Mother Stephania.

Because Novo-Shulba was a long way from the railroad, Sister Catherine had to join a column of Kazakh men going that way and to spend the night with them on the steppe. The steppe in the springtime is full of the fragrance of grasses and tulips, and it was here that Sister Catherine had an unforgettable experience. She was holding the Blessed Sacrament close to her heart, bringing it to Mother Stephania. Lying there on the ground, she looked up at the dark sky, covered with bright stars, and her soul was filled, as never before, with a sweet peace and a real sense of the presence of God, of union with Him and the entire cosmos.

Novo-Shulba has a harsh continental climate: in the summer there are sand storms and it is so hot that at times the wells dry up; in the winter the temperature goes to minus 40 degrees Celsius and lower, with snowdrifts and blizzards. The locals live either in huts or in dugouts. In the winter Sister Catherine had to get up at night to heat the stove so that in the morning they could dress in at least a little warmth. When she began to teach in the local high school, their lives improved and they no longer went hungry.

Once an amazing thing happened to them. They hadn't even a speck of sugar or anything sweet for Easter. Sister Catherine had futilely looked for sugar over the course of several days and she was returning home with nothing, walking across the snow-covered steppe. Suddenly she heard a voice: "Do you need sugar?" Lifting her eyes, she saw in front of her a Kazakh woman holding out to her a packet of sugar. After giving her the sugar, the woman very quickly disappeared from sight. This and other similar events touchingly tell us that God helps us not only in major, serious events and needs, but He also tenderly indulges His little, weak children.

Thus the Sisters lived together until 1947, the end of Mother Stephania's exile. Two or three weeks before her release, she said that she would not eat any more honey so that she could bring it as a present to the Sisters in Maloyaroslavets. In the post-war period one had to wait weeks on a train platform for a train; thus the return home was a long and difficult journey.

In 1946 Maria Filippovna Sokolovskaya, who had been living in Moscow, joined the Sisters in Maloyaroslavets. From her youth she knew she had a vocation to religious life but owing to unfavorable and difficult circumstances it was not until she was forty-four years old that she was able to respond to her vocation. She chose as her patroness Saint Catherine de Ricci. In the summer of 1946, after a twelve-year separation, I came to Maloyaroslavets from Uralsk on my first vacation from work. At the end of March 1947 I returned to the community for good, and the Sisters received me with great joy.

After me, Sister Margaret of Hungary arrived from Kazakhstan and then Sister Teresa, who had finished her five-year term in the Temnikov camps. Sister Margaret and I were unable to find work in Maloyaroslavets and after living in the community for about a month, we had to move to Kaluga. Mother Stephania and Sister Catherine arrived from Kazakhstan on the eve of our departure. As the Sisters had expected, Mother Stephania was upset by their desire to elect another Superior; she stormily protested, and there was no pacifying her. Life in the community became unbearable.

Here we need to take into account the fact that even when living at liberty the Sisters were nevertheless immediately put under surveillance. Their whole life – which even without this aggravation was full of deprivation and difficulties – passed under the unsleeping eye of the GPU, both at their places of work and at home. Of course all this did not give one a chance to relax, to give the nervous system even the slightest rest – and thus nerves were in an overwrought state during the arrests, in the prisons, on the convoys, in the camps and when living in exile.

And it was only the constant merciful help of God, prayer with deep faith and hope that preserved in the soul a deep peace and readiness to endure trials sent by the Lord as proofs of His acceptance of the Sisters' vow of sacrifice for Russia.

Sister Margaret and I found work in Kaluga – Sister Margaret as a hospital nurse, and I as an office worker. When I went for a couple days to visit the Sisters in Maloyaroslavets, I found there a very heavy, tense atmosphere. Sister Stephania was in high dudgeon, criticizing everything. During a general conversation at table her whole countenance and disdainful retorts seemed to say: "What can you say of any sense?" The atmosphere was becoming more and more heated, and this was reflected in the Sisters' spiritual state.

It was impossible to bear such a situation for long. Once informed about it, Father Laberge warned Sister Stephania, demanding changes in her behavior – and letting her know that after two visitations during the course of the year, he was prepared to remove her from the community. All of this was in such sharp contrast with the earlier atmosphere of unanimity, good will and mutual love in the community, and the Sisters took it very hard. And things had come to such a pass only because serious mistakes had been made on both sides.

At that time life was also materially difficult because of food shortages and post-war disruptions – and they went hungry. Sister Margaret and I lived in Kaluga only six months. After approximately one year Sister Stephania departed Maloyaroslavets for Kaluga, together with Sister Catherine, who was very attached to her.

We need to remind readers of these memoirs who were not living in Russia during these years of the distressing trials her citizens underwent. In the 1920s there was the famine along the Volga that devastated a huge territory and brought the people to the point of cannibalism. Even the aid rendered by America during that time of misfortune was not able to change anything for the famine-stricken regions. The authorities tried to ease the situation with the "New Economic Policy" (NEP), temporarily allowing a return to private trade. But at the same time, the persecution of the faith began in 1920: the authorities arrested priests and active parishioners and they closed and destroyed churches. They confiscated gold and valuables from the people. Denunciations and arrests began.

The NEP came to an end in 1928, and then collectivization and the de-kulakization of the peasants began. Again there were mass arrests, devastating villages and the countryside. A famine began in Ukraine, no less terrible than the Volga famine.

From 1935 we were under the dominion of an arbitrary dictatorship, the tyranny of Stalin, with arrests and executions of members of the government, comrades of Lenin, and members of the Party for the slightest disagreement or criticism. We saw the annihilation of the best part of the intelligentsia, representatives of the arts and sciences – "enemies of the people."

This persecution and hounding of people who were not guilty of anything was difficult to bear, and many, driven to despair, committed suicide. It was enough just to declare someone an "enemy of the people," and no evidence or facts would be needed – his execution was assured. They shot people by the hundreds, by the thousands.

Then there were the mass arrests in 1937 and 1938 – "Yezhovshchina" – with death sentences or sentences to Kolyma for ten to twenty-five years, and sometimes without any fixed term limit at all. All sentences were handed down without a trial, in absentia, by decision of a Troika or a Special Board of the NKVD. The whole huge territory of the country was covered with a thick net of prisons and camps.

Then the war! And after the war – more famine and, once again, mass arrests began. O unhappy, long-suffering country!

New Arrests, 1948-1949

Arrests began again after the war; some were in connection with the occupation, but most were repeat arrests of persons previously repressed. The following Sisters were arrested in the autumn of 1948 in Kaluga: Margarita, Philomena, Stephania and Catherine. The authorities brought Sister Lucia from Maloyaroslavets to the Kaluga prison. The rest of the Sisters, who had not long before this departed from Maloyaroslavets, were arrested six months later, in 1949. Only Sister Rosa Maria escaped arrest this time.

The prison was overcrowded: they squeezed in bunks and packed six or seven people into a small single cell. From 1937 onward the tribunals had been giving sentences of up to twenty-five years, and we found ourselves witnessing the grief, despair and nervous breakdowns of women with children still at home who had received twenty-five-year sentences. We were all in separate cells and each of us tried to support these poor women, enduring their grief with them.

We spent almost a year in the prison. During the investigation, the interrogator once shouted at Teresa that he would give her twenty-five years – to which she said, "It will be as God pleases. If He does not will it, you will not give me anything." He answered, "What's God to us?!" Walking back to the cell from her interrogation, Teresa prayed, "Lord, they think they are god and can do anything. Show them that they are but men." And indeed, despite the interrogator's threats, Teresa was set free. True, she was not able to leave the prison right away because she had fallen seriously ill during the interrogation and ended up in the prison hospital.

By decision of a Special Board of the Ministry of State Security (made, as always, in absentia), Sisters Antonina and Catherine each got fifteen years and the rest of us got ten years in the camps.[33] Soon we were loaded into convoy rail cars that were specially made for transporting convicts: the four-seat compartments were separated from the corridor by a grill from top to bottom, with grilled doors that were locked by the guards. There were narrow windows in the ceiling, also grated.

Sister Lucia and I ended up in a compartment with a few women we did not know; we women experienced no trouble along the way from our accompanying guard. The men were in other compartments and the convoy escort treated them cruelly. For the slightest breach of order – for example, if someone lit a cigarette or spoke loudly – the guards immediately put him in handcuffs. With even a small movement of the hands or fingers, these handcuffs automatically tightened and caused unbearable pain because they had spikes on the inner side that punctured the flesh. Wearing these cuffs, even healthy young men cried like children from the pain. When they let the men out to go to the toilet, they forced them to run down the corridor with their hands behind their backs, regardless of their age.

At this time the camps were of different types: general camps, camps with a prison regimen, camps with a strict prison regimen, and camps with a penalty regimen. We ended up in a camp with a strict prison regimen.

[33] Editor's Note: The sentences were dated August 17, 1949.

Tayshetlag, 1949-1956

During these years men and women were kept in separate camp sectors, and the sectors for those convicted under Article 58 ("politicals") were separate from the sectors for criminal convicts – which was good because it made life in the camp calmer.

We were transported to a transit camp in the town of Tayshet, 250 miles northwest of Irkutsk. It was already the dead of winter, with temperatures down to zero. From Tayshet we were transported to a camp sector that had previously been used for men, so it was filthy and run-down. They put us in a barrack that had ice and snow on the walls and floor. It was packed full with double-decker plank boards for sleeping, and there was no lighting. The person on duty, whose responsibilities included cleaning the barrack and heating the iron stoves, had to gather thin sticks, dry them out and then stand with a burning stick to illuminate the barrack in the evening until everyone was settled in, and then again in the morning, when everyone was arising. There was no water at the camp sector; water was brought in barrels, but only for use in the kitchen. To wash ourselves we collected snow or broke dirty icicles from the roof and melted them.

The jobs were as follows. First – they marched us in a column, in rows of five or six, several miles from the camp, where we were to gather as much scrap wood as we could and carry it back to the camp for cooking and heating the barracks. Often, walking with the column part of the way, the escort would give the command "Sit!" and we had to sit in the snow. After keeping us some time in the snow, he would shout "Stand!" And this could be repeated several times: "Sit! Stand! Sit! Stand!" It was bitterly cold and many women were poorly dressed – many had nothing warm to wear and no boots. They suffered frostbite and fell ill.

The second job was cleaning up the excrement. The small wooden outhouse for some reason was covered from floor to ceiling with frozen excrement and the ground all around it was covered with a layer of frozen urine six to eight inches thick. Using picks and crowbars we had to break up the excrement and urine, with chips and spray flying at our faces and clothing.

In the spring, at another camp sector we scooped up the excrement from the large outhouses with large scoops, poured it into barrels and then hauled it to a designated place where it was dumped. Joking, we would say that we could now be called "gold workers."

They fed us a spoonful of oat kasha and herring broth instead of soup. We slept on plank beds packed so tight together that we all had to take the same position – like sardines. If you had to get up during the night, when you returned you wouldn't find your place because all the bodies involuntarily rolled together, like water. Fortunately, we were not long in these camp sectors.

At the end of 1950 we were moved to a camp sector that used convicts in mica production. The work was clean and it was inside. Using special knives, we had to take sheets of mica that were one to one and a half centimeters thick and remove thin mica sheets that were only millimeters thick. The work quotas were high and the work was done in day and night shifts. In addition to mica production, there were other heavier jobs for the younger and stronger women, mainly at the wood mill. The food situation was bad and we went hungry. Various illnesses broke out (dystrophy, debilitating diarrhea, wounds that would not heal), and I was twice in the hospital.

A very sad incident occurred in the camp sector at that time. In one of the large barracks several women heard a noise during the night, as though a large soft object had fallen to the floor. I was working the morning shift and I noticed that as they set off for their jobs, the women were all looking to one side and whispering among themselves. Looking in that direction, I saw a pale woman sitting there with vacant eyes. Around her neck was a bloody belt, about two inches wide. This educated woman had been sleeping in the upper bunk, at the end, right near the door. Being in a depressed spiritual state and at some moment having completely despaired, she had decided to take her life. She noticed a hook over the door. But the hook was weak and not able to hold the weight of her body – it came loose and the woman fell to the floor, but remained alive. I truly pitied this despairing, unfortunate woman.

Sister Lucia and I did not always live in the same barrack, but we saw each other often and we always spent feast days together. At the beginning of the summer of 1951 they sent Sister Lucia and me by convoy to different places. When I arrived at the new camp sector, I was so happy to see Mother Antonina there! We were housed in different barracks, but we frequently saw each other. Because of a bad foot, Mother Antonina worked as a fire warden, on night duty. She constantly had to climb high staircases in order to check everything carefully. Once she slipped and fell and broke a rib.

The jobs at this camp sector were more or less heavy: in the camp itself there were cleaning and service workers, and outside the camp the work involved either dragging logs from the woods for several miles or digging ditches, clearing away snow, etc. The younger and healthier women worked at the wood mill and cleared fields. Once after work the women collected armfuls of flowers and brought them to gladden those who had remained in the camp because there was not a single blade of grass in the camp, just barbed wire, the fence and guard towers. But the guard at the gate told the women to throw the flowers away – which they did tearfully. Everything the camp administration did was aimed at making the life of the convicts more burdensome, unnerving them and depriving them of even the slightest relief.

When we were setting out for our jobs outside the camp zone, we were put in rows of five or six, and the head guard leading up the column would yell, "I'm warning you! Walk arm in arm, no looking around, no talking. We'll consider even a step to the side an attempt to escape and we'll shoot without warning!" But the way was long and the women would quietly begin to talk among themselves. It happened that the guard as a warning would shoot a round in the air from his submachine gun and some women, whose nerves were so overwrought, would burst into tears.

The convict population was very diverse, but most of the convicts were from western Ukraine, Subcarpathia, Belorussia and the Baltic States: simple peasant women and wonderful young people – mostly students, friendly, very close-knit. There were also many educated, cultured women: painters, performing artists, ballerinas, engineers, doctors, teachers, and scientific workers.

Young women from western Ukraine prayed together in the barracks on Sundays and quietly sang the Greek Catholic liturgy. On Christmas Eve (this was after the death of Stalin in 1953), girls came to the barracks dressed in costumes as Herod, Death, the devil and shepherds, and they acted out religious scenes in verses. The camp bosses, when they heard about it, chased after them, going from one barrack to another, but the girls managed to slip away. Then they set up a Christmas tree in the barrack and invited believers and anyone else who wanted to come celebrate. One of the girls gave a fine speech wishing everyone a happy Christmas. There were only a few who received packages from home, so we had to save up our food from dinner and supper for a long time – not eating herring or sugar, saving up our black bread – all so we could better celebrate the feast day.

After some time I began to work in the office. After Stalin's death in March, 1953, everything in the camp changed immediately: they took the bars off the windows, they stopped locking the barracks, the food improved, and at the camp sector they opened a booth where we could buy sundries. The camp sector, where there had previously been not one blade of grass, nothing but barbed wire, was gradually transformed by the amateur gardeners and flower specialists among us. People from back home began to send us seeds and everything round about was covered with flowers. It changed so much that one could mistake it for a resort.

They started to show movies in the camp and women became more and more involved in amateur artistic productions. The young women were capable and talented. They held concerts with choral and soloist performances, ballet miniatures and fragments of various ballets with a string orchestra of guitars, mandolins and balalaikas. Everything was well executed with fine costuming and sets, all made by hand out of gauze, pillowcases, sheets and sacks; there were also women who did carpentry work. Administrators from other camp sectors came to watch and listen to our concerts.

In 1955 they began a review of case files, with a commission for considering the files of the disabled for early release. At the end of 1954 I once again had to spend a month in the hospital for a serious pre-stroke condition.

After Sister Lucia arrived at the new camp sector to which she had been transferred, they assigned her to work in the outpatient clinic, helping the main doctor, Father Józef Borodziula.[34] Every day they worked until midnight, seeing patients without a break. Soon Father Józef was transferred to another camp sector where there were thousands of women, and they brought a doctor from Moscow for the outpatient clinic, a decent and respectable man. Also at this camp sector doing general labor was the Catholic Bishop Teofilis Matulianis; and there were other priests there as well, but there was no opportunity to meet with them.

[34] Much later, after his release from the camps, Father Józef lived with his sister in Riga where he set up a domestic chapel in the apartment. Once in 1977 he visited Sister Lucia, who was living in the little village of Maishiagala sixteen miles northwest of Vilnius and he gave her as a remembrance a large photograph of his graduation from the seminary.

After a few months Sister Lucia was re-assigned to general labor – tree-felling and stump removal. First the convicts would dig around the stump from all sides, then with crowbars and long picks they made pits in the ground and pulled out the stump. This work was of course beyond a woman's strength – it demanded such exertion that it seemed that one's intestines would burst. Sister Lucia also worked for some time covering railroad embankments with sod. This work involved cutting large pieces of sod and then dragging them up onto the embankment, crawling on one's belly, which for Sr. Lucia resulted in a prolapse of her inner organs. They later sent her back to the clinic to help the head doctor.

Once she learned that the person on duty (i.e., the janitor-guard) in the men's barrack was a Catholic priest. Sister Lucia sent an orderly to the barrack with a request that the person on duty immediately report to the clinic. A venerable, gray-haired man appeared. With a commanding tone, Sister Lucia said to him: "Please give me a list of how many people are in your barrack." He bowed and left, and when he returned with the list there was no longer anyone else in the clinic. She locked the door and the two of them remained alone. The priest immediately understood what was happening. He was an educated Roman Catholic priest from Tbilisi and spoke several European languages. He asked Sister Lucia in which language she would like to make her confession. How good and easy it was, and how the soul felt cleansed after confession! Soon they were both transferred to other camp sectors and thereafter never had another chance to meet.[35]

Sister Lucia now ended up in a camp sector where more than two hundred wives of "enemies of the people" worked in vegetable gardens – these were respectable and noble women. Their husbands had worked in the Kremlin and had fallen into disgrace; some had been shot, some had been sent to the prisons or camps without the right of correspondence or without any limit on the term of their sentence. Many had ended up in Kolyma, in the very far northeast, a completely undeveloped territory. Sister Lucia worked with the wives of the Soviet ambassadors to Sweden and Italy, cultured and decent women, and a lot of wives of government workers from Moscow. They went in their overalls to work in the vegetable gardens, and Sister Lucia treated

[35] This priest invited Sister Lucia to Tbilisi, promising to set up a house so that she and the Sisters could live near the church.

them in the clinic, gave them moral support and comforted them as well as she could.

In 1954 the convicts heard the joyful news that the authorities were beginning to release convicts from the camps. The bosses, overseers and guards began to treat the convicts more kindly, and their wives, when asked, would even buy the convicts fruit and small necessities. At first, all releases had residency restrictions, and convicts were only allowed to go to places that had submitted certificates from relatives or acquaintances who attested by their signatures and the stamps of the local government organs that they would take responsibility for the person being released from the camp.

Sister Lucia was released from the camp in 1955 upon the conclusion of the medical commission, fully rehabilitated (because she was completely blameless!), and allowed to return to Moscow. But she went to Maloyaroslavets, where Sister Rosa Maria was still living. After a few days Sisters Lucia and Rosa Maria left for Vilnius, where they had been invited by the Superior of Third Order Franciscans whom they had known back in Moscow and Orel. They lived several weeks with the Third Order Sisters, who prayed for them every day.

When Sister Lucia went to the Ministry of Health about working in Lithuania, the person in charge harshly declared: "For you, there is no work in Lithuania. Go back where you came from." But as she was leaving, one of the clerks secretly said to her: "Come back in a couple days – this guy will be gone and there will be a different person on duty." When Sister Lucia came back to the Ministry, there was indeed another person at the desk – a young Lithuanian, who immediately offered her a choice of two jobs: either with the disabled or at a hospital in the little village of Maishiagala outside Vilnius. In offering the job in Maishiagala, however, he warned her that the head doctor at the hospital was a young fellow and did not care much for older co-workers.

Sister Lucia arrived at the hospital in Maishiagala at exactly the moment when the nurse on duty was giving injections. The head doctor suggested that Sister Lucia help her. Right away he liked how deftly and accurately she found the veins, and he hired her on the spot. Over the years, the head doctor[36] always treated her well, and he even would say "I am solidly behind

---

[36] V. Verizhnikov. He later worked as the head doctor at a hospital in Riga.

you, Anna Kirillovna. As long as I am here, no one will offend you." Indeed, he was like a father to her.

The Sisters settled into a little house across from the church; nearby was the hospital where Sister Lucia worked successfully for twenty-two years (1955-1977), receiving several commendations for her good work. Sister Lucia went to Mass in the church in a neighboring village, where for five years she played the organ, as they had no organist. Everything was good and for the glory of God! Sister Lucia died of cancer in Maishiagala on November 9, 1978, at the age of seventy-eight.

Vorkutstroi, 1948-1956

Sisters Stephania and Catherine Rubashova, arrested in Kaluga in 1948, ended up in different convoys. Sister Catherine managed to arrange to be sent to the same place as Sister Stephania, who was now old and ill. They found themselves in the little village of Abez, beyond the Arctic Circle, not far from Vorkuta. Soon Sister Monica and Sister Catherine de Ricci, a recent member of the community, also arrived in Abez.

Construction of the camp sector at Abez had just barely begun. The barracks were damp and cold, and there were few stoves and little coal. It was terribly crowded, but it was their breath that actually kept them warm. There were no bathrooms and the water situation was bad. There was an outhouse – in the freezing cold. A person can bear a lot and people had to get used to such hardships. Bit by bit the camp sector was built: washrooms were built in the yard, the water situation improved, and even teapots for boiling water made an appearance.

Sisters Stephania and Catherine Rubashova received parcels every two months and they shared the food with the other Sisters and also with the sick and the neediest. During these years in the camp, Sister Stephania wrote her best poetry. Many in the camp loved her, and she maintained contact with some of her fellow convicts over the course of many years, even after their release from the camps.

Thus the years passed. People grew weaker, mostly from the lack of air in the barracks, especially at night when the barracks were locked up. The constant transfers from one camp sector to another were terribly exhausting. One had to go on foot, six to ten miles, carrying one's belongings, and even though they weren't much, they were nevertheless heavy for weakened women. At one of the camp sectors the Sisters ran into Sister Margaret (Krylevskaya), who was working as a hospital nurse. The convicts tried to ease each other's lives, regardless of worldview, nationality or social position because it was only together that they were able to overcome the difficulties of camp life.

In 1954 the healthiest convicts were sent to do farm work in the Karaganda camps, and being among the youngest, Sister Catherine Rubashova and Sister Margaret were among those sent. The convoy was excruciating – they rode for three weeks in a freight car with triple-decker plank bunks, packed in like sardines. The work on the collective farm was not easy, but it was in the fresh air, where breathing was easier.

In 1954 Sisters Stephania, Monica and Catherine de Ricci were all ill and were sent to a facility for invalids in Ukhta. The years passed, many in the camps were dying, and seeing how the dead were unceremoniously hauled off to the cemetery in common boxes, each one thought that this would be his fate as well. But God had other plans. Rehabilitations began in 1955: they released people for lack of evidence of a crime committed and restored their rights. At the end of May 1956 Sister Catherine of Siena Rubashova was the first of the Sisters released from the Karaganda camp and rehabilitated. She could now return to her native city, Moscow. She immediately began to petition for the assignment of an apartment, and as soon as she received a voucher for an apartment, she put Sister Stephania's name on it.

Sister Stephania was released from the invalid facility in 1956; she was rehabilitated and moved in with Sister Catherine Rubashova in Moscow. She was already sixty-eight years old, and on account of her age and health she could no longer work. She did as much as she could of the domestic chores and freely gave herself over to a regular spiritual life. Sister Catherine, now forty-seven years old, soon went to work at the Historical Library, where she worked until she went on pension, and even then she sometimes worked there for short periods of time.

The Sisters attended Saint Louis Church, which, after the closing of two churches in the 1930s, had become not just the church for embassy workers, but also the only Catholic church for all Catholics living in or coming to the capital. In Moscow there were still two or three families of the Russian

Catholic community and the Sisters immediately reestablished contact with them. In time it turned out that the Sisters became the unifying spiritual focal point of the community, and their apartment became a place where it was possible to gather, to speak heart-to-heart, to be strengthened, to rest and be renewed in spirit.

It became customary to gather on feast days at the Sisters' apartment as a small group of believers. It so renewed the soul and led them forward along the path of fidelity to Christ and His teachings. Young people, mostly university students, soon began to be part of this little group. A strong spiritual bond formed between Sister Catherine, young people and clergy.

At the end of the 1970s, when it became possible to establish contact with Dominicans in Poland, Sister Catherine spent some time there. In connection with her trip, I went to Moscow for two weeks to look after Sister Stephania, who was ailing. After Sister Stephania's death in 1974, Sister Catherine began to come to Vilnius a few times a year for ten days or so to visit Mother Antonina and the Sisters. As before, she remained the connecting spiritual link between the Sisters and the parishioners.

Of course the experiences of their difficult, sacrificial life could not but be reflected in the Sisters' health. Each one's health had been compromised and they were constantly ill with one ailment or another. Sister Catherine suffered from cardiac asthma and she died from an asthma attack on May 12, 1987, at the age of seventy-eight. For two or three years prior to her death she had almost never left her building; she lived alone and her young friends took turns coming to help her.

Sister Teresa was released from prison in 1950 and at first she went to her mother and sister's in Kostroma and lived with them for three years. But she was not able to come to terms with the absence of a Catholic church and the impossibility of receiving the Sacraments. Furthermore, she had in her soul an unrelenting dream: to gather in one place all the Sisters who had been released from the camps and prisons. She sincerely loved them all and wanted to reestablish the tranquil spiritual life of the community. In order to realize this dream, it would first of all be necessary to settle in a place where there was a functioning Catholic church.

A certain Franciscan who had been banished from Leningrad knew a Third Order Sister who had recently moved with a friend to Vilnius, where there was a Catholic church. Their address was given to Teresa, who was going to Vilnius, so that she would have a place to spend the night – and this was the first piece of good fortune. Lithuania was the only republic in the USSR where the population was predominantly Catholic. The wave of utterly brutal persecution of religion – the closing and destruction of churches, persecution and arrests of priests and parishioners, lawlessness, secret deprivations of human rights at work and elsewhere – this wave had not swept over Lithuania with such barbaric force. Not only in the cities, but in the villages as well, there were still functioning Catholic churches with devoted parishioners – Lithuanians and Poles.

And the government always had to take the Catholic population of the republic into account. The authorities were not able to put pressure on the Catholic Church for still another reason: it was in a somewhat different position than the Orthodox Church, which was firmly in the government's grip and had been deprived of any independence. The head of the Catholic Church, the Pope, was outside of their power. Harsh and unpopular actions on the part of the authorities in Lithuania could arouse outrage, active opposition and an uprising of the whole population, and this could then lead to the intervention of the West, which would complicate international relations.

Sister Teresa found the Third Order Sisters in Vilnius living in a tiny little room. When they heard the story of her life, they treated her very warmly and took her in, even though they themselves barely fit in such a small place. Teresa slept on the floor, in a narrow space between two beds. Every morning she went out looking for work. It had only been eight years since the end of the war and there were still many ruined buildings and torn up streets, but it was almost impossible to find a job.

The first job she found was working as a cleaning lady at a large market. It was a lot of heavy work, and with her health having been ruined in the camps, she had little strength. But armed with a broom, shovel and rags, she was glad to have found any work at all, so that she could at least earn enough for her maintenance (as was required at that time).

After some time Sister Teresa moved in with an elderly secular Third Order Dominican who lived in a small room near the church, where it was possible to squeeze in a cot. She soon began to work as a nurse at the railroad hospital. In 1953, when the authorities began the review of case files and opened medical commissions for the release of convicts from the camps,

Sister Teresa sent me an official commitment certified at the appropriate state offices, stating that she would take me under her guardianship. People asked her, "How can you, who are yourself just getting by, take on others?" But Teresa had no doubts and firmly counting on the Lord, she entrusted everything entirely into His hands.

I was released from the Tayshet camp at the end of May 1953, after Sister Lucia had been released and had gone to Lithuania with Sister Rosa Maria. I stayed about ten days with some Third Order Franciscans, then I went to Maishiagala, outside Vilnius, to Sisters Lucia and Rosa Maria because residency permits for Vilnius, the capital, were not being issued to persons coming from Russia, much less to persons from the camps. Even on the outskirts of the city, permits were being granted only to those who had work.

There was no work suitable for me, although I did find a job without any days off as a night watchman on a State collective farm. There were three things that had to be guarded and they were far apart from each other: the calf barn, a supply of lumber surrounded by barbed wire, and a field of cucumbers near the forest – and there was lighting only around the lumber. I had been classified as a Group II invalid since 1938, and furthermore I had high blood pressure. It was hard to run between the three places that had to be guarded. Twice there were troubles because of the theft of cucumbers from the field, and chasing people in the dark was simply impossible. So after working there three and a half months I had to quit.

At about this time, they needed a janitor in the clinic where Sister Lucia was working, so I went to work as a janitor. The work was heavy and completely beyond my strength – carrying water every day from a well that was not close by, heating two stoves, washing the floors and seeing to the complete cleanliness of the rooms. I was not able to endure it for more than three months. So I began to petition to be granted my pension, which required several trips to Vilnius.

At the end of July 1956 Sister Monica came to Vilnius from the invalid facility, and at the end of the summer Sister Catherine de Ricci also arrived. Monica settled in with Sister Teresa – they managed to find a partitioned-off corner in a room of a homeowner in Vilnius. Sister Catherine lived with a blind woman in a little room in a house not far from the church of Saint Teresa of Avila. The chapel of the church had the miracle-working icon of the Mother of God of the Eastern Gate (Our Lady of Ostra Brama), which gave Sister Catherine boundless joy. She lived there, caring for the blind woman (a very good and deeply religious person) until the woman died in 1974.

At the end of August Mother Antonina was also released, and she went first to her sister's in Lesnoy, Kaliningrad region. In 1957 she came to Vilnius to see how the Sisters were living and in 1958 she came to stay. Sisters Teresa, Monica and Antonina managed to live in a small room with a separate entry that had been built onto a small cottage. The room was very cold and the wind blew through cracks in the walls and the door. The Sisters were constantly getting colds. Sister Monica, who slept on the floor, developed an inflammation of a facial nerve and suffered from this for a long time.

The issue of residency permits in Vilnius was becoming very acute and the requirements for a permit here were strict: there had to be no less than 140 square feet of living space for the person granted a permit and just as much for any other person living in the place, in addition to the sanitary norms. In order to stay in Lithuania, one could register in a region outside Vilnius, but living in Vilnius itself with a permit issued in a region outside the city carried the danger of expulsion and punishment for violation of passport regulations, something the Sisters had to take into account.

Employees of all city institutions emphatically responded to all questions only in Lithuanian, even though most of them understood Russian. As part of the disorganization of post-war life in Lithuania, bureaucrats used any means to make it difficult and complicated to come from Russia. When I came from Maishiagala to process my documents, I learned by chance from one of the Third Order Sisters that a certain woman living alone in Vilnius needed a watchman for the garden around her house. The woman was living in the home of her father, a distinguished chemical engineer who had received the Lenin Prize for his inventions. He had died during the war and after the end of the war the two-story brick house had been nationalized. His wife and daughter were left with two large rooms with a veranda, a living space of 600 square feet, which was more than enough for their residency permit. The wife died seven years after her husband. The daughter remained alone, and she needed some help.

Sister Teresa took the processing of my residency permit upon herself. Armed with my application and that of the homeowner and other necessary documents, she went to the Residency Department of the City Executive

Committee. The waiting room was crowded, and those who went into the department head's office quickly came rushing out, agitated and distressed. Refused … refused … another, refused.

Sister Teresa prayed while waiting her turn. When she entered the office and submitted the documents, she was told that there would be no permit for anyone recently arrived, since there wasn't enough living space even for the city's citizens. Teresa began to ask, saying that I had been born in Vilnius, but without listening to her, the department head summoned the next in line. She did not leave the office. She just stood there and prayed, asking God to help. When the next person had come into the office, the department head noticed that Teresa was still there. Taking her documents, he angrily said, "Here, I'll write it right now so you don't have to hope!" But as she left the office Teresa read the order: "Granted" – as though someone's hand had guided his hand.

A new life had begun. The owner of the house left for work in the morning and I was left to guard the garden and do battle with little boys who wanted to harm the garden. Gradually I began to recover from all the overexertion and exhaustion and now I was finally able to attend tranquilly to my soul. I also began to study Polish, which I didn't know at all. I had Father Hamon's Reflections for Each Day of the Year and two other books in Polish and a dictionary. Happiness filled my soul.

The owner of the house was Polish – an educated, cultured Catholic woman and in essence a good person. She was deeply lonely. She had spent all the years after the nationalization of her family's home petitioning for its return, submitting documentation to administrative and judicial offices regarding the illegality of the nationalization. This effort had become the main focus of her life. It was unhealthy because, on account of the constant nervous tension associated with petitions in this matter, she herself began to manifest strange behaviors that then aroused conflicts with her neighbors, who were after all residing in the house in accordance with official vouchers. I saw how unhappy she was and felt sorry for her. Soon there arose between us such a spiritual bond that she stopped feeling so alone and she gradually livened up, which made me glad.

I then appealed to the International Red Cross for help in finding my sister Galina's address, as she had left for Paris twenty-four years earlier. Six months later I received my sister's address and almost simultaneously, a letter from her. We were so happy that we had finally found one another and could now correspond. Although I was six years older, we had always been close and loved each other dearly. In her first letter my sister wrote that she had already sent a package to Lithuania. But having experienced over the course of my wandering life the all-abundant value of poverty – the emancipation and freedom of soul – I immediately felt an involuntary protest and a desire to refuse packages categorically. I wrote this right then to my sister, but my sister answered that as long as she was alive, she would regularly send me packages, regardless of my protests. So I understood that through my sister God wanted to give us some assistance, which was helpful for putting the community's common life in order.[37]

Around this time Mother Antonina and Sisters Teresa and Monica made the acquaintance at church of Mother Imelda, the Superior of a community of Dominican nuns. Upon learning our Sisters' story, Mother Imelda helped arrange for their move to a small apartment in a private cottage across from the house where she herself was living with two sisters: Sisters Sophia Marie and Bronislava. These three, and two others who lived separately, were the last of the Dominican community in Lithuania, the rest having mainly left for Poland.[38]

The apartment to which the Sisters moved had two rooms: one that was not large and another that was quite small, with a tiny little kitchen, but with its own entry. The apartment was next to the owner's, with stove heating and electricity, but without water or a toilet, which was outdoors. The house was a long way from the shops and public transportation, but it had a huge advantage: it was at the end of a street and was a 25-minute walk from the large, beautiful church of the Holy Apostles Peter and Paul. The Sisters were happy.

They saw Sister Catherine and me rarely because we lived far from each other. Two years later Mother Antonina told me that I should come live with them, especially since their landlady, Bronislava, had found the opportunity

---

[37] My sister, with poor health and high blood pressure, sent packages for the next ten years, right up to her death of a heart attack in 1969. I later learned that her family – she and her husband, three daughters and a son – had always lived very modestly and that my sister, a painter, took commissions for paintings in order to be able to send parcels to Lithuania. And they continued to live as modestly, even as their children had their own families and they had grandchildren.

[38] After the war, Poles were given the opportunity go to Poland. Thousands left, including many religious.

to register one more person at her place. I told my landlady, Katarzina, that I would stay with her for one more year, to give her time to find a replacement as I knew that I could not immediately leave her all by herself. It should be kept in mind that with the acute housing shortage, finding a tenant was not easy because it was impossible to trust people. All sorts of swindles and even crimes were constantly occurring.[39]

Over the course of the year I reminded Katarzina several times that I would soon be leaving. When the day of my departure arrived she became very upset. Apparently she had not taken my warnings seriously, thinking that nothing would ever change. I was very sorry for her, but I could stay with her no longer. I did not leave her without being concerned because she had not found a replacement and she lived alone in a hostile situation, for which she herself was in many ways to blame. I visited her, and when her feet began to hurt a lot and it was hard for her to walk to the grocery store I would visit her every couple weeks to do her shopping.

Once I had moved in with the Sisters I saw that my help here was very much needed: Mother Antonia and Sisters Monica and Teresa (who worked in the hospital) were all ailing and it was hard for them to deal with the complexities of daily life. I had always loved and respected the Sisters very much and I wanted to work for them, so I immediately took on all the household work and concerns. And thus the years passed. Sometimes I would go to Poland for a while.

And we had guests from Siberia: Lyubochka with her eleven-year-old daughter Nadezhda and her nine-year-old son. During my first period of exile (1924-1927) I had lived with her family in Obdorsk. I had stayed in contact with this family over all those years, from 1927 to 1956. Lyubochka brought her children for their first confession and First Holy Communion; and when she went home, she left her daughter, Nadya, with us for a year for treatment with speech specialists (she had a stuttering problem). I gave myself entirely to my new cares – the little girl enrolled in school, where I was considered her grandmother.

---

[39] For example, a person would move into a room in an apartment with an agreed-upon rent, then after some time appeal to the regional authorities for a voucher to the room they had rented – as space that was in excess of the owner's allowance. Acquiring it – of course, not without bribes – he would now live not only on the same rights with the owner of the apartment, but he would also begin to harass the owner with the goal of driving him out and taking possession of the apartment entirely.

And now there were five of us living together. In 1963 Sisters Stephania and Catherine Rubashova came from Moscow for three days – but a simple, open, good exchange between Mother Antonina and Sister Stephania did not come about. Sister Stephania never came to Vilnius again, but Mother Antonina traveled to Moscow and visited Sister Stephania, trying to rekindle their earlier, warm-hearted relations.

Later on Bronislava, the owner of the apartment, who always treated us with sympathy and trust, told us confidentially that agents from the secret police had come and were making inquiries about us. It was clear that the security organs were not going to let go of us until we died. Even though the nightmarish period of Stalin and Beria had come to an end, its spirit was still alive and was maintained by representatives of the regime. One had to come to terms with this constant "guardianship."

When we moved to Vilnius, we were enthralled by the fact that we were going to a Catholic country where we would find churches and the Sacraments. We rejoiced that we would be in communion with people of the same faith and spirit, and we hoped that we would be able to establish friendly relations with them. After all, prior to this time we had either lived very isolated from the outer world, or else we were on convoys, in prisons, exile and the camps, and during the short intervals between them, we lived under the constant expectation of being arrested again and facing the unavoidable sentence. These short breaks were, in a certain respect, even worse than the camps. At least under confinement there was a roof over our heads and some kind of meager food, even in undeveloped camp sectors. But now free, to find oneself a little corner in which to live in an unknown city was very complicated. And then once you had found a place and a job, you were immediately again under surveillance both at work and at home.

It turned out that our hopes for a good relationship with Catholics were only barely realized. We encountered, above all, nationalism and antagonism. Of course, one cannot blame the local population because they had endured and suffered so much both under the Russian tsars and then, after the Soviet seizure of Lithuania in 1939, under the despotic regime of Stalin and Beria.

Parishioners at the church we attended, wanting to get to know us, would address us in Polish, and it was obviously unpleasant that we would answer in Russian. We had to explain why we did not know Polish. After this, attempts to become acquainted with us were not renewed – especially when the Poles found out that we were Eastern Rite Catholics and that our community included women of several nationalities. In a word, they did not accept us as their own, so even here we lived closed off, in isolation.

Sister Philomena, OP – Sophia Vladislavovna Eismont – was born in Vilnius in 1900 and died in Vilnius in 1993. The map on the following page shows her via dolorosa from her first arrest in 1924 to her exit to Lithuania in 1956.

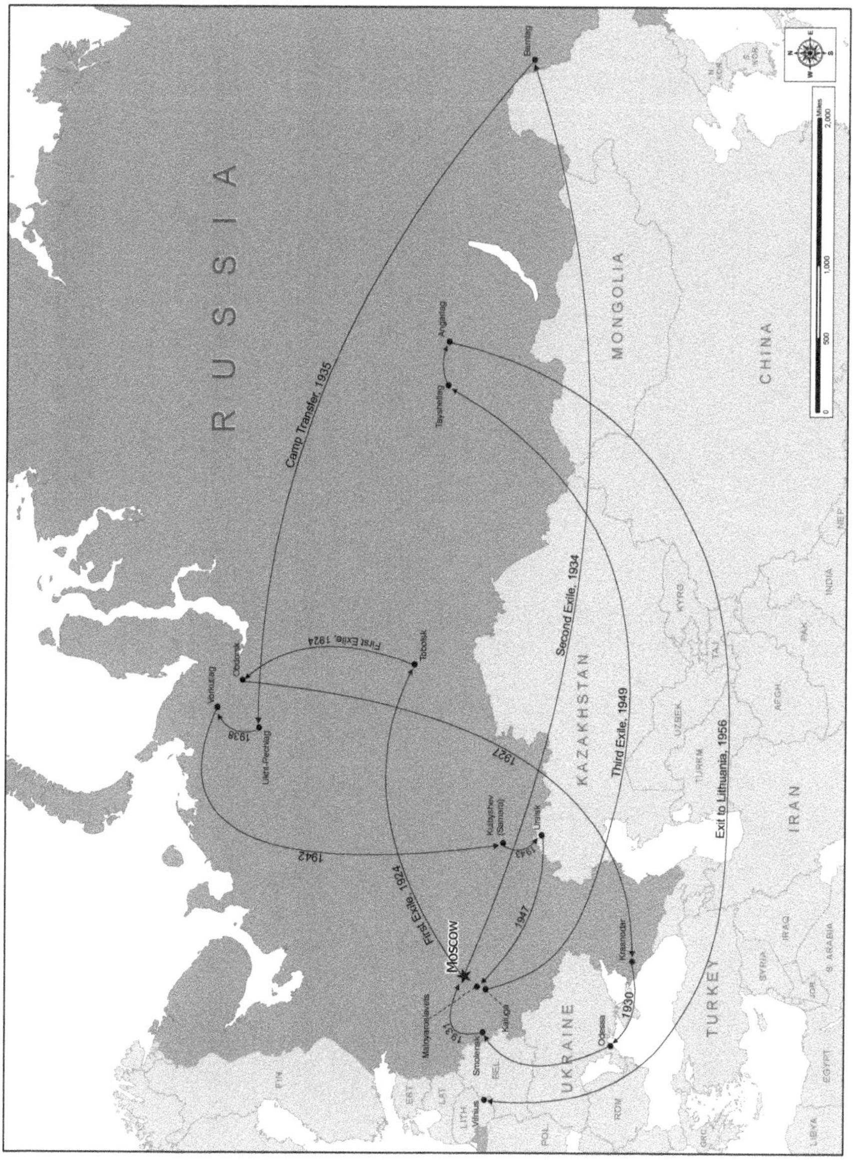

Map 4 – Sr. Philomena's *Via Dolorosa*, 1924-1956

Letters of the Dominican Sisters to the Political and Polish Red Cross, 1924-1935

LETTERS from the archives of the Political Red Cross were selected by Irina Osipova and those from the archives of the Polish Red Cross, by Ida Zaikina. The translation preserves the PRC staff's underscoring and notes.

The Political Red Cross had its origin in the nineteenth century and provided assistance to those imprisoned on political grounds, intervening for them with authorities, communicating with families, transmitting parcels, etc. It was headed by Catherine Pavlovna Peshkova (Maxim Gorky's wife) and functioned until 1937 when Stalin sealed the office.

The first letter presented below is a cover letter to the Political Red Cross regarding checks in various amounts. The addressee, Mikhail Lvovich Vinaver, served as Mme. Peshkova's assistant.

May 19, 1933

Dear Mikhail Lvovich,

I am responding to inquiries in your memorandum of May 9, No. 9.

The check in the amount of 2000 francs was sent to you at Mme. Peshkova's request for the prompt satisfaction of various needs.

The second check in the amount of 1300 francs was to be used for the satisfaction of the needs of those suffering for their faith. This is a special donation. Our associate, Vladimir Mikhailovich, provided Mme. Peshkova with all the necessary instructions with respect to this donation.

In addition, I am attaching to this letter a check for 200 francs made out to Mme. Peshkova, but designated for Catherine Osipovna Preobrazhenskaya, c/o General Delivery, Perm.

With best regards, [...]

Source: State Archive of the Russian Federation [hereinafter, GARF], f. 8409, op. 1, d. 848, s. 30.

Letters from Mother Catherine

March 19, 1924
Tobolsk

Dear Catherine Pavlovna,

With the opening of the navigation season the prison command will be transferring all the women being held here to Perm, including, apparently, me. Would you be so kind as to find out whether my transfer depends on the Moscow OGPU or the local prison command, because I understand nothing about my situation. I am permitted parcels only through the GPU and visits once a month in the presence of a representative of the GPU – but the local prison command can transfer me from place to place? Please, if possible, would you let me know if I am really going to Perm? For me, a transfer to still another prison is like a new arrest. And furthermore, I am being deprived of both parcels and visits. But of course this is not the place to discuss this – but I would really like to know in advance what kind of unpleasantness still awaits me. Forgive me for troubling you.

Anna Ivanovna Abrikosova

The secretary of the Political Red Cross made this notation on the letter: "Find out from the Secret Section where Anna Abrikosova is being sent." Source: GARF, f. 8409, op. 1, d. 348, l. 145.

July 28 and September 1, 1926

Today I received the ten rubles you sent August 7, under No. 2097, and I hasten to express my great gratitude.

Anna Abrikosova
Tobolsk Isolator

Source: GARF, f. 8409, op. 1, d. 113, l. 53, 54.

Letters of Sisters Rosa Maria (Vasileni) and Lucia (Davidyuk)

September 19, 1932

Dear Catherine Pavlovna,

Despite your long silence, we still appeal to you, as to a mother, with new and old needs. We ask that you help us return to our homeland, i.e., to Grodno province, or to America (Philadelphia), where our relatives live. Tell us, please, might we have any hope at all to be able to do this? The investigator in Poltava, Comrade Sereda, showed us two packets with documents from Warsaw – perhaps they can be requested from him and can now be useful? Please advise us, is there anything we can do in order to leave for our homeland or to our relatives? Our address: No. 47 Yadrintsovskaya St., Novosibirsk, Western Siberia.

Respectfully,
Anna Davidyuk and Nina Vasileni-Posharskaya

Source: GARF, f. 8406, op. 2, d. 1399, l. 10.

June 19, 1933

To: Moscow OGPU
From: Nina Iosifovna Vasileni

I was born in Matashi, Porozov county, Volkovysk district, Grodno province [in 1890], but for a long time I have lived in Moscow. In 1924 I was arrested and sent to Siberia, where I was until 1927, then, having a "minus 6" on my release documents, I went to live in Romny, Poltava province, where I worked in my specialty, as a seamstress. In 1930 I was again arrested and sent to the Siberian concentration camps. These years have been so difficult for me that I have lost my eyesight and now, being an invalid in Moscow, I am completely unable to earn enough for my subsistence. Therefore I am requesting that my "minus 3" status be changed to an exit visa to Poland, to go live with my relatives, who have a farm there.

Vasileni

Source: GARF, f. 8406, op. 2, d. 690, l. 5

June 19, 1933

To: Moscow OGPU
From: Anna Kirillovna Davidyuk

I was born in 1900 in Myshchitsy, Oryazh county, Grodno province and lived there until August 15, 1915, when I fled with all the other refugees into the depths of Russia. In Moscow I finished Lomonosov [Girls'] High School (25 Sivtsev – Vrazhek Pereulok). I studied two years at the university and upon completing the preschool education courses under the tutelage of Luisa Karlovna Shleger, I worked in various parts of Moscow. In 1924 I was exiled to Siberia – I worked a year in the Lenin Orphanage in Tobolsk, then they sent me to Obdorsk, where there was no work. From 1927, because I had a "minus 6" on my release documents, I lived in Ukraine, where I worked as a day laborer because I had no passport. In 1930 I was again arrested and sent to the concentration camps in Siberia where I was through 1933 – I labored there as an agricultural shock worker. I was the pacesetter for production and at the end of my term, by a decree of a Special Board of the GPU of the Ukrainian SSR I was internally exiled with a "minus 12." All my documents were taken from me when I was arrested and were not returned – in other words, I am again an undocumented non-person and I am unable to find a job. I have no one to help me because I am alone in Russia, and thus I ask that you change my documents from "minus 12" to "exit to Poland," my homeland, where my relatives live.

Anna Davidyuk

Source: GARF, f. 8406, op. 2, d. 1399, l. 13

October 12, 1933

Dear Catherine Pavlovna,

Now we are really in need, so if it is possible, please remember us in your efforts. Our earnings are only enough for a cold, damp place to live and dinner in a cafeteria. In recent weeks we have both been ill; our whole bodies swell up and we don't know exactly why, because we have 200 grams of bread each day and soup once a day. We have no residence address because we are staying in a flophouse and come here only to spend the night – so please respond to General Delivery at the post office.

I am also asking that you forward the enclosed letter addressed to my brother, otherwise I will receive nothing from him.

N.I. Vasileni and A.K. Davidyuk

Source: GARF, f. 8406, op. 2, d. 1399, l. 16

Letters of Sister Agnes (Vakhevich)

July 6, 1928

Dear Catherine Pavlovna,

I sincerely thank you for the money sent to me June 26, under No. V 221/2. I am now in a position to eat so that I can fully recover from my surgery, especially because my strength has been rather slow in coming back.

E. Vakhevich, Convict
Irkutsk Isolator

Source: GARF, f. 8409, op. 1, d. 252, l. 118.

May 23, 1929
Irkutsk

Dear Catherine Pavlovna,

Please advise me as to what to do to help my mother. A few days ago I received a letter from her saying that she has breast cancer and needs surgery. She thinks she will not survive the anesthesia and therefore will not consent to the surgery until she has seen me. They will not let me out of here, despite the fact that my term has been completed – as counted not just from the day of my arrest, but even if counted from the date of the decree of the Collegium – May 19, 1924. Obviously, no word has yet come from the Center [Moscow]. What will be my future fate? I would like to get to Moscow, if only temporarily, to visit my mother. Please advise me how to petition so that at least I might end up in one of the cities near Moscow where it would be possible to find medical assistance because my health is also always in need of attention. I have the necessary information about my health from the local doctor – and I have asked my mother to send me the information about her health. Please advise me how to proceed and please petition where it is necessary from your end, if this is possible. Among the cities close to Moscow, I would note that I have distant relatives in Yaroslavl. Graciously forgive me for troubling you, but I absolutely do not know to whom to turn for advice in this matter. Help me also, if possible, with money, because they've terminated my hospital ration but have not sent me anywhere. The small sum that was given for travel expenses will soon disappear for good if we begin to spend it, but we need to buy milk and bread otherwise it will not be possible to preserve what little remains of our health and strength.

Forgive me for writing you and troubling you.

Respectfully,
E. Vakhevich

Source: GARF, f. 8409, op. 1, d. 338, l. 184-185.

November 29, 1929
Kutimsky Village Council
Kirensky District, Kazachinsky Region

Dear Catherine Pavlovna,

I am writing to let you know that on November 27 I received the money sent for me on October 2, under No. V 224/3. I express my great gratitude for the money because my situation was extremely dire. We have been in debt for two months; they have even refused to give us Sisters food, and we had absolutely no money. In general here it is extremely difficult to acquire anything even with money. We hope very much that in the future you will not leave us without support because it is impossible to earn a living in my profession and all physical work is unsuitable because of the state of my health, and there is no other work.

Elena Vasilyevna Vakhevich

Source: GARF, f. 8409, op. 1, d. 338, l. 200.

March 13, 1932

Dear Catherine Pavlovna,

With great gratitude I am writing to let you know of our receipt of assistance from February 7 under No. 818.

Please let us know the date of the end of our term. Formally, the term had already ended March 9, 1932, because we were taken on March 8, 1924; the decree of the Collegium was issued May 19. We would very much like to know our future fate.

My sister's health, as well as my own, has completely broken down, and I have begun to have heart problems. In the doctors' opinion, the local climate is especially harmful for heart ailments.

We beg your financial assistance for getting out of here because traveling will be very expensive.

Elena Vakhevich
No. 32 Lenrabochy
Kirensk, Eastern Siberia

Source: GARF, f. 8409, op. 1, d. 809, l. 16.

March 1932

We appeal to you, asking you to find out about the end of our term and about our future fate, because on the basis of local experience we know that generally documents are not issued here, but only a certificate allowing one to go to Irkutsk and there to await future notification. This is absolutely not within our means. Please be so kind as to help us.

Elena Vakhevich

Source: GARF, f. 8409, op. 1, d. 809, l. 20.

Letters of Sister Dominica (Vakhevich)

October 4, 1924
Orel Prison Hospital – Women's Sector

Dear Catherine Pavlovna,

I am very grateful for the fifteen rubles that I received – this help was very timely. I am in the hospital with a leg inflammation. I am now better and most likely – perhaps even this week – I will soon be back in my own cell (Cell No. 57). I can write twice a month, but anything I write to you subtracts from what I can write to my own family. If you can, please pass along to my family (29 Prechistensky Boulevard, Apt. 34) that I am better but that they have taken us all off the hospital ration. I only receive [a ration] while I am in the hospital. I send my greetings to all – everything is going fine.

E. Vakhevich

I am very, very grateful for the help you have given me!

Source: GARF, f. 8409, op. 1, d. 39, l. 19.

November 12, 1925

To: Russian Red Cross for Political Prisoners
From: Elizabeth Vasilyevna Vakhevich and
Elena Mikhailovna Nefedyeva

We ask the Red Cross to come to our assistance and promptly send us a representative of the Red Cross. We were convicted May 19, 1924, under Article 61 to ten and five years, respectively; as of this date we are still in the Orel Special Purpose Isolator. Three days ago, i.e., November 10, 1925, we were told that we are being transferred on November 11 immediately with a convoy to the Solovetsky concentration camp for investigation, without having been given the opportunity to gather up our belongings, as should be permitted, or to visit with our relatives, whom we have not seen for six months. We do not have the most basic necessities for the cold climate, nor sufficient funds or food. In addition, our health is in very bad condition.

E. Vakhevich

Source: GARF, f. 8409, op. 1, d. 116, l. 245.

Letters of Sister Stephania (Gorodets)

May 31, 1929

Dear Catherine Pavlovna,

I beg you to inform me whether Anna Ivanovna Abrikosova has already arrived in Yaroslavl, whether she is in solitary confinement there, and whether it is possible to send her parcels directly or give her parcels there – or, if neither is possible and parcels are only permitted when sent through your office. I beg you, if it is possible, please petition on her behalf for permission for parcels and money transfers. After all, at her age, after spending six years in prison and with her poor health – this is a death sentence. Mailing parcels from here (Kostroma is a four-hour trip from Yaroslavl) can be done more frequently and nutritiously – whereas mailing through your office is more expensive and less could be sent. Items such as cutlets and eggs if sent from here would arrive in excellent condition, but if sent through your office they would spoil. Forgive me for troubling you with such details, but you most likely will understand how my heart aches for Anna Ivanovna; how will she survive this difficult phase, in complete isolation? Please, if possible, let me know whether she will be living there alone or together with [Anastasia] Selenkova.

With sincere respect and forever grateful,

Vera Lvovna Gorodets
Kostroma, Nikitskaya, #3

Source: GARF, f. 8409, op. 1, d. 348, l. 132.

June 27, 1929

Dear Catherine Pavlovna,

I am very grateful to you for your response to my inquiry. I hope that you will be able to petition on my behalf for the right to send small parcels directly to Yaroslavl – to Anna Ivanovna Abrikosova. In the meantime, together with this letter I am sending a package through you for Abrikosova and Selenkova in one box. On the top (you will unseal the box, right?) are lying separate lists of what is being sent to each of them. In addition, on each package is written "For Selenkova" or "For Abrikosova." Please forgive me if I should not have noted on the top of the box that it is for you, for forwarding to Yaroslavl, but I put this on the form in a personal address to you.

Please try to ensure that the prison will actually deliver the packages as addressed and that they will do so promptly. The two packages that I sent to Selenkova in Yaroslavl (before I knew that they would not be accepted) were returned a month later, the contents completely rotten, and the last parcel to Suzdal was lost altogether. Meanwhile, my friends and I deny ourselves even the barest necessities in order to put together parcels for our dear friends in prison, and it is very painful when they are lost.

Forgive me for troubling you, and if possible please let me know of the receipt – and also, if you should happen to know, what is the fate of Galina Jentkiewicz (the term of her sentence ended May 19)?

With sincere respect and gratitude,
Vera Lvovna Gorodets
Kostroma, Nikitskaya, #3

Catherine Pavlovna made two notes on the letter: "Respond that Krylevskaya is sending parcels to Abrikosova and mailing from several people is not permitted. They can send us parcels and we will forward." "Respond as to Jentkiewicz."

Source: GARF, f. 8409, op. 1, d. 348, l. 126.

August 8, 1929

Dear Catherine Pavlovna,

Thank you very, very much for the news about Galina Jentkiewicz's address. Again and again I turn to you with a request. I am very worried about whether my second parcel to Anna Abrikosova reached you – I sent it July 17 or 18, and your news about Galina Jentkiewicz, dated August 2, did not mention it. The parcel was valued at fifteen rubles. In addition, I sent you (later) ten rubles with a request that you forward it to [Anastasia] Selenkova (both the parcel and money to Yaroslavl, political isolator). Please, if possible, let me know if you received them. I now turn to you with another huge request – would you be so kind as to inquire of Selenkova, through the political isolator prison, what she needs, because she in fact has no one to be concerned about her – her brothers help her very rarely and ineptly. They are quite young fellows and not well provided for themselves, and they are rather frivolous. Perhaps if I were to know what she needs I could send at least part of it by winter. I would be so grateful to you. I know that I do not need to use sentimental words because even without them you will understand how difficult the situation of my dear ones is and you will not refuse to help.

In addition, the situation of Elena Vasilyevna Vakhevich (Irkutsk political isolator) is surprising. Her term ended May 19 (without taking account of the preliminary imprisonment) but on July 9 she was still writing from the same prison, not knowing her future fate. This is outrageous! To have to sit in prison until the time of year when the roads become impassable – this is very difficult for a person who is no longer young (she is the same age as Abrikosova), who has recently undergone a difficult surgery and suffers from rheumatism.

Please, please use your influence to speed up this matter. May the Lord reward you for all your hard, generous work.

With sincere gratitude,
Vera Lvovna Gorodets
Kostroma, Ivanovskaya, #33, Apt. 1

Source: GARF, f. 8409, op. 1, d. 344, l. 176-177.

January 6, 1930

Dear Catherine Pavlovna,

I beg you not to refuse the request that I have already sent you several times. You have always responded to our loneliness and grief so sympathetically and attentively, and it seemed that you so humanly understood our emotional attachment. And now the most difficult trial has befallen us – complete isolation from our dear and long-suffering mother and the almost complete impossibility of helping her! I once again appeal to you and ask you – have compassion for our grief and write to us. Have the money and packages that Komarovskaya and I (and most likely packages from Krylevskaya) have more than once sent through you been forwarded to Abrikosova and Selenkova? Write to us, please – are they well, and what do they need?

We are so depressed by our inability even to know what they need.

Please, please answer me! Please do all that you can to satisfy my request. Our second term soon ends – May 19, 1930 – can we hope to be freed?

With sincere respect and deep gratitude,
Vera Lvovna Gorodets
Kostroma, Ivanovskaya #33, Apt. 1

Note on this letter: "Respond and let them know when we sent help to Selenkova and Abrikosova." E.P. 1/23/29.

Source: GARF, f. 8409, op. 1, d. 520, l. 54.

Letters from and about Sister Rose of the Heart of Mary (Jętkiewicz)

March 7, 1932

To: Aid to Political Prisoners, Mme. Peshkova
From: Administrative Political Exile Galina Fadeevna Jentkiewicz, Residing in Kolpashevo, Narym Region

On April 20, 1932, my three-year exile to Narym region will be completed; this exile follows my five-year confinement in the Irkutsk Political Isolator (by decree of the Moscow Collegium of OGPU, May 19, 1924) under Article 61 of the Criminal Code, old edition. The decree of the Novosibirsk OGPU regarding my exile to Narym was issued in June 1929.

In view of the approach of that time of year when the roads will be impassable and postal communication with Narym will be interrupted, I am appealing to you ahead of time with a request to let me know my future sentence and, if possible, to assist me and dispatch without delay permission to leave here with the opening of the navigation season. For your information, I have spent all three years of my exile in Kolpashevo, where I have worked as a typist.

I also ask, in view of my limited means, for help with respect to travel expenses, either with money or a voucher for passage.
Please let me know what you are able to ascertain.

Galina Jentkiewicz

Source: GARF, f. 8409, op. 1, d. 724, l. 4.

July 15 1932

I am writing to let you know that I received today the money order you sent by post, No. 4104, April 21, in the amount of thirty rubles. Thank you.

Galina Jentkiewicz
Kolpashevo, Narym region

Source: GARF, f. 8409, op. 1, d. 819, l. 57.

January 25, 1931

Dear Catherine Pavlovna,

I am appealing to you, kind Madame, with an ardent, urgent request that you prevail upon the appropriate organs of power to allow my daughter, Galina Jentkiewicz, who is thirty years old and in exile for religious matters in the village of Kolpashevo, Narym region, Tomsk district, Siberia, to be transferred before the end of her term to Tomsk for the sake of her health and economic conditions (she has one and a half years left on her term of exile).

The goodness of your heart and your desire to come to the aid of the suffering are known to everyone – and thus the mother of one of those who is among the suffering may be so bold as to turn to you with an urgent request to share her grief.

Always ready to be at your service,

Janina Kaetanovna Jentkiewicz
Warsaw, Poland

Source: GARF, f. 8406, op. 2, d. 1668, l. 1

November 11, 1935

To the Information Sector, Polish Red Cross, Warsaw

Please be advised by No. 9676/35 that Galina Fadeevna Entkevich [Jentkiewicz] is being held in Voronezh under investigation. Her case is set for trial.

Authorized Agent of the Polish Red Cross in the USSR

Source: GARF, f. 8406, op. 2, d. 1668, d. 1.

Letter of Sister Hyacinth (Zolkina)

July 13, 1932

Dear Catherine Pavlovna,

Thank you very much for all the good that you have done for me during my imprisonment.

I want to ask, if it is possible, if you would send me a dress (something quite simple) and two pairs of stockings.

I remain deeply grateful,

Anna Ivanovna Zolkina
Burtyrka Isolator – OGPU
10 Workers' Corridor, Cell No. 43

I am grateful to Vera Grigoryevna Gradskaya.

Source: GARF, f. 8409, op. 1, d. 819, l. 59.

Letters of Sister Magdalina (Komarovskaya)

September 2, 1924

To: Nina Iosifovna Vasileni-Pozharskaya
Tobolsk 8, Ostrozhna 242, for [Lucia] Chekhovskaya

I received the parcel and the money sent to the Samarovo telegraph office in my name. I humbly thank you for everything. I am now living in Tobolsk, where I was transferred. Again I humbly thank you for everything.

M. G. Komarovskaya

Source: GARF, f. 8409, op. 1, d. 37, l. 207.

January 27, 1925
Obdorsk, Tobolsk region

With deep gratitude I want to let you know that I received the money you sent by telegraph – twenty-five rubles (fifteen rubles have been given to Anna Davidyuk), and I simultaneously received the money order for ten rubles from October 27, 1925, No. 5010, by post. I am very, very grateful for everything.

M. Komarovskaya

Source: GARF, f. 8409, op. 1, d. 121, l. 113.

November 27, 1925

With deep gratitude I am writing to let you know that on November 12 I received the twenty rubles you sent. The remaining forty rubles have been transferred as designated. Again I send my warm gratitude for the assistance rendered, which helped me a lot and which I presently needed greatly, because I was relocated from Obdorsk to Muzhi...

Komarovskaya

Source: GARF, f. 8409, op. 1, d. 121, l. 110.

June 12, 1926

With deep gratitude I am writing to let you know that on May 11 I received the sixty rubles sent by telegraph and I have distributed the money in accordance with the instructions in the telegram.
I remain with gratitude,

Komarovskaya
Obdorsk [...]

Source: GARF, f. 8409, op. 1, d. 121, l. 106.

January 5, 1928

Dear Catherine Pavlovna,

I am writing to you with a huge request concerning Anna Ivanovna Abrikosova, who, as you know, is in the Tobolsk isolator. The issue is that instead of two parcels a week, as she has been allowed until now, she is only being permitted one parcel a week. The reasons for this deprivation are unknown. Meanwhile, she is no longer young (she is forty-seven), and given the length of her prison term and her completely ruined health (her stomach can barely digest the prison food, she has tuberculosis, periodic acute headaches and heart dilations), it will be very difficult to get by on one parcel a week, especially because she does not receive financial help from her relatives and she has no money for minor personal expenses, such as stamps, paper, laundry, etc. Please petition for permission for her to receive two packages a week, as before, and also, if at all possible, please send her material assistance. It would be better not to send any money to the prison, but to Raisa Ivanovna Krylevskaya for delivery to Anna Ivanovna; her address is No. 32 Vershina, Tobolsk.

I will be very, very indebted to you. In addition, if it is possible, please let me know whether a reconsideration has granted anything to Anna Ivanovna or to me and to all those now in Romny (who received a "minus 6" – Davidyuk, Gorodets, Vasileni-Pozharskaya). Again I ask that you not refuse to petition on behalf of Anna Ivanovna because she is in a very, very difficult situation.

We received your inquiry about our situation in Romny. Thank you very much for your attention.

With deep respect and gratitude,

M.G. Komarovskaya
Romny, Poltava Region
Novo-Lozovka, d. Karmanovo

Secretary's note on the letter: "We sent twenty rubles in November and ten in December."
Peshkova's note: "At the first opportunity we will send more."
Source: GARF, f. 8409, op. 1, d. 259, l. 226-227.

August 6, 1930

Dear Catherine Pavlovna,

Forgive me please for troubling you now for the third time with my request. The issue is that they have still not taken me off the roster and I have to remain in Smolensk; but I cannot stay here because they are evicting me from my room (and to find another place to live is a hopeless proposition given the acute housing crisis). In addition, I need to try to get my voice back so that I can find more certain employment than I've been able to find so far.

I am placing all my hopes in you and I hope that you will not refuse my request that you petition on my behalf so that Moscow will timely send its order concerning the end of my term of exile. The local authority says that there has been no order from Moscow but from your telegram (in response to mine) it seems that Moscow has sent its order – and I am in complete bewilderment as to what is going on and whether everything will soon be cleared up. My term ended May 9. I offer you in advance my deep gratitude and I hope that you will expedite my departure from Smolensk so that I may go to my relatives.

I am so bold now as to add to my request yet another on behalf of Raisa Ivanovna Krylevskaya. She, like me, continues to remain in her place of exile – Tobolsk – because Moscow has still not sent the order concerning her to Tobolsk. Please do not refuse this request.

With deep respect and gratitude,

M.G. Komarovskaya
Smolensk, Kostelnaya Kozinka #18

Source: GARF, f. 8409, op. 1, d. 520, l. 449.

Letters of Sister Margaret (Krylevskaya)

November 29, 1926

Dear Catherine Pavlovna,

I received the sixty-five rubles you sent me by telegraph. Thank you kindly – I passed it along to [Father Alexey] Zerchaninov and shared it all equally. He is very grateful to you. I am sorry that I was not able to answer right away as I was sick in bed. I am now a little better. Once again, thank you. My address: Tobolsk, Vershina, Bldg. 6.

Raisa Ivanovna Krylevskaya

Source: GARF, f. 8409, op. 1, d. 121, l. 94.

Spring 1927

Dear Catherine Pavlovna,

Forgive me for troubling you so, but I am writing to you with a big request. I am the exiled Raisa Ivanovna Krylevskaya, and in the spring I was sent from Tobolsk to Surgut. In Surgut my vocal cords and larynx became paralyzed and for two months now I have been absolutely unable to speak. I was transported to Tobolsk for treatment. Would it be possible to petition for me for a small allowance in order to pay for my room? I am now in dire need. I cannot work anywhere, but the main thing is that it is difficult to speak because of the loss of my voice. If possible, please petition for me.

And the second request is for Anna Ivanovna Abrikosova – that if you send an allowance, please send it to me for food parcels, because it is hard to get anything at the prison canteen. If possible, please answer me. [...]

Raisa Ivanovna Krylevskaya

Source: GARF, f. 8409, op. 1, d. 121, l. 65.

April 8, 1929

Dear Catherine Pavlovna,

I received the fifty rubles from you for Anna Ivanovna Abrikosova. Thank you – I am sending you the return coupon for confirmation.

Today I visited Anna Ivanovna and she told me that she will be transferred to Perm, although when I asked the local GPU agent about her transfer he said that he himself does not know because Moscow handles her file. Catherine Pavlovna, if possible, petition that she be allowed to remain in Tobolsk. But if this is not possible, would it be possible to transfer me to Perm as well, for the sake of her food parcels, because she cannot use the prison ration at all. I would be eternally grateful to you. Please respond to my letter.

My address has changed: Tobolsk, Leninskaia 32.

R. Krylevskaya

Secretary's notes: Answer soon; send money to Abrikosova. Source: GARF, f. 8409, op. 1, d. 348, l. 140.

Letter of Sister Margaret Mary (Spechinskaya)

October 6, 1924

I sincerely thank you for the money you sent. This money truly came to my rescue because I am in a place where it is impossible to find oneself even the slightest income.

This unexpected help deeply touched me and once again I thank you from the bottom of my heart.

O. Spechinskaya

Source: GARF, f. 8409, op. 1, d. 37, l. 430.

Letters of Father Teofil Skalski to Father Vladimir Abrikosov (1932, 1937)

IN the autumn of 1932, Father Teofil Skalski was released from the Yaroslavl Political Isolator Prison as part of a prisoner exchange with Poland. From Warsaw he wrote to Father Vladimir Abrikosov, describing in detail his meetings with Mother Catherine during their walks in the Yaroslavl prison yard. Father Skalski apparently soon thereafter received a response from Father Vladimir with new questions, and in 1937 Father Skalski responded to him from Łuck, where he was living at that time. We present these two letters, which were provided to us by Father Georgy Friedman, OP.

October 15, 1932

Warsaw, Poland

Dear Father Vladimir,

I am Father Teofil Skalski, and one month ago I left the Yaroslavl Political Isolator Prison where I shared a cell wall with your wife, Anna Ivanovna, with whom I talked over the course of our two years of prison yard walks together. Anna Ivanovna considered me her spiritual guide, and during the whole time of our acquaintance I had the good fortune to call myself her devoted friend in Christ. You undoubtedly know, Father, that Anna Ivanovna has been at liberty since the last days of July, and most likely she has had the opportunity to correspond with you. I have learned from Mme. Peshkova that Anna Ivanovna underwent a successful surgery for breast cancer in Moscow. After her operation, the file regarding the imprisonment of the Eastern Catholics was reviewed and Anastasia Vasilyevna Selenkova and Father [Johannes] Deibner were both released from the Yaroslavl Political Isolator. I did not have the chance to meet with Father Deibner because of the extremely strict isolation; I spoke with Selenkova during our walks only over the course of the last two months, when they transferred her into our walking group after your wife's departure.

Anna Ivanovna endured her difficult lot as a Soviet prisoner with unimaginable tranquility and the humility of her deeply religious soul. She was subjected to enormous deprivations, including both a lack of food and clothing, but no one ever heard any squabbling or grumbling from her. She asked me to find your address and let you know that she considers herself fortunate to be able to suffer so much for Christ and for the good of the Church, and if it would please the Lord God to place this Cross upon her again, she is ever ready to take it upon her shoulders. She regrets nothing and she is always happy that she is a Catholic and content with the memory of all that has been her fate to endure as a Catholic.

I personally regard her as a truly righteous woman, most likely very dear to the Heart of the Lord and a creature pleasing to Him in the midst of the banality of contemporary life. She is likely very much in need, and now if you are able to send her money in foreign currency, she could stock up on all she needs in the so-called "Torgsin" stores in Moscow.[1] Soviet currency is worthless in the USSR.

Anastasia had rather shattered nerves, but she is a charming Catholic woman and also very poor. I am temporarily in Warsaw [....] I am always ready to let you know, Father, all the details I know concerning Anna Ivanovna and Anastasia Vasilyevna.

Pray for me, as six and a half years in prison did not pass without ill effects.

---

[1] Translator's Note: Torgsin stores were precursors to Russian hard currency stores. The name Torgsin is a Soviet compound word for "trade with foreigners" (torgovlia s innostranstami). Such stores appeared in Moscow around 1930, selling hard-to-find items in exchange for foreign currency, gold, silver or valuable items. Sheila Fitzpatrick, *Everyday Stalinism: Ordinary Life in Extraordinary Times: Soviet Russia in the 1930s*, Oxford, 1999.

February 16, 1937
Łuck, Poland

Dear Father Vladimir,

It took an illness that kept me in my apartment and freed me from all the usual occupations that swallow up every minute of my life nowadays in order to find the time to answer your inquiries about my recollections of my time spent together with Mother Catherine in the Yaroslavl Political Isolator.

We shared a cell wall, and although we did not learn the prison telegraph code, we somehow managed to tap out messages and were able to communicate through the wall ventilator. In addition, the guards took us out each day for our half-hour walk in the prison yards; we were in the same group for these walks. There were three other Catholic priests in addition to me in our walking group, so we four priests and Mother Catherine made up a like-minded group.

It was difficult to trust others. The prisoners were a very motley group, often changing – among them were open Communists and secret collaborators of the prison bosses. Anna Ivanovna naturally tried to be friendly to all. Some were studying English and Anna Ivanovna would devote a good half of her walk to English lessons, and in doing so interacted with an element that was alien and even outright repulsive to her.

Our walking group included other women, some even from the milieu of cultured Russians, but with their views and candor about their immoral behavior and affairs in the past, they repelled Anna Ivanovna.

The authorities transferred Anna Ivanovna from Tobolsk Prison to the solitary confinement block in Yaroslavl Prison because the criminals in Tobolsk, who were entrusted to her for literacy instruction, began to idolize her, whereas they scorned the Komsomolka who was also assigned to look after them.

OGPU agents on several occasions came to Anna Ivanovna with suggestions – or, more likely, tests – to see whether she would repudiate her Catholic convictions. In her responses, Anna Ivanovna showed herself no mercy, and was steadfast in her assertions about the unassailable truth to be found only in the Catholic Church.

It was an unbearable grief for her that her brother, a professor of medicine, had left the Catholic faith, had broken the bonds of holy matrimony and even dared to talk blasphemously about it in the Soviet newspapers. She was not able to forgive him for this, although she constantly prayed for him.

She was forbidden the right of correspondence – as was I. She received packages very, very rarely and the very poorest women – these Dominican Sisters who had been scattered in exile all over the country – sometimes managed to send her something. She received a little money from the Red Cross, but there was nothing to buy with the money in Yaroslavl at that time, and therefore she endured a lot of difficult deprivations.

Prior to my arrival in Yaroslavl, the priests were not hearing confessions, as they did not have an *approbatum*. I, having been in Kiev on the border of the Mogiliev eparchy, had received jurisdiction from the now-deceased Archbishop Cieplak for an unlimited time and the right to authorize other priests as well. Thereupon we began to hear confessions among ourselves, and Anna Ivanovna started to make her confession to me every two weeks during our walks.

She prayed a lot in her cell – she had Sacred Scripture and some liturgical booklets. She especially loved the penitential canon and the practice of spiritual Communion. I copied out several prayers from my breviary for her and she prayed them every day. She subscribed to the Soviet newspaper and was interested in the politics and life of her unfortunate fatherland. They published Communist newspapers in foreign languages as well – she had the English newspaper and perhaps the German. She also read books from the library.

When she told me she had a lump in her breast, I insisted that she go to the doctor. He somehow guessed that it was cancer and sent her to Moscow, to the prison infirmary. She had time to prepare herself before her departure, and her first priority was to attend to her soul. She asked me to hear a general confession for her whole life. This was in the spring and summer of 1932.

She often spoke to me of you. It was evident how deeply she

harbored feelings of homage and respect for you. For her, you were the embodiment of the priestly life of renunciation and asceticism. It was never "Vladimir" – it was always the holy "Father Vladimir." Your spousal abstinence from the moment of your ordination was for her something entirely natural, and she would not have understood either her own or your service to the Lord God without this voluntary celibacy.

I can attest that this worthy witness of the Catholic faith, always steadfast and even-tempered under trials, by the grace of God enjoyed perfect possession of spirit; she was reconciled to her bitter fate and was an example to others, even to us priests. I do not remember her ever grumbling.

After a six-year ordeal in prisons, they finally transferred me to Poland and I am no longer able to find out anything about Anna Ivanovna. I read recently that she died in Butyrka Prison, and I would like to know her fate following her surgery [in 1932].

After she was sent to Moscow for her surgery they transferred Anastasia Selenkova into our walking group, but I spent only about three months with her. She was a different type of person – although very devout, rather difficult to get along with. She also held you in very high esteem.

There was also with us at that same time a certain [Lidia] Gildebrandt from Petrograd, the wife of an officer, imprisoned for her Catholic faith, but I never had the chance to meet her. As for Father Deibner – he was an unhappy man, but by the end of his time in Yaroslavl he had calmed down.

Pray for me, Father, and write if there is still something you would like to know.

Respectfully,
Father Teofil Skalski

Galina Jętkiewicz, Sister Rose of the Heart of Mary, OP

Letters from Prison to Her Relatives in Poland (1923-1941)

THE letters of Sister Rose of the Heart of Mary presented below were sent to her relatives in Poland through the Polish Red Cross. Letters and parcels from her relatives in Poland were sent through the same means to Moscow and then forwarded together with parcels and letters from the Political Red Cross. The letters have been provided by the Dominican General Vicariate of Russian and Ukraine of Saint Michael the Archangel and translated from the Polish by Olga Salnit. The first is addressed to her sister and brother-in-law.

December 1926
Irkutsk Isolator

Dear Marysia and Genek!

[…] Did you have good holidays and did you remember me at Holy Communion? Remember that this is the best help you can give me and help for yourselves as well. Only those who have long been deprived of this food, as we are here, understand its daily necessity and the good fortune of being able to enjoy this wellspring of truth: for it is indeed the source of our true life, a life that has no end. I also hope to see you, but this does not depend on me: for as long as possible, we work for the glory of the Lord. […] As for letters, don't use so many Polish words because the censors underline them and if there are many, I won't receive the letter. Share my letter with Mama –

Your Galya

August 22, 1927
Irkutsk Isolator

My dear Mama,

[...] I think it is not a bad thing for you to be out in the fresh air. Most likely it's nice there in the countryside.

I also have been eating berries this summer, and we often eat cucumbers and other vegetables, so you see we are not bad off. Recently I was in the city – I had a few days' leave. I was so glad that I was able to visit a church.[1] Irkutsk is a very beautiful city, but in places it looks like a large village. The Angara River is very beautiful.

In the yard we have flower beds, flowers and a lot of sun in a good summer – but this year summer was very short. We work in the fresh air the whole day, so we don't need special walks. The work goes on all the time, and I also work in the office.

I don't know about finding work this winter – but I believe that the Lord God and good people will help me out. Don't worry about me – I'm living well and I don't need anything. For winter I will need felt boots and some sort of cloth to cover my hat, but I am sure the Lord God will provide. The store here is good now and one can get everything. I beg you, please think about yourself. I don't need anything except your prayers. I would really like to see a photograph of you and the children.

Farewell for now, dear one [...].

Your Galya

August 27, 1927
Irkutsk Isolator

Dear Marysia,

A few days ago I received a sweet letter from Józek[2] – he writes that your health has improved and that being out in the fresh air has

[1] Translator's Note: Assumption of Our Lady Roman Catholic Church was completed and dedicated in Irkutsk in 1884; it was built for Poles who ended up in Siberia, usually as political exiles. See photo in Rev. Christopher Zugger, *The Forgotten* (2001), p. 77.

[2] Her brother.

been beneficial. Praise God! I hope that you will soon be completely well after so much suffering. The children and worries are consuming you.

Remember that there is also beauty and joy in this regard, because it was your calling to create a family. Remember that one has to sacrifice for love, and then everything will be fine. Everyone has his vocation and only by fulfilling it completely can one really be happy; the main thing is to save one's soul. Right? I kiss you dearly and I wish you a happy name day, although most likely belated. I was almost offended when Józek wrote that he had received a photograph of you with the children – but I am waiting as patiently as I can. When you write to him, thank him for remembering me, and tell him I will fulfill his request. I pray for all of you. Did you have a good summer? Our summer this year was very short. There was almost no warm weather at all. It's already becoming cooler now and it's raining. It will be a pity if we don't have as beautiful an autumn as last year […] Write if you have time. I kiss you […] Everything is fine –

Your Galya

March 13, 1927
Irkutsk Isolator

My Dears!

I am sending you Easter greetings a bit early, but I know how long it takes letters to get through now. Better my greetings should arrive a little too early than too late! I've not received any letters from you for a long time; I hope that everything is all right. I've begun to get used to not receiving letters – they are lost somewhere or frozen. […] As you can see, I have little news. I live quietly, monotonously. I am learning in this seclusion how to be free in spirit and how to live by what I believe […] Our desires are deeply hidden and the whole world cannot fill the human heart. These are not empty words – this is reality – and every person who looks into his own heart experiences the same thing […]

I am healthy and have nothing to worry about. Materially, I am not perishing; by the mercy of God I am not going hungry, so Mama, please, don't send me anything. I have enough of everything. […] As for shoes and clothing, I have everything, and this is fortunate because right now there's nowhere to get anything, so it's just as well I don't need anything.

It will be warm for you at Easter – for us spring is coming late. We are still having frosts despite the fact that the sun warms things up quite a bit. It's sunny in our cell in the morning. (I don't know whether I wrote you that in November I moved to another place, on the third floor.) In this section we have central heating so it is very dry and warm. The only pity is that the yard here is small, without any greenery.

Time goes quickly, as always, if one is busy […]

I promise to entrust you to God, Mama, more than anyone. As often as possible, Mama, make use of what gives life [i.e., the Eucharist] – I am deprived of it, so receive Communion for me.

Your daughter, Galya

May 14, 1927

Dear Mama!

[…] My friend and I will no longer be receiving small sums for our work, as we have up until now, but this does not frighten me because it's the same as last year, and He never abandoned us […] Thank you for remembering me at Holy Communion – go as often as you can, and ask not just for me, but for yourself as well, that you will be able to be good, happy, calm, that you will be able to evaluate everything from the point of view of enduring truths – then life becomes very simple and nothing disturbs the deep peace of one's soul.

I am healthy. I feel wonderful. I am working just as before – I didn't manage to go on leave. Perhaps this summer […] I have again received your shoes. I am now wearing Marysia's and for the summer I have some other, lighter ones […] It's been a very strange year. The third of May we had snow, and after a few days it was almost hot, then again it turned cold and I still can't part with my short sheepskin coat. Nevertheless, our *bagulnik* hedge has blossomed. It has very pretty red-lilac blossoms, shaped somewhat like azaleas. We have two bouquets in our room and the walls are adorned with green branches [...] Mama, write, even if I don't write so often. I am now in a different situation and I have little news. Life flows on monotonously, time flies quickly, there is always work and in general I don't understand how it is possible to be sad [...] So long for now. Don't grieve, don't wait for letters. There is only one misfortune in the world – sin, and one can avoid it. Be well, my dear.

May the Lord God watch over you everywhere.

Your daughter

June 5, 1928
Irkutsk Isolator

My dear Mama!

[...] Take care of your health, my dear, and as for the rest, be calm, trust God in all things and you will see how easy and well one can live. This is how I live and thus I do not notice the time and conditions do not bother me.

We recently decided to lay out a garden because we cannot go [to the city]. I've not been in the city for a long time, since November, and most likely will not be going there any time soon, but I don't care. Our yard was completely bare, only rocks and bricks, but thanks to our work and the help of the authorities it has been decorated with flower beds and various plants. The flowers have not yet bloomed, but if, as they promise, they give us seedlings and everything planted sprouts, it will be very nice and pleasing to the eye. I really like to work in the flower garden, and plant and so forth. Nature is so enchanting and speaks so greatly about God, about His wisdom and love. And after all, the more you love, the better you know, and vice versa. Therefore, Mama, you must love God and others as much as possible, and then your heart will be light, you will have no fear, you will not regret anything, and you will possess spiritual wealth that is not diminished when it is shared with others – unlike material goods that quickly melt away [...] Only living thus, as I now live, can one understand what a blessing it is to live where at every step there is a Church and so many books that speak about the Truth, nourishing the mind and heart. After all you will agree that in the overall scheme of things, nothing is more important than our soul, and because it is so, then one must be concerned about the soul above all. Don't worry about me, "I will somehow get along" – as we say here to cheer ourselves up – in other words, all misfortunes are fleeting, and a person can endure everything if he wants. I have no real trouble, I live calmly, evenly, maintaining order – this helps save time, and it seems there's never enough time.

Relatives promised to send our neighbor a kerosene stove, and then we will be able to cook additional food, because it is more expensive to buy prepared food – sausage, etc. There's no substitute for hot food, and they usually give us only soup for dinner. In the winter we boil potatoes, but now they're not quite ready for eating. In addition, our rooms are not heated with stoves. We have central heating, not like in the women's sector where we had stoves and could fix what we wanted. [...] But of course we have to live economically. Sometimes difficulties arise because something will be in short supply at our little store. A bottle of milk costs eight kopeks – this is a primary source of nutrition and it seems that soon we will once again be without it. There hasn't been any butter recently – it costs sixty-five kopeks, which is a lot of money in Siberia. True, in the winter it was only fifty-five kopeks [...] bread is seven kopeks, sausage, forty to forty-five kopeks.

Spring this year has been late, and even now at the end of May we have severe frosts, but nevertheless everything has already leafed out and the cherry trees are in blossom [...]

Your Galya

August 15, 1928
Irkutsk Isolator

My dear Mama!

[…] Everything in Irkutsk is now very expensive and the prices are almost the same as in the capital, and in our little store they are the same as in the market. Our neighbor's kerosene stove has helped us solve the problem of cooking – we use it in common and fix things to supplement our ration. This is less expensive than buying everything, and more wholesome. It also surprises me that there is no good butter in Siberia – recently we've only had imported butter (lightly salted) and it costs sixty-four kopeks a pound – while, for example, eggs are thirty-five to forty kopeks. I am completely well. My eyes were hurting a bit, but that has now passed. On my cell-mate's advice I underwent a course of injections to fortify my health for the winter. I don't know whether I wrote you that I've had my hair cut completely short, because a lot of it was falling out and I thought this would help it to grow out better. Of course I have very little news. I live monotonously: I work, I rest. Our flower bed, where I've put in a lot of work, is now flowering and it brings us a lot of joy. Flowers are always dear and in our conditions, they bring even more joy. A person in prison becomes a little like a child, and every little thing brings him joy – and these flowers furthermore teach us a lot and speak so clearly about Him Who so wondrously created them […]

The frosts here are very severe – and this year we didn't have much of a summer, and spring was very cool. Now warm days are here, but we won't have the kind of heat that you have, and the nights are always cold. They say this is because we are so close to Lake Baikal and snow-covered mountains.

I'm still working as a typist, so I'm busy half the day and I never have enough time because I still have things to do in my cell. You won't receive this letter for a month – don't worry if there are no letters for a long time. I write rarely because, to tell the truth, there's nothing to write about and furthermore, it's not even worth sending letters because some of them don't get through anyway. I send everyone my best wishes. Take care of your health, be calm, be concerned only about eternity, which is the only thing that gives meaning to life and will not change. I remember you in my daily prayers.

Your Galya

P.S. Remember me on August 30[3] and pray for me that I will be good and faithful to the end.

August 29, 1928
Narym, Western Siberia[4]

My dear Mama!

[…] The nights have become cold and today it was gray, overcast and cool. Of course there will still be sunny days, but we will soon have overnight frosts. We will soon be digging up the potatoes that we planted. We and a few others have already eaten young potatoes a couple times, but we hope to gather more, which will be a big help in our small household. There's now a family living in our cell: a cat with two charming little kittens – wonderful company that brings us moments of joy. Mama, the cat is a Chinese breed, fluffy – the kittens are different, but also pretty, striped like little tigers. I know you don't like cats much, but these are very well-behaved and very clean. Of course when they are grown we will give them away to someone. Our flowers are fading – and local barbarians have also been picking them, wantonly, without asking, but we managed to gather some of the seeds. And today we even have a bouquet with some sweet peas, which I really like […] My cellmate Elena Vakhevich thanks you very much for remembering her. We are very close, and it is easier for us to endure the hardships of prison life together. The only problem is that she gets out three months after me. She still has her mother in Moscow – a seventy-year-old woman, completely alone, and Elena has no way of helping her because we

[3] Translator's Note: The feast of her patron saint in religious life, Saint Rose of Lima; now commemorated on August 23.

[4] Translator's Note: Apparently written while she was still in Irkutsk.

live on what we get, and life here, as I've already written you, is not cheap [...] Wheat flour and bread have long not been available. Praise God that we are still holding on, our ration is sufficient, we are still not going hungry, and as for the future, God will take care of it. He never abandons those who place their trust in Him [...].

Your Galya

November 1929
Narym, Western Siberia

My dear Mama!

[...] I will not be too lonely these days, although, generally speaking, loneliness is a somewhat better state than we think if only the Lord shares it with us. But it would be nice if the frosts were less severe, in view of the distances between places as we are constantly being transferred from one place to another. But it's not worth saying much about this. My time flies quickly, and when I go to work, then upon returning home after dinner and other household chores, I haven't even a minute for grief or idleness. Grief and idleness in general are forbidden. I may have a chance to move to another apartment, a little more expensive but more comfortable, but this is still unknown – we'll see. As for now I'm satisfied with what I have. Some time ago I made myself a dress – very modest, but nice – it looks nice [...] I wrote you that I began to take [English] lessons. I had only two lessons and then we called them off. The teacher didn't want to continue, so in my free time I read on my own. Perhaps you could send a dictionary? [...] I am healthy, I have not had frostbite on my nose or ears – it's just with my legs that everything's not quite right. Apparently, with time, my rheumatism has gotten worse [...] but then one must have some suffering or otherwise life would be too comfortable [...]

It's very beautiful outdoors now. It seems like everything is creaking and ringing, but if you stay outside for a long time it's hard to breathe. There's a white fog covering the river, and the glare of the sun hurts the eyes [...] Now that the road has been constructed, they bring in more food and the market (true, a small market) is open every Sunday. [...] Who knows whether things would be better somewhere else, but when we ourselves choose the place, it usually turns out worse. At least here there is enough meat, fish, and a crust of bread, which we didn't have in Irkutsk [...]

Your Galya

May 7, 1930
Narym, Western Siberia

My dear Mama!

[...] Spring here has been awfully cold – we even had snow on May 2. We hope that the second half of the month will be warmer. I've already written you that I have boots and that fortunately you don't need to send me any [...] I've long not been troubled by the fact that I have no job, and I've been earning a little by sewing. In addition, Providence, you, my dear ones, and patience have supplied for anything I lack. I recently tried my luck at the office of a horticultural enterprise located about a half mile away, but they also rejected me – very rudely (saying that they didn't need "such" people – i.e., exiles). They were so rude that quite honestly I don't even want to make any further efforts, at least not in the near future, because my nerves are somewhat giving way. But it is a useful lesson and I'm trying not to be upset. One needs to pity them that they have such ideas in their minds. I am absolutely healthy, even no headaches. With warm hugs, I entrust you to God. My regards to all the relatives.

Galya

November 28, 1930
Narym, Western Siberia

[...] Winter here has been very fickle this year, with warm spells followed by cold spells; in general, it's unhealthy and many have caught colds. My friend has also been ill and still has a slight fever and a cough. [...] Time flies so that you don't have time to look around and it's already the holidays. I hope that you will all spend this time very well – time that is very important for preparing well for those wonderful days [Christmas] that give us a foretaste of our eternal homeland – where there will be no more separations, no poverty and countless difficulties. But one must also struggle to attain this Kingdom, to use all the means that have been given us [...] I wish you health and peace. I send you hugs – I hope that you do not forget me. Kisses for the children.

Galya

February 17, 1931
Narym, Western Siberia

My dear Mama!

[...] I have already written you about the loss of my belongings – now I have no work, and this means no bread ration card – but thanks be to the Lord, I am still somehow managing and not going hungry although naturally I've had to resort to a strict regimen of frugality. But it's nothing, there have been worse times and we have survived them. I have not lost hope that I will find work and perhaps in my next letter I will be able to tell you about it. I have temporarily taken up embroidery in order to earn a little money for bread. It pays little, but it's still better than nothing [...] I have never lost hope. Providence has never abandoned me in need, and now in prayer I am literally asking for "my daily bread." Sometimes one can buy flour, but seventy rubles or more for a 36-pound sack is not for me, especially because I am not earning anything. The parcel from Mrs. L. that I unexpectedly received a few days ago will be a big help. [...] Perhaps I will manage to trade some of the clothing for food, because it's hard to live without bread, and there's only a little left of the flour that was sent me – I am saving it for the holidays, and during Lent it will not harm me to fast a bit [...] Our landlady went for some time to visit her son and my neighbor and I are left with new landlords – they are also not bad people, although simple. They installed electricity today, but there are no lamps, so for the time being we are just looking at the lampshades. Having electricity will be good because the government has not been issuing kerosene for a long time and we have already burned the last of what we had. I am healthy, and although it's not terribly to my liking (because it arouses my appetite), I do go out for walks a lot and I sleep well, because air is no less necessary than food. The weather now is fine, although it has been windy. There's been a lot of snow, sunny, and not too cold [...]

March 1931
Narym, Western Siberia

My dear Mama!

[...] Mrs. L.'s parcel was an unexpected help at precisely the moment when I needed it most of all. So as our Little Saint so rightly says – one can never trust God too much, and if He worries about even our material needs, then so much more will He give us all that we need spiritually [...]

August 9, 1931
Narym, Western Siberia

My dear Mama!

[...] Of course the sea is wonderful and I would like to see it, but I don't feel any regret or envy because I am satisfied with my lot and I believe that God will give us precisely those conditions that most favor the fulfillment of our vocation and tasks. Everything I have endured and everything that most likely awaits me helps me to live by faith and almost tangibly to feel the truth that faith teaches and above all, absolutely not to be attached to things and places, to surroundings, to people, to one's own tastes and preferences, and to understand the value to the soul of even the very smallest act called forth by faith and love for God. Why is there so much evil in the world? Because many Christians forget their vocation and live as though the teachings of Christ about self-denial, suffering and fidelity to Him even unto death – as though these teachings did not exist.

An unfortunate thing recently happened here – on August 4 after a long hot spell a severe storm broke out and lightning struck my landlords' household buildings (something like a barn). This was just a couple steps from our house. The flames began to spread quickly and it was only thanks to the energetic help of the neighbors that only a part of the cattle pen burned, and even the stable that was close by remained unharmed. The Lord so arranged it that even though during the last few days we had very strong winds, during the fire the wind was quiet and it took the flames in the direction away from the house, toward the fruit garden. We carried everything outdoors. You can imagine what a panic this would have been had it happened during the night! I am convinced that the Sacred Heart of Jesus, whose image hangs on my wall, saved us: He has promised that He will preserve those houses where this image is found. And just a few minutes before this I had returned home and, hearing claps of thunder, I remembered this promise and with this thought in mind I had blessed the house with this image – and then a couple minutes later the fire broke out… […]

Now I need to be thinking about setting aside money for travel, which is now expensive; and I cannot be certain that I will have work until the end of my exile […].

September 1932
Kolpashevo

[…] I've somehow learned to be less sensitive to various discomforts of life. All this passes quickly and, of course, it is much easier to bear everything when you are prepared in advance. Relations with the landlords were good, although this is not difficult and depends, to a great extent on the tenant himself – if he pays on time and is not demanding. The children scream terribly, especially at night, for absolutely no known reason – the landlords have no idea how to raise them. Sometimes I drop in on my former landlords, who very kindly greet me, but even though they are unhappy with their present tenants, I will not be returning to live with them – what once was will not be again […] Please don't be surprised if my letters don't come in order or if they are unsealed. I myself sometimes receive unsealed letters. Hugs to all the children and I am asking Saint Anthony, who has always helped me in such situations, to make sure that your postcards and mine not be lost.

Galya

October 6, 1932
Poshekhone, outside Rybinsk

My dear Mama!

[...] It is hard to believe how time flies and that I will soon have gray hair (and bald spots for sure because my hair has recently been falling out) – but this doesn't bother me. If only everything inside my head is in order, and if in my heart are good will and fidelity, which I constantly ask of God. One can endure a lot if one gives oneself without fear and unconditionally into His hands. He then works on our behalf and directs all things to one goal; true, this happens not without difficulties and it is often hard, but it is never hopeless or beyond one's strength, and He pays a hundredfold for the smallest effort and a droplet of love. He gives an enormous tranquility in life's burdens, as well as strength and new light in the understanding of eternal truths. These are the only things worth any efforts. It is from this point of view that I want to look at the present halting place in this journey, which is a continuation of my Kolpashevo exile. However I cannot ascribe any merits to myself because everything that He sends me is simply an integral part of my "profession" – and in these things I can be perfected and I ought the more to be ashamed of the fact that I am still so far from my intended goal. Perhaps it was not worth it to move here, but who can know in advance. I had to choose quickly and it wasn't worth even thinking about a large city (because I would soon have had to leave there), and it's easier to live in the provinces. After all, if the Lord so wishes, He will evict me from here, but He will preserve me, because only what He wishes happens. Of course I would not have left Rybinsk on my own will, but I had no strength to resist. Furthermore, I now have a small room here for the winter and if I have to move, then it is easier here. Prices are lower than in Rybinsk, and I can get, for example, meat soup – which I couldn't get in Rybinsk. I just need sugar and groats. [...] There is only one new nuisance: in the city this wasn't very necessary but here it is absolutely necessary because the mud here is impassable, as in Kolpashevo, and my favorite galoshes are already very old and have begun to crack [...] It's very muddy here in autumn and spring and walking along the streets is a major event. For example, last night we had our first snowfall – very heavy, and then it all melted, the mud became impassable, and I had to walk with a stick. Without it I would have ended up lying in a puddle, but I managed to just get a little water in my shoes. [...]

May 15, 1933
Poshekhone, outside Rybinsk

[...] Soon even here they will begin to issue passports; I don't know what will come of this for me, but I hope that my lot will change for the better. Providence keeps vigil and helps and if you have already put your whole self into His hands, then it is so sweet to bear one's cross because this is the only way to help people spiritually, if only a little, giving thanks to Love Supreme. I would not reject my lot for any of the world's treasures, because where His will is, there is happiness and the soul's peace, a hundredfold payment even on earth and only then is it possible to await calmly the final hour, because He is faithful to us and requires the same from us [...]

November 8, 1933
Poshekhone, outside Rybinsk

My dear Mama!

[...] My news is not very comforting – I am without work and, consequently, without an income. But what's worse, without a bread ration card for the whole month so I cannot buy flour or bread. This happened today completely unexpectedly. An order came from the Main Administration today about the reduction of jobs and as a result they let two workers go. This would not be a big deal if it were not for the fact that for me (as an exile) it is very hard to find a new job. I've already been to many places that need people, but as soon as they find out my status, the answer is always the same: "For the time being we are not hiring." From the point of view of the government agencies under whose jurisdiction we find ourselves, there are no obstacles – they say we can work, but it is up to the entity that accepts such a person "under its responsibility" to put us on the payroll – and this decision, of course, is unpleasant and dangerous [...] If it were not for my status I could find a job right away, and of course in Kolpashevo I had no problems in this respect because I knew how to work; but this second exile has turned out to be much more difficult because the food situation here is much worse than it was there – at least there was enough bread there and for me this is the most essential. Dinner can be bad, but when there's not enough bread you're always feeling hungry. But somehow everything will work out, and if I write you about all this it is not to complain, but just to share with you how things are. It doesn't suit me to lose heart. I prefer to endure new trials if the Lord so wishes. Tomorrow I should get an answer from a certain organization and perhaps they will take me on temporarily. I still have a little money, my pay for a half month's work, and maybe I'll be able to sell something and get through this period. I think that the negative attitude toward us will change [...] Meanwhile I am still not going hungry – but I have little bread, so please, don't send me clothing – it would be better to send flour or zwieback – and definitely sugar [...]

August 15, 1934
Rybinsk

My dear Mama!

[...] Today [the feast of the Assumption] I imagined myself in all the countries where in so many churches they are proclaiming the triumph of our wonder-working Mother of God (and even in the church not far from here, just a night's journey away). My soul would like to enter paradise – but not only its sins but something else as well will not permit it.

If you can, please request a Mass in honor of Saint Anthony with a request that he help me find a place to live. He's long been my faithful helper in life's matters. Could you send in a letter an image of the Immaculate Conception (Our Lady of Lourdes) – I would really like to have one [...]

January 2, 1935
Rybinsk

What will the new year bring? As always, many mercies and graces from God – let us use them better than last year because lost time can never be returned. We ought always to be sure of one thing – that nothing will come to us without His will, and how sweet it is to trust Him fully in all things [...]

There are no spruce trees here (how strange), just pines. There is a thick little pine tree still standing, and I am writing you this letter and looking at the little tree with pleasure. The kitten shares our joy – he jumps on the lower branches and ties to crawl on them, and I have to keep chasing him away. But even so, he is terribly cute [...]

August 28, 1939
Tambov

I arrived just fine, and in a couple days I'll begin to look for a job here. The city is very quiet. There's a lot of greenery, but no trams which means that one needs to walk quite a bit. It's already gotten cold and apparently it's often windy here. I feel okay – true, I'm a bit tired from the trip, but this will pass. I look forward to the parcel. My room is small but nice and the building is very quiet and peaceful. It's a bit expensive, and as soon as I find something better I will move. I'm eating all right, don't worry [...]

November 12, 1941
Maloyaroslavets[5]

My dear Mama!

[…] I hope that Providence continues to watch over you, that you are well and unharmed. As soon as the postal connection is back in order I will immediately write you in more detail. I, thank God, am healthy although we have recently been through a lot, but we have escaped injury; although not completely because we have been deprived of one of my friends. They arrested her before we came under the occupation. My soul aches for her, because I do not know where she is and when we will see her again […] I still do not have a job. The situation here is unstable and the times are difficult. I hope that Providence will not give us to die of hunger – the problems with food are very serious and for the time being it's impossible to get anything. Maybe they will let you send things like groats, flour, sugar, fat – please find out. I am completely well. The autumn is awful and damp and in our town there's mud like you've never seen. It's very sad without a church, and we won't be able to get to the city any time soon and who knows what is still there. But I am hoping in the Lord that better times will come and that He will give us strength […] Our former currency has no value, and the village residents still do not acknowledge the new currency, so they won't sell anything. But don't worry, I am not starving. Write me – address letters to Maloyaroslavets, to the Commandant's Headquarters […]

Letter from Mother Antonina about the Death of Sister Rose of the Heart of Mary

June 24, 1945

Dear Pani Janina!

Forgive me for addressing you so, but I do not know your patronymic. I have long wanted to write you but I did not have your address […] It is so difficult to tell you that Galya can no longer

[5] Editor's Note: Maloyaroslavets was at this time occupied by the Germans.

respond to your letters, as it is now more than a year since she went to a better world. January 10 it will be two years since she died in Semipalatinsk region where she went at the beginning of the war. I knew her the whole time, from our first sentencing in 1924. She was in Semipalatinsk together with Vera Lvovna (Sister Stephania), with whom she had lived earlier. I also lived with them and, like them, was in both Tambov and Voronezh. Then we all moved here together.

Her death was so unexpected. We had just received a letter from them, from which one could assume that they were both well – and then suddenly I received a telegram about Galya's death. Then there was a long period of silence and finally a letter from Vera Lvovna in which she wrote that at the beginning of January they had both fallen ill with a severe form of influenza and both lay in bed. The landlady had no time to look after them – on January 10 they decided together to go to the hospital. Each had a fever. Galya was always energetic and much stronger than Vera, but this time she took the illness badly. Her heart had been severely weakened after all her trials. On the morning of January 10 her temperature suddenly and sharply fell from 104 degrees to 100 degrees and even lower. Vera's temperature remained constantly at 104 degrees, but she felt better than Galya, who suddenly felt so weak that she was unable to speak, and they both lay flat on their backs. Suddenly she unsteadily got up, fell on Vera's bed and hugged her, but she was unable to say anything. I think that at that moment she understood that she was dying. Vera embraced her and tried to persuade her to eat even just a little bit and have some tea, which the landlady had made for them before departing in the morning. Galya ate a few bites of potatoes, drank some tea and indicated that she felt better; she lay down again. Not even a minute passed when she again got up, leaned against the stove that was near her bed, and thus she died. Vera began to ask her to lie down, but Galya did not respond or move. When the neighbors heard Vera scream, they came and found Galya already dead. Fortunately, at this moment an acquaintance arrived and bathed Galya and dressed her in white. Her face was serene and peaceful. Then the attendants came from the hospital and took Vera, who was barely conscious. The acquaintance buried Galya.

As soon as we received the telegram we prayed the Office of the Dead for Galya, as we also did on the anniversary of her death. We pray for her always at Mass. This has been a heavy loss for us that we have taken very hard. But we know that we will be together and we often distinctly sense that she is living in a better world. I embrace you, dear one. Such is God's will. He knows best what we need. Apparently Galya was ready for eternal life.

I enclose a small photograph of Galya.

Valentina Vasilyevna Kuznetsova

Biography of Galina Fadeevna Jętkiewicz

Henryk Jętkiewicz (Galina's Brother)

Galya was born in 1897 in a small village not far from Korsuvka Station on the Petersburg-Warsaw Railroad in what was then Vitebsk province. Our father worked there as a railway engineer. Ours was a home of comfortable means. In general, Galya's childhood was happy and peaceful.

In 1901 the family moved to Moscow where Galya attended the women's business school for a couple years. In 1906 she enrolled in the Girls' French high school at the Roman Catholic parish of Saints Peter and Paul, where the instruction was in French and Russian. She took private lessons in the Polish language. In her school years Galya was known for her peaceful and even-tempered nature, industriousness, great capabilities, persistence and purposefulness. She received her First Holy Communion on May 14, 1908, at Saints Peter and Paul Church, and in 1913 she finished school with high marks and awards.

From 1915 to 1917 Galya studied in the Chemistry Department of Moscow University, but she had to abandon her studies with the beginning of the Revolution in order to earn a living. She worked as a governess in a Kremlin kindergarten.

In the fall of 1920, after our father and his brother returned from Siberia, Galya left home and entered the Abrikosova community of Dominicans of the Eastern Rite, and then finally moved into the community, which sorely grieved her relatives. The family was very devout, with Christian traditions, but the relatives were unable to understand Galya's missionary ideals, ideals to which she remained faithful until her death.[6]

In December 1920 our father died of typhus, and on December 20 he was buried in the Catholic cemetery in Moscow. In November 1921 our mother with another daughter and son left for Poland, leaving Galya in Moscow, despite long, futile efforts to persuade her to accompany us. Here in Moscow she would fulfill the vow she had made "to suffer for Russia" – and she worthily walked the sorrowful road of prisons, convoys, isolators, camps and exiles.

Sister Rose of the Heart of Mary, OP

Anatolia Nowicka, OPL, Graduate, Bestuzhev Women's Institute, St. Petersburg

Sister Rose, a Pole by heritage and a Roman Catholic by confession, graduated from a French school in Moscow. During the First World War she worked a couple years as a foreign language teacher in a high school. She joined the community of the Third Order of Saint Dominic of the Eastern Rite in 1918 or 1919. Deep religious experiences and the fascination and prospects of the Catholic Eastern mission in Russia strongly attracted her. Hers was a great sacrifice, made out of love for God and souls who did not know the true Church. Having adopted the Eastern Rite and entered the Order of Saint Dominic, Sister Rose strove to sacrifice herself and her life for the conversion of Russia and its unity with the Catholic Church. In the community she served as Mother Catherine's secretary – and in that role she typed, copied out Mother's religious recommendations for the Sisters and transcribed translations of religious authors from French, English and Italian to Russian. These works were necessary for the Sisters' and parishioners' reading because it was impossible to get books from abroad or to print new ones.

---

[6] Our maternal grandfather, Kajetan Choliczewski, may have been for Galya a living example of self-sacrificing service. He had taken part in the conspiracy of Szymon Konarski, associated with the secret society "Union of the Polish People" that was organized in Vilnius province in the 1860s. For his participation in this conspiracy, grandfather was sentenced by the tsarist government to four years' imprisonment in the Warsaw Citadel and then eight years' exile in Siberia, in the town of Usinsk, Tobolsk province.

In 1918 and 1919 Sister Rose was still young – her face was rosy, her expression was good-natured. She was slightly taller than average, she held herself erect, and her movements were graceful. One could sense in her a tranquility, gentleness and friendliness toward people, and a deep inner concentration. In 1923 she was arrested along with the other Sisters. She was sentenced to five years of strict confinement. She served this term in Siberia, not far from Irkutsk, near Lake Baikal. She was with a friend, a secular Third Order Dominican. The prison building was built back in tsarist times and looked like a fortress – it was called a "political isolator."

These isolators for political prisoners were painstakingly separated from the outside world. The prison maintained a prison regime, not a camp regime. There was no hard labor, as in the camps – just complete isolation over many years. There were two in the cell. They rarely saw even their neighbors from other cells. Sister Rose's Warsaw relatives made several attempts to have her returned to Poland as part of a prisoner exchange.

We recently learned that Sister Rose died in Russia. Thus has been completed a sacrifice, perhaps a sacrifice that had little significance in the eyes of today's men and women, but one that had great significance before the throne of God. Such sacrifices yield much love and mercy in any country.

Letters of Dominican Sisters in France (1933)

In 1932 Father Jacek Woroniecki, OP, of Lwów wrote to the Master General of the Dominican Order with a request for help for the imprisoned Dominican Sisters, describing in detail their very difficult situation in prisons, camps and exiles after the devastation of the Abrikosova community in Moscow. He especially emphasized in his letter that any collection of funds for them had to be done in secret. Father Jacek's letter was circulated from Warsaw among the Dominican communities in Poland and sent to Paris for circulation among the Dominican convents in France. From the beginning of 1933 responses with enclosed "modest contributions" began to come from many cities in France and Belgium to Father Ernest Bodoni: in March, from eight cities; in May, from fifteen; in June, from seventeen; and so forth. All the funds collected were transmitted by Father Ernest through the French consulate in Paris by diplomatic pouch to the French embassy in Moscow and there entrusted to Bishop Pie Eugene Neveu, the pastor of Saint Louis des Français church. With the help of those Dominican Sisters and parishioners who remained at liberty, he sent these funds to the imprisoned priests and religious who had been arrested in the group cases against Russian Catholics.

We present here excerpts from some of the most typical letters from the prioresses of the Dominican convents in France. The letters were provided by the archive of the Dominican's General Vicariate of Ukraine and Russia of Saint Michael the Archangel and translated from the French by Hélène Kaplan.

Letter from the Convent of Mary, Mother of Mercy, in Pellevoisin

May 30, 1933

Dear Reverend Father,

We read your letter with great concern. We knew nothing of the existence of the Dominican Order in Russia – we even thought that this was absolutely impossible and that religion had been completed annihilated in Russia. Now hope has arisen in our hearts that perhaps these Sisters will be the embers under the ashes that one fine day – alas, in the very distant future – will flame forth the spark of faith in this unfortunate country.

In any case, their faith, courage and fortitude inspire us and are a good example for us. Their misfortunes have caused us real sorrow. None of us can imagine what exile in Siberia would be like, and life under constant surveillance would most likely be an existence not unlike martyrdom. These dear Sisters and pastors, so devoted to the Church, condemning themselves to persecution and perhaps even death, are such an example to us!

We hope for the salvation of this people who from ancient times venerated the Most Holy Mother of God and who have now fallen into madness. We have some kind of wonderful presentiment of this, and we will beseech the Lord that He hasten the hour of the return of this people to the holy faith. We hope that our patroness, Mary, Mother of Mercy, will hear our prayers and exert her powers toward their salvation. We pray for this with great zeal. We also pray to our Mother that our dear Third Order Sisters will continue their zealous service under the protection of our holy father Saint Dominic.

Our reverend mother has responded to your request – we had a Mass offered in the Convent for you and our heroic Sisters. She is also sending you our modest contribution – too modest in view of her wish to help them. The reason is that unforeseen expenses have overtaken us at the present time. If possible, she will later on supplement what we are now sending, but from the bottom of the heart of this ardent Dominican, she and the whole community are praying for them [...]

On behalf of the Prioress of the Convent of Mary, Mother of Mercy,

Sister Marie Thomas, OP

Letter from the Convent in Châtenay

May 10, 1933

Dear Reverend Father,

[...] I am sending you our contribution for our dear Sisters; enclosed with this letter is 100 francs. I regret that our poverty does not allow us to double or triple our offering. The Sisters of our convent were very troubled by the story of the suffering of the Sisters and their fortitude. We feel that we stand beside them [...]

Sister Catherine of Siena, OP, Prioress

Letter from the Convent in Montpellier

May 14, 1933

Dear Reverend Father,

Your letter has greatly disturbed us and the story of the troubles of our dear Sisters in Russia deeply touched us [...] But at the present time our own situation, alas, is especially difficult; we also have to help our relatives and friends. Because we ourselves are not able to help, we will try to find people who would be able to help our Sisters. And we will ceaselessly pray for them [...]

Sister Marie Madeleine, OP

Letter from the Convent in Lourdes

May 18, 1933

Most Worthy Father,

We are sending you without delay our modest contribution (two 100-franc banknotes) for our dear martyrs [...]

On behalf of Sister Marie, OP, Prioress of Holy Rosary Convent in Lourdes.

Letter from the Convent in Chateau-Chery

May 20, 1933

Most Reverend Father,

We read in your letter about the heroic life of R.P.A. [Anna Abrikosova] in Russia and also about our Third Order Sisters [...] We will pray even more diligently for our Sisters who are being subjected to such trials [...] We are sending you our modest contribution, regretting that we are not able to send more.

Attached to this letter please find banknote No. V 27934 for 100 francs.

Mother Marie Emma, OP, Prioress

Letter from the Convent in Monleon

May 22, 1933

[...] Your letter concerning our Third Order Sisters in Russia greatly disturbed us. We sympathize with them in their great sufferings and would very much like to help. But our meager means force us to limit ourselves to a small sum. We are sending in this letter a check in the amount of 100 francs for them. We realize that this is very small and we will try to supplement it with our ardent prayers [...]

On behalf of the Prioress,

Sister Marie Hyacinth, OP

Letter from the Convent of Saint Catherine

June 6, 1933

Reverend Father,

Your letter greatly troubled us, and in connection with what you wrote we would like to come to the aid of our dear Third Order Sisters in Russia. Until this time we have only prayed for this unfortunate country – now we can convey through Father Woroniecki our modest "widow's mite" on behalf of our persecuted and self-sacrificing Sisters. We always pray for them and we will also keep secret what you communicated to us in your letter.

Sister Marie, OP

Letter from the Convent in Lanzac

June 8, 1933

[...] We have already once been able to send to you from Warsaw our contributions designated for the Russian Third Order Sisters. Would you allow me to use your mediation to transmit to Father Woroniecki the attached check, which is our modest contribution on behalf of our heroic Sisters who are being so persecuted? We pray for them, keeping everything secret, as we were asked to do in the letter we received [...]

On behalf of the Prioress of the Priory of Saint Catherine,

Sister Marie Dominic, OP

Letter from the Convent in Montpellier

June 16, 1933

Dear Reverend Father,

I read with great interest and anxiety your kind letter of June 5.

The details that you communicated concerning the Third Order Dominican Sisters, victims of the persecutions that have befallen Russia, are very distressing. The fortitude of these holy souls in their sufferings, repeating the sufferings of Saint Dominic, evokes our pity and admiration.

With all my heart I will pray for them that the Lord will support them in all their sufferings and misfortunes, that they will maintain their soul's strength and tranquility in the hope that the trials that they have endured for so many years will finally be brought to an end. Our community feels bound to them and we will increase our daily prayers for them [...]

Our means are very limited, and the contribution that I am sending you is truly a "widow's mite," which I very much regret. We would be so happy to be able to help these Sisters more, as they are so deserving of our attention. It is a real torment for us that we cannot do more. We will make up for this with our fervent prayers [...]

Mother Alexandra, OP, Prioress

Letter from the Convent of the Sacred Heart of Jesus

June 25, 1933

We are full of compassion for the sufferings of our Third Order Dominican Sisters and we admire their courage [...] We are sending you our contribution – very modest, because we have very meager means and must take account of the cost of living [...]

On behalf of the Prioress,

Sister Marie Reginald, OP

Letter from the Convent in Le Puy

June 30, 1933

Dear Reverend Father,

Please excuse our delayed response to your very touching letter about the situation of our Third Order Sisters in Russia. We are sending you a very modest offering to help them. We had a Mass said for them and we will constantly pray for them [...]

Attached please find 80 francs.

Mother Marie Margaret, OP, Prioress

Letter from the Convent in Gramond

July 11, 1933

Reverend Father,

We are very happy to participate in rendering assistance on behalf of our Russian Sisters who are experiencing such torments. It is our duty to pray for them and also to send them our very modest contribution [...]

Sister Marie Edmund, OP

Letter from the Convent of the Sacred Heart of Jesus

July 13, 1933

Dear Reverend Father,

We are not indifferent to your letter, but having very modest means, we cannot send you the kind of contribution we would like to send. Nevertheless, small streams form large rivers, and we hope that there will be other help, more substantial than ours. We hope that many will come to the aid of our Sisters, and we will be praying for them.

Sister Marie Reginald, OP

Letters to Father Vladimir Abrikosov

August 26, 1933

Dear Reverend Father,

Your letter with 540 francs designated for the Dominican Sisters in Russia arrived twelve hours after the dispatch of the last diplomatic pouch. We only have contact every two weeks. We will now have to wait until September 6 to send post from Paris for Bishop Neveu.

I would like to know the best way to transmit these contributions – perhaps it would be worth using the Red Cross [...]

Devotedly yours,
Abbot Ernest Bodoni

September 1933

Dear Reverend Father,

I am writing to let you know that I just received a check for 400 dollars – which means that everything is fine. Bishopr Neveu has already been informed of this [...]. The next courier to Moscow will not go until October 4.

Devotedly yours,
Ernest Bodoni

The Last Words of Christ on the Cross

Mother Catherine of Siena, OP

ANY soul that sincerely desires to reach that blessed state where it can say with the apostle Paul, "It is no longer I who live, but Christ who lives within me," must live the sufferings of Our Lord Jesus Christ.

Fix your gaze on your wounded Jesus, and only on Him alone. Try ceaselessly with all your might to reach God, who became man so that you could attain knowledge of His divinity through the wounds of His humanity. Christ – Christ crucified – this is all we know, this is our whole life. This is because Christ came to earth in order to lift us up to the realm of the supernatural, to give us the chance to participate in His own blessed life and to give us the still greater joy and happiness of glorifying His holy name: to live and to suffer selflessly, having in mind only His glory. But the Lord's entire earthly life leads to the Cross and is concentrated in the Cross. It passes by way of Golgotha, to the glorious Resurrection – and this characterizes the life of each soul.

The Lord is not only our Savior and our Redeemer. He is also a Priest, and above all, a Teacher, since He is the Wisdom and the Word of the Father.

"Heaven and earth will pass away, but My words will not pass away" (Mk. 13:31). Every word of Jesus is a kind of creative act. It generates, creates and bears within itself the imprint of eternity. Without a doubt, His highest teaching cathedra was the Cross. On the Cross He gathered everything to Himself and gave Himself entirely to us: "When I am lifted up on the Cross, I will draw all men to Myself." On the Cross He taught us above all with His silence. The silence of the Cross. The silent contemplation of the wordless, crucified God – this is the best means of being penetrated by the spirit of Christ.

Then on the Cross He gave us His testament, His last testament, contained in seven utterances, seven "words." He included in these seven words all that the soul needs to reach its full blossoming, that is, holiness, and thus to glorify the Heavenly Father. The words of the Father – this is what brought delight to the Most Sacred Heart of Jesus.

"Father! Glorify your name" (John 12:28) – this is His favorite prayer. He came to earth so that, lifting men to the realm of supernatural life, He could communicate to them a new awareness – the awareness that they live for the glory of God and that their main motivating force ought to be this same prayer of Jesus: "Father! Glorify your name."

When we look at Golgotha, we see, on the one hand, creation: hostile creatures, friendly creatures – creation in all situations; on the other hand we see God – the Lord, the source and goal of every living being; and finally, we see Jesus Christ – Priest, i.e., Mediator, lifted up between heaven and earth, between God and creation, on His supreme teaching cathedra – the Cross. From that cathedra He spoke seven words, and with these words He set us upon the right, true relationship to God and creation and, consequently, to our very selves. In this is His entire testament, because He knew that without the establishment of this three-way right relationship (toward God, toward creation, and toward ourselves) there can be no truly spiritual life, there can be no perfection.

Father! Forgive them, for they know not what they do. (Luke 23:34)

Before us is a strange, grim picture. On the Cross – the exhausted, tortured, dying Lord. It would seem that all is finished. The spite, hatred, and loathing of creatures have led Him to complete exhaustion and to the Cross, from which He will not come down.

But what did He do to arouse this spite, this hatred, this loathing? He walked upon the earth, doing good. He taught and spoke in such a way that His admiring listeners said "Never has any man spoken thus" (John 7:46). He put before their eyes such holiness of life that He, the only one of the sons of men, could ask: "Who of you convicts Me of sin?" (John 8:46). How did such a complete and frightening reversal of the minds and hearts of men come about? Each time when the ray of divinity suddenly shone through His sacred humanity and imprinted, as it were, the stamp of obligation, duty and eternity on all His words – "Heaven and earth will pass away, but My words will not pass away" (Mark 13:31) – the spite, hatred and loathing swelled up in men's hearts like waves, their hands frantically grabbed stones, and one common feeling stifled them – "we do not want Him, we do not need Him, we do not want Him to rule over us."

And when He finally and decisively pronounced Himself God and thus imposed His entire law upon all people without exception as an urgent necessity, then that greatest of crimes, the satanic sin, was repeated once again on earth – the creature rose up against its God and rejected Him. The creature did not want to accept Him as He is – it wanted to choose its own god – i.e., it wanted to place itself in God's place. And so here it was – the most grievous, most terrible crime.

When He definitively said that heaven and earth will pass away, but His words will not pass away, because He is God, everything changed: all His words took on the nature of an obligation. It then became necessary not only to accept them, but also to carry them out, cost what that may – and the creature said: "I do not want Him, I will not serve Him, I will not submit." All the spite, hatred and loathing arose in order to stamp out, to annihilate God, this constant, living reproach. And what did God say in response, He who had clothed Himself in human flesh in order to save, cleanse and elevate this creature to divine life? The creature persecuted its incarnated God to His last breath on the Cross. When the exhausted, tormented, rejected God from the height of the Cross looked down, He saw before Him this rebellion of outraged creation, a raging sea of spite, hatred and loathing.

The Lord in His testament on the Cross established the law of the right attitude toward creatures: "Father! Forgive them, for they know not what they do" (Luke 23:34). And in our own days, when again and again the grievous crime of the creature's rebellion against its Lord and God once again occurs, the same voice of the Lamb of God resounds, enunciating once and for all: "Father! Forgive them, for they know not what they are doing." There it is – the solution of Divine long-suffering. But with this difference – since the time of Golgotha this voice is not just one voice. To it have been joined that choir of souls who have assimilated and made their own this law of the right attitude toward creatures enunciated by their Lord God on the Cross: "Father! Forgive them for they know not what they do."

Taking the correct attitude toward creatures is the major question of our spiritual life. Without it, there can be no correct attitude toward God. This is the foundation on which is built our entire spiritual edifice. The question of right attitudes toward creatures is a stumbling block and a temptation for our nature, damaged as it was by original sin. Our attitude toward God comes about differently: every religious soul is drawn toward God, is attracted to Him, sometimes even despite its will. God is so wonderful and so generous that He responds to every sincere striving toward Him with an abundance of grace and thus the soul is pulled more and more to God and will aim to enter into the closest communion with Him. With a creature, man finds himself in various attitudes: he is either attracted to it, he becomes engrossed in it, he seeks his pleasure and satisfaction in it – this is a pagan attitude; or he is hostile toward it, hates it, sees in it the cause of all his misfortunes, goes to war with it – but is entirely dependent on it – this is a savage attitude. Or then again, encountering a creature, he sees that "it lies entirely in evil" and he walks away from it, considers himself immeasurably higher than all the surrounding world, to which he believes it his duty to take on an attitude of indifferent contempt. All these attitudes are pagan, non-Christian. Finding oneself in the face of a hostile creature, the soul needs a directive, since this is a critical moment in its spiritual life, on which depends all subsequent spiritual growth. And this directive is given us from the Cross: "Father! Forgive them for they know not what they do."

In accordance with these words, the Christian attitude can be either simply a Christian attitude, or it can be elevated a degree higher and become sacrificial [i.e., that of a religious]. The Christian attitude to the surrounding world is above all characterized by the brightening of one's gaze and the penetration beyond what can be seen, into the essence of things. And also – and this is very important – by a certain distancing from oneself and by knowing how to evaluate all things independently of oneself and of their influence on us, having in mind only one unchanging and eternal criterion: God and the sacrificial offering of Christ on Golgotha.

Relying on this unshakable foundation, man begins to see everything in a new light. Above all, he comes up against the fact that all creation "is groaning," and that evil and sin are the only real misfortunes, primarily because they are an alienation from God, but also because they are an abnormal, perverted and wretched state, making man weak, ugly, ludicrous, but, above all, miserable. Here, instead of loathing, spite and hatred toward a hostile creature, the Christian ought to find within himself pity and mercy. Pity, because the Christian ought to have the awareness that evil is spiritual blindness and darkness, and how can one not pity a creature who unconsciously does not see or, even worse, consciously does not see the Sun of Truth and Love – Our Lord Jesus Christ?

Mercy, because this pity creates in the Christian a new, forgiving, merciful heart. Owing to this new heart, good will sprouts up – that is, the desire for good, the readiness to repay the evil of this outraged, hostile, but deeply unhappy creature, with good. The highest good, undoubtedly, is reconciliation with God, God's forgiveness; hence, when encountering a hostile creature the unceasing prayer of the Christian in union with Jesus Christ on the Cross will always be His cry for mercy, which resounds eternally, halting the punishing finger of God and covering the sinner with the cloak of patience: "Father! Forgive them." Where and in what can we find the cause, the reason for God's forgiveness?

Externally, everything can be terrible, but the Christian is convinced on the basis of his personal experience that only grace can give one knowledge of God and the proper light and awareness in order to avoid sin, and therefore in the hostile creature's blindness, darkness and the absence of the proper awareness he sees good cause for leniency, for forgiveness – "they know not what they do."

Mercy gives birth to the desire for the good, good will, which is nothing other than the beginning of love. Its result is a solicitous attitude toward the movement of the soul of the other, the recognition of the secret of the inner life of one's neighbor and respect for it. From this follows the practical realization of another great law of Christ – "Do not judge." You do not have the right to judge, because the inner life of another creature is a secret revealed only to God, and to Him belongs the right to judge. The Christian is bound by the law of Christ to do good for evil, while forgiveness and judgment belong exclusively to God – "Father! Forgive them, for they know not what they do."

But there is an even higher attitude toward a hostile creature – the sacrificial or religious attitude, because all those in religious life in a special way are called to share the feat of the Lord's Cross, and thus they are called also to Him. This attitude lies in the awareness of one's personal responsibility and sinfulness. Rooted in the Christian attitude toward the creature and deeply penetrated by the awareness of that blindness and darkness in which the majority of people live outside of God – "for they know not what they do" – the soul is filled with another awareness: they do not know, but we know or, in any case, ought to know, we are bound to know – everything has been given to us so that we could know. From this comes the awareness of one's responsibility before God and before the whole world for the slightest rejection of sinfulness, from which flow a sober strictness toward oneself and a merciful leniency toward others, and also not despondency, but cheerful, strong acts of remorse and a thirst for one's hastened purification. On account of such an elevated and wonderful state of soul, two dispositions grow and embrace it entirely, two dispositions that are in their essence sacrificial and co-redemptive.

The first of these is a living, deep compassion for creatures and a burning desire that they should "know and not do," a desire to gain for them the forgiveness of the Father by their personal voluntary sacrificial achievement in union with the great sacrifice on Golgatha. Such is the first disposition – but it does not reach its fullness without the second, which can be expressed as follows: first, in heartfelt gratitude to the long-suffering of the Lord Jesus Christ, who has overturned all our opinions, who has revealed His light to us, who has bestowed on us true life; and second, in a co-redemptive love and thirst together with Him and from pure love for Him, to extend over the world our hands, crucified and pierced together with His, ceaselessly repeating with our words, our life, and, most important, with who we are, since one in religious life prays not so much with her own words, but mainly by what she is: "Father, forgive them for they know not what they do."

Truly I say unto you, this day you will be with me in paradise. (Luke 23:43)

The thief says: "We are judged justly, for we are receiving the due reward of our deeds, but this man has done nothing wrong" (Luke 23:41). He said to Jesus: "Remember me, Lord, when you come into your kingdom," and Jesus said to him: "Truly, I say unto you, this day you will be with Me in paradise" (Luke 23:41-43).

The thief's attitude toward God is noted in two basic attributes: a selfless acknowledgement of the royal power of God, of His lordship over all. We see the right attitude toward creation first of all in the words of the thief, but also in Christ's response, which reveals to us the secrets of His Sacred Heart.

We see in the words of the thief a very high degree of awareness: he is sentenced justly, receiving his due reward for his deeds – this is a lofty way of thinking.... By contrast, our stubborn unwillingness to acknowledge ourselves as guilty and deserving of all that we so painfully receive from creation is a constant hindrance on our path of a right understanding of our situation, an understanding that is poured out upon us from the Lord's Cross, from the chalice and from all the wounds of Jesus. We are in every hour, in every minute, criminals, inflicting constant blows to the Heart of Christ.

From this sober and sound awareness of our sinfulness flow a real desire of purification and, as it were, a cry to all creation that it become an instrument in the merciful hands of God and help us to receive the due reward of our deeds. And our deeds? How useful in those minutes when our whole nature is seething, and from its depths arises a suppressed grumbling against our situation, against others' treatment of us, and so forth – how useful to be joined with the holy thief on the cross and to imagine how all his sinful life passed before his eyes – eyes that were dimmed with unknown-until-now tears of repentance – and for us in such moments it would be good to remember our past and, possibly, our present deeds – and there is no doubt that in the lives of any one of us there is something that ought to arouse us to a sincere acknowledgement, together with the thief, that no matter how other creatures treat us, "we have been justly sentenced because we are receiving the due reward for our deeds." This deep and lofty recognition of our sinfulness and thirst for purification lead to a high degree of humility, distinguished by a love for insults and gratitude for them.

"But He has done nothing wrong!" This is an ability to see and value another's superiority. It led the thief to the knowledge of Christ's divinity through the wounds of His humanity. "Remember me, Lord, when You come into Your kingdom!" This ability to see superiority in others, to value it and rejoice in it is a noble, beautiful attribute in a soul, but unfortunately, it is very rare. The saints had this charming ability to a high degree and they extended it to all people; this is a high ideal of an attitude toward a creature, built entirely on sound sense and logical consistency. Indeed, with humility one can find, and with desire one can see, in any living being a great superiority over oneself: one is more obedient, another is more devout, a third is more humble, a fourth is friendlier, etc. This ability to see another's superiority evokes, on the one hand, a proper respect for one's neighbor and ease in the struggle with temptations against him, and on the other hand, it places us thus in a proper, selfless, humble dependence on the Creator. The holy thief, having sunk to the bottom of his nothingness, measured the abyss of his sinfulness; having received what he deserved for his deeds – both his sentence and his death on a cross at the hands of creatures – he then rises through the wounds of the humanity of Jesus Christ to the height of acknowledgement of His divinity. He found himself before the face of His God in the proper disposition in order to complete the act of a complete giving of himself – that is, the act of perfect love – and from his lips comes forth a prayer, one of the most beautiful prayers ever to pour forth from the human heart: "Lord, remember me when You come into Your kingdom."

To attain holiness, one needs selflessness, satisfaction with having little for oneself, awareness of the lordship of God and joyful delight in His glory. He alone is Lord of all, His glory and beauty are in all things and for always – not me. Actually, the holy thief asks nothing for himself. Forgiveness? He perhaps even thinks that given his vileness, it wouldn't be possible. In general he does not think about himself; he looks at the crucified Christ and in the light of Christ's wounds he seems to himself not to have any significance; he longs that the Lord remember him, just remember him. Without a doubt, God's remembrance is already salvation, but he thinks nothing further about himself. "Remember me, Lord" – and this ends his thought about himself, since before him is unfolding another picture, one that absorbs him entirely, leading him to admiration, making everything bearable and easy, all the torments of his own crucifixion, all the torments of purification that he willingly accepts.

Through the wounds of Christ's humanity, he is lifted up to the knowledge of His divinity; he no longer sees Him humiliated, tormented on the Cross of His voluntary suffering; he sees him as King and Lord of the universe, to whom all is subject, without exception; He possesses all things, all creation – whether creation wants to acknowledge Him or not, it does not matter – it wholly and undividedly belongs to Him. What wretched madness and blindness it would be to rise up against this lordship, always good and merciful, freeing creation from its miserable slavery to the created world and elevating it to another, supernatural order of existence! He sees Him no longer in tortured immobility, nailed to the Cross, but free, gleaming after His bright Resurrection, in glory, at the right hand of the Father in His blessed kingdom. He watches with pleasure, he rejoices in this boundless glory of His Lord and God. With what solemnity resound these beautiful words: "...when You come into Your kingdom," "Remember me, Lord, when You come into Your kingdom."

To the thief's lofty acknowledgement of the royal authority of Jesus Christ, crucified, accursed, tormented, to this astounding victory of the spirit over flesh, of the invisible over the visible, of the supernatural over the natural, of grace over nature, came Christ's kingly response: "This day you will be with Me in paradise." This response is full of such royal generosity! They are across from one another, and each is on a cross: one finds in himself so much moral strength that, distancing himself from his personal sufferings, he acknowledges his sinfulness, he repents, traversing in one moment the way of purgation and illumination, renouncing himself, renouncing creation; fixing his gaze on Christ, he is lifted to the height of union, naming Jesus his only Lord and God. The other – from the height of His throne on the Cross proclaims that the union of a purified creature and its God has been perfected – "This day (and forever) you will be with Me in paradise" – not tomorrow, not some time after years of purification, but now, this hour, this day. You have acknowledged Me as your King and Lord and I choose you for my royal palace, and where I am, you will be with Me: you are My companion for all time, you have given yourself to Me and in your humility you have asked Me only to remember you – but I will give you everything – that is, Myself – and I take you with Me now and forever – "this day you will be with Me in paradise."

And there it is, the heart of Christ, not knowing any bounds to its generosity; it pours itself out entirely in its measureless love and gives what is most valuable and dear – its very self, forever: "This day you will be with Me in paradise." What does Christ's response teach us? The swiftness and the generosity of His giving of Himself. It cannot be postponed, the call comes – immediately one must answer: "This day" – but this is so difficult for us with our nature: tomorrow, I will wait a bit, I'll look ... No, not tomorrow, but today, right now, this day. And for every act done with respect to us we ought to give back many times over. The generosity of Christ, the generosity of His Sacred Heart – this is the measure of our love.

"You will be with Me!" The desire that all participate in our spiritual goods, the thirst to pour out on all the gifts we have received, to unite everyone to a life with Christ, a selfless generous giving of oneself – "You will be with Me in paradise." [One is] already in paradise here on earth in the closed garden of a secret life with Christ, in order to achieve the eternal possession and vision in heaven; the thirst for all creation to be united to Christ – both on earth and in heaven – and readiness to sacrifice everything for this, right up to death on a cross, if only so that the generous royal promise of the Sacred Heart might be heard both for oneself and for others, "This day you will be with Me in paradise."

Woman! Behold your son! Son, behold your mother! (John 19:26-27)

The moment of death is the point toward which our natural life and our spiritual life are moving. We ought always to remember, when we contemplate Christ's crucifixion, that we see before us not only our Savior, redeeming us on the wood of the Cross from all our transgressions, but also our model of the spiritual life, the example of our Teacher on the path to God – a purgative, illuminative and unitive path. It is as though the Lord has placed His crucifixion in our hands and has said, "Look and learn, this is all you need to know." Therefore we ought always to approach the crucifixion keeping this point of view in mind. Christ, having lifted us up with Himself onto the Cross, leads us along a certain way of crucifixion and mystical death, after which a true life of union with the Lord begins. These outstretched, wounded hands, the bowed head, the pierced feet and opened heart – this is our very life in the deepest and fullest sense of the word. Looking at the slaughtered Lamb, we ought to say to ourselves: "Here is the source and the fullness of our spiritual life. Only in Him and through Him – there is no other way. Through the wounds of His humanity we attain knowledge of His divinity."

Christ hung on the Cross in a terrible and agonizing immobility and, just as during His earthly life, He had nowhere to rest His weary head. All around Him surged a hostile crowd; He forgave the crowd and He taught us the right attitude toward the rebellious creature. With a single glance and with the grace that poured forth like a stream from His open wounds, He had called forth repentance in the heart of the thief and helped him by means of selfless humility and the acknowledgement of his complete dependence on God to be lifted up to the heights of union with the Sacred Heart. His heavy, exhausted head sank still lower, and at the foot of the Cross Jesus saw what was most dear to Him on this earth – His mother. She alone had always understood Him, she alone had known how to render Him the proper respect and had never in any way grieved His Sacred Heart and, finally, she had always known how to humbly step back and remain in the shadow, never in any way interfering with His holy sacrificial service. She belonged entirely to God and to Him – a holy, pure creature, a chosen vessel of grace.

Beside her stood John – a young, wonderful flower of the love of Christ. He had given Jesus all his youth and all his virginal purity, and the Lord had truly admired him because His Sacred Heart could be reflected in the transparent purity of John's heart. These two creatures – Mary and John – evoked in Christ feelings of tenderness and enchantment because nothing in them pushed Him away – on the contrary, their immaculate virginal purity was in harmony with Christ's pure humanity, with His Sacred Heart. Yet at this grand turning point, when all Christ's humanity is wholly directed toward God and God alone, He gives us his final great teaching on the complete renunciation of creation. This teaching is so important that one ought to proclaim concerning it, "Whoever has ears, let him hear; whoever can receive it, let him receive it!"

In the life of every soul that has decided to attain complete purification, no matter what should happen, no matter what it should cost, in order to open up a space for God's action in it – that is, a soul that has decided firmly and adamantly to do everything it can and leave the rest to God – in the life of every such soul comes this turning point of the great renunciation. At first it is renunciation of oneself, then renunciation of a beloved, dear creature to whom it is perhaps attached by a very noble tie; this creature has even led it to God; admiring and rejoicing in its enchantment, the soul was lifted up to God, praising and thanking Him. But it is just that the soul loved precisely this creature, the soul was happy with this creature, and some kind of unseen, very thin, barely noticeable thread attached it precisely to this being.

The soul had long believed that for God it was prepared to give up this creature, prepared to relinquish it – but for the time being the soul's attachment is not interfering with her, and to the contrary it is moving her toward God. Contact with this creature evokes in the soul a spiritual joy, the desire to speak about God, to serve God. Suddenly, the soul itself not understanding why, an uneasiness begins in the soul, and an inner voice, the voice of grace, stubbornly and persistently repeats over and over, depriving her sometimes of peace, that she is still not completely free, that although she is perhaps very elevated, nevertheless there is an attachment, and that God alone must rule; no one and nothing, it is God alone for those who want to walk unwaveringly through the Cross and wounds of Christ toward a mystical death in order then to rise for the blessed life of union; God is an indivisible unity and He does not tolerate the slightest division in a creature whom He has chosen for Himself. This is the highest step of the ascent in purification, when the soul completes the turn, once and for all, of its entire being toward God, without a single glance back, not a single glance to the side, a complete break from what is very beautiful, very lofty – but nonetheless, earthly, finite, created. God – Alone.

How many souls, reaching this turning point in the spiritual life, before the final renunciation of the most dear, close and beloved creature, to whose spiritual birth and growth they have perhaps given so much effort that it has become their beloved child, feel that no, it is not possible… and they say to God: "Lord, just not this – or at some other time, later…" But an indefatigable voice within them stubbornly repeats over and over: "Precisely this, and right now… God – Alone." In the spiritual life one must fear self-deception most of all and one must ask God to evoke in us a holy uneasiness and stubbornly repeat to us His holy desire until, finally, with the help of His grace, we will find in ourselves sufficient strength to make the last break from all that is created and finite.

Having bowed His head, Christ looked upon what had been most close and dear to Him on earth, and He said: "Woman! Behold your son!" and "Son, behold your mother." He calls her simply "woman" – one of many. But with her sensitive soul she understands everything, she accepts everything, and as always, with ease and promptness she immediately responds to this new call of grace and is lifted to new heights of humility and renunciation. It is as though this is no longer her son, it is as though He has already left her – before her is a great, frightening, universal sacrifice, her suffering and dying God. Yet she stands here for new service. This is the Virgin-Priest – she stands here to lift this New Testament sacrifice up to God the Father for everyone and everything. Through the wounds of His humanity, she also, only in a special higher sense, penetrates to the knowledge of His divinity, since no other human being had such a sensitivity for the divine as she. But even for her, the Cross and the Lamb slaughtered on it were her entire knowledge and wisdom, and she, contemplating them, is overflowing with even greater love and even greater supernatural virtues.

But her son is no longer; true, she will take His dead body in her pure hands, she will see how they place it in the grave, in the new tomb in Joseph's garden, where it will lie in secret peace until that moment when at the dawn of the third day He will rise in glory. She will follow in supernatural delight, how He, the victor over death and hell, will be lifted up in the splendor of eternal glory into the heavens to sit at the right hand of the Father; and then she will return home and wait in ceaseless acts of love until that moment when she will be united with her Lord forever. Her whole life, as the life of a co-redemptrix, was one of constant self-denial, right up until the final renunciation on Golgotha where, instead of her Son, whose humanity exuded charm and whom she so loved – she saw before her the great and terrible New Testament Sacrifice.

If one deeply enters into this mystery of the purification and as it were, the emptying out of the creature of all that is finite and earthly, of all that are even the most legitimate and lofty attachments, then unwillingly, the heart contracts and there appears a fear before this great emptiness. Theoretically we know that everything ought to be filled with God and that in Him is all our peace and joy. Yes, this is so – but in practice it seems to us that this is an excruciating emptying. The Lord, as always, comes to meet us and opens up to us the path forward. "Woman," He says, "behold your son." With these words He shows us the mystery of new serene, sanctified feelings that come through His pierced Sacred Heart.

This attitude toward creation that sets in after a complete renunciation of it, when a purified and clear gaze can completely objectively and dispassionately look on one's neighbor, and the soul derives all motives for its acts with respect to creation only in the Sacred Heart without the least admixture of self, can be best expressed with the words "virginal maternity." Actually, the soul, having made a complete renunciation on Golgotha, absorbs, as it were, from Christ His love and His divine feeling with respect to creation. "This is your son, this is your mother" – this virginal maternity, which makes its own the needs of all, which truly adopts all souls and carries them in itself, reached its full, perfected manifestation in the pure heart of Mary. This virginal maternity, the simplicity and loftiness of which can only be worthily sung by the angelic choirs, is an integral attribute of each soul in religious life, correctly and to the end understanding its own calling and exerting all its physical and spiritual forces in order to wholly bring it to life. By means of the three vows and in particular the vow of obedience unto death, death on the Cross, the soul of the religious has merited for itself the right to stand by the Cross and to take in from the Sacred Heart His last testament; He has entrusted to that soul the continuation of His work of saving the human race. "This is your son…this is your mother."

Here is the great gift of adoption, and it is extended to the whole world. This moment of complete renunciation fills us not only with fear, not only with a feeling of emptiness, but also with a feeling of a great loneliness. Christ knows that He must leave us for a time and that we find ourselves at the turning point of our spiritual life. The Lord turned His gaze to John. He knows that the virginal heart of His disciple is taking this very hard: in Jesus, John had everything – a father, a mother, a friend, a teacher, God, and the most wonderful of the sons of men whom he had become accustomed to watch with pleasure; contact with Jesus had brought John the highest joy. He loved Him not only as God, but also as a man. Jesus was all his happiness. And now…at the foot of the Cross… What a great loneliness… The Lord looked upon him and said, "This is your mother. Here is she in whose virginal heart you will find true support and who will help you to be lifted up to a new association with your Lord and God, in which God alone will reign."

John came down from Golgotha a new being, free and strong – his most striking symbol will be the eagle – but he came down from Golgotha together with Mary. The most holy virgin is a necessary figure in our spiritual life – she is our constant help. She takes us in her hands, she firmly and steadfastly, powerfully and gently leads us to God, pushing aside all obstacles with her maternal hand and defending us with her protection from all dangers and enemies. She knows how to maternally smooth out all difficulties, to plead on our behalf for the grace of the strength to accept and carry out courageous decisions. The Lord, knowing all this, in those most difficult moments from the height of the Cross says, "Behold your mother."

My God, My God, why have you forsaken Me? (Matthew 27:46)

The Lord, having spoken His last word to His mother, was now fixed with all His suffering humanity on His heavenly Father. The physical and spiritual torments kept increasing, the tide of grief, anguish, fatigue and isolation continued to rise, the level of these cruel waves rose higher and higher – all that was earthly had receded, disappeared from view, and only God remained. Christ's whole humanity seeks support in God and aims to find rest in Him. Rest, peace and quiet in God – this is what the tormented humanity of Our Lord asks. But all around is an impenetrable immobility that forges His limbs together and holds them on the Cross without motion, and only His exhausted head now lifts itself up, then lowers itself, not finding a point of support, even a moment's relief. The sky was hanging low, heavy, dull gray, merciless. All is silent. Down below creation is agitated and noisy. But creation does not concern him – He needs God, He wants God. And God is silent. God had always heard Him before, now He now longer hears Him; He had always answered Him before, now He now longer answers...

Here now is the great impenetrable darkness, complete abandonment, hopeless loneliness. Truly, on the Cross the son of man had nowhere to lay His head. Then in His great anguish He proclaimed His fourth word upon the Cross. It was a cry of His soul to God, of a soul that was unhappy, suffering, but faithful and not seeing or wanting anything but God: "My God, My God, why have You abandoned Me?"

After a final renunciation of the created world, a decisive period in life sets in to a certain degree. Sometimes the Lord does not bring the soul to Himself right away, giving it time to prepare itself and filling it with the joy of communion with Him, in order to lead her only later into great loneliness. One must always bear in mind that God wants our union with Him and disposes all things to that end. He treats the individuality of each soul with such solicitude, He so respects and values it, that He gives each soul what it needs that it might by the shortest and most direct path come to union with Him. Each ascent of a soul is like a new artistic work of God, His free creation. There are periods that almost have to be repeated in the life of each soul, but even those periods proceed differently. For some, they occur uninterruptedly over the course of several years, for others, in alternation with tribulations of a different kind; but we must know and believe that God disposes all things for the good of each individual soul. Thus, for example, a period of spiritual growth, which [is what] I call a great loneliness, and to which nothing better can be applied than the fourth word of Our Lord on the Cross – such a period is repeated in the life of almost every soul, precisely because it is the most essential for our movement forward; it is like a touchstone of the good will, sincerity and truthfulness of the soul – how much is the soul actually prepared to renounce everything and to endure all things for the sake of the glory of God by its union with Him?

But this period proceeds in different ways: sometimes it is uninterrupted over the course of a long time, sometimes it alternates with moments of sweet communion with God. Usually God leads most souls through the latter form of great loneliness – interrupted and periodic – and only strong souls will He place on a courageous, thorny, but very true path of complete abandonment over the course of more or less long periods of time. This state is similar to the state of the human soul of Our Lord Jesus Christ in that great moment when He cried out to His Father: "My God, My God, why have You forsaken Me?"

Usually God places a strong soul on the path of complete abandonment and great loneliness immediately after its renunciation of the created world, but it sometimes happens that before this He will give the soul a glimmer of joy in communion with Him. The soul has broken with creation, it no longer finds anything in creation that would in any way attract her, even what is dearest, what is closest – it is as though the created world were outside her field of vision – she needs something else. The soul acknowledges with all its being that its point of support is in God, that it needs Him more than anything on earth, as everything created and finite has left her, and the soul turns toward Him with all her bare and often exhausted and wounded being, but she encounters a complete, deathly silence. The heavens are closed – the soul is as though suspended in mid-air and completely alone: all the created world beneath her seems unreal, illusory, and – most significant – so unnecessary and boring; and above her is the low-hanging, leaden sky and nothing more. This is more than emptiness – it is like a vacuum or, even more like the immobility, the stupor of the Cross, when the acute pangs have already passed and a nagging, weary tiredness sets in, and the clear recognition that there is nowhere to lay one's head – and the one for whom the soul has left everything is silent. All that is left for the soul is to lift up its gaze with unwavering hope to the closed sky and, uniting itself with the slaughtered Lamb on the Cross, stubbornly repeat His cry: "My God, why have you abandoned me?"

This period of the ascent of the soul to God is characterized by two basic features – a feeling of complete abandonment and the recognition of one's loneliness and an emptiness that can be filled only by God – and it has an extremely important significance for the development of the soul that is passing through it. It is a major moment in the life of each soul, since it is precisely in this period that is forged that gold, that strength of soul, which will be necessary in order to endure later visitations of its Lord and God and it also burns away all the straw of the sensible and sentimental life. The typical features of this state are the following:

First, angst and boredom with the created world, sometimes going as far as complete repulsion; the temptation to leave everything, to avoid contact with creation. The soul must courageously resist; it must develop within itself a disposition, a patience with respect to creation and an unwavering, selfless fulfillment of its obligations no matter how boring and painful they may be.

Second, a great desire for support, the temptation to look for support in creation – but neither one's confessor nor superior can give it. The soul has come to the time when all its support ought to be only in God. God alone. Of course, guidance and obedience are more important now than at any other time; the soul must disclose its state with straightforwardness and the clean-heartedness of a child and unwaveringly follow the advice given it, since in the darkness surrounding it obedience will be its shining lantern. She has no other light: she sees nothing, she hears nothing, she understands nothing. But she can find on earth no support, no comfort, and therefore she ought to resist the temptation of fruitless despondency and debilitating sorrow, to resist with the recognition that her whole support and comfort can be only in God, and that she must patiently await him, and He will come – thus hope and obedience will tell her – and now there is nothing to do but to cry out together with her Lord on the Cross, "My God, why have you forsaken me?"

Third, boredom and angst with all spiritual exercises, particularly with verbal prayer. How difficult and even how unbearable it is to whisper with dried lips words that seem deprived of any sense when it seems that no one hears them. In prayer, feelings of abandonment and loneliness sometimes reach their greatness acuteness, because this is a time of conversation with God and encounter with Him, and when no one answers and no one comes. One can only wait, ceaselessly crying out "My God, My God, why have you forsaken me?"

And finally, spiritual reading also becomes painful, deprived of sense, once God does not respond and does not enliven each word with His life-giving breath. God, the heavens – everything is dead. And He is silent. There is a temptation to pare down one's spiritual exercises, to think up some physical work that will distract one from this constant angst. The counteraction here lies in the development of constancy, no matter what, persistence in prayer, in courageous expectation such that one's whole being would say "Lord, I am here, waiting!"

The following are dangerous temptations for the soul in this time:

- A desire to seek recreation and rest in activities that one thinks up or in work – sometimes very serious and important, but nevertheless distracting the soul from the immobility and angst of the crucifixion with the desire to come down from the Cross.
- A temptation against guidance and obedience – they are not satisfying, they do not give the support that the exhausted soul is seeking; on the contrary, it is as though they intensify the awareness of abandonment and the reality of loneliness. There is an urge to criticize, to avoid guidance and withdraw into oneself.
- The most excruciating and dangerous temptation here is the temptation against hope: "I will not endure if this continues for much longer." Yet a faithful soul with the aid of unseen and unfelt grace that is always pouring forth upon her, flowing from the wounds of Christ, who endured for her all this anguish, endures and delights the angels with its courage.

- But there is still one more kind of temptation against hope – the realization of the hopelessness of one's situation. The heavens are closed. God is silent. Tiresome gray days drag out. It is as though they have left me in some kind of frigid, dark basement: somewhere out there the birds are singing, there is light, and in general there is a different kind of life – but all that is not for me. I have been condemned for my whole life to vegetating without God, without sunshine, without joy, and there, beyond the grave, perhaps I have already been rejected by God and sentenced to a long, long purgatory or perhaps even to hell. And this is the beginning of hell on earth.

The soul must respond emphatically and firmly, that out of love for its crucified God it agrees to suffer thus for its whole life. One needs to develop in oneself patience, and constancy, and unshakable fidelity to one's Lord and God. And when the soul, fixing its gaze on the crucified Lamb and hearing His cry: "My God, My God, why have you forsaken me?" – courageously and firmly traverses the path of loneliness and abandonment, the length of which has been determined for it exclusively by the grace and love of God – then in the soul, under the influence of grace, beautiful fruit will ripen, making it capable for a further ascent to the heights of the spiritual life.

These fruits are (1) a deep awareness of the truth of the words of Saint Francis of Assisi: "My God is my all." God alone – in Him is all the support and all the life of the soul; (2) the ability to look on all things with the eyes of faith and to hope in God no matter how things may appear; (3) freedom from the power of the senses and feelings and independence of them; (4) self-mastery, in both inner and outer manifestations; and finally, (5) the most beautiful fruit of all, a deep inner tranquility, the peace of a soul that does not depend on any events in the external or internal world. The soul is ready to move on to a greater feat and absorption of Divine communications of grace.

What a comfort it is for souls who are going along the difficult path of abandonment and great loneliness that God loves them very much. He watches them, He follows them. Together with them He again undergoes His abandonment at Golgotha and in them He sees the embodiment of His cry: "My God, my God, why have You forsaken Me?" God looks at them with love and He awaits His hour, when He will come and reward them with His love for their fidelity, patience and constancy. But just let these souls understand that they must bear their abandonment and loneliness in the closest union with the sufferings of Jesus Christ on the Cross, that they must never lose from their field of vision the crucifix and the Lamb upon it, that they must constantly call out with their whole being, "My God, my God, why have you abandoned me?" ... to await their hour ... and the Lord will come.

I thirst. (John 19:28)

Our Lord Jesus Christ, having experienced all the anguish of abandonment and loneliness, expressed in His cry to His Father – "My God, my God, why have You abandoned Me?" – has given His entire holy human existence to a new feeling, one that directly flows from the recognition of His abandonment by God and His great need for Him. The holy soul of the dying God-Man was over-filled with that longing which He Himself so clearly and powerfully expressed with the utterance "I thirst."

For what did the Sacred Heart of Jesus so thirst? It thirsted, first of all, for union in heaven with God the Father and, thus, for the full completion of His great sacrificial offering, which was completed on the day of His glorious ascension. Jesus thirsted for what he prayed: "Father, the hour has come, glorify Your Son, and Your Son will glorify You" and He expressed this in a mysterious manner to Mary Magdalene: "Do not touch Me for I have not yet ascended to My Father." This thirst to go to the Father, to finish the great work of the glorification of God by means of the only New Testament sacrifice pleasing to Him filled the Sacred Heart of Jesus when He cried out "I thirst."

His heart also thirsted for the glorification of the Father on earth – "Hallowed be Thy name, Thy kingdom come" – the spreading of the additional glory of God. How the entire holy humanity of Our Lord thirsted for this! For this Jesus had a great desire to apply the fruits of His redemption to souls – the salvation of souls, the conversion of souls, as many souls as possible, perfected, self-sacrificing souls that have made it their goal, despite all obstacles, to attain the happiness of being His co-workers, His co-redeemers. He desired, above all, selfless souls, voluntarily nailed to the

Cross like Himself and firmly and unwaveringly determined not to come down from the Cross even if the whole world and all their flesh and even their reason were to ceaselessly cry out to them "Come down from the Cross, just come down from the Cross and then we will believe, and You will save the whole world – just come down from the Cross because it is unbearable not just to You, but to us as well." The Lord knew and saw that there would be such souls who would not come down from the Cross, even if their poor, exhausted nature would beseech them: "Rest for a minute, come down from the Cross for just this one hour." No – there is neither rest, nor any limit on the time – such a soul would be on the Cross until the end; it was for souls of this kind that the Sacred Heart of Jesus thirsted in His agony on the Cross when He cried out "I thirst." These souls, headed by the most holy Virgin Mary, were the comfort and joy of His heart during His sufferings on the Cross.

We must boldly and resolutely place ourselves in front of this exclamation "I thirst," and by an act of the will awaken in ourselves the realization that the Sacred Heart thirsts also for us, and it thirsts not for such as we are, but precisely in the selfless ideal which His heart has borne and ardently loved and desired. The soul has experienced all the anguish of abandonment and loneliness, it has remained faithful to its Lord and God, by acts of the will, drawn taut like a violin string, it has fastened itself to its own Cross of abandonment, it has humbly rejected all that is eminent, and it has agreed to serve Christ in darkness and loneliness. As a result, it has learned to value its Lord and God, to value the slightest sign of attention from Him, recognizing that in comparison with Him, everything is nothingness and has no value.

Gradually the soul begins to recognize in itself the awakening of a new life: the abandonment, loneliness, the recognition of the fact that God is and, finally, the desire for Him, a burning, insatiable desire. Yes, the soul at first desires, then thirsts for the Living God. "Give me God," the soul is constantly asking of all things that it encounters along the way, and indeed, it is as though the soul is constantly in motion, going, sometimes even running, impelled by its insatiable thirst. "I want my God and I ceaselessly seek Him, give me my God" – and it could repeat this word, "I thirst, I thirst," at all times, morning and evening, in prayer and in work, and even in its sleep. Its whole being ends up being a single desire – I want God.

Mary Magdalene says: "Tell me where you have laid Him and I will take Him away" (John 20:15). The power of her desire is so strong that it is as though it blinds her, it seems as though she does not see anything, she does not recognize the glorified Christ, and in an outburst of longing it seems to her that she can do anything: "I will take Him away." With these beautiful words, "I will take Him away" – we come to the second basic feature that distinguishes the soul in this moment. It is not enough to desire God, to be fixed on Him with all her being, to seek Him everywhere and in all things, to ask everyone about Him – "Where have you laid Him?" She must act for God – "I will take Him away" – she has already done much for Him: she has ceaselessly changed her ways, she has subdued her nature in every way, unwaveringly subjugated her spirit. She has fulfilled precisely all her obligations, she has tried to be obedient, she has served her neighbors.

But now she feels within herself a mysterious surge of strength, strength that exceeds her nature, "I will take Him away." Everything that she has done so far seems petty, pale, small. She wants to do something greater and more difficult. She wants a feat and a martyrdom on account of her love for her Lord. She wants to exhaust herself together with her crucified God, because His dying cry – "I thirst" – lives in her and ceaselessly resounds. She wants to be obedient unto death, death on a Cross. She winds a crown of thorns upon her head and with the rejoicing of the higher part of the soul and the indignation of all her nature, a blind obedience comes to life; she performs acts of humility against which her whole nature rears up, and all her soul is flooded with joy. She takes upon herself the most difficult and degrading obligations, and she is glad when they exhaust her body. She aims to work and labor for others. She takes upon herself difficult voluntary mortifications, even though her flesh often cries out against them; but somewhere within, she herself knows not where, some kind of stubborn and insistent voice repeats over and over: "Further, forward, still, this is not much." Chains, hair shirts, fasts – all these become the object of her desires. And it seems to her that even all this is not enough to satisfy Christ's "I thirst."

She begins to thirst not only to give all her blood for Christ, drop by drop, but to spill all her blood for Him, she thirsts for martyrdom. This is the final point of thirst with respect to herself; there is nowhere further to go. But then, the more intimately she comes to know the thirst of Christ on the Cross, the deeper she enters into the secret of the desires of His Sacred Heart, the more her own heart is expanded and there arises within her a new thirst, a thirst for the salvation of souls. The love of Christ gives her no peace; it impels her to bring all to Christ, even the most hopeless. This is a time when great missionary calls are born, when people, throwing aside everything, set off for distant countries to preach the good news of salvation and, if possible, to win their martyr's crown. Entire religious orders have been born precisely out of this cry from the Cross of Our Lord Jesus Christ, "I thirst," to quench the thirst of the Sacred Heart, burning with this same thirst.

But this is not much. The soul feels very limited and it seems to her that she is not enough, she alone is too little in order to quench and share this thirst of Christ, and she begins to thirst for zealous souls, souls who have set as their goal this desire to quench the thirst of the Divine Lamb for perfected souls. She begins to pray and work in this direction. She tries in any way she can to motivate souls she encounters along the way to follow the Cross, to love and take on themselves wholly the Cross of Christ. "I thirst not only for my own perfection, but for that of others as well, and if I am not able to quench the thirst of the heart of Christ, then may others more ardent and more consistent than I do so – but just let this thirst be quenched." The presence of this altruistic element is extremely important – it shows the sincerity and unselfishness of this "thirst," so beautifully expressed in the words of the Lord's prayer, "Hallowed be Thy name!" If not I, then others – but I am ready to serve these others my whole life.

The first and most essential virtue of the thirsting soul is zeal, manifesting itself in all spheres: zeal for all that is most difficult for nature – therefore giving oneself the most difficult works, the joyful acceptance of all troubles; zeal and service of one's neighbor and readiness to take upon oneself all burdens and all the fatigue associated with this service. The fruit of this state is the development of true zeal, detached from personal feelings and experiences, and having its basis exclusively in the desire to quench the thirst of the Sacred Heart.

But this state of the soul has also its own great dangers:

1. Unreasonable zeal with respect to oneself, aiming to go beyond the bounds of obedience and overestimating one's personal strengths; from this comes criticism of one's director – imagination that my

director does not understand me, that she is holding me back and does not value me;
2. This then leads to self-aggrandizement and pride, to an exaggerated understanding of one's spiritual growth. From this instead of altruism come egoism, the exclusion of others, and a false notion of one's personal chosenness, as greater and higher than others';
3. Ill-advised zeal with respect to others; an aim to lead all along one's own path, charging headlong and showing impatience with respect to any opposition on the part of one's neighbor, both in the realm of conversion and in the realm of movement toward perfection.

From this can come an extreme demandingness toward others, and as the extreme point of this improper direction – love of power and impatience toward any manifestation of independence on the part of one's neighbor in the spiritual life. But remember that guidance and obedience conduct the soul along a thorny path, avoiding all these obstacles. One needs only – despite all the indignation of nature – to accept everything and to lay everything at the pierced feet of Our Lord. For most souls, spiritual thirst, just like great loneliness, is repeated periodically and alternates with other states, but its significance for our spiritual life is very important. Therefore in conclusion I give you two pieces of advice:

Do not stifle this thirst in yourself – on the contrary, try to expand and deepen it, leaving yourself, your feelings and sufferings to the side, and entirely making it supernatural and uniting yourself with the thirst of Our Lord on the Cross.

Never reject grace and its inspirations. God, seeing the soul's thirst and its desire to do something for Him, very often will come Himself to the soul's help and instill in her resolutions, often going against her nature. Instead of verifying these resolutions with obedience, the soul under various excuses tries to slip away from them or, not having decided directly to reject God, it does not immediately follow His voice and postpones them for an indefinite time. Fear such refusals. One such refusal and sometimes all spiritual thirst vanishes; and remember that in the life of the soul there are no small things. Sometimes the Sacred Heart asks us only for a swallow of water, a small insignificant service, and you, under the excuse that this is a small thing, perhaps set it aside; you think it is not important, so you refuse Him. Let us try to learn to hear the voice of Our Lord from the height of the Cross and learn to quench the thirst of His Sacred Heart.

It is finished. (John 19:30)

The most holy Virgin, who was standing motionless at the foot of the Cross and contemplating the great New Testament Sacrifice, suddenly saw in the eyes of her Son and God a new light that gradually spread across His whole face. The agony had disappeared... The breathing once again became free and full, His whole body suddenly straightened up under the charge of some powerful feeling, and He found in Himself the strength not only to speak but to let out a cry of triumph that frightened the soldiers standing guard. This cry resounded and always will resound as the cry of the King and Victor: "It is finished!" In a single instant Jesus parts forever with sorrow, grief and fatigue. "It is finished." God is glorified. In Christ He receives all the glory that only He can receive from creation. All the damage inflicted upon the glory of God by all the sins of the world, beginning with the sin of Adam, has been paid in abundance. Christ's work is finished and nothing else is needed.

His mercy, grace and love give us the possibility with the help of His grace to participate in the work of redemption and the glorification of His holy name. Friendship between God and man has been enkindled again in the body of Christ. The irreconcilable struggle between the sin of the creature and the justice of the Creator, between the depravity of souls and the holiness of the Father of these souls has been ended. Salvation is opened for sinners; there is no longer a sin that cannot be forgiven.

But this is still not all. Christ's "it is finished" opens for us not only a simple friendship, but along the stages of this life it can lead to the perfection of holiness. David could thirst for God, he could yearn to please God, but before the death of Christ no one could reach this final goal of Divine and human desires – and now it is opened for any soul that sincerely desires to take upon itself all the necessary sacrifices. By the grace of the sacraments and the power of the most holy Blood given to us by its shedding, any action, word and thought can be not only done in obedience to Christ, but with the help of this grace the soul can reach such full living union with

Him that it can truly cry out "No longer do I live, but Christ lives within me" (Gal. 2:20).

"It is finished" – Christ's work is completed not in the sense that it is locked in immobility – no, it is more like the human body in its mother's womb and born in pains for new life. Now the sufferings of Christ will increase in intensity in His mystical body. The Church will begin and complete that which is lacking in these sufferings – that is, applying them to souls and not only for their salvation but, primarily, for the full achievement of the likeness of the soul to that of the crucified bridegroom. The victorious cry "It is finished" relates precisely to these souls.

Jesus knew that His human soul would render the fullness of glory unto the Father. In Him the Father's name had reached the highest degree of its splendor, and now – "It is finished" – and what remained was only "And now, Father, glorify Me in Your own presence with the glory which I had with You before the world was made" (John 17:5). In addition, He saw the royal path opened for the soul: by way of Golgotha and a mystical death toward the bright Resurrection, union in eternal life with Him in heaven.

It is finished! He saw the snow-white retinue that always surrounds the Lamb – the fruit of His "It is finished," His victory over the world, the flesh and the devil. He knew of course that in Him alone is all the fullness of the manifestation of God; that with his glorified wounds He was a fully completed work of unusual beauty. But as St. Thomas Aquinas said, the greatest good must expand, as the Sun emits rays even though it does not need these rays. Souls that have followed Him to the end are like these rays of the sun of Christ. "It is finished" and the height of the Cross belong to these souls, because this is the act of the creation of the world.

In Creation God created out of nothing and nothing opposed his creative word. "He spoke and it was done; He commanded and it appeared (Ps. 33:9). "And God said: let there be light. And there was light" (Genesis 1:3). What ease, freedom and promptness of action one feels in these words. Nothing opposes, and the act of creation is a work of Almighty God. But when the Son of God takes upon Himself the re-creation of creation and exclaims "God, I come to do Your will" – He must not only as it were do violence to His own divinity, having clothed Himself in human nature – "You have prepared a body for Me" – but on the path of His blessed, merciful feat, not only the salvation of man, but also the ascent of His purified, illumined soul to the level of marriage with Him, He encounters a serious obstacle – the free will of this creature and its indignant, rebellious nature, but – mainly – its free will since the whole work is in the will, supported and directed by grace. The Lord had to defeat and overcome the most evil enemy of man – his own personal "I." The enemy of man is the petty, domesticated demons, says Holy Scripture, and the closest and most dangerous "domesticated demon" is a person's own self. The Lord took the conquest of this demon upon Himself, and this is why the work of the redemption and sanctification of man is an act of selfless, pure love.

There are two fruits that come from this sixth utterance spoken on the Cross:

First, learn to contemplate this "It is finished" as the perfected glorification of God in Jesus Christ Himself in order that you might see Him, adorned with glorified wounds, as the "full sun of the Father's glory," and in order that all your being might learn, in renouncing itself and all that surrounds it, to admire this beauty and to rejoice together with the angels and archangels, the thrones and the powers, the dominions and principalities: "Then I looked, and I heard around the throne and the living creatures and the elders the voice of many angels, numbering myriads of myriads and thousands of thousands, saying with a loud voice, 'Worthy is the Lamb who was slain, to receive power and wealth and wisdom and might and honor and glory and blessing!'" (Revelation 5:11-12).

Second, be filled with a deep gratitude toward your bridegroom and knight, the Lord Jesus Christ, who has freed us from the ferocious enemy – that is, from our very selves. Apply the great "It is finished" to the life of your soul. In the life of every soul that is sincerely aiming to glorify God with its perfection and ready for all sacrifices for the sake of God's glory, there comes a great moment when the Lord from the height of the Cross bends down toward it and with inexpressible love says: "It is finished, you are Mine, there is no turning back, everything has left you, except Me. I am your all, and outside of Me there is nothing for you. It is finished."

This special extraordinary kindness can be granted to individual souls not in the ordinary course of things; no, the soul hears nothing and is thinking of nothing with regard to itself – but it knows that something has happened. She cannot precisely define the time, but she knows that in her life there was a moment, prior to which she was one thing, and after which she was completely different. All that used to seem unclear, confused, incomprehensible and even outrageous in the realm of the spiritual life suddenly became so evidently clear, simple and logical; and indeed thus it is – calmly, without any emotion an inner voice declares it to be so; some kind of strange separation of the internal from the external has taken place. The word of God is alive, and efficacious, and sharper than any two-edged sword – it penetrates to the division of the soul and the spirit. The word of God – because this state is characterized mainly by light and understanding. In this state the soul somehow especially lives on the truths of the faith; it is even difficult for it to say "I believe" – it would rather say: "I know that this is so, I see." The light of the word of God really penetrates into its depths, like a two-edged sword, and there takes place in the soul a mysterious separation of the soul from the body – that is, of the lower part from the higher part, the spirit.

The soul senses this separation very powerfully, like a new light within itself. Indeed "It is finished." In the soul appears an innermost, purified eye that is drawn toward eternal truths and aims to derive the basis for its behavior in them: the clouds that were concealing the summit of the soul, that snow-white beautiful summit that the Lord reserved only for Himself, have dispersed; true, this summit does not yet shine – for this, one must still pass through the winter of rest, the Sabbath in the grave; but it is already here, rid of all obstacles and ready to take in the rays of the sun of love, and it will come in its hour, in the Lord's hour. But already "It is finished" – everything is ready. Christ's sword has made the necessary division in order to free the spirit for deeper inner communion with God. Perhaps all this seems somewhat foggy to you. Perhaps there were glimmers of this separation in the soul even earlier, but now we are speaking about a constant state, since it is only to a state that the cry "It is finished" relates. [With respect to this state, we can observe the following traits:]

1. The first is an unusual reality, sometimes even frightening the soul: the contours of the invisible world and the truths of the faith are so sharp and definite, and as a result, so are the truth of one's own personal earthly existence, and the clear awareness of eternity, of one's calling and betrothal with Christ. From this come a holy indifference to all that has happened and, above all, to one's person and a complete independence from circumstances and people – a holy

freedom, despite complete obedience, both internal and external, and a great reverence for authority as a result of the reality of the truths of the faith.

2. Eternal truths become the basis of one's behavior, and from this, as a result, come an ease and skill in the exercise of the virtues. From this it is simple, easy and natural to see God in one's confessor and superiors and to render them prompt, calm obedience, both externally and internally.
3. Objectivity: complete liberation from creation and separation from it; an objective and sober view of everyone and everything, a steady, distanced view of oneself, and checking oneself by an objective criterion. From this come a calm clarity and even merriment, an ability to see the comic side in oneself, a good-natured humor.
4. In the realm of spiritual exercises, it draws the soul more and more toward a motionless standing before God, to the reception of light from Him and toward savoring Him. For the soul, a single word from verbal prayer, from a psalm or from spiritual reading is enough to give it nourishment for a whole day, and not for reflection, but for internal penetration into divine realities. For the soul, a mysterious light is revealed in all things, and for her nourishment she needs the very simplest words – complex constructs of ideas do not satisfy her, but the sweet name of Jesus, or a saying from Holy Scripture – and the whole soul goes headlong into motionless contemplation. "It is finished" – the secret of the life of divine truths has been revealed for her.
5. Independence from temptations. Yes, there are temptations, somewhere, far away on the surface. But the soul looks at them from a distance. Sometimes the soul smiles at herself, at her petty nature. But most often she makes acts of humility, reacting to her temptations in such a way as to call as much attention to them as necessary in order to humble and abase herself, and insure herself from the slightest urges of pride; she constantly makes acts opposed to her temptations, recognizing that she has within herself an impregnable bulwark where temptations cannot penetrate, since "It is finished" – the two-edged sword of Christ has rid her summit of all obstacles,

where there is nothing and no one can enter, except his grace. It is his stronghold, his property.

6. From all the preceding traits there flows one last one: a tempered, unwavering fidelity to God, to one's bridegroom Christ, and to everything that represents Him here on earth, above all, the Church, its head, its pastors and teachers, and then to one's own immediate superior; a high-minded fidelity, independent of anything external, temporal or passing, resting exclusively on the invisible eternal truths of the faith. Fidelity, detached from all that is concrete, from all visible facts. The soul will have no criticism or even discussion of the behavior or person of the one who is vested with the authority of God; there are no grounds, there is no place for these – it simply does not concern her because she sees not this, but something else – the inner essence, the principles of faith, God acting outside.

And from all these result freedom and devotion, steadfast devotion to the interests of Christ, His church, one's Order and the representatives of the Order for the given soul: her superiors; one can say that in grief and in joy, she is their faithful, fearless co-worker, and they can always and in all things rely on her; she will not falter nor waver, even though the whole world should rise up and all visible facts were against her. The Lord can rely on her – she is entirely His, wholly and indivisibly. "It is finished." He is for her the only really essential God, Alone, and she will go, without emotions and feelings, perhaps, but with unshakeable fidelity, to martyrdom, to exile, to disgrace and shame, if such will be God's calling with respect to her; she will go to the end. She will not come down from the Cross; they will only take her down dead. There remained one step to complete mystical death, or rather one final breath, and there, at the dawn of the third day, the Bright Resurrection of the full joyous union with her Lord and God – "It is finished."

Father! Into your hands I commit my spirit! (Luke 23:46)

The moment of great rest has drawn near. The Lord knew that His last night on earth was upon Him, and after it on the dawn of the third day would begin an eternal, cloudless day, and as His most pure mother had taught Him in His childhood at night before going to sleep – sleep is a symbol of death – to entrust His soul to God, just as now, on this singular night, He entrusted His soul into the hands of His Father: "Father, into Your hands I commit My spirit." Having said this, He gave up His spirit. The evening of rest had descended, and that Sabbath is drawing nigh, when He will cast His gaze upon all that He has done.

"… And God saw everything that He had made, and behold, it was very good. And there was evening […] And on the seventh day … He rested …. from all His work" (Genesis 1:31 – 2:2).

The contemplation of this rest of death, into which Jesus Christ has entered, is one of the most fruitful for the life of the soul and, unfortunately, we very often leave it aside. We do not know how to be with Christ during His mysterious rest in the grave; we have not developed within ourselves a reverence for the dead Christ; we forget Him. He worked over the course of thirty-three years from the day of His first breath in the cave in Bethlehem. He had not rested for a moment; even at night His heart kept vigil, since His work was the complete reversal, both internal and external, of the whole world. Not a single culture can exist and develop if it is not conformed with Him and His law.

So that He could live constantly among people, He founded the greatest kingdom in the world, standing outside all nations and states – His church. At the same time He healed all ailments and all wounds; He had the strength and the time for all people; and, finally, He revealed the royal road of the Cross, leading to His kingdom in heaven.

He did all this. Of course, God Himself could have directly accomplished all this with a single act of His almighty will, but He wanted to accomplish this through human nature; human lips pronounced these eternal words: "Heaven and earth will pass away, but My words will not pass away."

A human brain served as the means and it put Divine dreams into action, making them a reality. God knows no tiredness, but God, having become a man, can become deeply tired, both in soul and in body. He earned His rest, but before taking His rest for all time, Jesus offered His Father the great gift, His holy, human soul: "Father, into Your hands I commit My spirit."

Before going any further, I would like you to learn to contemplate the whole beauty of this soul that Jesus has placed into His Father's hands. He lived thirty-three years only for the glory of the Father – "Father, glorify Your name" (John 12:28). His soul burned with the desire to make people understand God and to help them love Him. "And this is eternal life, that they know You, the only true God, and Jesus Christ whom You have sent" (John 17:3). His food was to do the will of His Father – "My food is to do the will of Him who sent me and to accomplish His work" (John 4:34). "… that they may be one even as We are one, I in them and You in Me, that they may become perfectly one, so that the world may know that You have sent Me…" (John 17:22-23). He took on and loved suffering for our sake: "I have a baptism to be baptized with; and how I am constrained until it is accomplished!" (Luke 12:50). His soul aims to reveal to us the path of life and true happiness. The beauty of all the angels, seraphim and cherubim cannot compare with the beauty of the soul of Christ, which He commended into the hands of His Father. "Father, into Your hands I commit My spirit."

This soul, having sorrowed unto death, has now entered into its great rest, but do not think that this is a state of inactivity, quietism. No, God is pure, simple, indivisible act, and the soul of Christ, the most closely approximating the image and likeness of God of all human souls, continues to glorify God and do good; it has descended into a place of stillness, coolness and light, where souls faithful to grace await the coming of their Redeemer, the Conqueror of hell and death. His body, having endured all the burdens of the intense heat of the day, exhausted by work beyond its strength, bent under the weight of the Cross and grief, exhausted and beaten up by the hands of those for whom He suffered all this, His body will be placed in a new grave, carved out of a rock, and there it will rest in great peace and await the bright dawn of the third day. His countenance, the countenance of the dead God … what rest and peace … "[…] and there was a great calm" (Matthew 8:26). "'Father, into Your hands I commit My spirit!' Having said this He breathed His last" (Luke 23:46).

And indeed there was a great calm – such is the state of the life of the soul, corresponding to the last word of Our Lord's testament from the Cross. How logical and consistent this is – at His appearance on earth the angels sang "Peace to men of good will." When the time of His voluntary suffering was approaching, wishing to give His most valuable gift to men, He said to His disciples: "Peace I leave with you; My peace I give to you" (John 14:27).

The peace of Christ is peace with God, peace with the world, and consequently, peace with oneself – the great need of our soul. But it is as though there were two kinds of peace. One – the peace of the Christian soul, conscientiously and honorably fulfilling its obligations to God and neighbor, not allowing itself voluntary sin and feeling a tranquility of conscience from having fulfilled its duty to God and man. This is also the peace of Christ and His valuable gift to people of good will. But it is not about such peace that I want to talk with you, since there is a different peace, which precedes the struggle on Golgotha and all those moments of the spiritual life about which we have spoken. This is no longer the peace of a right conscience only, but peace of the spirit, the higher part of the soul, a mystical peace of Christ.

The triumphant word "It is finished" has penetrated to the summit of the soul like a two-edged sword, and it has begun to act through a liberated and reigning will. As a result of this "liberation of the will," there is a great calm: the passions and feelings, having been quieted, obediently nestle close to their mistress – the will; and the will, free and joyful, like Mary Magdalene, has taken its seat at the feet of Jesus to listen to His commands. "Father, into Your hands I commit My spirit." What He will show her makes no difference to her – she has conquered the world, the devil, flesh, and herself – and now, free and tranquil, she rests at the feet of Christ. She needs nothing. "Father, into Your hands I commit my spirit." Into Your hands I give everything. The time has come for you to act in me – do with me all that you wish. The soul together with Christ has earned its rest: the struggles have passed and there is a great calm.

Evening has come, when all has come to a standstill, as though awaiting something. The soul is like the smooth surface of a quiet lake that is silent and waits, while at dawn on the third day, after a great rest, the sun of love and truth will rise and suffuse the whole lake with its rays, and a new life begins, a life of union and love, but for the time being it has grown quiet and it waits – but it knows that the sun will rise. "Father, into Your hands I commit My spirit."

Do not think that this great calm and rest are a lethargic dissolution in God, a quietism that is false and yet enticing to our nature. No, this is not a dissolution of the soul; it is more like the soul's self-collectedness, when all the soul's capabilities press against its center, the will, and it is joined with God, its unchanging, simple, single point of support, through pure acts of faith, hope and love; but love is the main virtue, and it reigns, it brings the soul close to its greatest resemblance – to the Creator, who is pure act. The soul, without alternation or division, is poured out wholly in a single and simple act of giving: "Father, into Your hands I commit my spirit." A great peace has come, and there is a great calm – the calm of an evening before the onset of the eternal, cloudless day. Nothing and no one can take this peace from her.

"Who shall separate us from the love of Christ? Shall tribulation, or distress, or persecution, or famine, or nakedness, or peril, or sword? [...] in all these things we are more than conquerors through Him who loved us. For I am sure that neither death, nor life, nor angels, nor principalities, nor things present, nor things to come, nor powers, nor height, nor depth, nor anything else in all creation, will be able to separate us from the love of God in Christ Jesus our Lord" (Romans 8:35-39).

The active life of this great rest is all within, at the summit of the soul. "The kingdom of God is in your midst" (Luke 17:21). The soul does not depend on anything external. The events and circumstances of its external life can bring tears, but these will more likely be tears of compassion, like the tears of Christ over the dying Jerusalem that rejected its God and had become hardened in evil. But these tears cannot disturb the peace of the soul because the soul sees in all events that happen to her, in all contradictions, the manifestation of the wisdom and grace of God's providence. What can disturb her, make her anxious, trouble her, or cause her doubts? "Father, into Your hands I commit my spirit." She is wholly and entirely in the hands of God.

The Lord has taken her into his blessed and powerful hands, and the soul rests in peace and calm upon His breast. She needs nothing and nothing frightens her because nothing and no one can tear her from Him. Theoretically she can fall and leave Him – but in practice this almost never happens. He Himself firmly holds her. He – the powerful, mighty, all-loving and faithful God – and everything has been given into His hands. "Father, into Your hands I commit my spirit" – the soul is on the eve, on the threshold of a complete life and union and she awaits His hour in peace and rest...

He will come at the dawn of the third day, glorified and shining, in order to lead her, free and joyful, into His marriage chamber. For the time being He has left her to rest: she suffered together with her crucified God, she struggled, and despite everything, despite the onslaughts of the world, the flesh and the devil, she believed, she hoped and she loved. Now she is victorious, having conquered the world, and together with her Lord she has earned her rest.

Evening has come. Around the Cross "there is a great calm." The Sabbath draws near, when the Lord rested from all His works... Jesus looked at the heavens with a peaceful, clear gaze and quietly said, as He had said in childhood, "Father, into Your hands I commit My spirit." Having said this, He bowed His head and gave up His spirit.

Try to make your Easter communion tomorrow under the banner of the Cross and in great peace and quiet of soul – "and there was a great calm." By an act of the will, set aside all thoughts and all sufferings of a personal nature and immerse yourselves in the contemplation of the calm and rest, the rest of the sacred Soul and Pure Body of our dead God.

Indeed, what rest, what peace and calm. "And there was a great calm." Here precisely in such peace and rest of all our passions and faculties, under the influence of the liberated – although temporarily – will, await the coming of Our Lord and God. Before his arrival, try to arouse in yourselves three dispositions:

Detachment from yourself and the external world. God Alone. "He must increase, but I must decrease" (John 3:30).

A pure desire to glorify Christ. "Father, glorify Your Son." "May Your name be glorified." And finally,

A great gratitude for all that God has given you, all He has given to all souls, and most important, for the fact that "God so loved the world that He gave His only-begotten Son" (John 3:16) and that He is so beautiful, powerful and good.

When you receive communion, take your soul resolutely and firmly and place it in the powerful and good hands of Our Lord and God, through the intercession of the most holy virgin Mary: "Father, into Your hands I commit my spirit."

Anna Ivanova Abrikosova

Sr. Stefania

Sr. Lucia

Sr. Rose Maria (Vaseleni-Pozharskaya)

Sr. Rose of the Heart of Mary

Sr. Rose of the Heart of Mary. Moscow, 1910

Minna Kugel (Sr. Teresa)

Sr. Teresa, 1972

Sr. Monika

Sr. Monika

Sr. Philomena. Ryazan, May 1933

Mother Antonina

Srs. Margaret Mary and Philomena

Srs. Antonina and Philomena. Tayshet, July, 1955

Srs. Monika, Antonina and Catherine (Rubashova)

Srs. Romualda and Philomena. Vilnius, June, 1967

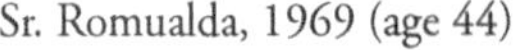

Sr. Romualda, 1969 (age 44)

Sr. Catherine Sokolowska

Srs. Philomena, Romualda and Philomena. Vilnius, June, 1967

LITANIES

THE Litany of Saint Dominic, originally composed by Saint Alfonso Rodriguez[1] and translated by the Sisters, came to be, according to the words of Father Georgy Friedman, OP, the "spiritual, sacrificial program of life for the Sisters of the Dominican community."

Unfortunately, we do not have the translations of the original, but only a copy of another copy, so that the partial revisions in the resulting text engender doubt as to their placement because it was impossible to verify them against the original.[2]

Litany of Saint Dominic

Lord, have mercy.
Christ, have mercy.
Lord, have mercy.
Christ, hear us.
Christ, graciously hear us.

God the Father of Heaven, *have mercy on us.*
God the Son, Redeemer of the world,
God the Holy Spirit,
Holy Trinity, One God,

Holy Mary, *pray for us.*

---

[1] Saint Alfonso Rodriguez (1531-1617), Spanish writer and preacher. His well-known work "On Christian Perfection" has been translated into nearly every European language. (Translator's note: "On Christian Perfection" was actually written by another Jesuit of the same name, who has not been canonized, Father Alfonso Rodriguez, SJ (1526-1616). The two are often mistaken as being one and the same person, as herein.)

[2] Translator's Note: The Litany of Saint Dominic has been reproduced here in its entirety and in the traditional format as it is prayed by Dominicans worldwide. Lines and phrases denoted with parentheses are additions made to the Litany as they appear in the Sisters' version.

Holy Mother of God,
Holy Virgin of virgins,
Holy Father, Saint Dominic,
Light of the Church,
Day star of the world,
Torch of the ages,
Preacher of grace,
Rose of patience,
Most ardent for the salvation of souls,
Most desirous of martyrdom,
(Great leader of souls),
Evangelical man,
Doctor of truth,
Ivory of chastity,
Man of truly apostolic heart,
Poor in the midst of riches,
Rich in purity of life,
Burning with zeal for perishing souls,
Trumpet of the Gospel,
Herald of heavenly tidings,
Rule of abstinence,
Salt of the earth,
Shining as the sun in the temple of God,
Enriched with the grace of Christ,
Clothed in heavenly robes,
(Golden bloom in the midst of blossoming flowers),
Thou who didst water the earth with thy precious blood,
(Wheat, gathered in the heavenly granaries),
Resplendent in the choir of virgins,
Father and leader of our Holy Order (of Preachers),
That at the hour of death we may be received into heaven with thee,

Lamb of God, Who takes away the sins of the world,
Spare us, O Lord.
Lamb of God, Who takes away the sins of the world,
Graciously hear us, O Lord.

Lamb of God, Who takes away the sins of the world,
Have mercy on us.
Christ, *hear us.*
Christ, *graciously hear us.*

Let us pray. Grant, we beseech Thee, O Almighty God, that we who are weighed down by the burden of our sins may be relieved by the patronage of Saint Dominic, Thy confessor and our father, through Christ Our Lord. Amen.

Holy Father Dominic, rise and fall down lovingly at the feet of the Lord. Reconcile us to Jesus Christ by your holy prayers, for great is our guilt before the Creator. Beg forgiveness for our sins, peace for our souls and joy in Heaven. Amen.

Litany of Thanksgiving

Lord, have mercy.
Christ, have mercy.
Lord, have mercy.
Christ, hear us.
Christ, graciously hear us.

God the Father of Heaven, *have mercy on us.*
God the Son, Redeemer of the world,
God the Holy Spirit,
Holy Trinity, One God,

Holy Mary, *pray for us.*
Holy Mother of God,
Holy Virgin of virgins,

For light, for life and for all of creation, *we thank you, Lord God.*
For revealing to us the secrets of the Holy Trinity,
For the Holy Spirit,
For sending your Son into the world,
For the Queen of Heaven, the Mother of your Son and our mother,

For the purity and chastity of the Blessed Virgin Mary,
For the assistance of your Angels here on earth,
For your saints, whose example gives us hope,
For those who intercede for us before Thy throne,
For giving us a rational and immortal soul,
For ennobling our will with freedom,
For stirring up kind motives in us,
For Holy Baptism, which cleanses our souls,
For the blessing of Confirmation, the standard of your warriors,
For the sacrifice of Christ's Body and Blood,
For daily strengthening us with the Bread of Heaven,
For Jesus, Who remains with us always on your altars,
For the remission of sins in the sacrament of Penance,
For anointing with holy oil for the salvation of the sick and
the relief it brings,
For the blessings and gifts you give to priests,
For the dignity, honor and nobility of marriage,
For the Church, who unifies and ennobles each of us,
For the rock of Truth in anxiety and the storm,
For Saint Peter and the keys to Heaven which were given to him,
For the supreme and infallible governance of the Church given in
the person of the Holy Father,
For Your royal priesthood and for our pastors,
For the laborers of our Holy Order in the Church,
For absolute evidence of the truths of the faith,
For the hope of seeing You face to face,
For happiness, whereby we may glorify Your Name,
For Sacred Scripture and the teachings of the Church,
For the great victory of Your Kingdom,
For the full splendor of the feasts of Your Church,
For Your condescension toward our prayers for the dearly departed,
For those who direct us to Your Church,
For our fathers and mothers, family and friends,
For our native land and its marvelous language,
For the heroes and defenders of our homeland and
the Catholic Faith,

For daily bread, shelter and daily work,
For consolations, for health and protection from danger,
For acts of penance, which You gave us for our correction,
For the bitter yet strengthening chalice of patience,
For Your Providence, which graciously guides us through life,
For the light which illumines us in the dark moments of life,
For the voice that called us in the darkness of temptation,
For the hand that firmly held us when the ground shook under our feet,
For the sorrowing Heart of Jesus Christ,
For the blessings You bestowed upon us instead of punishment,
For our future resurrection,
For the coming of Christ in the Final Judgment,
For Your just judgments,
For our joyful procession to heaven on the last day,
For the promise of eternal reward for the slightest merit,

That we may not forget Your blessings and good gifts,
we beg You, Lord God.
That we may ever glorify You and offer up our thanksgiving worthily,
That in our sorrows and grief we may remember Your goodness,
That we may offer thanksgiving for blessings and consolations as well as for sufferings and crosses,
That You would lead us to glorify You in heaven after this life,

Lamb of God, Who takes away the sins of the world,
Spare us, O Lord.
Lamb of God, Who takes away the sins of the world,
Graciously hear us, O Lord.
Lamb of God, Who takes away the sins of the world,
Have mercy on us.

Our Father…
Hail, Mary…

V. We thank You, Lord God, for Your great glory,
R. Which You revealed to us, Your servants.

Let us pray.

Lord God, Who through the mouth of Saint Paul the Apostle said "In everything give thanks, for this is the will of God in Christ Jesus," we humbly beg You to grant us the grace that we may begin to offer our thanksgiving to you here on earth and continue to do so forever in heaven, through Christ our Lord. Amen.

The Abrikosova Dominican Sisters As Remembered by Russian and Polish Catholics

IN this section we present interviews of twelve Russian and Polish Catholics who knew the surviving Sisters of the Abrikosova Dominican community after their release from the prison camps, from the 1970s until the death of the last of the Sisters in 1993. The interviews were conducted in 1998 and 1999.

Father Evgeny Geinrikhs, OP

Interview conducted and text transcribed by Irina Poltavskaya

I had the good fortune to be acquainted with three of the Russian Dominican Sisters who were part of the Third Order Regular community founded in Russia by Mother Catherine Abrikosova, OP: Sister Catherine (Nora Rubashova), who lived in Moscow; Sister Antonina (Valentina Kuznetsova), who was the superior of the community at the time of my acquaintance with the Sisters and was thus called Mother Antonina; and Sister Philomena (Sophia Eismont).

Mother Antonina and Sister Philomena lived in Vilnius, at different ends of the city: Mother Antonina on Dzuku Street, and Sister Philomena on Zhermuny.

The first Sister I met was Nora Rubashova. A mutual friend brought me to visit her at her apartment in Moscow on Prospect Vernadskovo in the autumn of 1978. From that time I visited her regularly, right up until her death in 1987.

In 1981 I was ordained a Catholic priest and each time I was in Moscow, which was often, I would celebrate Mass at her apartment. If she needed me to, I would leave her a supply of the Sacred Hosts for her to receive daily communion in the absence of a priest (by the time of our acquaintance her mobility was already very limited).

Nora Rubashova was not tall, and her facial features were quite unlike what you might expect of a typical Jewish woman: she was pug-nosed and broad-cheeked. Despite all her orthodoxy, her fidelity to church tradition and obedience to the teaching of the Church, she distinguished herself by a kind of boldness and a somewhat man-like courageous wisdom, as well as a certain decisiveness and an authoritative nature. When she spoke of God she might say things that were very bold, on the forefront of the development of Church teaching. She had fully assimilated the spirit of the Second Vatican Council; she had a lively interest in the latest documents outlining Church teaching, and above all in Papal encyclicals, which she discussed with great animation.

Because of her mental alertness, the youthfulness of her thinking and the wise boldness of her views, Nora Rubashova was like a magnet who attracted people to herself. Many young and educated people visited her, and they visited her not just out of charity, as one might visit a grandmotherly figure, someone who needed help or needed something brought from the store, but rather for the sake of being with her.

I have to say that being with her played a very large role in my own life. She was one of those people who opened up for me the spiritual beauty and goodness of the Christian faith. Some questions about the Church from its more or less distant past disturbed me and I did not know how to answer these questions that arose from time to time. She helped me find a precise, convincing and satisfying answer to these troubling questions.

She was constantly working, right up until the last days of her life: translating some piece of theological writing, or working on some small assignment from the library where she had worked after her last release from the camps and before retirement. These little assignments supplemented her pension. She dedicated a lot of time to spiritual exercises – prayer, meditations, spiritual reading. Various people visited her every day. She had a constant need to help people in some way, to be in solidarity with their lives despite all the limits on her opportunities to do so.

Because of her heart ailment, she was often completely unable to leave her building. Furthermore, it was difficult to talk by telephone for fear that her conversations might be of interest to the security organs because of the people who were included in her circle of acquaintances. It was hard to guess what very innocent piece of information might be used to fill out the paranoid picture they had created, and to whose harm.

Furthermore, at that time we did not understand all this as well as we would later, when many things became clear. When everything crumbled to pieces and it all fell apart before our very eyes, it became clear that we had been watching the death throes – the dying agony – of the regime. Back then it seemed terrible and hopeless. Perhaps the tragedies of the distant past were not so interesting to us because the reality of the terrifying present was being dramatized in the fates of individual people, our contemporaries, who drank this cup of suffering practically before our eyes.

From among those who had contact with Nora Rubashova – but not as a result of that contact – some would fall into the KGB's field of vision. KGB agents would "summon" someone for questioning, or they would visit someone else. Some, because of this surveillance, broke off contact with her. She did not blame them, but she took these losses hard. Nowadays much is described differently, but back then, some stopped going to church, avoided meetings with acquaintances, and even asked to be readmitted into the Party. She condemned no one, but of course it pained her.

I continued to visit her. I had no concerns about contact with her at that time, but I nevertheless submitted to the rules she established. By the end of the first half of the 1980s we communicated to a great extent by using a pencil and a roll of toilet paper on which we wrote down what we wanted to say and what must not, in the event of possible eavesdropping, be heard by "listeners."

I remember the story of the nail on the landing in front of Nora's apartment. A nail had mysteriously, as some said, appeared in the wall. I only know about this from what I was told. I paid no attention to these walls. The landing was in semi-darkness, but once, according to Nora, a nail that had not been there before suddenly appeared. She practically never slept at night because of her heart ailment and, as she said, one night she suddenly heard a commotion on the landing. When all had quieted down, she went out to the stairwell and she saw the ill-fated nail.[1] In any case, almost everyone poked fun at the nail.

It seems to me that until her last days Nora Rubashova had an unrealized need for motherhood. She was your textbook Jewish mother and grandmother, solicitous to a fault. She would tell full-grown men, professors who had come to visit her, to cover their throats or to fix their scarves, and she would exclaim "what do you have on your feet! It's cold!" Her care for others was very touching.

She loved some people blindly, bestowing on them qualities that they absolutely lacked – or so it seemed to me, although perhaps I was mistaken. This self-giving of poignant love always astounded me. So what does it matter if she saw a conceited, dull egoist and manipulator as very good and very wise? There's no shame in such mistakes. I myself experienced her solicitude for the trifles in my own life. I once jokingly said to her: "Nora Nikolayevna, you probably think that if you do not know the train schedule, the trains won't run!" She really wanted to share in others' lives, and not because her own was boring.

In the final years of her life, she suffered almost every night from heart problems and she had to sleep in a half-sitting position; as the years went on she was more frequently unable go outside because of her weak heart and dizziness. In the early years of our friendship she would nevertheless go out somewhere; later she only left her apartment a couple times a year, mainly in the summer when one of her friends would have time and could help her go outdoors just to breathe some fresh air.

Her death was both expected and sudden. Given the state of her health, death might come to her any day. Realizing this, she likely had a presentiment of her death. I can remember it as though it were right this moment. She called me on a Monday evening when I was at home, in Leningrad, and asked, "Are you planning to be in Moscow tomorrow?" I already had a ticket for the following evening, and I said, "No, I will arrive Wednesday

[1] I don't know what it was, but it certainly wasn't what she imagined. After all, they certainly could have done their eavesdropping through the windows that faced onto the yard without any such technical complications. When she died, on the day of her funeral, I pulled this nail out of the wall and picked around inside with a knife. I of course found nothing. True, I didn't thoroughly explore the walls. For me, this was not the mere satisfaction of curiosity; it was a kind of tribute to her memory. I had simply done away with something that had caused her so much suffering during her life. Of course, this was already 1987, when it was possible to have an entirely different attitude toward such things than in the first half of the 1980s.

morning." She said, "Fine." I asked, "And why do you ask?" "I'm not feeling so well, and I'd like to chat – it's been a long time since I've seen you. I miss you." But we are so accustomed to the fact that a person of her age and poor health would feel, as a rule, unwell, that I found nothing surprising or anxious about her remark, especially since she then said, "Well okay, call me right away on Wednesday, and come by to see me." And we said our good-byes.

When I arrived in Moscow on Wednesday and, as usual, called her from the train station, an unfamiliar woman's voice told me that Nora Nikolayevna had died. I arrived to an already cold corpse, lying in state on a table. Witnesses said that a doctor or nurse had come to give her an injection and at that moment her veins had collapsed and she was pronounced dead. She was not taken to the morgue. She lay at home, in a coffin, on a table. It was May and the weather was hot.

It astonished me that she looked so good. There was no waxen pallor of death, although it was evident that she no longer remained, only her mortal remains; however, on her face was the eternal imprint of life. She was just as she had departed from this life. On her lips was a kind of half-smile, reflecting the joy of meeting. People who had been close to her were there; a priest whom she had loved very much had come on Wednesday to pray the Office of the Dead for her eternal repose.

I did not go to her coffin immediately after being informed of her death, since there was no need of my presence. I went on the day of the funeral. People who had been especially close to her gathered for the funeral – her friends, each of whom I had seen several times at her apartment, and several with whom I maintain a close friendship to this day. Some of these persons have already journeyed on to that place where we, I hope, will someday meet again. I accompanied Nora Nikolayevna on her last journey.

I became acquainted with Sisters Antonina and Philomena somewhat later, after I had already been ordained a priest, in Vilnius where I visited rather often in those days. Father Andrey Kasyanenko celebrated daily Mass for the Sisters in the apartment on Dzuku Street and thus had contact with them practically every day. Sister Philomena did not come to Mass every day, but she was regularly there on Sundays and feast days. On Sundays and feast days, the small community, its Vilnius branch, gathered in the apartment on Dzuku Street which was like its center, inasmuch as Sister Philomena came there.[2] Today one can regretfully say that this branch of the Dominican family has died out, although it did give life to other communities.

The Sisters were very different. Sister Antonina was a plump elderly woman with a severe limp. When I met her she was no longer able to get out and about because of an injury she had sustained to her leg. She practically never went out of her building and she moved around her tiny Khrushchev-era apartment with great difficulty. A kind, touching old woman, very devout, like all of them, she held on to traditional views, old-fashioned and in their own way touching for a woman of her age and fate. With respect to personal traits, she was very different from Nora Nikolayevna; she had less energy and was more gentle.

Sister Philomena was tall, exhibiting traces of a former beauty. At the time of our acquaintance she was already of a very venerable age. If my memory serves me right, she was approximately eighty years old, but it was evident that in her youth she had been very attractive. She had a disease of the spine that came with old age, and therefore she walked very bent over when she was out in public. At home she had developed a strange and unusual gait: she walked bending her legs slightly in order to hold her head erect. In other circumstances, this might have seemed grotesque, but here it was obviously a desire not to give in, not to submit to the debility. I would say that her opinions, for the most part, had a more enthusiastic, innocent flavor than those of the other Sisters. When expressing her opinions, either in a kind of unusual outburst of delight or, conversely, of poignant wrath, she reminded one of a pre-Revolutionary schoolgirl. She was a very touching old woman.

I knew that the life story of each of these women was heroic. Each of them had accepted the gift of faith and entered the community of the Dominican Sisters in their early youth. They had studied at the universities or at the music conservatory, and this old-fashioned kind of education was very perceptible in them. Each of them knew foreign languages well – the stuff of the gymnasia and boarding schools. They had embarked upon the path of being confessors of the faith as young girls; not once did they later betray their chosen path, despite all their difficulties. It befell them to endure many hardships: prisons, camps, and many years of internal exile. Their

[2] There were other Sisters but they are not part of this story because they had a later "calling." Basically they helped the elderly Sisters in their increasingly difficult life.

paths played out differently. For example, Sister Philomena spent practically all her years in prisons, camps and exile by herself alone, without any of the other Sisters. For other Sisters it turned out that in exile, and sometimes even in the camps, they were together with one or two other members of the community; in other words, they were able to communicate, to support one another and to pray together, which of course lightened the load of their life in camp, prison, or exile. Not once did they betray their chosen path.

In their stories about their experiences, what is interesting is not the details in and of themselves, as these are typical of all camp memoirs – the horrors of the barracks, the plank beds, the overcrowded barges or "Stolypin" rail cars. In their descriptions of these common features of camp life there was nothing new to be told. What always astounded me in their stories was a kind of spiritual realism. Not optimism, but spiritual, Christian realism. Throughout all these horrors, through this gloom, they saw revealed to them a genuine reality, the reality of the love and goodness of God.

There was suffering and there was, of course, fear, which remained imprinted upon their lives practically to the end. But when they recalled their camp life, for the most part their memories were absolutely devoid of any trace of bitterness, of any lingering resentment, or of any vindictiveness – the lack of which, I have to say, astonished me and still astonishes me to this very day. They described events, episodes, and meetings, each time finding in them something positive. All the gloomy details of camp life were already familiar to me from literature, but in their stories the reality of goodness astonished me and became a revelation.

For example – Nora Rubashova, diminutive in stature, is walking along with a huge bundle of her belongings. Perhaps the bundle isn't all that big, but for her it is big. They are on a journey of many miles and she is beginning to fall behind the convoy of other convicts trudging along a worn-out road. She is falling behind, growing weaker, she has no strength, and she well knows the notorious instruction that says, "a step to the left, a step to the right will be considered flight." Then a guard, uttering unprintable obscenities, grabs the bundle and with a sprint he hurls it into the wagon; thus he saves her life. And Sister Catherine remembers him with unfailing gratitude.

Another Sister remembers the little flowers and the shoots of grass growing beyond the Arctic Circle. A third remembers her kind, simple-hearted camp companions instead of the embittered and incorrigible criminals. I don't recall the Sisters relishing any of these horrors, and if anyone tried to get them to tell stories of such things, the Sisters would somehow brush it all aside with a "Yes, yes," – and then steer the conversation to descriptions of more joyful moments. For example, how in the midst of these horrible conditions they gathered together somewhere in two's or three's, in exile or in the camp zone, to celebrate Christmas, and where conditions permitted, they cut out little lanterns from colored paper, out of candy wrappers or anything handy to decorate their little shrines. Suffering transformed into something else – that was the discovery, the manifestation of peace. This is the path of Christian asceticism, and the Sisters, of course, were on this path. This is what astounded me more than anything during my interactions with them, despite all their differences.

Sometimes of course it was tiring, all their old-womanish, seemingly restless solicitude about things that were of little significance, or so it seemed at that time. The distance between a nearly classic asceticism and this all-so-human daily existence seemed enormous at times and it was disconcerting. I have no doubt, however, that were they to experience something similar to the events of their youth, they would act exactly as they had in their younger days – they would never have betrayed their chosen path.

Undoubtedly, in their youth they were not fearless, otherwise this would not have been a feat of asceticism, but some kind of narcotic intoxication with their own fantasy. Surely they were afraid, certainly the Cross frightened them, and most likely they did not want to take up their Cross, just as Christ had not wanted to take up his own Cross. (If you think otherwise, just read the Evangelists' account of the night in the Garden of Gethsemane!) Surely it was the same with our Sisters: they did not want to, but fidelity impelled them to act as they did. In everyday life, however, when the Lord gives us the opportunity to relax, people, in their weaknesses, reveal themselves as completely ordinary, without any zealous convictions.

What surprised me most in my contact with them was that they were so different from one another. They were already quite elderly and had suffered much: at the same time they were faithful to the end and carried within themselves the horrible imprint of fear to their last days. Their anxieties, as it seemed to us back then, bore a somewhat exaggerated character; I think that at that time there was no threat whatsoever to the Sisters, as they lived utterly retiring lives. Of course they always were plagued with fear based on what they had experienced. Each of them was certain that people were eavesdropping on all sides, that everything was being "watched." Maybe it was, but I am not so sure. No one had any troubles on account of contact with them. There were more grounds for fear in Moscow, understandably, than in the Baltic States.

With respect to Father Leonid Feodorov [Exarch of Russian Rite Catholics], they all maintained an exceptional reverence. Some of them had known him personally. Nora Nikolayevna met him – if my memory serves me right – only once, when he was returning from one period of exile and before being sent on another. He celebrated Mass in Moscow at Eastertide; she met him first on the tram, not knowing who he was. At that time clergy still wore clerical garb in public. She saw an unfamiliar priest on the tram, then later recognized him at the Cathedral of the Immaculate Conception on Malaya Gruzinskaya Street, where he celebrated the Easter liturgy in accordance with the Eastern calendar.

With respect to Julia Nikolayevna Danzas, however, one could not but notice some hostility among the Sisters regarding certain opinions expressed by this woman who had figured prominently in the life of the Russian Catholic community in Saint Petersburg. These opinions appeared in a voluminous book about Exarch Feodorov that also included quite a bit of material about Julia Nikolayevna – including her letters, and memoirs.[3] The Sisters polemicized with the book's assessment of both Mother Catherine herself and the Moscow community of Dominican Sisters, and in this there was a kind of (in a good sense) rash, deliberate, "chivalrous," daughterly fidelity. They would accept no arguments to the contrary – although truly I had no occasion to argue with them.

Much of what Julia Nikolayevna wrote made sense to me: Mother Catherine and Julia Nikolayevna were completely different people – in temperament, in their views, and simply in their fates. Both women were complex persons. Two rigid, powerful temperaments thus collided, like two opposite poles of a magnet. The Sisters, however, were irreproachable in their esteem of their spiritual mother; without question, they always took

[3] Deacon Vasilii von Burman, OSB, *Leonid Fyodorov: Zhizn' i deyatel'nost'* [Leonid Feodorov: Life and Work], Rome, 1966. Translator's Note: See Appendix 2 for Sister Philomena's "Rebuttal" to offensive statements about the Abrikosova community and its beloved foundress.

her side and indignantly cried out like children about what to them seemed to be an injustice.

During the whole time of my acquaintance with the Sisters, Nora Nikolayevna was in Vilnius only a few times, during the early 1980s. Later she could no longer undertake such a lengthy journey. I visited the Sisters in Vilnius for the last time sometime at the end of the 1980s. They died after 1990, when travel to the Baltic States had become more difficult to undertake; unfortunately I did not see them during their final years of life.

As long as Father Andrey was living in Vilnius I received news about them and had the opportunity to convey my greetings and inquire about their health and how they were getting along. Unlike Nora Nikolayevna, the Vilnius Sisters had strong hearts, and thus they "faded" very gradually. Their hearts continued to function, while their bodies steadily weakened, and as I heard from Father Andrey, by the time of their deaths they were already in a state of semi-consciousness.

Ivan Lupandin (Brother Vincent, Secular Tertiary)

Interview conducted by Margarita Kurganskaya and transcribed by Evgeny Krasheninnikov

I met Nora Nikolayevna November 12, 1978, when Georgy Friedman brought me to her place. I had met him at the home of Olga Vladimirovna, who was also a Dominican, but of the Saint Petersburg Third Order community.[4] When he brought me to Nora Nikolayevna's, he said to her: "Here is a young man who is interested in Catholicism – perhaps he can help you

---

[4] Bishop Jean Amoudrou, a Dominican, had accepted Olga Vladimirovna into the Dominican order. She was an individual lay member of the Third Order; she did not become a Regular sister. She married the captain of an ocean fleet and although they had no children, her family life somehow distanced her from regular contact with the Dominicans. After her husband's death she became more active, and young people, as well as some who were slightly older, gathered at her place. Georgy Davidovich was among her guests. He brought to her a certain young man who was a bit ill, in flight from Orthodoxy on account of a priest who was constantly exorcising him in the belief that he was in the grips of an unclean spirit. Somehow after an unsuccessful exorcism the priest had him admitted to a psychiatric hospital. Traumatized by such treatment, under the influence of Georgy Davidovich, he began to attend a Catholic church where he became acquainted with Olga Vladimirovna and other Catholics. It was he who brought me to Olga Vladimirovna. She was already an elderly woman, very loving, good, cultured and even refined in a certain sense and fluent in French. At her place I met Georgy Davidovich. I later saw her several more times. She died, I believe, at the end of the 1980s or beginning of the 1990s.

with some of your chores." True, it was not a question of helping her at that time, but gradually I did in fact begin to help with household chores. She was an elderly woman living alone; it was not possible just to sit at her place and not do anything. The main thing, however, was that we spoke a lot on spiritual themes. That was what brought us close. I began to visit her often: basically, every other day, but there were times when we saw each other every day. This close contact with her continued until her death, almost nine years. She shared with me some recollections, and I met many of her acquaintances at her place.

One sensed in Nora Nikolayevna a person who was entirely dedicated and had given herself to Catholicism, to Christ, and to the Dominican Order – I do not know in which order to name these; she was a person who had suffered much and not been broken, had not been bent under the weight of the sufferings she had endured. Yet she had none of that educated softness or refinement, and perhaps she lacked sensitivity. Obviously such qualities would not have fostered survival in the circumstances in which she had lived.[5] Thus she was a stricter, one could even say, sterner person than Olga Vladimirovna. She may also have surpassed Olga Vladimirovna in her keen knowledge of people and their psychology, a knowledge that would have been sharpened in the camps. Thus she of course immediately saw right through me; she saw my shortcomings,[6] unlike Olga Vladimirovna for whom I was just a young man, "pleasing in all respects."

Naturally she understood immediately the kind of person with whom she was dealing, and I sensed this right away. This introduced into our relations an element of very deep seriousness, such that it was impossible simply to break off these relations – for example, not to come visit her for some time without any explanation, and so forth. I understood that with Nora Nikolayevna one would have either a serious relationship or none at all. I noticed later that many people around her understood this as well. She was a person of deep convictions, some that were Christian, specifically Catholic and Dominican, and others that were simply common to humanity. She always spoke seriously, weightily, and even, one could say, without a particular

---

[5] Obviously one should not expect that people who had lived in the camps would be gentle, meek and sensitive. Such people either died or went insane.

[6] My lack of restraint and my worldly foolishness and a certain softness that could turn into depravity.

sense of humor. This did not shock me because prior to this time I had been with the monks of the Pskov Cave Monastery, who were very serious people. On the contrary, it even pleased me. I understood that one could not deal otherwise with Communists; only people like Nora Nikolayevna won. Such people knew how to survive, but in the event of something worth dying for, they knew how to die without losing their dignity, without lowering their heads. Later Father Alexander Hauk-Ligowski, OP, said of her that she had all the qualities of a leader: intellect, will and personal sanctity. She really did have both a strong will and a firmness of character – without a doubt, qualities of a leader. She was capable and she was obviously called to guide people; she did this well, with knowledge of her responsibility and duty.

She talked about her childhood in a Jewish family in Minsk, how she had often cried there, that things somehow didn't work out for her. She loved the theater; she was a big fan of the actor Mikhail Chekhov and went to all his performances at the Moscow Art Theater. She was baptized in 1926 [at age seventeen] on the basis of her convictions, when she was a first-year student in the Historical-Philological Department at Second Moscow State University,[7] where she had matriculated with difficulty as the daughter of an "enemy element."

She told me that she thought then about the meaning of life, that she even had thoughts that life was meaningless and that it would be more honorable to commit suicide, just to put a bullet to her head. Obviously she was undergoing some kind of crisis, and faith then saved her from suicide. Why she had chosen Catholicism, in particular the Greek Catholic Church, why she had gone to Father Sergey Soloviev for baptism – I do not know. She did not speak of it. Soon after her baptism in 1926 she became a secular Third Order [Dominican]; she went to visit Sister Stephania (Gorodets) in Kostroma and met with the Sisters there. All the while she continued to go to the theater and lead an ordinary life; the Sisters placed no special restrictions on her.

The Abrikosova community had already been broken up. The Sisters and Anna Ivanovna had been arrested and sentenced in 1924, but Father Sergey continued to serve more or less legally at the church on Malaya Gruzinskaya

[7] Translator's Note: Moscow Higher Women's Courses, also known as Moscow University for Women and, from 1918 to 1930, Second Moscow State University, which admitted men as well as women.

Street at one of the side altars. He even had, I believe, some kind of authorization from Bishop Neveu as the deputy of Father Leonid Feodorov, Exarch of the Russian Catholics. Furthermore, he met with Father Feodorov when the latter came to Moscow.

Nora Nikolayevna once told me of how she was sitting in the tram to go to the church on Malaya Gruzinskaya Street and noticed that some very imposing person in clerical garb sat down next to her. She thought it was an Orthodox priest. Then she noticed that he was getting off at the same stop and walking to the same place. Later it became clear that this was Exarch Leonid Feodorov.

Nora Nikolayevna became Father Soloviev's spiritual daughter and served as sacristan. During the last two years before his arrest [in 1931], when the authorities forbade him to celebrate Mass on Malaya Gruzinskaya, members of the community gathered in their homes to pray. One day in the six-month period before his arrest, Nora Nikolayevna was led into a little room at the university to have a "conversation" with someone who was apparently a representative of the security organs, who proposed to her that she collaborate with them. In her words, she gave him the "double fig," in other words, she flatly refused – and with the kind of response that of course did not lighten her future fate. True, they politely responded, "You'll have no one to blame but yourself."

She was unable to finish the university and receive her diploma because on February 15, 1931, she was arrested along with all the members of Father Soloviev's community on charges of espionage and sentenced to five years in the camps. This particular article of the indictment – espionage – was especially damaging because it meant a strict escort on convoys and general labor in the camps. Thus she endured plenty, serving five years from beginning to end and under all the severity of the law, just for participation in a prayer group. There was no mitigation of the sentence, nothing, even though at the moment of her arrest she was only twenty-one years old.

Nora Nikolayevna emerged from the camps a completely different person. She now understood what was what in this life – that the Soviet system embodied evil – and she had already decided that she would seriously dedicate herself to God and the Dominican Order. She spoke rarely about life in the camps, but sometimes she would recall individual events. For example, how on the day of Kirov's murder [December 1, 1934] the camp administration, as vengeance on the "enemies of the people," made all the convicts sleep in the frost in tents without blankets.

After the camps she was released with residency restrictions and lived for two years in Michurinsk where an acquaintance from the university had given her a job in the botanical garden. (This friend later became an Orthodox priest.) She renewed her contact with Sister Stephania and after Michurinsk she went to live with the Sisters in Maloyaroslavets. They were living there as a community, six or eight of them, and Sister Stephania was the superior. Life there was strict in all respects: a lot of work, very strict discipline, prayer and fasting.

They went once every one or two months to Saint Louis Church in Moscow where they received Holy Communion, went to confession, and received some monetary assistance from the pastor, Father Leopold Braun,[8] through whom they maintained their connection with the Vatican (even though this was forbidden). There could be no reconciliation with the authorities because these were two ideologies that were completely incompatible with one another.[9] Of course Father Leopold undoubtedly did all he could to ease the fate of Catholics and, in general, of Christians. Nora Nikolayevna helped him in this regard in any way she could and most likely informed him of everything that she was able to find out.[10]

In 1941 Sister Stephania was arrested, but then the war broke out and they gave her only five years in exile – perhaps just to get her out of the way. At first Sister Rose of the Heart of Mary (Galina Jętkiewicz) went out to eastern Kazakhstan to help Sister Stephania, and then after her death of pneumonia in 1944, the community sent Nora Nikolayevna out to help Sister Stephania. Sister Stephania lived as an exile; Nora Nikolayevna worked in a school as a free employee.

During the war the Sisters in Maloyaroslavets were for a short time in

[8] Bishop Neveu was no longer there. He had gone to France in 1936 and the Soviets would not issue a visa for his return to Russia. He saw Nora when she returned to Moscow after her release from the camps and she approached him at church. He embraced her very affectionately – but after this conversation the authorities detained her and then immediately expelled her from Moscow.

[9] Whereas in Orthodoxy the ideology in general is contemplative, and could thus somehow coexist with the Mongol invasion and possibly with the Communists, Catholicism could not coexist with the Mongols, or the Turks, or the Communists – in other words, for Catholicism it was a struggle not to coexist, but a struggle to the death.

[10] What could one priest and a group of women do? But at least they did something. Thanks to the activity of Father Leopold and his reports, the West knew what it was dealing with.

a German-occupied zone. The German contingent occupying the city was accompanied by two Catholic priests. They of course established contact with the Dominican Sisters and celebrated Mass for them. One of them, as Nora Nikolayevna recalled, was (in her words) a "Hoch Deutsch" – that is, a very nationalistically inclined priest. I asked Nora Nikolayevna, "Did that 'Hoch Deutsch' not betray the fact that there were two Jewish women living among you?" "Well, he was a Catholic priest. He was nationalistic, but not that nationalistic." In other words, a Catholic is a Catholic and a priest is a priest, and in general there was some kind of Catholic solidarity.

When the Soviet forces arrived, however, they arrested Teresa Kugel and sent her to the camps for five years on the presumption that she had collaborated with the Germans; how else could she have worked in a hospital and not been shot by the Nazis? Valentina Kuznetsova (Sister Antonina) was under investigation for the same reason, but they later let her go. Thus once again the community was for all practical purposes extinguished: Sister Stephania was in exile with Nora Nikolayevna, Sister Rose of the Heart of Mary had died in exile, Sister Teresa was in prison. Almost no one was left in Maloyaroslavets. Sister Antonina continued as superior.

Sister Antonina came from a family of Pentecostals. She was a mystical person. The political aspect of the East-West dichotomy, the Catholic Church and the democratic West, the Soviets and Communists – none of this interested her. She was immersed in some kind of interior, spiritual, meditative life, a person not of this world. Thus I think that there were no special interactions with Father Leopold, and until Sister Stephania returned from exile the authorities did not touch anyone else.

By 1946 new people began coming to [St. Louis] Church: Irina Sofronitskaya, Margarita Sharova (actually, by 1946 she had already been arrested and exiled to Siberia), and some university students. In general, a new generation had appeared. State Security was of course well aware of all this. Two Sisters from the Abrikosova community returned to Maloyaroslavets: in 1946, Sister Stephania returned from exile in eastern Kazakhstan, then Sister Philomena arrived from Uralsk, in western Kazakhstan, having been released after the lengthy sentence she was given in the case against Anna Ivanovna in 1933. These two, with Sister Antonina, were the backbone of the community, to which were then added Nora Nikolayevna and Sister Teresa Kugel upon her return from the camps.

It must have seemed to State Security that this community was like a many-headed Hydra. They had chopped off several heads but they had grown back again. If they sent these women to the camps, they returned after twelve years in the camps, like Sister Philomena. They didn't go to the ends of the world to save themselves, but they came right back here, to the same place, to the very thick of it – Sister Teresa Kugel and Nora Nikolayevna and others. If I had been in the KGB's shoes, I too would have been alarmed. It was almost mystical how State Security hounded and hounded people, and people kept coming back to life, especially since now a new round of the "cold war" had begun.

In short order, a large group of parishioners of Saint Louis Church was arrested in 1948: Alisa Benediktovna and Alisa Albertovna Ott, Irina Sofronitskaya, and others, as well as all the Sisters in Maloyaroslavets. Vera Khmeleva, even though she no longer lived in the community and only rarely visited the Sisters, was under arrest for a short time and sentenced to exile, but soon thereafter released. The authorities eagerly used the statements of Irina Sofronitskaya who, of course, because of her youth, signed everything they put in front of her. Nora Nikolayevna told me that Irina signed everything, confessed to everything, even to saying that she prayed for Stalin's death! These were the main charges.[11] Vera Khmeleva gave, as I understand it, generalized ideological statements against the Vatican and the Dominican Order, explaining how dangerous they were for the Soviet regime, and the interrogators also used her statements against the Sisters from Maloyaroslavets. The interrogators were not able to extract the required statements from the mother and daughter – Alisa Benediktova and Alisa Albertovna Ott – or from the Sisters. They all received long sentences (ten or fifteen years in the camps), except of course those who had signed everything.[12] Nora Nikolayevna received a fifteen-year sentence. The only one who was more or less lucky was Sister Teresa Kugel. They ruled her insane and sent her for forced treatment, from which she was later released. By 1951 she had already settled in Vilnius.

Everyone else remained in the camps until 1956 when the mass release

[11] Editor's Note: An agent-informant was brought in from the camps to give the main charges against the Otts (mother and daughter) and others.

[12] Editor's Note: Except Alisa Albertovna Ott who went insane during the investigation and was sent for forced treatment at the special hospital run by the Ministry of Internal Affairs.

of convicts gradually got underway. By 1959 the Sisters were at liberty. No one had died. They had all survived and returned, and now something strange took place. As Margarita Sharova later told me,[13] the Sisters gathered and elected Valentina Kuznetsova to serve as superior of the community. I personally did not know Vera Gorodets, the earlier superior, but on the basis of Nora Nikolayevna's stories I can very vividly imagine her. She had two higher academic degrees, she was a socially active person, politically progressive, a philosopher, and a gifted poet. She was totally, as it were, of this earthly world, and her rallying cry had always been for "the reconstruction of the earthly world."[14]

Valentina Kuznetsova, on the other hand, as I have already mentioned, was a contemplative, a mystic, as though not of this world; in her thoughts she was far away, in the future world. The mundane had little interest for her. Apparently the Sisters liked this better, or perhaps during the time of Sister Stephania's absence they had become accustomed to Sister Antonina's ways. Thus it was decided that they would all live in Vilnius, under the direction of the new superior. Sister Stephania was not able to swallow this, to overcome her pride, so she remained in Moscow[15] with Nora Nikolayevna who, as a persecuted person, had received an apartment in Moscow since that is where she had been arrested.[16]

Nora Nikolayevna worked in the library; Vera Lvovna was already on pension. They lived very modestly; all their furniture had been retrieved from piles of discarded belongings. People began to gather at Nora Nikolayevna's – both well-known people such as the poet and translator Arseny Tarkovsky [1907-1989] and unknown but completely "other" people[17]; there was also some contact with Solzhenitsyn. Something new came into being. From 1951 the priests serving at Saint Louis Church were from Lithuania and

[13] Nora did not tell me of this.

[14] Thus we imagine active Catholicism.

[15] I know the Sisters were not in contact for a long time, but later things somehow mellowed and after Vera Lvovna's death the Sisters began to come from Vilnius to visit Nora and Nora began to go to Vilnius from time to time.

[16] Nora's brother lived in Moscow; he had helped her a lot, sending her parcels when she was in the camps and, one could say, saving her from starving to death. He was married and Nora dearly loved her niece, born in 1956.

[17] Translator's Note: "Other" here means "not in step with the Soviet system."

Latvia (and hand-picked by the KGB), and the Sisters had no contact with them or any support from them.

Then Father Georgy Friedman, a young priest, full of energy and enthusiasm, showed up at Nora Nikolayevna's and watched over her, spiritually and materially.[18] Of all the Sisters in Vilnius, he liked Sister Teresa Kugel the most; he had a spiritual friendship with her right up until her untimely death. As a rabbi's daughter, she most likely understood him best. Obviously, Nora Nikolayevna was also closer to him in spirit and blood, and he began to come to Moscow. Close friendships with Polish Dominicans date from approximately 1972, when Father Zigmunt Kozar, OP, and Father Alexander Hauk, OP, began to come to Moscow and stayed with Nora Nikolayevna.

Georgy Friedman was an active person. There were always young people around him and he became the center around which a new community began to take shape: his friend Gennady Goldshtein became a Third Order Dominican, Dominican Sisters came from Poland – for example, Sister Róża. Thus another Dominican center was formed in Leningrad. Georgy himself dreamed of becoming a priest, but the problem was that he was married, which would not be possible for a Latin Rite Catholic priest. With the help of Father Zigmunt, he was ordained a priest by an underground Greek Catholic bishop in October 1979.[19]

He was very close to Nora Nikolayevna. I also met Andrey Georgyevich Makhin[20] at Nora Nikolayevna's. He later also became a Catholic priest, but his fate played out much more tragically. Nora Nikolayevna loved him dearly and placed a lot of hope in him as a Catholic priest who would carry forward the idea of the Dominican Eastern Rite. He was accepted into the Dominican Order by Father Georgy Friedman and, in the opinion of both Nora Nikolayevna and Father Georgy, he was ready for ordination.

In 1980 they sent him to Poland with their recommendation; he was ordained [and became a Dominican priest], but upon his return he refused to serve under the Eastern Rite. As a person who knew very well all the

[18] He was a musician – a saxophonist – who at the age of thirty-two had fallen into depression, so-called "black melancholy," and was baptized into the Catholic Church on the advice of an artist friend who had become a Catholic in the camps. At the beginning of the 1970s he became acquainted with the Sisters in Vilnius and then with Nora. He was ordained in 1979.

[19] He and his wife took vows of celibacy and thereafter lived as brother and sister.

[20] A thirty-five-year old psychiatrist, unmarried, Orthodox; he met Nora Nikolayevna through her Polish acquaintances.

details and refinements of the Orthodox Rite, he was convinced that clandestine liturgies did not allow one to fulfill all the required conditions of an Orthodox service.[21] Nora Nikolayevna was somewhat upset by this turn of events but she hoped that all would nevertheless change. Then Father Andrey fell seriously ill.[22] When he was in the hospital Orthodox priests from the church he had at one time attended came to visit him and heard his confession. In confession, he told them everything, and they absolved his sins under the condition that he would not serve as a Catholic priest. After his release from the hospital he no longer served or received Holy Communion at the Catholic Church.[23] He died May 14, 1982, having made his final confession to an underground Orthodox priest.

Nora Nikolayevna attended Mass with Father Vladimir Nikiforov's community several times, but then Father Vladimir took fright and stopped inviting her because of his "ideas about conspiracy."[24] Later, when it became clear that under interrogation Father Vladimir had betrayed everyone and had been released as a result, Nora Nikolayevna had nothing but contempt for him.

Thus it turned out that Nora Nikolayevna witnessed the collapse of many illusions and hopes. Also around that time everyone was demoralized by the arrest of two Greek Catholic priests in connection with a letter to the Party Congress with a demand for the legalization of the Greek Catholic Church in Ukraine. One of them, Father Rafail, used to come to Leningrad and taught Father Georgy how to celebrate the liturgy [in the Greek Catholic rite]. He had been sent by Bishop Pavel Vasilik, who had ordained him. During Father Rafail's arrest the authorities found a photograph of Father Georgy and tried to extract statements from Father Rafail about Father Georgy. They even

---

[21] I would note that underground Orthodox priests conducted their secret liturgies and all the details perfectly well. For example, at Solovetsky [prison camp] they said secret liturgies where they even used the back of one of the convicts as the throne [altar].

[22] He had kidney cancer. He underwent surgery in December of that year but the cancer metastasized. For his mother, a Jew, the fact of his baptism into the Orthodox confession – and then his ordination as a Catholic priest – was like an act of betrayal. But his death changed her spiritual consciousness and she began to confess and receive Holy Communion from Father Georgy. She died a Christian.

[23] It seems that A.G.M. was not firmly convinced that the Faith is One. These doubts very likely explain both his contacts with Old Believers and his arguments with them about who had the better liturgy, Orthodox or Old Believers.

[24] In my opinion, the main reason was that Father Vladimir did not want to have two "centers" in his community of neophytes.

cried with hysteria "Uniatism has penetrated into Leningrad!" They forbade Father Georgy to appear anywhere or do anything. "Otherwise, you'll be behind bars with the rest of them." Thus from September 1981, on account of being blackmailed by the KGB, Father Georgy "sank into oblivion."

Others among the people close to Nora Nikolayevna included Julius Shreider, a member of the Party who was especially unable to extricate himself;[25] the young priest Father Andrey Kasyanenko, ordained as a Dominican priest in 1980 but forced to leave Vilnius on short notice in 1985; Father Evgeny Geinrikhs, ordained by Bishop Pavel in December 1981 and also a Dominican (he was a contemplative by nature and never interested in politics); and two lay sisters – Anya Godiner and Natalia Trauberg.

There was no leader among them, no one who really became her direct successor, but she did not expect a successor. She knew very well that when she died there would be no one to whom to entrust the idea that sustained the Abrikosova community; she knew she was the "last of the Mohicans." In this lay her tragedy – that with her death the Abrikosova community and its Eastern Rite spirituality disappeared.

Major changes were underway in the Catholic Church, renewal and liberalization. Nora Nikolayevna understood that the Church had to be opened up to the world and to engage in dialogue with the world, and she fully accepted the spirit of the Second Vatican Council. The Council, however, was not just about openness to the world. It adopted reforms: it introduced a relaxation of religious discipline; it simplified its liturgical worship and changed it from Latin to the more understandable vernacular languages, and so forth. As a result it turned out that the Church no longer needed people of such a resolute tempering as Nora Nikolayevna, and interest in the continuation of the tradition of the Eastern Rite collapsed, especially in Poland.

When speaking of the regulations and discipline in Anna Ivanovna's community, Nora Nikolayevna was convinced that any religious community ought to be built on strict discipline, obedience and repentance, on the need to sacrifice everything – for example, intensifying Lenten penances by adding kerosene to the soup to ruin its flavor, not changing one's undergarments for weeks, not showering, and so forth. Nora Nikolayevna considered

---

[25] Translator's Note: He became a Lay Dominican; taught at Moscow State University; died August 12, 1998.

the mandatory and unbounded sharing of one's soul with the Sister Superior a natural feature of religious life; nor did she object to being forbidden by the Superior to visit relatives for a week, a month, a year – or even to having to break off relations with family altogether.

She did not understand that Soviet society had constantly made and is making spiritual wreckages of people, "spiritual ruins," who are filling up the Catholic and Orthodox churches and the sects. One has to work very gently with such people, and the pastor who will be able to do the most will be one who has softened his own heart and who tries to understand the problems of these people, oppressed and broken by life.

Nora Nikolayevna was not able to understand this: here before her stands a young person, already a complete spiritual invalid – how could this be? She had been raised in a normal family, where both the father and mother were believers and, as a rule, decent people. For her it was simply preposterous that people who were living in decent conditions – who didn't sleep on plank boards, who had good nourishment three times a day, who didn't have to work the whole day in the freezing cold and fulfill an insuperable norm – that such people could be deeply unhappy, that they could risk their necks, end up in the insane asylum, fall sick, suffer and be depressed. She did not realize that "Solovetsky Camp" can be created in any home, and that the devil can create a camp anywhere.

One had to bring almost ideal people to visit her, and then she would lead them to the final luster. When a crushed and demoralized person showed up, she was flummoxed, she did not know where to begin. She had no sensitivity, no understanding of what and how much people today have to endure, since in her day people endured so much more. Nowadays one must be stricter toward oneself, but more merciful toward others. The Sisters never had this understanding, they did not want simply to be nice or affectionate toward anyone – and in this lay the secret of their loneliness.

This double standard – strictness toward oneself and leniency to neighbors – was missing in their community. In this, which was a failure to understand the mercy of Christ, they departed from the spirit of both Anna Abrikosova and Julia Danzas. Their attitude toward people would have it that out of a hundred sheep only one was suitable for the work of Christ and they needed to find that one, to teach her and make of her a worthy member of the Dominican community. The Sisters wanted to carry their unstained banner of spirituality to the end, regardless of sins of the flesh, greed, and so forth, but when the world is groaning and crying out with pain, to think at such a moment that Dominicans ought only to preserve the treasure of their spirituality – that is not completely right.

With her passing from this life into eternal life, Nora Nikolayevna was perhaps enrolled in that cohort of the early confessors and possibly received into heaven; but in these times we need the kind of ecumenical spiritual guides to whom people can come to ask for healing – pastors who can mourn with people and comfort them. People do not turn to pastors who are strict and stern, nor will they confess their sins to them. They do not find it enough just to thank God for the fact that at least they are not sitting in a cell or toiling somewhere in the camps. After all, the first commandment in Christianity is Love. Much more is demanded now.

Thus Nora Nikolayevna was somewhat sad in her final years. True, she rejoiced in the beginning of the downfall of the Communist system that was taking place before her eyes; she caught a whiff of the springtime of perestroika. She had a rather animated reaction to Gorbachev and said, "I can believe any beast, but as for him – I'll wait a bit" – but this sentiment was more like the kind of caution one might hear in the camps. In general she looked upon him with interest.

Anna Godiner (Sister Genevieve, Secular Tertiary)

I met Nora Nikolayevna Rubashova on Thursday of Easter Week in 1979. One of my acquaintances, a religious, invited me to go visit someone, saying "I will introduce you to an elderly nun and you will like each other." Thus it turned out. Nora Nikolayevna and I were friends for eight years, right up until her death, not once arguing – not a tiff ever arose between us, even though we saw a lot of each other. I would be at her place often, two or three times a week.

We spoke mostly about current events and rather rarely about the past. History was for Father Georgy Friedman and Ivan Lupandin, to whom she told a lot, specifically so that they would remember and they (especially Ivan Lupandin) would someday be able to tell about the Abrikosova community – and now that day has come!

I was always calm and comfortable at her place; it was obvious that in some respect we were similar. For me, her place and contact with her were, above all, contact with some part of a "former life," pre-Soviet life, when everything was more or less in its proper place, where there was a certain decorum and a normal view of things. It is beyond all comprehension how people of that generation, who lived through all the stages of the Stalin era, were able to remain normal in their daily life and in life in general, and to maintain the uniqueness and the spiritual strength of their personality.

Here are some fragmentary recollections and feelings about those "eight years of happiness," which is what I call that time until her death. It would be impossible to present them in any order.

First of all, Nora Nikolayevna was a person of deep inner stillness. Although her personality was obviously rather explosive, how well she knew how to control it!

It always astounded me how much she spoke of the fact that one must "beware of people." For this reason she rarely gathered many people in her place; she would think up "conspiratorial" nicknames on the telephone; she tried not to give her name when calling on the phone – she would just say "It is I" – and she wasn't the only one who took such precautions in those days. But this was in combination with the greatest readiness to face whatever may come. She once outright said to me that she was ready and waiting, should they come again to arrest her. I was astonished to think that at her age someone would arrest her – but she knew better than I the kind of government we were dealing with. But really, it would have been impossible that they would arrest her. God knows…

The whole time of the camps was like the background of her life. Once she told me that she just had to lie down at night and close her eyes and she would begin to dream of her life from that time. During the Andropov period, when the government began persecutions of certain believers, Nora Nikolayevna forbade anyone from speaking in her room about anything except ordinary, superficial things. Conversations about what was important – not just information, but spiritual things as well – now had to be conducted either in the bathroom with the doors closed and water running or written on a roll of toilet paper. For me this was normal, even though I thought it unlikely that this room would have been "bugged."

In addition to the fact that she fed those who had material difficulties, she also simply loved to share dinner with someone. On those days when

I was planning to go to see her, she would often call and ask what time I would be arriving and whether we would be having dinner together. In the final years, when from time to time I would prepare her something to eat under her direction, her words would sometimes astound me, as when I mechanically poured the prior day's water from the teapot to fill it with fresh water: "How much clean water is wasted – I always regret that."

She had an undeserved pity for her apartment-mate, a Communist who was crippled and embittered by the camps and who had at times stricken her and even her guests. She had a remarkable respect for him, which was especially evident in the communal kitchen where everything of his was considered respectfully untouchable.

When Nora Nikolayevna was telling me some things from the rather drastic asceticism of the life of the Sisters of the community – for example, how they would add a drop of kerosene to the cabbage soup during Lent to ruin its taste – I was interiorly repulsed. Obviously she noticed, smiled with embarrassment and grew silent, and then did not return again to this conversation. In her room, diagonally from the table, in a corner, stood a small table and there (I don't remember in what) was kept the Blessed Sacrament. In her final years she often said "I am alone a lot, and I simply sit and timidly talk with God." (She always used precisely this word, "timidly.")

I was also amazed by how many things in life she called "good." For any service at all she would say "he did me a good deed," or about food "good fish," or she would request, "buy me something good at the market."

It was remarkable that through all the searches she was able to carry and save her rosary, which had beautiful, brown, elongated beads, like coffee beans. I believe she left it to the Dominican Sisters in Poland.

Elena Lupandina

Interview conducted by Margarita Kurganskaya and transcribed by Olga Mironova

I met Nora Nikolayevna on February 20, 1980. It was not long before the attempted assassination of Pope John Paul II [May 13, 1981]. I remember very well arriving at her place on the day of the assassination attempt. She was living in a communal apartment, and once inside the door one stepped into a long corridor. Usually she would lead me right away into her room, but on this day she suddenly said to me, "Lenochka, what a misfortune!" I sensed that she was not feeling well; she leaned against the wall and said, "There was an assassination attempt on the Pope."

Ivan Vladimirovich [Lupandin] had brought me to visit Nora Nikolayevna, but for my part, visits to Nora Nikolayevna were not entirely for religious motives. (Vanya and I had become acquainted in 1978; he proposed to me, then we later split up, and when I began to try to renew relations, Vanya brought me to Nora Nikolayevna.) She needed help with household chores and I was happy to serve her in some way. I understood that she lived alone, that she had suffered much in her life, and that she could teach me a lot.

Nora Nikolayevna had a rather difficult neighbor who, like she, had been in the camps and by nature was extremely hard to get along with; he would even get into fights with her guests. I realized that one simply needed to understand him, to help him somehow in his daily life, since he was a lonely man. I washed the corridor and common areas and it seems that I reconciled him a bit with Nora Nikolayevna and with life.

In general, Nora Nikolayevna tried not to have large gatherings of people. The times were still rather dangerous for such "informal religious" gatherings, and thus I knew only a small number of the people who visited her.

I remember Julius Shreider and Father Alexander Khmelnitsky, and how Nora and I discussed the idea of Alexander's ordination. Of course I also remember Father Georgy Friedman, to whom I began to go to confession. Then there was Father Andrey Kasyanenko, but we saw each other rarely. I remember Father Evgeny Geinrikhs – I attended his ordination and he married Ivan and me. There was also a very young girl who began to visit Nora Nikolayevna – Tanya Konovalova. (I remember her very well because she became, as it were, my successor; she helped Nora with the housework, did her shopping and supported her daily life.) Irina Sofronitskaya, Tamara Kazavchinskaya and Natalia Trauberg also visited, but I did not see them much.

Generally, the guests' family names were not used – that was not accepted. Instead they used silly nicknames. For example, they called Julius Shreider "Julienka," a girl's name, which I found amusing. I remember Gennady Faybusovich. I saw him a couple times. He was a very colorful person and one couldn't help remembering him, especially some of his quips. Vladimir Likhterman often visited Nora; she fed him and in general supported him materially. Vera Alekseyevna and her son Alyosha often came from Malakhovka.[26]

Sergey Averintsev came to visit, but Nora always arranged things so that I would not be there when he came. The poet Arseny Tarkovsky also visited. Then there was Anya Godiner, but I seldom saw her. Of course, the person I met most often at Nora's was Vanya – he was her favorite person. The circle of Nora's contacts was simultaneously large and small. Later Alexey Yudin began to visit her, but our paths almost never crossed. Then in 1984 my son was born and thereafter I was very seldom at Nora's.[27]

Nora was in contact with her brother, Alexander Rubashov, and his wife, Valentina. She dearly loved her brother's daughter, Veronica, who then in her turn had two sons, Lenya and Volodya. I remember this because Nora and I went to Children's World to buy a little toy for the little one when he was about three years old. It was already very hard for Nora to walk and the toy, in my opinion, was insanely expensive.[28]

Sometimes a priest came from Poland to visit her; I later learned that this was Father Alexander Hauk-Ligowski. She always spoke very highly of him. She said he was so gentle that it was as though she could not sense his presence; he, knowing he was visiting an elderly person, ensured he caused her no inconvenience.

Nora lived not far from the University stop on the metro. The "Fish" store was in the same building. She was in Apartment 122, on the third floor, and the entry was from the courtyard. Nora said it was not accidental that she lived near this store, because God had so arranged things that she

---

[26] Nora did not like to speak of this – Vera Alekseyevna was the daughter of one of the Sisters who had gotten married when the community was broken up. For Nora, this was a deviation, a weakness, on the part of that Sister.

[27] Translator's Note: Gennady Faybusovich (b. 1928) writes under the pseudonym Boris Khazanov; he emigrated from Russia in 1982 and now lives in Munich. Sergey Averintsev (1937-2004) was an expert on ancient cultures and religions, a professor at Moscow State University and University of Vienna. Arseny Tarkovsky (1907-1989) was a prominent poet and translator. Alexey Yudin (b. 1963) is on the faculty at the Center for the Study of Religion, Russian State University of the Humanities.

[28] Alexander Nikolayevich was terribly afraid that Vanya would write something about Nora after her death. He was a timid person and he feared that this would somehow harm him. These fears lived for a long time in this family, but I think the family has very happy memories of Nora. They now live in America. Alexander died in Brooklyn [in the late 1990s].

would thus be able to see when goods that were in short supply were delivered and she would be able to buy them. It was not always possible to buy what one needed in those difficult times, and to make life easier for those of us who helped her, she would let us know when it was a good time to go to the store.

Her room was rectangular in shape, almost square. Near the entry was a little green sofa. To the left, in a corner was a tabernacle, and whoever entered, without fail, genuflected before it. A little lamp always burned before the tabernacle – not an oil lamp, but a modern, electric lamp, very beautifully made. To the left, on the same wall, hung an image of the Sacred Heart of Jesus. I remember it well because it was so different from Orthodox icons. Above this little altar hung a reproduction of Raphael's Sistine Madonna. Actually, it wasn't even a reproduction. It was a very plain black and white photograph, under glass. It was held together with band-aids on the sides.

In the corner, on the left side, stood an old and very beautiful glass cupboard with a single door. Here Nora kept the dishes that she brought out only on special occasions. In the middle of the room stood a table, and over it hung a lamp with a polyhedron lampshade. On its sides had been cut out a little branch and a bunch of grapes. The inside was covered with a dark blue fabric that had faded and was now covered with dust. Although this lamp had no bulb, its lampshade held a special value for Nora. The cut-out work had been done by a man who had spent time in the camps and died in a home for the disabled. For Nora it was a living reminder of this man, and her attitude toward this lamp had something of reverence about it, as though it was a relic. One just has to understand that mystical life where everything acquires a secondary significance.

In general, although all the furniture had been retrieved from junk piles, it was nonetheless fine. Toward the very end of her life we acquired a new bed for her, which we placed near the wall in front of the cupboard. Somehow I happened to arrive at her apartment when a hypertonic crisis had set in and I had to call the ambulance. It later became clear that her blood pressure was very high. I remember her lying there on that bed. They gave her an injection, which was rather painful, but she somehow endured it all very calmly and staunchly. Even the doctor from the ambulance was charmed by her.

There was one other interesting thing in her room, something that nowadays you will not see anywhere – an étagère. It stood to the right of the window by the wall. I don't remember what was lying on it – some little things that were precious to her, photographs, letters, books. She was translating something from the French from a booklet that was lying there. It was the table, however, that occupied the central place in the room. Mass was celebrated on this table; and we all gathered around it to discuss all manner of significant things. I also remember her rosary. I do not remember where she kept it, but I do remember how she would kiss it. I remember her dress, which she wore for her most solemn occasions. It was a black sleeveless dress; on the left side she wore the Dominican black and white cross.

Nora listened to daily Mass on Vatican Radio. She took Holy Communion from the tabernacle, which at that time I did not fully understand. At first Father Mark Smirnov celebrated Mass and heard confession at Nora's – later, it was Father Georgy Friedman. We gathered around the table, which was covered with a special tablecloth, Father Georgy stood up, handsomely and properly vested, and Mass began. We stood around the table, Father Georgy stood facing the small little altar and said Mass. We knelt around the table. In general, everything was rather simple; there was nothing particularly solemn. Strange as it may seem, this was exactly what won us over. We were people who had converted from atheism and at Mass there came over us a feeling that we, who were now believers, who were rejecting our customary way of life, could adapt to this spiritual world.

This Mass gave me the sense that I was a normal person. I needed to be self-affirmed because there was a feeling that we were in a spiritual vacuum. It was barely possible to find souls with whom one could speak of God. Therefore when you finally found such people it was very important simply to feel that you were in the midst of such people. Others might think them bad people, but when you found yourself in this setting, you realized that they were ordinary people, perhaps with their own weaknesses, but nonetheless they believed in God and could speak of Him. Furthermore, no one here was going to think that something was not going right in your life and therefore you "needed this religion."

At Nora's that part of the soul that could be called mystical found an outlet. Everything at these Masses was simple, and the people who attended were mature, no longer young: Nora, Georgy Friedman, Julius Shreider. It was obvious that these people were not zealots. Nora prayed a lot for specific people she knew. Many people turned to her with their problems, and she took the problems of others, as though completely her own, and tried to bring them to Mass. Her telephone was rarely silent. She was both an information center and a center of support for all.

Nora dearly loved Pope John Paul II and prayed regularly for him, especially after the attempt on his life in May 1981. It was not by chance that she had an image of the Sacred Heart of Jesus – the heart was entwined with thorns. In this sense she was a solid and complete person. She never preached in a spirit of catechesis; she definitely had this personal participation, this prayer of the heart. I never encountered another person after her who could accept another as closely as she did.[29] Nora was a very astute person, in the sense that she understood and accepted people's sinfulness. I always felt that she read me like an open book.[30]

Nora taught me how to pray. She was the first person who spoke to me about prayer. She explained the meaning of prayers, so that they weren't just a repetition of certain words learned by heart, like poetry. She said very interesting things – for example, "you, Lena, are helping me, and the Dominican community will always pray for you after your death." She said that this was in the Dominican tradition, that Dominicans prayed for their benefactors, for those who had helped them, after their death – not at the death of those whom they had helped, but after the deaths of those who had helped them.[31] I do not know, perhaps in this sense she was more astute than I, and a person really has more need of prayer after his death.

Nora's attitude toward food came from her years in the camps, and it wasn't that she was worried about the tiniest crumb, but there was some kind of ritual with the food. Perhaps this belongs under the category of her weaknesses; I know that some in fact saw this as a weakness. I too saw it as a weakness, but not the kind of weakness that was the expression of a fall, but a comprehensible weakness that I understood. It evoked in me something

[29] True, there was an instance when this bothered me a bit. When I had trouble with labor during Seryozha's birth, I took it as grounds for personal resentment. It seemed to me that Nora should have been able to intercede successfully on my behalf, that things should have gone well, not poorly. It seemed to me that she was able to take my sins upon herself.

[30] Not everyone had the sense that Nora was extremely wise, although I certainly did. It seemed that when she looked at me it was not to see my deficiencies, but in terms of being drawn toward either sin or holiness.

[31] I remember that I was terribly offended. I needed prayers now, not after my death!

more like respect, because it made it clear that the hunger she had endured was real, genuine.

I want to emphasize once again that Nora was not a political person. She tried to avoid conversations about politics. What I liked most about this was the proposition that a person ought to be able to preserve his faith under any regime, and that one should disregard, not give any attention to the regime itself, its qualities, and peculiarities – provided that this regime did not prevent one from being a believer. In general, there was some danger associated with visiting Nora, and although that now seems hypothetical, back then everything was seen as completely real. You felt that you were not playing games, and you tried to erase certain information and impressions from your memory so that there would be no extra information.

This did not concern me, but it concerned Nora and it was reflected in the form of great fears and some very specific things. For example – surveillance. There definitely was surveillance that even I observed. Once I arrived at Nora's and found in the hallway two young men who, when they saw me, made it look as though they were just there smoking and eating, but there was something feigned about their behavior because they appeared to be rather educated. They were approximately twenty-five years old, no older. There was someone visiting Nora at that moment, and I think they were tailing him.

Then there was the very well-known story of the nail. Someone had come at three in the morning and pounded a nail in the wall in the stairwell. Nora heard the pounding during the night and in the morning saw the nail in the stairwell. The wall of her room was right against the stairwell. I think it was just an ordinary nail, but that's not the point. This was simply a means of putting psychological pressure on a person, knowing full well that these people were already quite frightened. Nora lived in a state of fear, but it was a controlled fear; it did not cross over into anything like a psychosis. She simply took measures to protect herself from danger.

I will say, however, that important conversations took place only in the bathroom with the water running and that guests tried not to name names. Nora was very anxious for Julius Shreider when they kicked him out of the Party, worrying about how his future would play out. I remember conversations about Father Alexander Khmelnitsky. Nora seemed to feel the depth of his yearning for the priesthood. These conversations, however, were more intellectual than spiritual. Nora told me nothing about the camps or about her periods of exile. She avoided these conversations, except she did tell me a little about the community in Maloyaroslavets.

Despite the fact that after her conversion to Catholicism Nora had broken with those around her, she nevertheless remained a Jew to a great extent. For example, she received both Sergey Averintsev and Boris Khazanov (who later emigrated). With respect to Khazanov, she always emphasized that if Khazanov, who was the more talented, had not been a Jew, he would have gone much further than Averintsev. (I saw Khazanov several times and I did not have the same impression.) As another example, I was studying in the Psychology Department at Moscow State University, and Nora said that MSU did not accept Jews. I myself was studying there and there were very many Jews studying with me and teaching, but Nora did not want to hear this. She was convinced that MSU discriminated against Jews.

She did not tell me much about Mother Catherine Abrikosova, but from her words I realized that obedience in Mother Catherine's community was rather strict. When Nora Nikolayevna and Vera Lvovna began to live together, Vera Lvovna was the superior in their small, two-person community. Nora believed that Vera Lvovna's demands of her were rather harsh. For example, she demanded that Nora not maintain relations with her brother. Nora was not able to give herself a rational explanation for such a requirement and it bothered her. She did not accept it because she did not at all understand why it was necessary, but her obedience in this matter was unconditional. She fulfilled the demand of her superior, and relations with her brother were renewed only after Vera Lvovna's death.

When I became acquainted with Nora, it had already become difficult for her to go out anywhere. Shortness of breath plagued her. It was hard for her to move, and we would have to call for a taxi. I don't remember her ever going to Saint Louis Church, nor do I remember her going out to walk about. She came to visit us a couple times after the birth of our daughter. She was godmother to our daughter, and she also dearly loved our son. Her last photograph was taken a few days before her death – Georgy Friedman, Seryozha and Nora. She is smiling, with her hand extended toward Seryozha.

In general, Nora died a happy death because she was on her feet until the very last day. She had always prayed for this, because she was afraid that in her final days she might become paralyzed and be a burden to those around her. She was afraid of dying somewhere other than in her own surroundings, in a strange place, a fear that had worn on her both mentally and physically from the time of her release.

Father Georgy Christopher Friedman, OP

In the autumn of 1974 God led me to the Dominican Sisters of the Eastern Rite who were living in Vilnius. At the initiative of, and with the blessing of, Father Algirdas Motsius, a heroic priest who had served two eight-year prison terms for the sake of Christ, I was seeking a Greek Catholic bishop who could ordain me to the priesthood. In those times, this was a very difficult matter because the Greek Catholic Church in the Soviet Union was deep in the underground. First one needed to find the Greek Catholic priest, who, I was told, was living in Vilnius. I was lucky. After several attempts to learn his address from local priests, I fell on the right track and found him in a little wooden house on the outskirts of Vilnius.

It was Father Vladimir Prokopiv, a priest who suffered much in his lifetime. During the occupation the Fascists had thrown him in a pit, from which he was rescued by a miracle. Then our partisans had put a noose around his neck and were ready to hang him – but his execution was commuted. He sat for a long time in Soviet prisons, and even after this the KGB would not leave him in peace. I arrived at his place just as he was going to visit the Dominican Sisters. When he learned I was a Jew by nationality, he thought it would be interesting for me to meet the Sisters, some of whom were also Jews by heritage, and so he invited me to go with him.

They were living in a small apartment in a Khrushchev-era building on Dzuku Street. We found Mother Antonina and Sisters Teresa and Philomena at home. I remember how the atmosphere of quiet and peace in their quarters delighted me. On the walls hung large images of Saint Dominic and Saint Catherine of Siena. In the tiniest little chapel they had made an altar out of a dresser, and on the altar stood a crucifix. A lamp flickered in a beautiful vessel to show that the Blessed Sacrament was reserved there.

Mother Antonina was petite, very venerable, with a sweet, child-like smile, dressed in a black outfit. She had some time ago suffered an injury to her leg and now walked with a severe limp. She spoke quietly, with few words, but very weightily. She was then approximately eighty years old.

Sister Philomena was a lean, elderly woman, an eloquent witness to the Faith who spoke Russian beautifully, which was rare in Lithuania. She was then approximately seventy-five years old. Sister Teresa, sixty-two years old, was tall, stocky, and plain. Her face reflected a selfless faith. She was then still working as a nurse at the hospital.

The Sisters received me with such goodness and sympathy that despite my innate shyness, I immediately felt myself at home. I do not recall what we spoke about at that first meeting. Perhaps they asked me about how I had come to seek God. Mother Antonina told me that in a year Dominicans were coming from Poland and that I would be able to enter the Third Order of Saint Dominic and that possibly they would be able to find me a Greek Catholic bishop.

Mother Antonina and I corresponded for a full year. I still have her deeply spiritual letters.[32] A year later, I visited them on Christmas Eve and met three Fathers from Poland: Michael Mroczkowski, OP, the Dominican provincial; Alexander Hauk-Ligowski, OP; and Zigmunt Kozar, OP. I made three-year vows in the presence of Father Michael. The Fathers promised to send me theological literature in Polish for my preparation for the priesthood.

At that time I also met Sister Catherine Rubashova, who had come from Moscow to visit the Sisters. She was then sixty-six years old. Petite and plump, she had a fine intellect and a strong and resolute character. Since there were no male Dominicans in Russia at that time, Father Alexander attached me to her as the directress of my spiritual formation. "She has the nature of a leader," said Father Alexander, "and she is a holy person." I was to go see her in Moscow every month for several days. I also visited the Sisters in Vilnius every month.

All the Sisters knew Polish [by that time]. Mother Antonina also knew French and English; Sister Catherine knew French and German. They were both engaged in translations of spiritual texts. The Fathers sent the Sisters a beautiful Liturgy of the Hours in Church Slavonic and they unfailingly prayed morning, evening and night prayer. In addition they prayed the rosary of the Mother of God and the Way of the Cross. The Sisters always treated the Most Holy Father with great reverence and love, and they never allowed the criticism of any priests in their home. After my ordination in

---

[32] Four of these letters are presented in the following section of this book.

1979 I had the honor of celebrating Mass in their home every month. All the Sisters were confessors of the Faith, having spent no less than thirty years in prisons and the camps. Their path had begun back in the first years of the Soviet regime under the guidance of an unusual, richly gifted woman, Mother Catherine Abrikosova.

What I will write about the Sisters will, unfortunately, be rather fragmentary because in Soviet times the Sisters, understandably, did not allow me to take notes of their stories. Some of what I recall may not be completely accurate.

This is how it all began.

The married couple, Vladimir Vladimirovich and Anna Ivanovna Abrikosov, came from a wealthy and cultured merchant milieu. Anna Ivanovna studied at Cambridge and, as the Sisters told me, until the end of her life she had a slight English accent. They both belonged to the young fashionable set, the "White Linings."[33] By tradition they were both Orthodox, but barely religious. Vladimir Vladimirovich used only the very smallest and briefest prayerbook.

Once during their travels in Europe, the couple was walking in the evening at the seaside at sunset, watching people strolling along. Suddenly – and simultaneously – they saw that these were not living people walking along, but dressed up skeletons. "What is this?" they asked each other. The both saw the skeletons. The vision quickly dissolved and once again there were just ordinary people sauntering along, but the vision left a deep trace in their souls and, of course, it caused them to become more religious.

Later, they visited the Church of Saint Dominic in Siena where the head of Saint Catherine of Siena is preserved in a reliquary upon the altar. In the presence of this relic, their souls underwent a profound conversion and they decided to join the Catholic Church and take religious vows. In an audience with Pope Pius X in Rome, Vladimir asked his blessing to become a Latin Rite priest. The Pope blessed him, but with the condition that he become an Eastern Rite priest. "This will be more useful for Russia," said the Pope. Later, back in Russia, both spouses took religious vows for Dominican service, and

[33] Translator's note: This nickname originates from the pre-revolutionary era, referring to students from wealthy, aristocratic families who were considered unfriendly to revolutionary and democratic ideals. It is based on school uniforms with a white lining typically worn by wealthy students, in which the students of lower classes could not afford to dress themselves.

in 1917 in Petrograd, in the Malta chapel, Vladimir was ordained an Eastern Rite priest by Metropolitan Andrey Sheptytsky.

A women's Dominican convent was soon formed in their Moscow quarters with Mother Catherine at its head and Father Vladimir as their chaplain. In addition to the three usual religious vows, the Sisters took a fourth vow: to suffer for the salvation of Russia. God heard their desire, and soon they were to suffer much, for many years.

The discipline in the convent was strict. The Sisters slept on the floor in a large room on little mats. Some placed books under their heads instead of pillows. Upon rising, they had to dress, put away the mats, wash and take their places in the chapel within five minutes for Matins, and then Father Vladimir would celebrate Mass. There was absolute silence before Matins and after Vespers. They also rose during the night for prayer. The Sisters were allowed to use the "discipline."

Mother Catherine and some of the Sisters were engaged in translating. They translated and published Lacordaire's Life of Saint Dominic and they composed numerous original spiritual writings that all later ended up in the basements of the NKVD. The only composition of Mother Catherine that survived intact is "The Seven Words of Christ on the Cross." It was not an exact copy that was preserved, but what we have gives us an idea of the very lofty spirituality of the author. I would even be so bold as to say that the level of this work is no less than the writings of Saint Teresa of Avila. Especially in "The Third Word" one can see the personal, burning pain of voluntary suffering borne by Mother Catherine – the renunciation of, and then even the separation from, her ardently loved spouse. This work became, as it were, the spiritual-sacrificial program for the Sisters' life in her community.

Father Vladimir was arrested and sentenced to be shot, but the sentence was commuted to expulsion from the country. The Chekists suggested to him that he bring his wife, but Mother Catherine could not leave her Sisters behind and she chose instead the path of sufferings. She was very worried about Father Vladimir and when Julia Danzas was emigrating, she asked her to look after him. This request was not meant to be realized.

The Chekists began their surveillance of the convent by making a spy hole in the ceiling, but this did not bother the Sisters at all. Then when the Chekists came for them and carried out a lengthy search in the apartment, one of the Sisters even lay down under the table and calmly fell asleep. After their sentencing, the Sisters were sent in heated freight cars to the east. Along the way they merrily sang spiritual songs and hymns.

Once the convoy escorts brought them to some kind of camp sector toward nightfall. The convicts were assigned to a barrack where they saw people sleeping on the stairway. The Sisters thought that the barrack must be overcrowded, but when they entered they saw to their surprise that it was completely empty. Mother Catherine had not had time to lie down on the plank bed when huge bedbugs rained down from above. The Sisters tried to brush them off her but she said, "Leave them alone, let them eat me."

In one of the prisons, they put Mother Catherine in a cell with criminals in an attempt to break her spirit, but she made such an impression on these thieves and prostitutes that they were filled with great respect toward her. Once the guards brought a woman with syphilis into the cell, where there wasn't a free spot on the plank beds. Mother Catherine placed the woman next to herself. The convicts said, "What are you doing, mother? You'll get an infection!" She calmly answered, "And so? If I do, I'll get it treated."

Even the Chekists treated her with great respect. "Such an intelligent woman," they said to her, "ought to collaborate with us." When they put her in solitary, there were always flowers in her cell…

Strict in the fulfillment of religious discipline, Mother Catherine always showed kindness toward those who had fallen. Once it became evident that one of the women who was close to the Sisters, frightened by the Chekists, had become an informant. Out of compassion for this unhappy woman Mother Catherine doubled her tender attention to her.

When Mother Catherine and the Sisters were in Siberia, in one of the small villages, one of the residents, a father of small children, had suddenly lost his wife to illness. Out of compassion for him, one of the very exemplary Sisters who was there in exile began to visit him to help with the housekeeping. It turned out bad: she broke her vows and married the man. When she tried to attend Mass, Father Alexey Zerchaninov, who was also exiled in Siberia, ranted and raved at the defector. Mother Catherine went up to the unhappy woman and tenderly embraced her.[34]

This poor woman was unlucky. She gave birth to a child who died soon

[34] Editor's Note: This could only have happened after Mother Catherine's early release from prison after her surgery in 1932 because when she was in Siberia she was in prison and could not have approached and embraced this unfortunate woman.

thereafter, and hungry dogs dug up his little grave and tore apart his little corpse. Some of the Sisters saw this as God's punishment. The man whom this woman married also died tragically – he fell under a car. Now alone, she asked to be once again accepted into the religious community, but the higher authorities of the Church would not permit it. Mother Catherine showed kindness toward her to the end.

I would like to share with you a poem by Father Sergey Soloviev dedicated to Mother Catherine.

To Anna Ivanovna Abrikosova

That moment, when you suddenly appeared before me
Within the precincts of Lefortovo,
Like an unearthly apparition –
That moment could not have been by chance.

Tall, like a white swan,
Cold, like mountain snow,
Your image imprinted itself
Upon my memory forever.

Amidst the fearsome prison buildings,
You glided serenely along;
Undistressed amidst sufferings,
Supernaturally bright.

In modest monastic garb,
You already foresaw the Cross,
The years in chains, in a darkened cell –
The rewards of the Brides of Christ!

And like that other Maiden of Siena,
You calmly looked upon the iron bars and walls,
As though surveying
Lovely flowers in Paradise.

In prison, you sat among criminals,

Murders and thieves – like He
Who, crucified by the Jews,
Gives Himself to us as food.

Mount of Love, Mount of the crucifixion –
This was your mountain. In that brief moment
A drop of grace
Fell into my dried up spring.

At the Irtysh River they put the Sisters on a steamer going downstream (i.e., north to its confluence with the Ob, and on to the Arctic Ocean). Sometimes they were allowed to go onshore under guard. This was a great delight for them. On the shore these Sisters, who were still quite young, found a beautiful little caterpillar and brought it onto the steamer. It needed to be fed and the Sisters asked the convoy guards to pick leaves for it on the shore. The guards wondered, "What kind of a kindergarten class are we transporting?"

Along the way the Sisters were discharged in pairs to live out their sentences in small villages along the river. The very young and very beautiful Sister Philomena, by education a pianist from the conservatory, was taken right up to the Arctic Ocean and was to have gone still further, to some island, but the merciful captain of the cutter saved her from this fate. "I won't take this little snot any further – she'll die up there."

Now I will try to tell what little I have preserved in my memory from the stories of the individual Sisters about themselves.

Mother Antonina [Valentina Kuznetsova], by nationality a Karelian, was born into a Baptist family and came to the Church by way of a complicated path. She left the Baptists and converted to a group of Pentecostals. When they spoke in tongues she felt her soul tremendously uplifted. She had a strong singing voice and she sang as she had never been able to sing before, but she was disturbed by what was going on around her. The senselessness of words and sounds – for example, "tu-tu, tu-tu!" – led her to believe that, in a psychological sense, not everything here was quite right. She then became a member of the Salvation Army where she reached the rank of corporal. She humorously told me of her experience as a soapbox preacher. Below the soapbox stood a bench where those who felt called to God by the preaching were to come and sit. Our preacher labored long, but in vain – no one came.

She was about to cry from disappointment when suddenly someone out of pity came up to her and sat on the bench…

Once she agreed to stand watch at the bedside of a dying person who was from among the circle of friends of the Abrikosov family. Having noticed her, Mother Catherine said to the Sisters: "Pray for Valya. She has a good heart and she ought to be with us." Their prayers were heard: Valentina Vasilyevna became a Catholic and entered the community of Dominican Sisters under the name Sister Antonina.

Sister Catherine of Siena [Nora Rubashova] was born into a Jewish family. She was baptized by Father Sergey Soloviev; she served as his sacristan at the Cathedral of the Immaculate Conception on Malaya Gruzinskaya Street. To her parents' grief, she entered the community of Dominican Sisters. Her father soon came to terms with this and when she would come home with some of the Sisters, he would jokingly say, "Here come my in-laws!" She was arrested the same day as Father Sergey.

Father Sergey Soloviev was a talented poet, translator, university professor, a person of refined spirituality. He was subjected to methods of interrogation by the NKVD that his psyche could not endure and he fell ill. For example, Sister Catherine told me, the Chekists deceived him, saying that Bishop Neveu had been shot. "What!!" he shuddered. The Chekists drilled it into him, "It was you who betrayed him!"[35] His soul could not bear it. The obsessive thought constantly tormented him: "I am a traitor, I am a traitor!"[36] Sister Catherine wrote wonderful memoirs about Father Sergey.[37]

Sister Catherine behaved audaciously at her interrogations and told the investigators exactly what she thought of them. Thus they gave her the longest prison terms. Once when she was in prison she found out that Mother Stephania, who was in a different cell, had fallen seriously ill. She demanded that the prison administration transfer her to the sick woman's

---

[35] Editor's Note: Judging by the materials in the investigation case file, the Chekists did not say anything to Father Sergey about the execution of Bishop Neveu. To the contrary, in his letter of repudiation, Father Sergey refused any future contact with Bishop Neveu as a representative of the Vatican.

[36] Editor's Note: The feeling of guilt tormenting Father Sergey was not groundless: In the interrogations he had named the names of all the members of his community, including the names of Sisters whose religious vows he had secretly accepted.

[37] These memoirs were published under the name of Sister Mary in *The Life and Artistic Evolution of Vladimir Soloviev* (Brussels, 1977), pp. 13-15. [Translator's Note: *Vladimir* Soloviev was Father Sergey's uncle.]

cell so that she could care for her. When she was refused, she declared a hunger strike and ... she won – which was absolutely unheard of during that harsh time… I still have her deeply spiritual letters.[38]

The Lay Dominican Sister Josafata Nowicka wrote that Sister Catherine "endured imprisonment more easily than the others. This was because of the purity of her soul and her deep faith. She dearly loved people and always tried to be useful to them."[39] As a true Dominican, she spiritually enlightened her poorly educated fellow prisoners. These catechetical efforts occasioned a few amusing moments as, for example, when one of her simple listeners, upon hearing that the Virgin Mary was a daughter of the Israelite people, became terribly upset and, running about the camp, shouted, "Have you heard what Pani Rubashova said? That the mother of God is a Jew!"

Sister Catherine, according to Nowicka's memoirs, "quickly found herself something to do in prison; she helped those around her. Even many of the prison supervisors treated her very affectionately."[40] In a concentration camp somewhere up north, they assigned her to clean up the garbage around the edge of the camp. Huge black crows swept down, and just being with these wise birds brought her true joy.

During exile she managed to receive the Blessed Sacrament from an exiled priest. Wanting to bring this joy to Mother Stephania, who was then living in exile very far from her [in Semipalatinsk, Kazakhstan], she set off on a wagon going out that way with men she did not know. They had to spend the night in the field. Lying in the straw with the Blessed Sacrament upon her breast, she looked at the starry sky with delight and felt herself in complete safety among these coarse men.

Between two prison terms Sisters Catherine and Teresa found themselves during the war in occupied territory. Perhaps because they were fair-haired and with facial features that were not typical for Jewish women, they avoided persecution at the hands of the Nazis. Sister Teresa worked as a nurse in a German hospital, where Russian wounded were also being cared for. She became acquainted with two Catholic priests – one of whom, an officer, was a military chaplain, and the other, a soldier, served as a male nurse. When these priests found out that Catherine and Teresa were Dominican Sisters

[38] One of them is included in the following section.

[39] Nowicka, *op cit.*, p. 38.

[40] Ibid.

and that they were Jewish, they wanted to celebrate Christmas with them. What a strange company: an officer and soldier in Fascist uniforms and two Jewish women. The chaplain solemnly then said concerning this event: "A Catholic is at home everywhere." In truth, this was a corner of paradise in an ocean of evil!

After her release from the camps under Khrushchev Sister Catherine made it back to Moscow on foot from eastern Kazakhstan. Along the way she had to spend a night in the home of some "son of the steppes." During the night she discovered something hairy next to her. In her innocence in such matters, it would not even have come into her mind that this was the head of the house! She thought, "it must be some kind of animal." "Get away!" she shouted loudly. Frightened that his wife might have heard this scream, this "son of the steppes," as such it was – quickly withdrew.

According to the rules of the community the Sisters were not allowed to look at themselves in the mirror, which was the cause of an amusing incident. After her release, Sister Catherine went to the store to buy herself some clothing. The clerk suggested she go behind a curtain to try it on – there was no one else behind the curtain. But when Sister went behind the curtain, she saw some old lady there. She said to the woman, "Oy! Excuse me, I thought there was no one here...." Only then did she realize that it was her own reflection in the mirror.

In Moscow Sister Catherine and Mother Stephania were allotted a small room in a communal apartment on Prospect Vernadskovo. I never met Mother Stephania, who died in 1974, at the age of eighty-one years. Before entering the Order she had been an actress; she was talented and intelligent. She had even been able to win one of the cases against the Sisters without the help of an attorney – after her brilliant speech in a closed trial in Voronezh the Sisters were acquitted and released straight from the court room. She was also a gifted poet. I have a notebook with her poetry.

Living after rehabilitation if not in poverty, then in very modest conditions, Mother Stephania and Sister Catherine still managed to help the very poorest around them. In some shelter they found an unfortunate paralytic who had fallen into complete despair. They helped him find his way to God and supported him materially. Mother Stephania believed that if you were going to help someone, you needed to help him generously. The paralytic was so touched by the Sisters' goodness that upon every suitable occasion he sent them touching letters of gratitude. Here is one of them:

> My dear and best friends, Vera Lvovna and Nora Nikolayevna,
>
> I received the letter from Vera Lvovna. I was very touched by your words, in which I sensed much spiritual warmth. I have become very weak and apparently my end is near, and thus at night I cannot keep from crying. I am endlessly grateful to you for the fact that you taught me to believe in God, which gives great relief to my soul at night. If you believe in the kinship of souls, then you must sense at night that I am praying to God, drowning in tears, asking him to help you. I am very sorry that you are not feeling well. With all my soul I wish you good health, well-being and spiritual tranquility. Each must have his end, but you have done so much good that you can calmly await your passage into the other world, since all your good deeds will be credited to you. You do so much good to people, and especially to me, and I so often pray to God for you, that you can easily await your earthly end, being firmly confident that, for all your good deeds, God will grant you all that you ask and deserve. I firmly believe that the Lord God has prepared for you a place at his right hand.
>
> Our situation is terrible – almost every day a new nurse's aide comes – they are illiterate and don't know how to do anything. They can't even write notes, but they know how to sneak into the night table and steal. The only thing that helps me is this deep remorse for my errors and sins, the realization that what is sent to me by God is a punishment that I richly deserve. No one visits me, and you and Nora Nikolayevna are the only ones who have not forgotten me. Once again I sincerely thank you for the moral and material support that you have given me and especially for the fact that you converted me from being an atheist to a deeply believing Christian. This greatly eases my end. I kiss your hands. Devoted to you until my last breath, and forever indebted to you,
>
> Konstantin Nemechek

I was at Nora's on Prospect Vernadskovo to celebrate Mass once a month. She attracted many believers and her room became a little center of the Catholic underground. At her place one would see, for example, the now-deceased Professor Julius Shreider; Alexander Khmelnitsky, who is now a Dominican priest and editor of the journal Istina i zhizn' [Truth and Life]; Ivan Lupandin, now a professor at the Catholic College; Anna Godiner, now the editor of children's religious literature; and many others.[41]

Since Nora was no longer able to get out and about, her visitors would bring her groceries. This, and the fact that I would spend the night there, really annoyed her elderly neighbor. He had some idiotic ideas and would never respond to my greetings. Once he became completely enraged. From Nora's room I heard some obscene profanity in the corridor and when I ran out into the entryway, I saw that he was kicking this elderly Sister. I had to resort to nightmarish threats. This frightened him and he disappeared from the apartment… I describe this unattractive scene for one reason: when he fell seriously ill and there was no one to look after him, Nora, not remembering this assault, took it upon herself to look after him and thus completely tamed him. When he recovered he even began to bring her groceries (but his hostility toward me remained unchanged).

Nora and I dearly loved each other. She was always a very valuable and wise advisor, but when I would come to Moscow, we almost never had time to talk. Before my arrival she would plan out my work. She would have me going to different ends of the city, and even outside the city, to celebrate Mass for people who were afraid to come to church – I would hear confessions, bring Holy Communion, celebrate Mass and sometimes baptize. By the time I returned to her place at night I no longer had the strength for conversation. We would simply sit side by side in the silence, but how wonderful this silent communication could be! When we would have enough time, Nora would read aloud, perhaps from the spiritual reflections that she was translating from the French.[42]

Nora visited me a few times in Saint Petersburg. We would pray the

[41] Several of these visitors were or became Third Order Dominicans and can be identified by their religious names as well: Julius Shreider – Brother Thomas; Ivan Lupandin – Brother Vincent; Anna Godiner – Sister Genevieve.

[42] She was working on a translation of *Sur se pas*, spiritual reflections by Father Jacques René Boucher, OP, the Dominican provincial in France whom she knew personally. Her translation was published under the title *Sledui za mnoi* in 1993.

Liturgy of the Hours and I would celebrate Mass in my little domestic Gothic chapel. "How do you like my chapel?" I once asked her. "The finest in the world!" she said. Once in the summertime when she was visiting I took my dog Mishka out for a walk before Mass. On my way back, I noticed that some kind of animal was thrashing around, drowning in the Kryukov Canal. I ran home for a bucket and rope, and when I got back to the canal I saw that it was a crow. While I carefully lowered the bucket into the canal, the crow completely gave up and dropped its head beneath the water. There was no other way – I had to jump into the canal myself, but what I dragged back onto the shore was already almost dead. I carried the bird home and placed it in the entryway, on the windowsill, and then went into the chapel to celebrate Mass. Nora and I prayed for the poor thing during Mass, and when I was finishing the post-Communion prayer with the words "through Christ Our Lord," instead of our "Amen" there resounded from the entryway a loud "Karrr!" The crow was jauntily walking along the windowsill. When we opened the window, it flew off, leaving behind a large piece of plasticine, the likely cause of its nearly drowning in the canal.

Nora was very grieved by the unreflecting conformism of our people, our intelligentsia, and even our believers (though of course not all of them). They were so malleable to the deceits of official propaganda. She herself was absolutely honest and uncompromising in this respect. I remember – this was during the days of the Soviet Army's invasion of Afghanistan – Nora and I went to a village outside Moscow to celebrate Mass in the home of a now-deceased long-time friend of Nora who was lying ill. This educated lady, who had worked a lot on translations of fine spiritual books, alas, harbored a feeling of trust toward the lie with which the mass media had brain-washed our citizens. My homily during the Mass, in which I touched upon our national misfortune, the war in Afghanistan, provoked an outburst of indignation from this poor lady: "Why are you speaking about Afghanistan? Why not about Nicaragua?" I tried to reason with her, but in vain. "You are just the typical anti-Soviet!" she shouted. Poor Nora grew pale. She pleaded, "Please end this conversation or I will have a heart attack."

After Mass, on our way back to Moscow, we consoled each other, lamenting our fellow citizens' susceptibility to deceit. Nora had not an ounce of conformism. When I read her statements as recorded in the protocols of her interrogation – "I believe it necessary to declare my hostile attitude toward Soviet power" – my heart overflowed with pride for this brave confessor of the Faith who was my beloved spiritual mother, sister, daughter and friend.[43]

When the Moscow KGB stoked up the case against Father Vladimir Nikiforov and persecutions began in the form of job dismissals, we were all anxious because we did not know how far this would go. At that time, Nora heard someone during the night drilling into the wall of her room from the stairwell. In the morning she discovered a deep hole that had been carefully drilled. The following day she fumbled around and found some kind of metallic device deep inside this hole, but on the next day the hole was plastered over and painted, and in its place a metal dowel protruded. She was sure there was a microphone in the wall. I wanted to tear out this dowel with pliers but she would not let me. From that time, whenever I would celebrate Mass in her apartment, at her insistence, it was an absolutely silent Mass. In our conversations we would change the names of our friends – for example, Zinka instead of Zigmunt. Important conversations were written on toilet paper and then immediately burned by candle.

Nora died in May 1987. As I had promised her, I came to Moscow right away and, at her coffin in the empty apartment, said the Mass for the Dead. For me, her death was an irreplaceable loss. I hope to meet her and all the Sisters in a better world.

Sister Teresa [Minna Kugel] came from a Jewish family. In her youth she was a Komsomolka; in other words, she was ready to defend the Communist idea zealously. She lived not far from the Sisters – I can't remember in which city. She was inclined toward works of mercy. Seeing her kindness, the Sisters agreed among themselves to pray regularly for her conversion. God heard their prayers and what happened to Minna was similar to what had happened to André Frossard[44] and Hermann Cohen.[45] She once went into a Catholic church and saw the Sacred Host (the Body of Christ) in the monstrance on the altar. Instantly her soul experienced a complete conversion. She asked the priest to baptize her, and after instruction she was baptized and soon

[43] See Appendix 1. See also Irina Osipova, *V iazvakh svoikh sokroi menia* [Hide Me Within Thy Wounds] (Moscow 1996), trans. Malcolm Gilbert (Fargo, ND, 2003).

[44] André Frossard (1915-1995), author of the well-known book on religious orders, *Le Sel de la terre* [Salt of the Earth], 1956.

[45] Father Hermann Cohen, OCD (1821-1871) was an outstanding pianist and pupil of Franz Liszt.

thereafter joined the community of Sisters and was arrested with them in 1934.

She recounted two remarkable incidents from her prison life. In the words of the other Sisters, Sister Teresa was a shapely, strong and beautiful young woman. One of the supervisors at the camp set his eyes on her and choosing a convenient moment when they happened to be alone, he tried to grab her. She gave him such a blow that she knocked him out. When he came to, so ashamed was he that a young woman had knocked him out that he did not file a complaint against her. His pestering also stopped.

The other incident she described was rather barbaric and occurred in the same prison. In an effort to deal with a louse infection among the women, the wardens sent men with razors into the women's cell. They shaved hair from all parts of the women's bodies. The women criminals even found this fun! Sister Teresa, a nun and virgin, refused to submit to them. "Even if you kill me!" she said. As a punishment they stood her barefoot outside in the snow. She patiently stood there until one of the educated Chekists saw her from the window. "What's going on?" he asked. They explained. "Put an end to this barbarism!" he ordered and this practice was abolished once and for all, and Sister Teresa was set free from her punishment.

Sister Teresa died of bladder cancer in one of the Vilnius hospitals. Father Vladimir Prokopiv and I went to visit her. From her frightfully changed, almost corpse-like face, her eyes looked upon me, radiant with love and joy. I quickly left the room because I was afraid I would begin to cry. When I returned, Sister Teresa was asking Father Vladimir, "Father, why are they prolonging my sufferings with these pills?" Father Vladimir bent over her and quietly asked, "Do you not want to suffer a bit more for the sake of the salvation of souls?" "I do," she quietly answered, and thereafter not a single complaint fell from her lips.

Sister Philomena [Sophia Eismont] was Polish on her father's side and Russian on her mother's side; she had a courageous, ardent nature. She converted to Christ under the influence of the Protestant preacher Marcinkowski who at that time headed up the Christian Student Union. She then entered Mother Catherine's community and was very soon thereafter arrested with the other Sisters. At eighty years old, despite her physical limitations, she took upon herself the task of flying to Saint Petersburg to let me know that the matter of my ordination had been resolved. She was a passionate conversationalist on theological themes. In the final years of her life, at the insistence of Father Zigmunt and me, she labored over the writing of memoirs that are now so precious to us, describing the sufferings of the Eastern Rite Dominican Sisters for Christ and Russia. May the Lord reward her!

We must also mention the Polish Sisters, whom I, unfortunately, did not personally know. They converted from their native Western rite to the Eastern rite (I can imagine how hard that must have been for them!) in order to suffer with the Russian Sisters for the salvation of Russia. When they were languishing in prisons and concentration camps, the Chekists on the petition of Mme. Peshkova decided to release them to Poland in exchange for Soviet spies. They refused to go – they had resolved to suffer everything to the end and they died, like Mother Catherine, in captivity.

The anxieties I described above touched not only the elderly Sister Catherine in Moscow; in their later years the Vilnius Sisters also experienced their share of worries. Here was what happened. In 1980, a year after my ordination, I brought my bishop a new candidate for the priesthood, Andrey Kasyanenko. At his ordination, someone showed up with a camera, allegedly a candidate for the priesthood, and he began to take photos during the liturgy. I tried to protest. "Don't be afraid, Father," people said, "it's for history. The photos will be well hidden." After the ordination I said to Father Andrey, "This is bad! These photos will turn up someday."

Father Andrey was at that time working as a communications engineer in Vilnius. He had no residence – he would just take a corner at various peoples' places. Once the Ministry of Internal Affairs [the ministry that oversaw police and surveillance operations] proposed some work in his specialty, promising to put him in line for an apartment. He agreed, intending to leave the MIA when he got the apartment. He worked for them a year, then two, three years, but they didn't give him an apartment. He had already reached the rank of senior lieutenant. So in his closet hung both his Dominican habit and his police uniform!

Suddenly the general – the head of the Lithuanian branch of the MIA – summoned him and asked, "Are you a pop?"[46] "No, I am a Catholic priest," Andrey answered. "That's even worse!" said the general, grabbing his heart.

---

[46] Translator's Note: Pejorative word for Orthodox priest.

"Do you have any Validol?" They both took some Validol. It turned out that someone had submitted a denunciation to the MIA with a photograph showing our bishop, Father Andrey and me in full Greek Catholic vestments. The general was painfully trying to grasp what hostile forces would have embedded a priest into the militia. Fearing reprisals from the KGB, since this was during the Andropov period, he ordered Andrey to write a notice of resignation immediately, after which Father Andrey departed Vilnius.

Obviously, the elderly Vilnius Sisters could not have been unaffected by all this. Grant them rest, Lord, there where there are no more anxieties, no more grief, and you, confessors of Christ, pray for us sinners.

Father Andrey Kasyanenko, OP

Interview conducted by Margarita Kurganskaya and transcribed by Olga Mironova

In 1977, Nora Nikolayevna (Sister Catherine), who was living in Moscow, helped me become acquainted with the Sisters of the Abrikosova community who were living in Vilnius at that time.

Exiles and prison terms had swept the community away, and now only a remnant lived in Moscow – Nora Nikolayevna Rubashova and Vera Lvovna Gorodets – and the rest, thanks to Sister Teresa Kugel, were in Vilnius. She was the first to have been released from the camps, and she had found herself a job as a nurse in a hospital in Vilnius and obtained a residence permit. Later she managed to bring Sisters Antonina Kuznetsova and Philomena Eismont to Vilnius, after they were released from the camps as disabled. (They were given a pittance of a pension, but not rehabilitated.) Thus Teresa Kugel, a Jew who had been converted by the Sisters' prayers and baptized during the war in Yaroslavl, had established herself in Vilnius and brought the Sisters to join her – and a small community was founded.

By the time I appeared on the scene, the Sisters were living in two buildings. In the building on Dzuku Street lived Sisters Antonina, Teresa and Leokadia – this last Sister had at that time not taken permanent vows and subsequently left the Dominican community. A second apartment was located on Zhermuny Street, where Sister Magdalina Segen is even now still living. At that time Sister Philomena lived there with her. Sister Antonina was the Superior of the small community. The Sisters gathered every week in the apartment on Dzuku Street for Mass, conversation and a shared meal. The older Sisters were already retired, but Sister Magdalina worked as a bookkeeper in the forestry division.

I arrived on the day when Sister Teresa died, and thus I did not have the chance to know her, but on the other hand, I saw all the other Sisters together. The apartment on Dzuku Street was in a five-story Khrushchev-era walk-up. It had two rooms with a shared bathroom. One tiny, very narrow room, perhaps 100 square feet, was used as a chapel: a dresser served as the altar and the Blessed Sacrament was on the altar; the room also accommodated a desk and sofa.

Father Vladimir Prokopiv regularly celebrated Mass for the Sisters in this chapel. He was a Greek Catholic priest, a Ukrainian who had at one time studied at the Russicum in Italy.[47] When he came home to Lviv on holiday, he found himself in the Soviet occupied zone. Being a Catholic priest, he was sent to the camps, thus sharing the fate of many. After his release from the camps, he did not return to Ukraine, but settled instead in Vilnius. He celebrated Mass in the underground church, although the authorities in general knew that he was a priest and that he was saying Mass, now for some Sisters and now for others. Of course the authorities knew about the existence of these religious communities but in Lithuania they somehow closed their eyes and did not make particular difficulties for anyone.

Father Vladimir celebrated Mass for the Sisters in accordance with an Eastern Rite (a Galician Rite, in Church Slavonic). The Sisters prayed the Liturgy of the Hours in Church Slavonic, but with some "adjustments." For example, if they thought the opening psalm for evening prayer was too long, they might divide it into two parts, praying one part on the first evening and the other on the following evening. Nonetheless they did it very faithfully.

I think it is important to describe what the Sisters did, in addition to prayer. They were very well aware of the task of the Dominican Order – preaching – but inasmuch as they were elderly and furthermore were in a foreign setting, they did not feel at home in the local church. (The church was Polish-Lithuanian, not Russian.)

---

[47] Translator's Note: Established in 1929 by Pope Pius XI, the Collegium Russicum trained seminarians in Russian culture and spirituality for the purpose of ministering within the USSR. Its establishment followed upon failed efforts by the Vatican to consecrate bishops in the USSR for the ordination of native priests. It is in charge of the Society of Jesus; graduates include Father Walter Ciszek, SJ, and Father Pietro Leoni, SJ.

A year later I found a job in Vilnius and I began to have contact with the Sisters practically every day. By that time I had become a Third Order Dominican; it was Sister Philomena who worked with me on my formation and we would unfailingly meet once, if not twice, a week. She would tell me about the history of the Dominican Order and in particular about the history of the Abrikosova community, and mainly the history of the Sisters' wanderings. She herself had entered the community – as best I can remember – in 1920, when she was twenty years old. She was a student at the conservatory, Orthodox by religion even though she was half Polish – but she was rather indifferent toward the church.

Through the Christian Student Union and the Nowickis, Sister Philomena became acquainted with the Dominican Sisters and later, having adopted their spirit, she decided to leave the conservatory and dedicate herself totally to the Dominican Order. The first repressions of this community began in 1923 – there were searches and arrests and later they arrested Sister Philomena as well. Their wanderings began in Siberia, in Tobolsk; from Tobolsk they were sent down the Irtysh River to the Ob River and some even further north, to the Arctic Circle. These were young women, ages eighteen to twenty-one, perhaps one was twenty-five. The convoy escorts discharged these young girls one by one at various landings, and they lived there among the native population. Apparently they were not given the right to work so it was of course very difficult to survive. It is interesting that one fruit of these exiles was the conversion to the Catholic faith of those local residents in whose homes the Sisters lived. I remember how the grandchildren of these people who had converted thanks to the Sisters came to Vilnius from Omsk – in other words, the Faith had been preserved into the third generation.

The Sisters worked on translations of books, especially Sister Antonina who knew several languages: she knew French and English very well, and in my opinion, German as well – in any case she was constantly translating from French and English. She had a huge pile of handwritten translations of various spiritual reflections and a book about Saint Thomas Aquinas. In addition, she and Sister Philomena carried on a very active correspondence which in its own way was a variant on preaching. They wrote many letters, corresponding mainly with people who lived in places far removed from a Catholic Church, but were nevertheless faithful to the Church. The Sisters invited these people to come visit them and during my acquaintance with them such Catholics indeed came from Karaganda[48] and from Omsk, where the Catholic Church did not legally exist. These people came once a year for lengthy stays – long enough to go to confession, receive Holy Communion, and somehow be spiritually fortified.

These were not the best of times, but of course they were not the years of the Stalinist repressions; they were the years of the Brezhnev marasmus, when repressions of dissidents and believers were gradually being renewed. Many priests were brought to trial in Lithuania – Tomkevichius and Svarinskas – as well as the Catholic activist Jadwiga Beliauskina. All trials resulted in the accused receiving sentences to the Mordovian camps.

The Sisters began to be afraid that their life – and contact with them – was becoming dangerous. Thus the liturgy that was conducted in their home gradually became a Latin Rite liturgy and furthermore, silent liturgies, without a homily. Surprisingly, I once came upon an Eastern Rite liturgy, complete with singing. Imagine, in one of these tiny Khrushchev-era apartments, with paper-thin walls, people gathered and singing in full voice during a Byzantine liturgy being celebrated in a large room around a round table!

I should also note the entry of new Sisters into the Dominican Order. For example, Sister Magdalina Segen, who came under the German-occupied zone during the war and later ended up working in a forced labor camp in Germany and somehow there became deeply aware of her vocation. After the war she returned to Rostov-on-the-Don, where there was no Catholic Church; she realized she could not imagine herself as anything other than a religious. So she set off for Vilnius without knowing anyone there, and somehow she met a strange branch of the Dominican Order, a branch of the Eastern Rite, which was completely new to her. They were Russian Sisters, for some reason in Lithuania, where there were not that many Russians, and it seemed that no one had any particular need for them. So by some miraculous way she bound her life with them. She adopted the Eastern, Greek Rite, which, in my opinion, remained something incomprehensible to her, but it was a fidelity and obedience to a voice that she had heard in Germany, in the forced labor camps, when she was sixteen years old. She was with them

[48] I remember, for example, a German family coming from Karaganda.

practically to the very end, the only one of the Sisters who is living to this day.

Sister Magdalina was much younger than the other Sisters – perhaps thirty years; in any case, they were old enough to be her mother. I suspect it was not easy for her to live with these people of an older generation and a different culture; the Sisters were well-educated, whereas Magdalina was not. Nonetheless they somehow lived very harmoniously with one another and even though there was some friction, even in this regard each was being purified along her path toward God.

The renewal of contact with the Dominican Order was a very important event in the life of this community. Somehow in 1969 and 1970 they managed to establish contact with the Nowicki family, who had been returned to Poland in the 1930s as part of a prisoner exchange. Father Donat Nowicki, clandestinely ordained a Catholic priest of the Eastern Rite while serving a term in Solovetsky Camp, and his wife Nina (Sister Josafata, OPL) lived somewhere not far from Zielonka, outside Warsaw. They were living in a Latin rite country, where their own Eastern Rite was not understood by anyone at all.

The Sisters renewed correspondence with the Nowickis and through them the Sisters were able to visit Poland. When Sister Philomena travelled to Poland, the timing of her visit was quite fortuitous because Father Fernandos, OP, the General of the Dominican Order, was in Poland at that time. When he learned that in Soviet Russia, over the course of all these long, difficult years, a small group of women religious had remained faithful to the Order, he realized it was absolutely necessary to do something for them. He therefore appealed to the Fathers of the Polish province to help these Sisters in some way.

Three priests came forward as volunteers: the now-deceased Father Włodzimierz Kuczarek, OP, Father Alexander Hauk, OP, rector of the College of Saint Thomas Aquinas in Kiev, and Father Zigmunt Kozar, OP, who now lives in Fastiv. These three priests, very different from one another, volunteered to serve as a link between the Dominican Order and the Sisters, and each one of them helped the Sisters in accordance with his own gifts.

Father Włodzimierz, the "cherubic father," was a man of a meditative disposition, who came to Vilnius and gave spiritual exercises for the Sisters.

He often just spent time with the Sisters and his presence was unusually important for them.

Father Alexander Hauk, an intellectual and an aristocrat, came in order to establish and support contact with the intelligentsia, especially contact with Moscow Catholics.

Father Zigmunt Kozar, who could be called the "seraphic father," with six wings that he flapped over everyone, out-maneuvered the Soviet customs guards to bring us illegal literature. He illegally traveled throughout the whole country, baptizing people, then bringing them baptismal certificates, and secretly celebrating the sacrament of matrimony for those who needed it and did not have the opportunity to receive it. Having obtained visas from Vilnius, he traveled to Rostov-on-the-Don, even though in those days it was generally impossible to travel more than twelve miles from the place where your visa originated without permission of the local authorities.

Contact with these Fathers seemed to reanimate the life of the Sisters. They began to receive literature from Poland. Of course it was in Polish, which almost none of them knew other than Sister Magdalina, but each of them learned Polish and read the books brought to them and translated them into Russian.

I should say something about the Sisters' personalities. Sisters Antonina and Philomena were very different from one another. Each had come to the Dominican Order by her own path. Sister Antonina was from a Protestant family. Her family was Evangelical, and she herself was, I believe, a sergeant in the Salvation Army. She ended up with the Sisters of the Abrikosova community in a remarkable way. She was a nurse and to earn a little extra money while she was a student, she had gone to the bedside of someone from the community to give an injection. A theological discussion began between this Protestant nurse and the Catholic Sisters, and the Sisters won. She remained with them.

Sister Antonina was a person of unusual tranquility; it was as though peace flowed forth from her. Sometimes I visited her when I was upset or not at peace. Usually it was enough for me just to speak a little with her or listen to her, or just to sit near her. She said nothing unusual. In other words, everything was about the plain and simple truth that "the cat has four paws," or "Praise God!" for this or that, but every time it was something stunning, and this phrase, "Praise God," was absolutely sincere.

When I visited the Sisters in Vilnius in 1989 on one of my last visits, Sister Antonina was still alive, but she was bedridden and always in some kind of half-twilight state. I celebrated Mass and she received Holy Communion – and it was evident that she did this consciously, but then once again slipped into this twilight state. She died October 9, 1989.

I have already spoken of Sister Philomena, the conservatory student, a non-believer and furthermore someone not interested in religion, who also converted to God in a miraculous way. Now she was a Sister with "fire in her eyes," as Frossard described his hosts when writing about ardent intellectual discussions at breakfast with Dominican friars. When Dominican Sisters begin to speak about theology, sparks of the bonfires of the Inquisition appear in their eyes. These sparks constantly appeared in Sister Philomena's tender blue eyes. She also spoke about such plain and simple truths as that "the cat has four paws," but when she did so, her eyes were as inflamed as Savonarola's. Sister Philomena lived several more years and died in 1993, leaving Sister Magdalina as the only survivor of this branch of the community.

The Sisters' active years, when a person would want to establish his career, to be the head of something or in charge of something – these years for them had passed in exiles and camps, and they were years of purifying sufferings, properly accepted by the Sisters, in the situations in which they found themselves. Although suffering does not always purify one, in this case their sufferings purified them from passions and from any pettiness; what came to the foreground of their life was their faith and fidelity.

The Sisters were people who would not for anything, under any circumstances, have turned back from the path on which they had once embarked, from the vows they had taken, from the Spirit that had drawn them, the Spirit of the preaching of the Gospel. God's love had pride of place over everything in their lives, and I think that in those very years when all kinds of pettiness, passions and even foul deeds come forth from a person, it befell the Sisters to live through those years in suffering when all those things somehow were wiped out and went up the chimney with the smoke. After those years, they were already old women. Thus what a person has heaped up for his life is what he is left with in old age. It is remarkable that the Sisters were left with the same character traits with which they had set out. For some it was peace; for others, like Sister Philomena, it was the thirst for truth.

I sometimes had rather heated arguments with Sister Philomena and then thought we would not speak with each other the following day; but she was always the first to make a step toward me, a step of reconciliation, and it became clear that in reality none of these disagreements was all that important.

The Sisters' contacts with their neighbors were interesting. For example, in the neighboring apartment on Dzuku Street lived a family in which the mother had converted to the Baptist faith, but the father had not. When the mother began to attempt to convert their daughter, the husband came to the Sisters, as experts on the Faith, to ask whether what the mother was doing was all right: he had once gone into the kitchen and found her on her knees doing something completely incomprehensible. The husband was very upset about this, but the Sisters assured him that the forms of faith can be different – the only thing that was important was whether it was the Gospel or not.

Some young girls often visited the Sisters. In my opinion they were rather intellectually underdeveloped, but nonetheless, they came in order to listen to the word of the Gospel, since their mother was not a very enlightened person and it was impossible to hear anything new or interesting from her. So they sat, with their mouths hanging open, and listened to what the Sisters told them. It was the most ordinary catechesis, but it was given not in a dry, but in a very understandable and living form.

I brought Vitas Alishauskas[49] to visit the Sisters, and later on, through him came Algirdas Saudargas, now the Lithuanian Foreign Minister, who always treated the Sisters with very great respect, even reverence. He was a very educated person, and he would sit and listen to their stories, literally with his mouth hanging open.[50] Algis asked me whether it would be possible for him to become a Secular Third Order Dominican, but the circumstances were not favorable at that time.[51] I remember talking with him by telephone

[49] He now works for one of the major journals in Lithuania.

[50] I remember how he later came up to me and said, in Russia the nobility dreamed of giving their children to serve in the Hussars, here in the Republic – in Poland and Lithuania – they gave their children to the convent or monastery.

[51] Then in 1985, in those completely marasmic times, they dragged Algis himself to the KGB. Then came the years of struggle for Lithuania's independence and in 1990 Algis became the Foreign Minister. Translator's Note: He served in that post until 1992, and then again from 1996 to 2000. In 2009 he was elected to the European Parliament.

in 1990 and 1991, and he would very warmly inquire about the Sisters; he was interested in them and had kept memories of them in his heart.

We usually imagine convents as places of enclosure, Gregorian chant, Gothic architecture, and so forth. This convent, however, was a little Khrushchev-era brick building with small windows, a tiny balcony, paper-thin walls, and some absolutely wretched furnishings – for example, a plywood cupboard that the Sisters called a chiffonier, painted with brown floor paint. Sometimes I looked at it and wondered, why did the Sisters do that? (for they themselves had painted the cupboard this color). Was it some kind of aesthetics, or was it asceticism? I finally understood that it was more important to them that the cupboard not be cracked or peeling than how it looked. In other words, for people who had passed through the crucible of the Gulag with faith, external appearances were absolutely unimportant.

My hypothesis was later confirmed in a conversation with Sister Catherine about rites. For some reason we were talking about theology. I really enjoyed such conversations, especially with her, because she was an unusually deep thinker with a theological cast of mind. She did not just praise God and sing Alleluia. She set everything out wonderfully and explained things such that everything was fitted into a graceful system.

I do not recall what we were discussing at that time – perhaps Sacred Scripture because at that time books by Alexander Men[52] had been smuggled into the country, books that were very important at that stage in our history and were being enthusiastically discussed – but perhaps we were speaking of a more scholarly book on Sacred Scripture. I was interested in all sorts of liturgical niceties: Eastern Rite, Western Rite, Armenian Rite, the rites of the ancient churches. It seemed to me that this was important because liturgy is a kind of [semiotic] theology. Liturgists say that liturgy is the first theology.[53]

Sister Catherine said to me: "You know, liturgy – fine, I love all liturgies, Latin, Eastern – but liturgy is like an outfit: you can wear one outfit or another. What is most important is what is in the heart."

For the Sisters, that is how it was. To someone looking on from the

[52] The books of Alexander Men (1935-1990) were exactly right for us, as people with little education in these matters, people who did not know Sacred Scripture from childhood. Through these book Scripture became more easily understood and popularized.

[53] One cannot disagree with them, because man establishes his contact with God through sign, symbol, gesture and melody.

outside, it might seem that they were powerless women who sometimes spoke words that were not very wise, who sometimes acted in ways that were not the best. It might have been better, in their situation, to have acted otherwise; but the main thing was that they had this inner core, this vertical beam, and everything else was unimportant. I think that their place in history will be precisely this, that they had this inner core, this hook by which they had been caught, and later everything received a new impulse, everything began to develop further. This branch no longer exists, and one may or may not regret its disappearance.

I remember how Father Mark Smirnov responded to my remark that this branch was dying out and how sad it was that there were no new vocations: "You know, so many new branches arise and so many old branches die off. This is absolutely unimportant." At that time it seemed to me that it was very sad that this branch was dying off without new vocations. Now I think it is probably unimportant. What is important is that it was, and that the Lord somehow saw that it was needed during that span of the life of these people.

Nora Nikolayevna Rubashova was the first Dominican I met. I expected all sorts of things, but not what I saw. Friends in Moscow brought me to Prospect Vernadskovo; we went up to the third or fourth floor where she was living and we rang the bell. A small, gray-haired, plump, elderly lady opened the door and led us into a room in the communal apartment. This, it turned out, was Nora Nikolayevna, a Dominican, the "last of the Mohicans," as others had told me. I expected anything, but not this, as I had my own notions about intellectuals, Dominicans, and nuns.

I must say that we began to speak very straightforwardly and immediately abandoned all formalities and extraneous matters.[54] It was very easy

[54] I was then still quite young – I had finished the institute and was what they called a "hippy": long hair and jeans. But I remember how later on, perhaps six months or so after our first meeting, Nora said to me, "You know, if we were somewhat better acquainted, there is something I would say to you." To which I responded, "Well perhaps we are already well enough acquainted for you to be able to say it." She then said, "Could you not cut your hair – because that long hair is so strange." I had come to Moscow for Holy Week and Easter; in the morning I went out to Mass, then the whole day I knocked about Moscow – I had some things to take care of, but I was also just walking about the city. The whole time the idea gnawed on me: "To cut my hair – if I were to act on principle, I would not cut it; but on the other hand, I want Nora Nikolayevna to see me as a grown up." So as if diving into a hole in the ice, I jumped into a barber shop and said, "Cut my

because Nora was a very tolerant person. This was one of her very important and main qualities. I remember that at our first meeting she asked me what I read, in general. When she heard my response, she said, "You know, it would really be worth it for you to read a catechism."

At that time I had already been in the Church five years and it seemed to me that I had no particular need for a catechism; but the fact of the matter is that the catechisms we had contained short questions and simple answers of the type "Why did God make you? – To be happy, to love him" and so forth. I had never given this much thought, but she gave me a different catechism, in Polish, which, praise God, I mastered. When I had read it, I realized that this little book was in fact extraordinarily important, that our faith ought to begin with the Gospel and the Catechism, with the truths of the Faith, and if not, then all the rest is just window dressing that no one needs; nor does it save anyone. Nora began with me right from the beginning. In other words, we did not talk about the theology of Saint Thomas Aquinas or about philosophy, but instead we put the most basic things in place, and then all the rest. For me, Nora was a godsend.

Nora's visitors included, in my opinion, very remarkable people. I remember one Easter when a large crowd was at her apartment, perhaps fifteen people, including descendants of the Third Order Sisters and some people from church that Nora had known from her youth. Natalia Protopopova was there and perhaps one of her daughters. Nora's apartment was a very unique place, where people could talk, receiving even some parting words and admonitions from Nora. She never gave these words categorically; she would just make a suggestion, and a person then had to draw his own conclusion and decide for himself what he ought to do. This was something that was unusually valuable in her.

It was there that I first met Father Alexander Hauk-Ligowski, OP, and Julius Shreider, about whom I had heard so much from the first day of my acquaintance with Nora. They were legendary people to me. When Julius Shreider crossed the threshold of this room, I suddenly saw a completely ordinary person, in whom what was extraordinarily valuable was the fact that, with all his education, with his position, his life experience and age, he nevertheless spoke with me as with an equal, and because of this,

---

hair a bit shorter." And it was done. When I returned, she expressed no surprise, as though nothing had happened.

conversation with him was easy and fruitful. Everyone who spoke with him benefitted immensely – conversation with him gave one a kind of inner growth, it caused one to want to learn more.

Nora's visitors included other interesting persons as well; for example, Sergey Averintsev, who treated Nora with very great respect; and Gennady Faybusovich, about whom I had heard a lot of interesting things. Nora treated him very tenderly, in spite of the fact that he was not only not a church-goer, but an unbeliever. Nora once gave me correspondence between Julius Shreider and Gennady Faybusovich, where they wrote about what was most important – about faith, about the philosophy of faith. I heard that Arseny Tarkovsky also visited Nora, but I never had the occasion to see him. He had a great respect for Nora and the Dominican Order.[55] Such was the kind of open house that Nora had.

Sometimes people ended up at Nora's by chance. For example, Father Zigmunt Kozar, OP, having come to Moscow, was sitting on a bench in some little park and saw seated next to him a young man who was copying something out of a book. Looking over his shoulder he saw the young man was copying out the Gospel. In very broken Russian, Father Zigmunt turned to him and said: "Do you need a copy of the Gospel?" The young man answered in the affirmative, and that was how he ended up at Nora's.

Ivan Lupandin also came to Nora's for the first time through very strange circumstances. As a new convert to Russian Orthodoxy, he had gone to see Starets Tavrion at Elgavskaya Pustynya in Latvia, and there he met Mark Elkind, a parishioner of one of the Catholic churches in Saint Petersburg. The starets was receiving a few people at a time, and it happened that Vanya [Ivan] and Mark went into the starets' cell together. The starets told Vanya, "Follow that man [Mark] wherever he goes." They didn't know what to make of his words – whether they were some kind of prophecy, or what.

Mark took Vanya with him to Saint Petersburg and introduced him to some Catholics, some Dominicans. Then in Moscow Vanya became acquainted with Nora and one can say that until her death he was the person closest to her. He loved her tenderly and she him in return, treating him as a favorite child and participating in his life in every way she could.

---

[55] They say he spent some time in Dominican priories in Poland.

Romualda Segen (Sister Magdalina, OP)

I personally became acquainted with the Sisters of the Dominican family of Mother Catherine in Vilnius in the autumn of 1961. At that time five Sisters were living in Vilnius itself: Mother Antonina Kuznetsova and Sisters Philomena Eismont, Monica Zvidrin, Teresa Kugel and Catherine de Ricci Sokolovskaya; the last named was living in another apartment with a poor blind woman. There were two other Sisters living outside Vilnius, in Maishiagala: Avgustina Davidyuk and Stephania Vasileni-Pozharskaya.[56] Very soon after I met them, the Sisters from Maishiagala left the Dominican family of the Eastern Rite and joined a community of Latin Rite Dominicans.

Unfortunately, I know little about the Sisters, even though I lived with them from 1962 – I was seldom at home because of my work schedule. Every day by seven in the morning I would walk with the Sisters to church for Mass, and from church I would go to work. After work, I would go to the evening service and then be home by nine for common night prayer, after which everyone went to bed. On my days off there was a lot of work to do around the house, then prayer and spiritual reading; if I had several days off, I spent them in recollection.

When I met the Sisters, they had all been rehabilitated and most were already advanced in years. Mother Antonina, the eldest, was sixty-four years old; the youngest was Sister Teresa, who was forty-nine years old. Mother Antonina was a Karelian; Sister Monica, a Latvian; Sister Teresa, a Jew; and Sister Philomena was half Polish and half Russian. All the Sisters were good-looking, but the best-looking of them was Sister Teresa.

She was tall, with a solid physique. As the youngest of them, she considered herself the strongest in the family and took all the heavy work upon herself – the laundry, preparing fuel and vegetables for the winter, and so forth, even though she was also working at the railroad hospital in the tuberculosis ward, frequently working around the clock at time-and-a-half wages. Thus she was often not at home.

She dearly loved all the Sisters and revered Mother Antonina. She spared them, as much as she could, from all burdens and unpleasantness, and she was very concerned about each Sister. She had been the first of the Sisters

---

[56] Editor's Note: These two were known in the Abrikosova community as Sister Lucia and Sister Rosa Maria. Perhaps their religious names were changed when they transferred to the Latin Rite.

to be rehabilitated and she came to Vilnius, where in a miraculous way she managed to get a residence permit and a job, and later even an apartment. All the other Sisters, after their release from the camps and rehabilitation, were living at that time in Russia in homes for the disabled. Sister Teresa took them all under her guardianship and gathered them in Vilnius. The Sisters living with Sister Teresa were receiving a miserly pension and for all practical purposes were her dependents.

They were living in a small apartment in a private little wooden cottage without any amenities. The apartment was heated with coal; water had to be hauled from a well; and the toilet was outdoors. They washed the laundry by hand, heating the water on the coal stove in the winter and in the summer, on the kerosene stove. They also cooked on the kerosene stove. The kitchen was tiny and narrow, and poor Sister Teresa, after her night shifts, would launder the bed linens in this tiny kitchen. I used to wonder why they didn't just take the linens to the laundry. It would not have cost much to do so.

No matter how Sister Teresa tried to be the strongest and healthiest in the family, it did not work out that way. She was very sick but continued to work almost until her death. She died December 2, 1977, after surgery for bladder cancer, when she was only sixty-five years old.

Sister Monica died July 1, 1972, at age seventy-one; Mother Antonina, October 9, 1989, at age ninety-three; Sister Philomena, February 25, 1993, at age ninety-three; and Sister Catherine de Ricci, March 28, 1985, at age eighty-five.

Natalia Trauberg

Interview conducted by Margarita Kurganskaya and transcribed by Olga Mironova

The elderly Vilnius nuns were, of course, women of their own times, and one had to make accommodations for this fact, which I somehow managed to do. I moved back to Vilnius in 1979 and met them almost right away, although I don't remember how. I liked them a lot. It was already twenty years since I had first met Catholics, and in my first acquaintance with Catholics I saw something exceptionally touching in many features of everyday Catholicism. At the end of the 1970s it no longer seemed that way to me. Nonetheless the Sisters made an extremely dear impression on me because they were kind. For the past fifty years of my life I had loathed nasty people who professed to believe in God, and twenty years of knowing Catholics had been enough. Every denomination has its very fierce, absolutely crazed members – and how this fits with the Gospel, I don't know. I saw none of this among the Sisters. They were gentle, humanly kind and sweet women, and in the course of the four and a half years that I was in touch with them, this feeling remained just about the same.

Two of them – the simple peasant woman Liodia (Sister Margarita) and Mother Antonina – were truly warm-hearted women who sincerely commiserated with anyone who fell ill. They simply loved to help the sick. They lived in a tiny little apartment on Dzuku Street, with daisies and forget-me-nots on the balcony, and served cozy, touching dinners with the absolutely necessary dessert. They lived in poverty, but Liodia put up berries in the summer and then made jam from them in the winter, and they bought "Korovka" candies. All this gave their life a very cozy touch that reminded me of the French Catholicism in my childhood storybooks.

Sister Philomena was different. She was very well educated, refined, and from the old Polish-Lithuanian aristocracy. She made a very tender impression with her little yellowish-violet eyes, but what she said sometimes just astounded you. For example, with her eyes flashing, she would say that "every person is responsible for all his deeds," intending this to mean literally absolutely every person, regardless of whether he was of sound mind or had succumbed to the influence of others, or was in general capable of independently thinking and choosing. None of these very fine points that had been worked out so precisely in Catholic doctrine meant anything to her. Her opinions were utterly severe, as though she were a Calvinist.

I remember our young Fathers, who served in the underground church, listening as she said, with her eyes flashing, "every single person, without exception, will be punished," since each one is responsible for everything – "each and every one, under the knife!" She so gleefully repeated this that one of them said, "I will forthwith instigate a trial on charges of Pelagianism!" But Sister knew nothing of such things and it only added an element of playfulness to her intolerance.

Once, in 1982 or 1983, a very difficult period connected with Afghanistan and the arrests of our friends, we went to a church with Sister Philomena and while we were sitting there on a little bench she suddenly began to explain gleefully that people were now being punished. I cannot describe the horror that came over me – how a person who so fervently believed in God could rejoice that people were being punished so cruelly. But what could be done? It was impossible to reprove her; she was a very old woman who had spent half her life in the camps. Some of the other Sisters were also ready to talk about bonfires, but Mother Antonina immediately quashed such conversations.

Our community comprised Mother Antonina, Sisters Margarita, Magdalina, and the very elderly Catherine de Ricci, Father Dominic and me. Occasionally someone else would join us for Mass, which was celebrated every Sunday at Mother Antonina's tiny apartment. The liturgy was remarkable. A few times the doorbell rang during Mass, but none of the Sisters ever answered the door. Once it even rang precisely during the Eucharistic canon, but everyone remained kneeling and the ringing stopped. I have no idea what this was all about.

Sometimes we had adoration of the Blessed Sacrament. When there were just a couple people present in the chapel, it was truly a little domestic church, but when there were a lot of people standing and kneeling before the Blessed Sacrament it was somehow not right. The Sisters were deeply pious women who had paid for their faith with horrific sufferings. It was touching to see one of them go into the little chapel and pray before the Blessed Sacrament for a couple hours.

Sometimes we didn't agree with them. Once when they were arguing with a certain priest who had come from the village about how to translate the "Ave Maria," I thought I was watching a scene from Ionesco! They were all saying practically the same thing, but no one understood anyone and each was becoming angry about it all. Yet even in this there was something worthy of note: their whole life was piety, not just a layer of life, but their whole life; and if they were naïve, how could it have been otherwise?

In those frightful years of the Andropov era, 1979 to 1984, it was as though I found myself in some kind of children's tale, in something that was very Christian and touching. I remember their tiny apartment on Dzuku Street as something wondrous, but absolutely something that could not be transmitted to us, to our heavy souls, our completely different experience. If we were to try to pretend to live in their world, nothing would come of it. We could be touched by it, but we could not create it. We are completely different. It was like a wondrous island in a fantasy made of gauze – with daisies, forget-me-nots and Korovka candies, such a childlike, un-tragic Catholicism. It was given to me then as a comfort.

The Sisters were very sincere. There was nothing Pharisaical in them; they had a kind of special purity. In their apartment at different times of the year one could see a special light that was so strangely reflected from the opposite windows. Whether it was early morning or late at night, there was something sparkling in the apartment that created a childlike and very touching effect. In general, I would say that through the practice of Catholicism in its childlike aspect one comes to belong to a specially transformed world, a world that Chesterton loved to describe.[57] I, such a Biblical rebel, was at peace there, in their apartment, very likely because everything was unbelievably sincere – and not just sincere, but suffused with a kind of angelic, childlike piety.

Father Zigmunt Kozar, OP

Interview conducted by Margarita Kurganskaya and transcribed and translated from the Polish by Olga Salnit

I met the Dominican Sisters from Vilnius in approximately 1969.[58] At that time I often had to visit parishioners in Lida (Belarus), which is only seventy miles south of Vilnius. I would bring as many religious books for the Sisters as I could, and these would then be sent from Lida to Vilnius. Later, during the Brezhnev era, it became possible to send books through the postal service, but I still found it easier to send them through Lida.

In my meetings with the Sisters we would often discuss historical as well as theological-liturgical and philosophical-ethical problems. On any topic they expressed themselves precisely, clearly and with detailed grounds for

[57] Translator's Note: Natalia Trauberg (1928-2009) was a prolific translator of literary works from English and most of the Romance languages. Her translations of G. K. Chesterton's essays date back to 1959, but could not be published in the USSR at that time. C.S. Lewis, P.G. Wodehouse, Dorothy Sayers, and Graham Greene were among the many authors whose writings she translated over a span of nearly fifty years.

[58] I had not undertaken anything [with respect to the Sisters] prior to that time because I was still not very bold in my priestly ministry. It was only after my getting to know my parishioners, when I began to understand who was who, and from where, and believers began to come to me, to complain and to cry, that I decided to become acquainted with the Sisters.

their opinion. This was not surprising inasmuch as they constantly read religious and philosophical literature. I discovered that they had disagreements among themselves with respect to how religious life ought to be lived in contemporary conditions. Some wanted to be closer to Orthodox customs, preserving the rules of the Eastern liturgy; others wanted to be closer to Western models. I know there were serious disagreements among them, and one of them, Janina, even left them to join a Latin Rite community.

With all these disagreements, they were nevertheless always open to reconciliation and unity. I noticed that they had contact not only with Orthodox, but with Protestants as well. They knew how to strike up relations with all confessors of Christ that they met along their way. This spoke to the fact that their life was a life of the church – religious and Dominican, but also ecumenical.

The Sisters also participated in clandestine meetings, conferences and liturgies with Third Order Sisters from Dorogobuzh and Boleslavets, in western Ukraine. These events were a form of mutual support, both spiritual and material, as they provided us an opportunity to fulfill various errands and requests for the Sisters. I brought them money and other small things from Poland, but the main thing was that we had deep spiritual bonds with them.

Of course, sometimes they talked about how they had been persecuted and tormented, how difficult it had been for them in the camps and exiles, and what kinds of catechesis had been possible in various places. They recounted some very funny and amusing stories, but more often, sad stories. Now what can I say about the Sisters themselves?

Sister Philomena had a very tough character, very demanding of herself and rather stern in relation to others. She was confident that her decisions were always correct and she didn't want to hear any objections. In discussing a question regarding religious life, she had such a firm and definite opinion that she believed everyone simply ought to listen to her alone. In her presence it was impossible – and senseless – to express one's own opinion, but I was also rather stubborn and not always willing to submit to her. I brought her to tears a couple times.

Sister Philomena told how they had been arrested more than once, sentenced to various terms, and then released and again arrested. About the prioress, Mother Catherine, she remembered that while in prison Mother

Catherine was a source of comfort for many unfortunate, deceived, and weary women who had often been brought to the point of insanity by the interrogators; the convicts respected her very much. Sister Philomena always spoke of Mother Catherine as a person of lofty spirituality who worthily endured heavy trials.

The Abrikosova community of Dominican Sisters included both young novices and professed Sisters, university students and a professor, and it was multi-national. There were Poles, Jews, Ukrainians, Latvians, and Russians, and they all lived in unity and love. Discipline in the community was very strict; the rules of religious life were unfailingly observed. This became the cause of the GPU's increased interest in the community and its prompt liquidation of it. The Sisters ended up in prison only because they had carried out an energetic catechetical and ecumenical effort among the intelligentsia, which the authorities found absolutely unacceptable.

In their wanderings the Sisters were subjected to intense persecution only because of the fact that they continued to believe in God, and in the face of all these trials they brought the Faith of Christ to others whenever they could. After their release, their acquaintances and friends from those places of exile and internment, people whom they had converted to the Faith, came to visit them from all over the Soviet Union to seek their advice and support. So even in freedom they continued their apostolic service.

When I became acquainted with Sister Nora Rubashova, I would constantly ask her, who would continue their work, as there was no one to whom to pass it on; the Sisters were dying and there were very few new candidates. Sister Nora would answer, "It's all right. We have finished our work. Yes, we have finished. Very likely, we will die out, but others will come after us. Perhaps everything will be different and religious life will take a different form."

Sister Nora was a remarkable person, so open to God and people, always so joyful, with an enormous hope for the future. She lived in Moscow under rather peculiar conditions – a listening device had been set up outside her door, so we often conversed with signs or wrote each other notes – she would ask, I would answer. Or we would go out of town and tranquilly discuss everything where surveillance was less likely. She took me about Moscow, and it was with her that I first experienced the Moscow Metro. I often spent the night at her place. She doted over me and fed me. We had some amusing moments – as for example, the episode with the oranges.[59]

When Sister Nora came to Warsaw I took her everywhere. I later convinced her to visit Częstochowa, even though she did not much want to go – "Why should I go there? The Mother of God is the same everywhere. I don't want to go." But I said to her, "Sister, you will see the very eyes of this Mother of God." In Częstochowa I managed to bring her right up to the altar and seat her there. Then she took part in another two or three Masses at the shrine. Later she said to me, "Yes, you were right." I answered, "Sister, it is the same Mother of God, but she looks at us with eyes from different icons, from all places, but she is the same." She agreed with me.

Sister Róża Krszyna, OP

Interview conducted by Margartia Kurganskaya and transcribed and translated from the Polish by Olga Salnit

First Sister Philomena came to visit us in Zielonka and then Father Zigmunt went to visit the Sisters in Vilnius. He went dressed in his clerical garb. He thought he was going there like Saint Jacek and that upon arriving in Grodno and deboarding the train, he would walk out of the train station and go about the town dressed like that, preaching along the way to everyone he met. But as soon as he went into town, he discovered he was being followed. So he changed into a plaid shirt, pants and rubber boots, put his things in a sack, and began to walk about like everyone else.

Nora Nikolayevna came to visit us in Zielonka later. I had met her earlier, when our Superior had blessed me with the opportunity to visit the Sisters in Vilnius and Sister Nora Nikolayevna in Moscow. I had the good fortune of living with her, speaking with her at length and meeting her friends. When

[59] Once I wanted oranges so bad that I bought some on my way to visit Sister Catherine, since they were inexpensive, and I began to eat one right away. She noticed this and bought a few more – she begrudged me nothing. In the morning I discovered swellings on my forehead, arms and legs, and they were all itchy. She saw that I was scratching myself and said, "Well, you ate too many oranges and now you are ill." The following morning I got up and was again scratching all over even though I hadn't eaten any more oranges. There were icons and pictures hanging over the bed – I looked and saw – bedbugs! True, they were all dried up. So I said, "Sister, look – there are your oranges!" She laughed and answered, "I've lived here so many years and they've never bitten me." To which I said, "Your blood is either holy or sour." And we had a good laugh. Now whenever I eat oranges I always remember her laughter.

I spent the night at her place I noticed that the Lord was in her home, in a small tabernacle, where the Blessed Sacrament was reserved. She communicated with the Lord as with someone dear and close to her. One could sense how happy she was from her communion with Jesus. It was quite obvious that the Lord had chosen her for service.

Sister Nora was firm in her behavior and in her prayers, and this impressed me deeply. I was younger then, and she became an example for me. She was so intelligent and well-read; she explained and interpreted everything so splendidly and she was serious in her communication with people. There were no empty words; all conversations were directed to the good of the other person. She was so self-sacrificing and modest; she never wanted anything from Poland, even though things were very difficult in Russia at that time. She was always good-natured and smiling.

I have good memories of both Sister Nora Nikolayevna and Sister Philomena. I liked these Sisters most of all because they were outstanding individuals, with very serious attitudes toward life, an amazing honesty and self-denial, and a complete giving of themselves to others. As religious, they were distinctive for their extraordinary zeal in prayer, their righteousness and steadfastness, an amazing modesty in their daily life, in clothing and food. When they came up against misunderstanding or even contradiction in their encounters with others, they accepted it as given by the Lord – like saints. It was these Sisters who nourished our Fathers from the East; these Sisters became more like their spiritual mothers. We often spoke with them about their difficulties and trials, but in the end of ends they referred to God's will as His gift. They became for us an example and a model. One could even say that they were like stars shining on us.

When Father Andrey [Makhin] died, the Lord sent me a dream of Sister Nora, and when the telephone rang in the morning, I already knew that it was she who was calling to let us know of his death. I had the same happiness of communion with a saint after Sister Nora's death. I dreamed that in the morning I was in her room and I saw her quietly sleeping in her coffin. Obviously, the Lord, having given me this dream as a sign, gave me to understand that something had happened to Nora. In the morning I said to the Sisters that some misfortune had happened in Moscow, and just then Father Zigmunt arrived and informed us of her death.

I can say the same about Mother Antonina from Vilnius; she was an amazing individual who was a model of piety and sanctity. Even her presence created around her an atmosphere of joy; light simply radiated from her eyes. The other Sisters – both Sister Philomena and Sister Nora – created the same sensation. I often observed them in conversation with people, how modestly they conducted themselves, how much and how fervently they prayed, reciting the rosary more than once each day, how timidly they treated animals and flowers. I felt prayerful in their company. After returning from a visit with the Sisters I always felt as though I had been on a spiritual retreat. They filled me with a great spiritual strength that impelled me onward to acts of self-sacrificing charity, fasting, self-denial, penitential pilgrimages and further apostolic service. One could say that contact with them brought me closer to heaven.

We used to travel in large groups to visit shrines in Poland to pray for the conversion and salvation of Russia. We have many wonder-working shrines associated with the Mother of God and at these holy places we would fast, go to confession and pray. All of this was done, in accordance with the wishes of the Mother of God, for the good of Russia. Our Catholics, and even non-believers, Polish and Russian Communists, helped us greatly, carting religious literature, catechisms and Bibles from Brussels, Paris and Milan across the border into the Soviet Union. Through good, often non-believing people, we distributed all these books throughout the Soviet Union. We brought them tons of books. We constantly prayed for these, our Communist brothers. Thanks to the efforts of many people, some of whom held high positions in the Party, churches began to be opened in Russia.

Now of course people feel their need to have contact with the Lord and it is evident how strongly they need this. It is so important that religious sisters go about in religious habit openly so that people can approach them and so that they can teach prayer and talk of God, giving an example. This is now very, very necessary and important. One can sense a great hunger for knowledge of God. Everywhere I have been it is evident that people are insistently seeking God. Man's unhappiness stems from the fact that he does not find the Lord or, if he finds Him, he does not know how to speak with Him. Man can be happy only in a tremendous friendship with the Lord.

When I would go to Kiev, I walked about the city in religious habit, and soldiers at the train station stopped me and requested, "Mother, pray for us." On the train, going to Fastiv, people came up to me in the car, sat next to me and said, "Pray for us." Once in an airport when I was flying to Kiev, a young pilot began to speak with me about piety and sanctity, even though he did not know me and I was wearing secular clothing. On my last visit, I was at the market buying groceries. Although I was wearing secular clothing, the Georgian vendor turned to me and asked, "Which convent do you live in?" I looked at him and wondered, how did he know I was a Sister?

Our Catholic brothers in Poland hosted people from Russia, children and adults, who stayed with them, watched religious films, observed our pilgrimages and spoke with many believers who were an example for them. Our entire religious community, the Dominican Missionaries of Jesus and Mary, prayed to Saint Thérèse, the patroness of Russia, for the return of this country to the Lord. By the mercy of God, for almost forty years I taught during the school year, and on summer and winter holiday I would travel to the Soviet Union to help believers. I appealed through Saint Thérèse and many other saints with the prayer, "Please remember the merits of all these saints and together with their prayers, please hear us and fulfill these requests that we make of you: that we be called to holiness and that it be possible to travel to Ukraine and the depths of Russia, to bring souls close to Jesus Christ and the Mother of God."

People came to Poland from various places and they warmed and inspired us with their piety, self-sacrifice and courage, and we were strengthened in our faith to pray constantly and be engaged in this penitential work for the salvation of Russia. Now, when the churches have been re-opened in Russia, convents have been established and people openly confess their belief in God, I remember with such joy and gratitude to the Lord our self-sacrificing labors, our efforts together with these surviving Sisters of the Abrikosova community who passed through the prisons, camps and exile. It is so important to gather recollections about them and to compile their biographies in order to raise these holy Sisters to the altar as Confessors of the Faith.

Sister Kazimiera Morka, OP

Interview conducted by Margarita Kurganskaya and transcribed and translated from the Polish by Olga Salnit

When I first came to Vilnius, Marysia Gostynuvna, who knew the Sisters well, brought me to visit them on Dzuku Street. There I met Mother

Antonina and Sisters Philomena and Romualda (who at that time was still a novice). I saw Sister Teresa only once, when she was passing by me and slightly bowed. Then I met Father Georgy Friedman, OP, from Saint Petersburg. Later, when going to visit him, I would drop in on the Sisters; or if going to visit the Sisters, I would go on to visit him as well.[60]

I did not converse much with the Sisters inasmuch as they were constantly in fear that their apartment had been bugged. Once I spent the night on Dzuku Street – the second time, with the other Sisters on Zhermuny Street. I was astonished that the beds were so uncomfortable. Romusia gave me such a bed and I asked her, "How can you sleep on this? What kind of a bed is this?!"

Sister Philomena was merry and lively, always joyful, good-natured and smiling. She had likely been joyful her whole life. Even when she was setting the table she was always smiling – and she had such a beautiful smile. She did everything herself and when I offered to help, she answered "No, you are the guest, sit – I will do it myself!"

She showed me photographs of herself when she was a charming young girl and told me a little about her life – how she had entered the community as a very young woman, the kind of order they kept and how strict the life was, requiring much self-denial. The life was strict, but nevertheless joyful because there were many young girls in the community. Of course the discipline was strict, but this discipline turned out to be very helpful as preparation for their later life in the prisons, which was much harder.

She told of how frightful it was in the camps and what she had endured during those years. In one of the camps they had to break up a pile of frozen excrement, and all this filth flew about and hit them in the face and got all over their clothing. Prior to this, in exile on the Ob River up near the Arctic Circle, the hunger had been so bad that they had to eat raw fish, and even though they got used to it, it was nevertheless frightful. I consider Sister Philomena a saint.

Mother Antonina was serious, even-tempered, good-natured and very devout. She had severe leg pains and got around with difficulty; then she broke a leg and her mobility was even further impaired. She had suffered a lot in her life, but she had not lost her self-composure. I consider Mother

[60] Translator's Note: Vilnius is approximately 250 miles east of Warsaw; Saint Petersburg is another 400 miles northeast of Vilnius.

Antonina also a saint. For me they were all models and examples of real people of God.

They also spoke a lot about Mother Catherine, a woman so poised and calm. She was always joyful, even in prison. Neat and tidy, she was very concerned that everything around her be beautiful. No one knew, no one even suspected that she was seriously ill and how much she was suffering. The authorities released her from prison after an operation in 1932, but the Chekists immediately set up constant surveillance on her. If someone were to come up to her on the street with a question, the Chekists would summon her and question her as to who this was and what he had asked about. Then they arrested her again in 1933 and she died in prison [July 23, 1936]. No one knew what became of her and how she was buried.

I knew Father Andrey Makhin in Moscow. I liked him because he was so devout; he prayed so earnestly. He was simply a person of God, as though not of this world. He had a real vocation and received great strength from the Lord. Once in the evening when the flowers smelled so wonderful he said to me, "I feel as though I am already in paradise." And soon thereafter he died. Each one had his weaknesses, but in those times of persecutions, to serve the Lord, as he did, was a tremendous act of self-renunciation. A person in those times always had to conceal his faith within himself.

Sister Ancilla Swatowska, OP

Interview conducted by Margarita Kurganskaya and transcribed and translated from the Polish by Olga Salnit

I don't remember in which year Sister Philomena came to visit us, but it was after the Second Vatican Council (1962-1965). She came to study the documents of the Council; she compared documents before and after the Council, made many notes and was keenly interested in the life of the Church. She was full of strength, energy and enthusiasm, and gave the impression of a person of high culture and a deep inner life. She had no need of the purely external interests of a tourist; she tried to imbibe the monastic spirit of our community, inasmuch as the Sisters in Russia at that time were not free to express their views, nor could they lead an openly religious life. She spent every spare minute in the chapel; she read many books in Polish.

She visited us two or three times, and then we corresponded for some time thereafter. How she had been called to the religious life, how she had survived, how certain rather strict forms of religious life were dying out – we spoke a lot about these things. She firmly held to precisely those strict methods of religious practice. I suggested that it was necessary to meet young people halfway, and thus it was necessary to soften the conditions of religious life, but she would not agree with me. She was stubborn and stuck with her own opinion.

Of course she had her own ideas on this question and she based her opinions on her own experience; external factors of contemporary life had little interest for her. She led a modest life and she never sought comforts in her everyday life; on the contrary, she even created trials for herself in her everyday life. When she would come visit us, she would not let us prepare special dishes for her; she would not allow herself, as a guest, any leniency, which showed a degree of spiritual centeredness.

In the apartment on Dzuku Street at that time there were only three Sisters left; I knew the rest only by stories of them. In her youth, Sister Philomena had obviously been quite a beauty, but she did not care to talk of her youth. She spoke more about her parents: her mother was Russian, her father Polish. At the time of her arrest she was a novice, having entered the community only in 1922 or 1923. She professed her vows later, in exile.

With respect to the life of the Abrikosova community, when she had her own opinion it was difficult to change her mind. For example, she was convinced that the community was already doomed and that it would survive only as long as the Sisters were living, that it was completely impossible to renew it. When she looked at the elderly Sisters, it was evident that she did not believe in a miraculous rebirth of the community.

She was afraid that she would be subjected to new persecution if she should begin to write her memoirs. We tried to convince her to overcome this fear and write about the sorrowful path of the Sisters of the Abrikosova community so that the work of their life would not be lost. Although she constantly praised and idolized Mother Catherine, telling us many details about her, we were not able to convince her to put this in writing and thereafter we stopped bringing up this subject.[61] Later our correspondence broke off, but I remember her as a brilliant and very sharp-witted conversationalist.

---

[61] Editor's Note: She did of course eventually overcome these fears and wrote the memoirs that are presented in the first section of this collection.

LETTERS OF THE DOMINICAN SISTERS, 1975-1977

Letters of Mother Antonina

[1975]

Glory to Jesus Christ!

Dear Georgy,

I received both your letters.

"In tranquility and hope is your strength!" First of all, you need not worry or hurry. There is a tremendous strength in tranquility. Remember Abraham who waited dozens of years for the promised son. The first mark of a human activity is haste. The greater and the stronger the plant has to be, the slower its seed grows. If you want to fulfill the will of God, wait for his indications and calmly work on the acquisition of virtues. Plant good seeds all around. Be prepared for whatever God calls you to do. You have Valya – help her to grow in knowledge and love. The will of God is the sanctification of all people. She most likely has less free time for reading. You can share with her what you yourself are learning. Don't be an egoist – think about her. Don't hurry. Entrust yourself to the will of God. He knows best what you need; place everything in his hands.

As for Esau's fate,[1] one must say that the Lord God does not predestine some to salvation and others to damnation. "Those whom he foreknew, he also predestined" (Romans 8:29). You most likely know the story of Esau? He preferred a bowl of porridge to his birth right. It seems as though Jacob sinned against Esau in taking from

[1] This is the continuation of a conversation on the theme that in his mother's womb, the Lord "loved Jacob but he hated Esau." See Romans 9: 11-13.

him his father's blessing – but Esau had scorned his father's blessing as something of no value. God sees the fates of people and he knew Esau's behavior in advance. Man can at any moment call to God for mercy, and God will be merciful. But God owes no one anything. The fact that he gives more to one than to another – in this lies his free will; but man can dispose himself to the acceptance of a greater or lesser gift. God does not place a limit on anyone's perfection, but God is free to give more or less. If all gifts were the same, then all creation would lose its harmony and variety.

I must finish. I wish you tranquility, and may you entrust yourself completely to the will of God. Hugs – please give my greetings to Valya (may I call her Valya?)

Teresa sends her greetings to you and Valya.

Valentina Kuznetsova

[October 18, 1975]

Glory to Jesus Christ!

Dear Georgy!

I've finally gathered my thoughts to write to you!

Teresa thanks you for your greetings. It is difficult for her to write because she is so busy with household chores.

Falling into despair is not befitting a Christian. In and of ourselves, we are absolutely nothing – but we can do all things with the help of the Lord Jesus. It was for this that he became one of us. All humanity is a single organism. In order to help us, Jesus Christ became a man; for this, he wanted to have a mother who would give him a human nature. He is true God and true man. His riches are our riches, his father is our father.

"I can do all things in Jesus Christ who strengthens me," said the Apostle Paul. This does not mean that we do not have to struggle. But our most basic faults are our pride and self-love, and the Lord allows our falls for our humility. Thus we should take a calm attitude toward these falls, and we should immediately get up in order to press onward. Whoever says that he is without sin deludes himself.

We need our falls as medicine against pride and self-love. There is no need whatsoever to fall into despair; calmly accept your nothingness and then God will give the grace for victory. There are various ways to struggle with one's shortcomings. One can try to overcome them – or one can try to acquire the opposing virtue. It seems to me that the second means is more effective. The acquisition of virtues is the work of a lifetime.

Rodriguez says that most people pass through life, striving for virtue as though walking along a sandy road, dragging their feet with difficulty in the deep sand and only, possibly, by the end of their life do they arrive at the mountain of perfection, which, with great effort, they climb by a steep slope. With every step the horizon expands, opening up wondrous vistas. But here, in the mountains, "roads have no exits – it's either up or down."

I wish you, my dear, to struggle with all your strength, but calmly, humbly, recognizing your own nothingness, but not going into despondency. There can be no talk of despair. Do you know what "mental prayer" or contemplation is? Most likely you've read about this [...]

May the Mother of God cover you with her protection from all troubles [...] Hugs.

Valentina Kuznetsova and Teresa

[1976]

Dear Georgy Christopher!

So now you have begun your new life of service to God and man! You wanted something different. But nothing is done right away. One must steel oneself. The Lord Jesus Christ prepared himself a long time for his service, and you have already begun this service. It is a service of the spirit, not the flesh, and therefore it can be less noticed, but it is very real nevertheless. You began to work a long time ago, but now new spiritual strengths have been poured into you. But the main thing is that you are not alone, you are in the [Dominican] family, which will remember you. Construction begins with the foundation, and the deeper the foundation is sunk into the ground, the taller the building will be. "In tranquility and hope is your strength," says the Sacred Scripture. Busy yourself with inner work. Deepen your learning of Sacred Scripture, pray, grow in love of God and man [...]

Dear Georgy Christopher, deepen your inner life and prayer. First of all is the salvation and sanctification of one's own soul [....]

Hugs.

Valentina

[March 19, 1976]

Glory to Jesus Christ

Dear Georgy!

As always, I was glad to receive your little note. Lengthy letters are absolutely unnecessary. No external expressions can convey well what is happening in the realm of the spirit, which blows where it will and can embrace a huge field of activity. One can do a lot, remaining in one place and not speaking a lot of words. The strength of prayer is colossal. This is the greatest activity. "In tranquility and hope is your strength." There are no limits on the activity of prayer.

I am writing out for you a few lines from a new book about Saint Thérèse of the Child Jesus, wherein she says that humility manifests itself not in merely accepting our state of dependence and powerlessness, but in coming to love this state. We must be satisfied, seeing ourselves as we are, and endure those imperfections that are inseparable from our nature. We will then be happy, as we recognize our nothingness more and more. To discover our imperfections does not mean to act in accordance with them. It means that we now see the imperfections that previously lay hidden within us. Their discovery has shed light on them, showing us our true state. The more we recognize our state, seeing ourselves as we are, the more we find ourselves in the truth, and in this we become more pleasing to God; we become more sensitive to the working of his merciful love. We forget about ourselves. "She wanted to be a grain of sand, hidden from men's eyes, under everyone's feet. A grain of sand that only wants to be forgotten; not despised, for that would be too honorable for a grain of sand. In order to be despised, she would have to be seen – she wanted to be forgotten." "But I want to be seen by Jesus because I am very much in need of him."[2]

Saint Thérèse willingly consented to her shortcomings. This should not be understood as consent to sin. Saint Thérèse here had in mind only the weakness of human nature, for example, dryness of perception, involuntary distraction, drowsiness. When she felt the effect of natural weaknesses in herself or when she saw her imperfections, she was not surprised by them – instead, she was happy and used them. "I always find a way to be happy and to use my shortcomings – Jesus prompted me to walk by this path. He teaches me to use everything I have in myself, both good and evil."

We eagerly await your arrival with Valya.

Hugs, my dears.

Valentina

Letter from Sister Catherine Rubashova

[March 8, 1977]

My dear!

How many times day and night I wonder how you are doing, whether everything is okay, whether you have done something flighty or rash to your own or others' detriment. If there is something about which you have a lot of doubt or are unsure, it is better not to make a decision until we have had a chance to discuss it. You are no longer a boy, but you have not reached full maturity and at times it seems to me that you never will. Unfortunately, we see each other little and of course there has not been enough time to speak of many things and to clarify what you need. You have many good impulses, pure aspirations toward all that is true and beautiful, but

[2] Translator's Note: Sister Antonina writes that the book was published in 1974 and gives its Russian title as *Soglashat'sia na svoe nesovershenstvo i poliubit' ego* [Consenting to and Loving Your Imperfection]. The book would presumably have been translated from a western language; original title unknown.

your feelings predominate and your will cannot keep up with them. You must learn to think before you act, to master yourself, your wishes, your first impulses. Consider that you are just beginning to walk (as is in fact the case).

Walk up each step on the staircase – don't skip steps or else perhaps you will have skipped and not mastered the one that is most essential for you. It is useful to everyone to consider himself a beginner. Such a great saint as Saint Augustine repeated to himself every day: "Today I am beginning." One must guard against unevenness – surging upwards and plunging downwards; rein in bursts of excess ecstasy, remembering how it is often not the spirit, but passion, that is being felt. This can keep you from collapses.

No matter how high you are lifted up, there are no "rest stops" allowed; if you succeed, self-satisfaction quickly creeps in and will bring all your efforts and achievements to naught.

A constantly depressed mood or sharp fluctuations from ecstasy to depression are signs of spiritual setbacks. I share your joy with respect to the book by Saint John of the Cross – read it, but remember that he reached the heights of perfection and union with God. For now I recommend you make an examination of conscience with respect to your obedience to the commandments and the rules of our [Dominican] family. Believe me, this is a lot and it is not easy. Struggle with your shortcomings and weaknesses – this is what the inner life is all about. First of all, look at your own shortcomings, and then turn your attention to your neighbor's imperfections – and do this not so much with words but with your personal example. Do not think that you know yourself well and that others are mistaken. Learn not to trust yourself or your opinions, learn to reject them when they point you toward anything that is wrong or unjust. Forgive me if you've had enough of my advice, but I so much want you to grow, to mature so that our family will receive from you the good that it is due, but mainly for the glory of God. And I would be glad to pour my entire soul into you if only this could be helpful in some way.

When I "preach" to Alyoshka, my eight-year-old godson, I sometimes see such weariness in his eyes and I read in them "Godmother, when will you ever finish?" I cannot see the expression in your eyes, but if I have made you weary, please forgive me. Your "Godmother" has finished for now.

Until we meet again, dear, let us pray for one another. Let us try to be our very best, and then all around us will be better. Good gives birth to good – and vice versa. Any kind of evil is very contagious. May the Lord preserve, strengthen and comfort you. I am with you in mind and heart.

Saint Catherine

Appendix 1: Documents of the Investigatory Cases Against Russian Eastern Rite Catholics, 1923-1935

THE first closed group trial of Russian Eastern Rite Catholics (hereinafter "Russian Catholics") took place in May 1924. In advance of the trial, from November 1923 through March 1924, fifty-two persons had been arrested: a priest and several Sisters and laity of the Abrikosov community in Moscow and clergy and laity in Petrograd. The sentences for the leaders of the communities and the active members of the laity were harsh – five to ten years in prison or the Solovetsky Special Purpose Camp.

For the second group trial of Russian Catholics in February 1931, eight members of the Soloviev community were arrested along with Father Sergey Soloviev and Father Alexander Vasilyev. In August 1931 they were sentenced to three to five years in the camps or internal exile.

By 1932 most of the Sisters of the Abrikosova community who had gone through the prisons, camps and repeated exiles had been released, mostly with residency restrictions not allowing them to live in the six major cities. Anna Abrikosova had been released early from the Yaroslavl political isolator prison.

In the beginning of 1933 she met with Dominican Sisters in Moscow and held several conversations with university students. In the summer of 1933 she and twenty-four others were arrested – Sisters from the Abrikosova community and young participants in the meetings with Anna Abrikosova – on charges of participating in a "counter-revolutionary monarchist-terrorist organization." A third group trial of Russian Catholics was held in January and February 1934 and resulted in harsh sentences: eight to ten years in prison or the camps for those who had refused to cooperate with the investigation, and three to five years in the camps or internal exile for the rest.

A large group of clergy and laity belonging to the suppressed Vysoko-Petrovsky Monastery was arrested in the autumn of 1934. This group was headed by the Orthodox Archbishop Bartholemew Remov who had clandestinely converted to Catholicism. The secret parish community included both Orthodox and Catholic members. A fourth group trial of Russian Catholics was held in January and February 1935, resulting in five – to ten-year sentences for the active participants of the community and the death sentence (by firing squad) for Archbishop Remov.

In February 1935 the NKVD arrested four Dominican Sisters of the Abrikosova community who were living out their internal exile in Tambov and included them in an investigation of a group of Catholic priests. The nine-month investigation led up to a closed group trial in Voronezh that resulted in a victory for the Sisters, who categorically refused to sign the charges. They were acquitted and released from the courtroom.

The last group trial was held in August 1949 in a case against five Dominican Sisters of the Abrikosova community who were arrested in November 1948. They were charged with criminal contacts with representatives of the Vatican and giving them "espionage information"; they were given sentences ranging from ten to fifteen years in the prison camps.

We present below the most telling excerpts from the documents of the investigatory files of the group trials for the period 1924 to 1949.[1]

Investigatory File of Russian Catholics, 1923-1924

"Investigatory File of A.I. Abrikosova and Others, 1924," Central Archive, Federal Security Service, Russian Federation

From Statements at the Interrogation of A.I. Abrikosova

> The goal of the community is the spiritual perfection of its members, by means of prayer, penance and serious work on their shortcomings [...]
>
> Each Sister, in accordance with her personal desire, could dedicate

[1] Translator's Note: Documents from the 1949 trial were not included.

herself to a specific idea by means of a special vow. Such a dedication was made with the knowledge of the Sister Superior alone – none of the other Sisters knew of it.

From Statements at the Interrogation of A.S. Serebriannikova

Q.: If your spiritual superior were to order you to do something outside the bounds of your spiritual relationship – for example, to shoot someone or something like that – were you, in accordance with your rules, supposed to submit without protest?

A.: My spiritual superior would never give me such an order. Such an order would be completely alien to the whole tenor of our life. I have never been given such orders and I do not even want to imagine that any order like that could be given.

Conclusion

On April 24, 1924, I, T. Guttsay, plenipotentiary of the IV Division of the Secret Section of the OGPU, reviewed the case with respect to the charges [...]

Background of the Case

In September 1922 the OGPU deported abroad the following persons for their anti-Soviet activity: the former counter-revolutionary factory owner V.V. Abrikosov,[2] who had been ordained a Catholic priest during the Soviet period; Professor Kuzmin-Karavayev, a prominent Constitutional Democrat; Professor Tsvetkov, a participant in 1920 in the organization of the National Center; and Professor Voznov, Professor [Alexey] Arbuzov, and Prince [Sergey] Trubetskoy, a prominent Constitutional Democrat, all of whom were involved in the National Center affair.

After the expulsion of the aforementioned personages, the OGPU set up surveillance of their correspondence. From that correspondence it was established that during their time in Moscow Abrikosov and Kuzmin-Karavayev

[2] Translator's Note: He himself was not a factory owner. His family had a factory, and the Bolsheviks accordingly assigned him to the factory-owning *class*.

had organized a Catholic community that was not registered anywhere, and its activity was continuing under guidance from abroad. In the summer of 1923 there appeared in foreign newspapers [...] notices that a group of exiled anti-Soviet intellectuals (Kuzmin-Karavayev, Kuskova, Abrikosov and others) was gathering material that disparaged the Soviet regime, for the upcoming trial of Maurice Conradi and Arkady Polunin.

In the autumn of 1923 Citizen Sh. appeared in the Secret Section of the OGPU and gave statements about the existence of a Catholic community in Moscow, all the activity of which had aroused his suspicion.

Among other things, he stated that members of this community were getting materials for the foreign White Guard for the trial of Conradi – and that he himself had been a member of this community for a time and that his friend Shafirov presently belonged to it.

With further intelligence work it was established that the above-mentioned community is extremely conspiratorial. Its members include former prominent members of the bourgeoisie and aristocracy, highly qualified intellectuals and representatives of both the Orthodox and Catholic clergy.

On the night of November 13, 1923, the OGPU conducted an operation for the arrest of persons belonging to this community, in the course of which the following documents were discovered:

Tamara Arkadyevna Sapozhnikova

The following documents were found in the possession of Tamara Sapozhnikova:

- Brochure in French entitled "Directive to the Priests of the Paris Eparchy." The brochure advances the position that Eastern Rite Catholicism ought to become a symbol for unifying Russian emigrés, that it ought to be a symbol and a banner around which all should closely rally. Excerpts: "Most Russian people so dearly value the preservation of their own ritual and their religious way of life that they look upon it as a constituent element of their national heritage. This way of life, these rituals are for the majority of emigrés a symbol of their tormented homeland, a banner around which they rally. For this mass of refugees the Orthodox faith represents the last bastion of their national society, gathering around itself all who are faithful to the precepts of Old Russia." And further it says: "They [Russian emigrés] do not know about Slavic Rite Catholicism, which is completely identical with that for which they harbor such a deep and completely legitimate attachment."

- A stenographic letter in Italian, "The Pope's Speech in the Consistory," dedicated exclusively to Soviet Russia, connected with the trial of [Bishop Jan] Cieplak and [Msgr. Constantine] Budkiewicz, and in which Soviet Russia is presented as "a cloud appearing on the horizon, obscuring the population of entire countries with darkness, bringing immeasurable harm not only to holy religion but to the entire population and culture." Touching on the trial of Feodorov, Cieplak and others, the Pope says "At the same time that we are rendering aid to our starving brothers in Russia, high-ranking representatives of the Catholic Church are on trial there."
- A letter to Archbishop Anastasios, printed in Constantinople and signed by thirty Russian Catholics [...] This letter maintains that the Russian Orthodox Church with its weakness and lack of cohesion has played no small role in Russia's sorrowful plight, and it puts forward Eastern Rite Catholicism as a force capable of saving Russia from such disaster.
- The original of a letter from Exarch Leonid Feodorov to Jurgis Baltrusaitis, authorized representative of the Lithuanian Republic, with a request to assist Abrikosova in sending various materials abroad since they were urgently needed and [Father Edmund] Walsh, the head of the Papal Mission, could not send these materials for another five weeks. At the end of the letter Feodorov recommends Abrikosova as a person "deserving full and perfect trust."
- A third letter dated September 14, 1923, to Anna Abrikosova, in which there is talk of an impending departure abroad in an exchange [of citizens] and the instruction, "send the attached letter to Golinsky by registered mail. He asked me to send his wishes for his Lordship's recovery."
- A typed document over the original signature of [Peter] Volkonsky, a notice about the Committee of Russian Catholics that had been

organized, with instructions on where to turn in case of need (according to our information, Volkonsky is one of the prominent leaders of the former Monarchist Union, now known as the Supreme Monarchist Council. Thus this "Committee of Russian Catholics" is nothing other than the Roman branch of the "Supreme Monarchist Council.")

- Formulas of vows taken by the Sisters at the completion of a two – or three-year period of belonging to the community, wherein each of them dedicated herself to a specific idea. Typical of them is the idea to which Sister Rose of the Heart of Mary dedicated herself (in public life, Galina Fadeyevna Entkevich [Jętkiewicz] – formerly of the nobility, a Pole, and now a typist in the community); the formula of her vow was as follows: "I, Sister Rose of the Heart of Mary, to the honor and glory of God the Almighty Father, Son and Holy Spirit and the Most Blessed Virgin Mary and Saint Dominic, in thy presence, reverend Father Vladimir (Abrikosov), head of the Moscow community, Third Order of Penance of Saint Dominic of Moscow, authorized by the Most Reverend Father General (the Pope) [sic], do confess and declare that I give myself to God as a sacrifice for the salvation of Russia, so help me God."

Citizen A. I. Abrikosova

Abrikosova was found to have in her possession an extensive correspondence between Exarch Feodorov and Leningrad Catholics, from which it is apparent that, sitting in prison, he had not ceased to direct the activity of the parish and the community in Moscow and the corresponding organization in Leningrad. The community gave him an account of its activity and reported back to him on the fulfillment of his assignments. Among this correspondence the most substantive documents are the following:

- "My conversation with Secretary of the Petrosoviet," written by Leningrad resident [Julia] Danzas. In this document, evidently widely disseminated, the Soviet regime is portrayed as persecuting Catholicism in the person of Cieplak and others for counter-revolutionary acts, for Catholicism as such.

- A letter of Danzas in which she reports to Feodorov that a "grandmothers' rebellion" had been organized in Leningrad – a demonstration involving more than 2,000 persons that had been clandestinely led by the mother of the priest [Father Edvard] Yunevich and [Anna] Posseypol, a representative of the Upper Council of [Saint Vincent de Paul] Conferences. The goal of this demonstration was to influence the Soviet government, to force it to free convicted priests. From the same letter it is apparent that directives for the demonstration had been received from Citizen [sic] Walsh from the Papal Mission – directly from Rome.
- A letter of [Father Epifanius] Akulov, a report to Feodrov, in which he (in six finely handwritten pages) reports about the activity and development of the work of the Catholic parish in Leningrad; Akulov informs him in this letter "it is true that the work of our evangelization is very slow, but it moves forward," and in another place, "The Conference of Saint Vincent is growing and functioning, a circle of those who love God flourishes in our parish" (followed by a list of leaders).
- A report of [Sergey] Prilezhayev (member of the Leningrad community) to Exarch Feodorov that throws a bright light on the nature of the aforementioned groups. This report sets forth a whole list of themes for discussions with parishioners and requests the permission (blessing) of Feodorov – these themes are preliminarily refined in small groups "in order to avoid awkward expressions." Thus it is clear that these small groups are cells of the organization, where one or another question of agitation is worked out in advance among believers.
- Letter of [Kapitolina] Podlivakhina to Feodorov, where she provides an analysis and gives an assessment of [Patriarch] Tikhon's appeal. In doing so, she claims that this was all fabricated while he was imprisoned, where they had furtively given the defendant a blank form and then dubbed in "remorse, repudiation" and so forth in the newspapers, as though written by the prisoner himself. In reality, this is all a lie. If a person is of little importance the form is kept under wraps; if the person is a prominent figure, then they use it as they see fit. From the letter it is apparent that she also took part in meetings of [St.

Vincent de Paul] Conferences. Podlivakhina attached to this letter another "letter sent from Moscow, which has been circulating from hand to hand and read everywhere."
This letter (that was being circulated) analyzes the activity of the "Living Church," its interrelations with Tikhon, its failure among the faithful and a campaign against it. The letter indicates that some sort of authorized person, who would be immediately arrested for counter-revolutionary activity and stirring up the popular masses should his name become known, is traveling back and forth between Moscow and Leningrad. The letter concludes with the words: "Inform the church people of Petrograd. It is time to act. Moscow expects it of Orthodox Petersburg."

- An excerpt from a speech given by the Pope, written in Feodorov's hand. The same excerpt was also discovered in the searches in Leningrad.
- The indictment in the case against Cieplak and Budkiewicz and a separate excerpt from the stenographic account and speech of Feodorov, handwritten.
- An informational communication compiled by [Vladimir] Balashev about the situation of the Orthodox Church.

Vladimir Vasilyevich Balashev

Balashev was in possession of numerous newspaper clippings concerning the Church and the current situation in the USSR, and also his own handwritten accounts about the debates of church leaders that had taken place – all this was being sent through Abrikosova to the Pope in Rome.

In general, Gotovtsev, Nowicki, Balashev and Abrikosova were in possession of numerous clippings from Soviet newspapers [...] that were being prepared for sending abroad. These clippings related to a whole series of questions, such as the situation of both the Catholic and Orthodox churches in the USSR, the trial of Cieplak and Budkiewicz, current events, etc.

These then are all the results yielded by the search of the Moscow community – but we must also note that everything in the community had already been prepared for a search, such that, in the first place, not a single letter from V.V. Abrikosov [now in Rome] was found, and second, at Sapozhnikova's interrogation she stated that after the search she had by chance asked Anna Abrikosova whether there might have been anything compromising in the file that she had, to which she received the response, "no" – and Abrikosova at her interrogation stated that she had destroyed letters she had received from Vladimir Abrikosov from Rome. As for the investigation in this case, the documents speak for themselves, and as later became evident in the investigation, the acknowledgement by Aleksandrov that their views and goals were expressed in the "directives" – one can only conclude that this organization, in addition to religious tasks, had specific political tasks.

After the operation conducted in Moscow, it became apparent from its results that an analogous organization existed in Leningrad. Directives were then issued to conduct searches and arrests of the prominent figures of the Leningrad national community. The Leningrad searches yielded results that conclusively established that the entire activity of the community was the continuation of the activity of Cieplak, Budkiewicz and others and that it was analogous to the activity of the Moscow community.

The following documents were discovered in the Leningrad searches:

- The brochure "Directives to the Priests of the Paris Eparchy," analogous to the one found in Sapozhnikova's possession in Moscow;
- The same excerpt from the Pope's speech as that found in Sapozhnikova's possession;
- An article entitled "The Question of the Existence of God," which, however, has nothing to do with its title, as it has the following: "the twentieth century has been born. In honor of its arrival, dressed in red clothing, it brought the peoples violence and blood. And here and there were heard the groans and cries of the dying and the violated. The human mind, inebriated with fraternal blood, is engendering various doubts within itself. A fog, having covered its vision, interferes with its ability to distinguish truth from falsehood." And further: "fortunately, the soil does not everywhere assimilate it in the same way. It has found such fertile soil only in the depths of Russia, where the granaries of this kernel are found in the hands of communism."

Further on there is a description of the "horrors" of rations, grain seizures, lines, and at the end of the article appears the slogan: "If the medicine will not cure, iron will cure; if iron will not cure, fire will cure; if fire will not cure, death will cure." At the top of the article is a dedication "to Russian Catholics."

[…] it is evident from the discovered documents that one of the aspects of the activity of this Catholic organization was the creation in the parishes of Conferences of the Saint Vincent de Paul Society.

These conferences were illegal organizations and were created with the goal of aiding the sick and political prisoners. Such conferences were organized at each parish, and from these conferences were elected a chairman and a secretary, and from all the chairmen was created the "Upper Council of Conferences," which was subject exclusively to the Roman Pontiff.

[…] a notebook was discovered, from which it was evident that meetings of the conference took place once every two weeks and every month a list was made of those who had joined the conference as well as those who had left and for what reason […]

Established by the Investigation

On the initiative of the former factory owner V.V. Abrikosov, expelled from the country, and Exarch Leonid Feodorov, convicted in the trial of Cieplak, there was set in motion at the end of 1921 the creation of a unified anti-Soviet front. For this purpose, in accordance with their plan, it would be necessary to bring about the unification of the Roman Catholic and the Orthodox Churches under the primacy of Saint Peter. (The task of this group was to do away with the discord that existed between these two churches, a discord that weakens the church in its struggle with the growing influence of socialist ideas that are enveloping the broad masses.)

The fact that persons drawn into the discussion of the question of the unification of the Roman Catholic and Orthodox Churches included Prince Urusov, Prince Trubetskoy, Kuzmin-Karavayev, Boikov, Prince Shakhovskoy, Shchepkin, and a whole series of prominent figures well-known through the National Center and the Tactical Center – speaks to the fact that the idea of unification was an exclusively political goal of the fight against Bolshevism.

Everything set forth above was entirely confirmed by the results of the operation and the statements of the participants in the organization's meetings at the home of V.V. Abrikosov when he resided in Russia. The arrested Arsenyev, pastor of the Church of Christ the Savior, who was at the meetings at the Abrikosovs, stated at his interrogations that "as for the Catholic side of the essay by Kuzmin-Karavayev, in this essay he expressed the idea of the creation of a Unified Anti-Socialist Front for the struggle with the lack of faith [atheism] and the Bolsheviks, under the guidance or leadership of the Roman Pontiff. There was talk of the creation of cells of believers that would comprise the foundation for the organization of the struggle with socialistic ideas." Arsenyev also indicated that Kuzmin-Karavayev in his essay had said that "the organization, resting on the authority and weight of Papal power, could, in his opinion, carry out a significant fight."

N.N. Aleksandrov, who basically replaced Abrikosov after the latter was expelled from the country, and who was an active participant in the meetings at the Abrikosovs' where Kuzmin-Karavayev had spoken, when questioned on this matter in simultaneous questioning with Arsenyev, stated: "I remember nothing about the creation of a Unified Anti-Socialist Front." He said, "I know that when Professor Boikov made a political statement, they immediately cut him off, and Abrikosov, presiding at the meeting, was the first to do so."

Professor Boikov's statement on this topic was "an appeal to the Pope for help against the Bolsheviks."

In his first interrogation, asked whether he had contact with Kuzmin-Karavayev and Abrikosov, Aleksandrov stated "they do not write me anything personally; they send postcards to the parish, but they are for the whole parish."

When questioned as to the gist of the brochure of the Vatican "Directives to the Priests of the Paris Eparchy," Aleksandrov, the head of the Russian Catholics, stated: "This brochure in its essence is an expression of our view and of the role to which we aspire."

This brochure was received from Rome, from Abrikosov, in two copies, translated by Abrikosova in the community, signed by Feodorov and Aleksandrov, as secretary of the community, and sent to Leningrad – and on the translated copy was the stamp of Sheptytsky (metropolitan of Lviv) and thus it had the character of an official document.

Further on Aleksandrov indicated that he has contact with those in prison who were convicted in the Cieplak case. He translated and circulated brochures, such as the above-mentioned "Directives" which he had indicated expressed their goals and views. He carried on all the while a correspondence with Leningrad Catholics, conveying to them the "will" of Exarch Feodorov.

To the question, what was the connection of Father Feodorov with Metropolitan Sheptytsky? Aleksandrov stated that he refused to answer the question.

In his statements of December 29, 1923, Aleksandrov writes that religion was being taught in the community, i.e., the Abriksova community, and that he was the leader.

At first he stated that he had not sent Abrikosov any clippings or in general any information. By his next interrogation, on December 29, 1923, he stated "I change my statements from December 14 concerning the fact that I did not know about the newspaper clippings sent by Abrikosova to Father Valdimir, and I state that I recall that Abrikosova told me that she was sending clippings, but I do not know what they were about" [...]

Also with respect to the question on the interrelationship of Catholicism and politics and the state, Aleksandrov stated that this interrelationship changes, depending on the conditions of the politics of the given state. Concerning further development of this view, Aleksandrov refused to answer this question. Further, according to Aleksandrov's statement, Abrikosova was the head of an illegal school where religion was taught, located on Afanasyev Lane at the residence of Vakhevich, a member of the parish.

Concerning the brochure found in her possession ("Directives to the Priests of the Paris Eparchy"), Abrikosova stated "I share the point of view expressed in the brochure, as expressed by Popandopullo (author of the brochure)."

Concerning Feodorov's letters to Baltrusaitis, the Lithuanian representative [...], Abrikosova refused to answer, stating that she did not remember what Feodorov said to her when giving her the letter.

Since at her interrogation Abrikosova stated that they were Catholics of a "pure quality," – to the question posed to her, "whether Catholicism was compatible with politics," she refused to answer, since she "considered herself not competent in such questions."

Questioned in connection with her gathering of information for the trial of Conradi and how she regarded this case in general, Abrikosova stated: "I cannot say whether those who contributed to Conradi's acquittal committed a crime, since I do not know the details of the matter." As for the punishment of those persons who enabled Conradi, she did not know whether they deserved this punishment, i.e., it depended on their awareness.

As to assigning Balashev and Nowicki the task of gathering materials about the situation of the Russian Church and other information, Abrikosova stated that she "did not remember" this.

To the question of whether she had sent an excerpt from the Pope's speech to Leningrad, she stated that she had not sent it; after being shown Danzas's statement that she had received this note from Abrikosova, she confessed, stating that "if Danzas says that I sent it, then it must be that I sent it."

Questioned in connection with a document discovered in her possession that had been signed by Volkonsky (secretary of the Supreme Monarchist Council), she stated: "I received this document from V. Abrikosov in a letter in which he wrote that this Committee had been formed for Russians living in emigration so that they could preserve their Eastern rite."

"I do not remember to whom I may have spoken about this Committee – perhaps to Father Nikolay, Feodorov, and Sapozhnikova."

P. V. Shafirov, a former member of the community whom they had been preparing with the goal that he might become the head of the men's Dominican community that was in residence on Afanasyev Lane, stated the following:

> Nothing of the activity evidencing the political features of the parish was communicated to me and therefore during the entire time of my presence in the community I was not able to imagine that I was in touch with, and to some degree depending on, an organization that, in the personage of its representatives, was carrying out political work – which I became convinced of by documents that were later shown to me at the GPU. Of those documents, the letter of Exarch Feodorov to the Lithuanian representative especially convinced me of the conspiratorial nature of the actions of individuals heading up the parish – somehow V. Abrikosov and Kuzmin-Karavayev from abroad (according to documents published in the newspapers) and

> here Anna Abrikosova, who was a confidante of Exarch Feodorov who is now in prison.
>
> In principle, I believe any such cooperation unacceptable, given the availability of regular means of communication with the West – I was forced to conclude that it was politically conspiratorial [...] And then there was the trial of Conradi and the dirty, disgraceful means that the jurors used, justifying the murder of ambassador Vorovsky – I connect this with the activity of persons who engaged in the collection of materials and information for the trial – as I became convinced from the letter to the Lithuanian ambassador from Feodorov through Anna Abrikosova that was shown to me – I consider political dealings reprehensible and blatantly not neutral.

Another of the arrested persons, Tamara Sapozhnikova, with respect to materials belonging to Abrikosova that were discovered in her possession (the "Directives," the document signed by Volkonsky, the letter from Feodorov to Baltrusaitis, and others), stated that one of the Sisters had left the file, but during subsequent interrogations it became clear that the material had been left by Abrikosova after she had been searched. Sapozhnikova was the treasurer in the community and she worked for Feodorov and Aleksandrov. She would go to the Papal Mission to receive parcels. According to Sapozhnikova's statements, she was very close to Anna Abrikosova and fulfilled her directives unhesitatingly. With respect to the brochure "Directives," she stated that she had read it, but she had not seen any political element in it.

Balashev was for all practical purposes the secretary of the community, being in contact with Feodorov and having been an active member of the gatherings at the Abrikosovs' – he stated that he collected (newspaper) clippings and various other information about the situation of the Church at the direction of Abrikosova, and that these were then sent to the Pope in Rome.

To the question as to what was his attitude toward Vorovsky's murderers and what ought to be done with the murderers by the court, he responded: "Since I consider this question political, I refuse to answer." To the question about his attitude to the circles that encouraged the acquittal of Conradi, he stated that "this question was outside his competence."

At the same interrogation, on the question of the (newspaper) clippings found in his possession, where there was an article that was purely political, for example, "On Polish-Russian Relations," [...] he stated that they were interesting to him since he, as a Russian, was always opposed to the interference of Polish political interests in Church matters. Concerning the letter "to Archbishop Anastasios," a typewritten copy of which was found in his possession, he stated that "it was unknown to him how this had ended up on his desk" [...]

Anastasia Vasilyevna Selenkova stated that Aleksandrov had given her his authorization to teach religion in the school. On the question that was posed about whether she would consider it necessary to dissociate herself from Abrikosova in the event she became aware of Abrikosova's counter-revolutionary activity, she stated that she would not find it necessary to dissociate herself under any circumstances from persons with whom she was in a spiritual union.

Galina Fadeyevna Entkevich [Jętkiewicz] was a typist and typed all kinds of materials, including the "Directives," Feodorov's letters, the letter to Archbishop Anastasios and so forth. At her interrogation she stated that she did not remember this. Having relatives in Poland, according to her words, she corresponded with them, but upon receipt of their letters she tore them up. Concerning her dedication to the idea of the "salvation of Russia," Entkevich stated that this meant to pray for "Russian souls." To the question regarding her attitudes toward "social questions," she stated that she would not presume to make judgments on such matters since she had neither the experience nor the knowledge.

Serebriannikova stated that she was at the meetings of Kuzmin-Karavayev, that she had contact with the imprisoned Feodorov, that she received letters from him to read at meetings, that she informed him about matters that had occurred at liberty. She received illegal letters from Feodorov, but not directly through him. She refused to answer through whom she received them. To the question as to whether the murderers of Comrade Vorovsky ought to be punished, she answered, "I am not answering because I am not engaged in politics."

Subsequent intelligence work and the investigatory materials both in Moscow and in Leningrad established the active participation of a number of persons listed below in those Catholic communities. Arrests were made. At their interrogations, the arrested acknowledged their active work in the community, that they were connected with the previously arrested leaders of the community and that they had rendered assistance. Their statements yielded nothing new for the investigation.

Further intelligence data established the following:

- The leader of the entire Catholic rite, Metropolitan Sheptytsky, had concluded an agreement with Petliura concerning assistance to Petliura in the spreading of Uniatism in Ukraine.
- Sheptytsky had concluded an agreement with Dontsov, the leader of fascist organizations abroad, that he would give Dontsov funds for work toward the strengthening of fascist organizations.
- Abrikosova's connection with Kirill, the "guardian of the Russian throne," and Baron Wrangel was established.
- In an intercepted letter from Kuzmin-Karavayev to Khrapunov, the former writes: "In my letter to Vrangel I have for the time being not written anything about the possibility of work in Italy, since I do not want to clutter things up with a number of questions and, furthermore, I think at the present time, when the Italians are going through a "honeymoon" with the Bolsheviks, one can hardly count on any kind of fruitful work for a new organization."
- Subsequent intelligence data established that the "National Union of Catholics in Italy" (an Italian fascist organization) considers the education of children and parish work to be the primary focal points of its efforts – and thus the head of the parish has a special responsibility and the task of the inculcating fascist ideas into the broad masses.

Illegal schools of this sort were organized in Moscow and in Leningrad.

Conclusions

On the basis of documents discovered in the arrest of the above-listed persons, who belonged to and were active members of Moscow and Leningrad communities of Eastern Rite Catholics, subsequent investigation, and agent data, it was absolutely, precisely established that:

- These organizations, under the appearance of religious-Catholic instruction, have pursued purely political fascist goals, identical to the goals of international fascism.
- The leadership of this activity was abroad, in the Supreme Monarchist Council and the Vatican.

Concrete activity of Catholic organizations in the USSR is expressed in the following:

- In connections with the "Italian Division of the Supreme Monarchist Council;
- In connections, organizational and financial, with [diplomatic] missions – mainly the Papal, Polish and also the Lithuanian missions.
- In connections with persons convicted in the Cieplak case, receipt of directives from them and informing them about the activity of Catholic organizations in the USSR.
- The gathering of materials that discredit the Soviet regime for the trial of Conradi and Polunin and the sending of these materials to "the Supreme Monarchist Council."
- Receipt and distribution of illegal counter-revolutionary brochures, both foreign and domestic.
- The organization of illegal groups and conferences which were a component element in the organization.
- The organization of illegal schools for the education of children in a religious-fascist spirit.

Given that White Guard groups have undertaken the creation of fascist organizations in various places within the USSR, and in view of the extreme social danger of the further development of these organizations, the Secret Section of the OGPU proposes to file a petition to the All-Union Executive Committee for the extra-judicial disposition of the present case [...]

T. Guttsay, Authorized Representative

IV Division, Special Board, OGPU
Concurring: Genkin, Andreyeva, Deribas

Investigatory Case Against Russian Catholics, 1931

"Investigatory Case against S.M. Soloviev and Others, 1931," Central Archive, Federal Security Service, Russian Federation

S.M. Soloviev's Statements at His Interrogation, February 16, 1931

From year to year I accepted new members into the community. They gathered at my apartment or at the apartments of other Eastern Rite Catholics. We often talked of current political and economic themes. In addition, we discussed and shared our impressions regarding the situation of Eastern Rite Catholics in prison or administratively exiled, with the intention of organizing material assistance to them.

[...] Neveu was the source of our funds for aiding those in prison. Neveu gave us funds every month, systematically, from foreign sources.

From Statements of Dominican Sisters at Their Interrogations

A.I. Nowicka:

I was responsible for assistance to Eastern Rite priests sent by the Soviet regime to Solovetsky for counter-revolutionary activity and espionage. I personally, and all Eastern Rite Catholics, believe that they were exiled not for counter-revolutionary activity and espionage, but for religious activity, and we regard this as religious persecution.

L.N. Polibina:

[In response to the question: What activity of the Eastern Catholic group helps the building of industry and agriculture and elevates the cultural level of the peoples of the USSR?]:

This group has no position with respect to this question. I believe that the Soviet regime is engaged in the persecution of religion, and a flagrant example is the case of the Abrikosova community and the case of the priest Sloskan. All of Moscow is talking about these sensational cases.

V.A. Sapozhnikova

[from a letter to her spiritual daughter]:

The more the burden of the cross is intensified, the more one needs to be prepared for everything, to the end. The cross – and such a cross as suffering for the Lord God, for the faith – is something so great, something we are not worthy of, and the Lord gives it to us only out of his mercy and exceptional love for us.

N.N. Rubashova:

In general, I consider it unnecessary to give the names of my acquaintances and I refuse to do so. I believe it necessary to declare my hostile attitude toward the Soviet regime. I believe that Communism is incompatible with Christianity, that a struggle exists between them, and in this struggle I am entirely on the side of Christianity against Communism. The struggle of the Soviet regime against religion and 'religious narcotics,' as the Communists call it, also forces me to take a hostile attitude toward the regime.

Investigatory Case against Russian Catholics, 1933-1934

"Investigatory Case against A.I. Abrikosova and Others, 1934," Central Archive, Federal Security Service, Russian Federation

Statements of A.I. Abrikosova at Her Interrogation, August 6, 1933

[…] I consider myself a proponent of a social-political system of state government that finds expression in a democratic republic with a unicameral system of popular representation based on the following constitutional statutes: full equality of the entire population before the law on the basis of civil freedoms: freedom of conscience, freedom of speech, freedom of the press, the inviolability of the individual person, and so forth.

In the economic sphere, [I believe that] major landholding interests and the interests of the financial oligarchy ought to be limited.

I consider myself a supporter of a democratic Christian party that takes as its goal the realization of the ideals of a bourgeois-democratic parliamentarianism that is not based on class.

I consider myself a principled opponent of the Soviet system. A policy of terrorism and the oppression of the individual, in particular, have found expression in the Soviet system. The dictatorship of the Communist Party over the people has been realized and is being carried out in the USSR.

Statements of A.I. Abrikosova at Her Interrogation, August 8, 1933

[…] At the meeting of the group I led a discussion on the theme of the situation of the young people of Soviet Russia and working out the problem of an anti-Soviet worldview.

The basic theses of my conversation were as follows:

- Soviet young people cannot speak of their own worldview, since they have blinders over their eyes.
- Soviet young people are developed in a way that is too one-sided; they only know Marxist-Leninist phrases.
- A political and spiritual worldview ought to be worked out on

the basis of a free, critical study of all facets of philosophical and political thought.

In Catholic educational institutions young people work out their worldview on the basis of the full freedom of a critical study of the works of Marx and Engels, as well as other economists.

Speaking of the Soviet system as a whole and Soviet economics, I asserted: in the practical experience of the USSR we see that Marxism is bankrupt, and as proof I cited the economic situation in the country, which I characterized as being in a state of near total collapse; the country is dying thanks to the Party's policies.

[...] Being a principled opponent of the Soviet regime, I criticized the organization of the political system: the absence of civil freedoms, freedom of the person, and so forth, and I also showed the unsustainability of the way in which the national economy was organized, which has brought the country and its people to the point of famine and destitution.

Statements of A.I. Abrikosova at Her Interrogation, September 10, 1933

Upon my release from the political isolator, and being in Moscow, I reestablished contact with a group of persons who had been sentenced by the Collegium of the OGPU in 1924 as members of a counter-revolutionary organization, and as the head of which I myself had been sentenced by the Collegium. The group with whom I reestablished contact included Vera Tsvetkova, Elena Vakhevich, Sofia Eismont, and Raisa Krylevskaya.[3]

I knew their political disposition prior to their arrest; I knew that they were of an anti-Soviet inclination. Renewing contact with them, I wanted to know their political and spiritual state after having endured arrest, administrative exile and life under residency

[3] All of the women named had been arrested earlier or were arrested together with Anna Abrikosova.

restrictions. After meetings with them I was convinced that they maintained their earlier worldview.

From Statements of Dominican Sisters at their Interrogations

K.N. Kruczelnicka[4]

"I consider myself an opponent of the Soviet system. The main, deciding element for me is the absence of civil freedoms in Soviet Russia [...] As a believer, I find it impossible to confess my faith openly in Soviet Russia. The Church is persecuted [from] various directions, and the finest children of the Church are repressed."

E.I. Gotovtseva

"I do not consider myself obliged to make any statements since, in the first place, as to what concerns me, this is my spiritual life and I am not about to give any account of it to an investigator for the OGPU; and secondly, the others have the right to give or not to give statements to an investigator themselves, since it is a matter of their spiritual life."

R.I. Krylevskaya

"I have expressed counter-revolutionary views, directed against the policy of the Party and the Soviet regime. I maintain those counter-revolutionary views even now – I have not changed them and I do not plan to change them. I am a principled opponent of policies being carried out by the Soviet regime in the cities and the countryside. I am a staunch proponent of Papal theocracy and I have made, and will make, my goal that of the realization of a theocracy in Russia."

[4] Translator's Note: The Servant of God Camilla Kruczelnicka was the hostess of at least one evening gathering, but she herself was not a Dominican.

V.A. Khmeleva

> "Anna Ivanovna is a person most devoted to her work – she is intelligent and well-read. She follows politics and she has a firm, unbending will that allowed her to endure nine years of solitary confinement and a difficult, serious operation. She will go to all lengths for the sake of her goal. She is an organizer and a leader by nature. After sitting in prisons from 1924 to 1932, she came out full of strength and energy and once again set about her work. All the Sisters once again came under her guidance."

Indictments in the Case of the Counter-Revolutionary Terrorist-Monarchist Organization

Formulation of the Accusation

A counter-revolutionary, terrorist-monarchist organization, which had taken as its task the overthrow of the Soviet regime in the USSR and the establishment of a monarchist system was liquidated by the OGPU.

The organization had been created and was headed by the superior of a clandestine Catholic Dominican Order, Anna Abrikosova, daughter of a former prominent Moscow factory owner. It was guided and financed by the Russian Commission "Congregation of the Eastern Church," which exercised its guidance through the Moscow Catholic Bishop Eugene Neveu, a French subject.

In accordance with the charter of the Dominican Order, the organization carried out counter-revolutionary work primarily among the old intelligentsia and university youth, preparing the latter for an active fight against the Soviet regime.

K.N. Kruczelnicka, the leader of the organization's youth group, was preparing a terrorist act against the leadership of the All-Union Communist Party (Bolsheviks). She designated A.V. Brilliantova, a member of said youth group, to be the perpetrator of the terrorist act.

In the course of its counter-revolutionary work the organization established contact with the counter-revolutionary Black Hundred group, led by a former official of the criminal investigation police and former member of the "Union of the Russian People."

Twenty-four persons were arrested in this case, the overwhelming majority of whom were former members of the nobility [...]

Programmatic-Political Tenets of the Organization

The organization had taken as the ultimate goal of its activity the overthrow of the Soviet regime in the USSR and the establishment of a constitutional-monarchist system. In the sphere of political-economic questions, the organization stood on a restorationist platform, putting forward the following demands:

- The establishment of a constitutional-monarchist system;
- The direct government of the country to be transferred into the hands of the intelligentsia "as the culturally and politically progressive, leading segment of the Russian people";
- The establishment of Papal theocracy;
- Full restoration of capitalistic relations: denationalization of industry and the abolition [restoration?] of land ownership, including estate land ownership [...]

The Origin and Composition of the Organization

In 1932, Anna Abrikosova was released early from the political isolator and sent into administrative exile in Kostroma. She had been sentenced to ten years in a political isolator prison in 1923 [1924] by the Collegium of the OGPU under Article 58-6, – 10 and – 11 for leading work in a counter-revolutionary organization of Catholics and active assistance of the espionage work of the priests Cieplak and Budkiewicz.

A group of clandestine Dominican nuns

Under the pretext of medical treatment, Abrikosova periodically came from Kostroma to Moscow in 1932 and there renewed her contacts with former members of the counter-revolutionary organization of Catholics who were living in Moscow, the clandestine Dominican nuns: S.V. Eismont, V.E. Tsvetkova, E.V. Vakhevich, R.I. Krylevskaya, V.A. Khmeleva.

Concrete Counter-Revolutionary Activity of the Organization

- Recruitment of new members [...]
- Counter-revolutionary work among the youth, gathering and distribution of counter-revolutionary literature [...]
- Preparation of a terrorist act against the leadership of the All-Union Communist Party (Bolsheviks)

[...] In numerous conversations with Brilliantova, K.N. Kruczelnicka systematically indoctrinated Brilliantova in a counter-revolutionary tendency, spoke to her of the "sufferings of the Russian people," "of the cruelty of the regime," "the guilt of the Bolshevik leadership." Kruczelnicka obtained a detailed description of the floor plan of Comrade Stalin's dacha. [...]

The materials of the investigation in this case have established that Kruczelnicka's terrorist activity was the organizational formulation of an ideological indoctrination, to which members of the organization, including Kruczelnicka, were subjected by Bishop Neveu.

In conversation with a number of members of the organization, Bishop Neveu systematically sharpened their counter-revolutionary dispositions with stories "about the massive dissatisfaction of the populace with the Soviet regime," "the large number of anonymous letters received by the French embassy whose authors ask Europe to free Russia from the Bolsheviks," about rebellions of the Red Army and young people that were brewing on the periphery, and about the fact that "Russia is an unfortunate country, its people are suffering, and the leaders are guilty in these sufferings."

[...] Taking into account the significance of the Dominican Order in the work of preparing obedient cadres of counter-revolutionaries and fanatics, ready to fight the Soviet regime by any means, the leadership of the organization put before the organization the task of converting newly recruited members of the organization to Catholicism and involving them in the Dominican Order.

The method of the initial approach to recruits – the missionary preaching of Catholicism – was determined by this task.

Connection with the Vatican and the Role of Bishop Neveu

The organization had contact with the Russian Commission "Congregation of the Eastern Church" (Vatican) and Pope Pius XI, who, through his representative, the Catholic Bishop Eugene Neveu, a French subject living at the French embassy in Moscow, exercised direct leadership of the organization.

The investigation established that Anna Abrikosova, upon coming out of the political isolator in 1932, appealed through Bishop Neveu to Pope Pius XI for directions for further work and through the same Neveu received the Pope's response, in which he confirmed Abrikosova's appointment as superior of the Dominican Order in the USSR and blessed her "for her struggle for the Russian work."

Abrikosova later received guiding instructions and funds for her work from Pope Pius XI and the Russian Commission.

[...] In conversations with members of the organization, Neveu systematically affirmed in them their confidence in the inevitability of an imminent intervention and the overthrow of the Soviet regime; for all practical purposes he guided the counter-revolutionary work of Kruczelnicka and others and through them he gathered information about the situation in the USSR. [...]

Investigatory Case against Russian Catholics, 1934-1935

"Investigatory Case against V.F. Remov," Central Archive, Federal Security Service, Russian Federation

Indictment in Investigatory Case No. 976

Information came to the Chief Administration of State Security concerning the existence of a Russian-Catholic counter-revolutionary organization of church people in Moscow, created under the directives of the Russian Commission at the Vatican by a secret Vatican representative in Moscow, the Catholic bishop, Eugene Neveu.

Neveu had recruited to assist him the Orthodox Archbishop N.F. Remov, who had secretly converted to Catholicism and in 1933 had been officially confirmed by the Vatican as illegal assistant to Neveu.

The counter-revolutionary group is made up of two groups – a Catholic group and an Orthodox group, with both groups uniting at the illegal Petrovsky Monastery in Moscow, organized at Remov's initiative.

The organization had as its basic task the preparation of active counter-revolutionary cadres for fighting against the Soviet regime. The creation of these cadres was conducted by means of recruitment of intelligentsia of a predominantly anti-Soviet disposition – recruitment was preceded by a lengthy and all-sided testing and indoctrination in the spirit of a "readiness to go to all sufferings and torments" in the struggle with the Soviet regime.

Along with this, information also came to the Chief Administration of State Security concerning the fact that the organization was supplying Neveu with slanderous information about the situation in the USSR, and it was receiving from Neveu foreign counter-revolutionary literature that was being disseminated among like-minded people.

On this basis, the active participants in the Russian-Catholic counter-revolutionary organization – twenty-two people – were arrested and a preliminary investigation was conducted, as a result of which the counter-revolutionary activity of the organization was fully established.

[...] A wide variety of methods was used in cultivating and recruiting counter-revolutionary cadres. Regarding this, Remov stated:

> We recruited the most suitable and trustworthy into a clandestine religious order, and in doing so provided those designated for recruitment with literature of an ascetical tendency. In addition, all kinds of obligations were placed on them for work in the church... We also created an institute of novices, the task of which was the nurturing of steadfast Christians who would be able to replace dying monastic cadres and if necessary to suffer for the faith.

[...] The witness S. was questioned concerning the nature of the counter-revolutionary organization and its method of recruiting new members, and he stated:

> Active members of the organization systematically and insistently inculcate in church members that every true Christian is obliged to direct his efforts toward hastening the day of the fall of the Soviet regime.

> A large number of those indoctrinated were dedicated to a secret religious order, and these secret religious fill various positions in Soviet institutions and, in their turn, indoctrinate new persons from among those of their acquaintances who are of an anti-Soviet disposition.

Counter-Revolutionary Activity of the Catholic Group of the Organization

Being directly connected with Neveu and under his ideological influence, the members of the Catholic group of the counter-revolutionary organization supplied Neveu with counter-revolutionary information about the situation in the USSR.

When questioned on this topic, Remov stated:

> Materials collected for Neveu were used in many presentations against the Soviet Union given abroad by church members. I helped Neveu in this; I supplied him with counter-revolutionary information and slanderous documents.

[...] Others among those arrested also acknowledged being in illegal contact with Neveu – [Elena] Rozhina stated:

> I served as a link between Neveu and the clandestine Catholic Bishop Remov. I received foreign literature from Neveu and I informed him on current questions. In particular, I informed Neveu about the arrests of the priests of the church on Malaya Dmitrovka. Neveu told me that a special Russian Commission had been created at the Vatican, and it is working on the realization of the idea of the unification of the churches. Neveu told me that in France there is a monastery school that educates people in a love for Russia and the

> Russian people. Neveu dreamed of the possibility of sending me to that school.

[...] Neveu provided the members of the organization with counter-revolutionary literature published abroad. He gave Remov a brochure by D'Herbigny that contained slanderous information about the situation in the USSR and called for a fight against the Soviet regime. Remov gave this brochure to [co-defendant Aleksandra] Kachalova, who translated it into Russian from the French with the goal of circulating it [...]

Appendix 2: A Rebuttal

Sophia Eismont (Sister Philomena, OP).

IN his lengthy book about Father Leonid Feodorov, the Exarch of Russian Catholics, Deacon Basil von Burman, OSB, includes superficial impressions of the community of Dominican Sisters and its leaders, Anna Ivanovna and Vladimir Vladimirovich Abrikosov.[1] These are the impressions of a person who was not closely familiar with either the community or the Arbikosovs, and they are permeated by a strange, hostile tone. It is hard to understand the source of such hostility. What he has written distorts reality. Note, for example, his very strange description of the Sisters:

> Locked in their own tight little circle, isolated from the people, having not the slightest understanding of the people's spirit or needs, they are like those elegant, alabaster marble statuettes with which ladies of the time of Louis XV adorned their étagères. (p. 534)

I, as a Sister of this Dominican community, who entered the community as the next to last, a few months before all, including me, were arrested, must say – my conscience insistently orders me to do so – that I was extremely upset and, reading this book with sad bewilderment, I wondered: "How was it possible to treat with such hostility and such injustice such a grand work of God, presenting everything that related to the Moscow community of Dominican Sisters and its founders in such a distorted form?" It was this that forced me to write this rebuttal.

One must not forget that the Sisters of the community were not secular parishioners, but nuns – and at the same time, given the circumstances and the fact that they were Sisters of the Third Order Regular of Saint Dominic,

[1] Deacon Vasilii von Burman, OSB, *Leonid Fedorov. Zhizn' i deiatel'nost'* [Leonid Feodorov: Life and Work] (Rome, 1966). Unless otherwise noted, all page citations refer to this work.

they were not "locked up in their tight little circle." The majority of the Sisters – professed, novices, or newly entered postulants – worked in various institutions, and coming home to the community in the evening, they led a strict ascetic life. Many of these "marble statuettes," in order to enter the community, had gone through great trials and difficulties, encountering a complete lack of understanding on the part of their parents and relatives. Some of them had been forced to break off ties with their relatives. In doing this, the Sisters fully understood what they were getting into, what difficult trials lay before them – but despite their youth, they were ready for whatever lay ahead and they did not waver in their vocation. Later some of the Sisters would give their lives, dying in the prisons and camps.

The future exarch of the Russian Catholics, Leonid Feodorov, had become acquainted with the Abrikosovs in 1910, and he also visited Moscow in 1911 and in 1912. Observing the activity of the Abrikosovs, to which they had dedicated themselves entirely, Father Leonid wrote of their work in a letter to Metropolitan Andrey Sheptytsky:

> Concerning this family, one can say with the words of the Apostle Paul: "I hail this domestic church!" Rarely can one encounter young people in the blossom of their years who are so dedicated to the work of the Church and so religious. (p. 171)

> The heart of the mission beats in the home of the Abrikosovs. May the Lord God reward these humble workers in His field. In their home one can regularly encounter a whole circle of Russian Catholics (predominantly women), who are doing all they can just to extend the light of the true faith. The genuine, warm-hearted piety, the tireless zeal, with which this worthy couple works for the glory of God would give honor to any missionary of the Holy Church. (pp. 198-199)

What changed in Father Leonid's attitude toward the Sisters of the community if in the next letter to Metropolitan Sheptytsky, after a full week of "real debates in private" with the Abrikosovs, he would write something so utterly different:

> "Holiness, holiness," they repeat like parrots. "The goal of Catholicism is the sanctification of people, i.e., the personal holiness of every individual member of the Catholic Church. The Russian mission ought also to aspire primarily to this holiness of its members. We want our Catholics to be saints! This is our goal!"

Well, who can argue with this? But the Abrikosovs accuse us Petersburg Catholics of not understanding how to achieve this goal. (p. 534)

In any great work of God there must be, first of all, an essential, inner spiritual preparation, as each person needs to create a spiritual foundation within himself. It is not us, not our external actions, that will foster our success. Only God within us and through us will complete His work, if we prepare a way for Him. We ought to be the obedient instrument in the hands of God. All the saints, Saint John the Baptist and the Lord Jesus Christ Himself bear witness to this.

And in this regard, Anna and Vladimir were right in considering the main thing to be not external activity, but internal, spiritual activity. One should have both, and they are tightly bound together.

> All the Russian Catholics in Moscow were subject to the local Latin jurisdiction… Thus, prior to the formation of the Russian eparchy, Moscow Catholics had only a distant and indirect relationship to the mission of Father Leonid. Out of this arose, even in this sphere, that Petersburg-Moscow distrust and mutual failure to understand one another, further intensified by that ever-present antagonism between the two Russian capitals, under the spiritual and cultural influence of which both groups of Russian Catholics found themselves. (pp. 94-95)

And thus it always is, when believers are not permeated by the truly Christian evangelical spirit of brotherly love, which precludes all manner of antagonism.

Von Burman more than once speaks of and emphasizes that Anna and Vladimir came from "eminent Moscow merchant" families, but there is no emphasis on the social origin of anyone else. It is as though this origin is a "minus," casting a shadow on them. This is incomprehensible and absolutely incompatible with the Christian spirit. What significance can this or that social origin possibly have before God?!

Von Burman also speaks more than once about the fact that Anna and Vladimir dearly loved one another, again, as though this were something unfitting. Those who knew Anna and Vladimir closely from their earliest years spoke of them as people of a noble soul with lofty aspirations and a complete unity of views, which then became the firm bond of their union.

There have been so many instances in the church where married couples have zealously served God and achieved holiness. One of the many examples is that of Saint Jane de Chantal, who dearly loved her husband and seriously grieved his unexpected death, but this did not keep her from becoming a saint. All these attacks, mainly against Anna, reveal a prejudiced attitude and a complete lack of knowledge and understanding of many of the basic principles of Christianity. Further on the criticism of Anna and the community itself become even more biased, and it is based solely on superficial contact.

> They lack any experience or that proper order that is developed over many years of practice, a way of life precisely set forth by monastic [religious] rule. None of this can be replaced by that external discipline which Anna Ivanovna had successfully imposed and strictly maintained in accordance with her own views of the matter. Much here smacked of improvisation, the fulfillment of a role she had taken upon herself. Unfortunately, this has to be attributed to the one whom the Sisters chose as their Superior and who played the role of head of the community, diligently trying to be their "mother." Alas, strict monastic experience, which was unknown to her, tells us that good will, common sense and some portion of fantasy are hardly enough to become the "mother." It is not enough to be domineering and even "autocratic" by nature. For the guidance of souls, and especially under such difficult conditions, the head of the community ought to have had a serious and lengthy school of humility, obedience and self-renunciation. Moving the furniture around in the apartment, establishing new relations with one's beloved husband while continuing to live side by side with him – these do not elevate one to the role of the head of the community, the spiritual mother of the Sisters, because for this it is necessary that one be spiritually

> mature, a real religious. In order to acquire the gift or simply the ability of working on the souls of those entrusted to one, one must first progress along what is no short or easy – and for some, a very lengthy and painful – path in a religious community. Secular people, who judge the spiritual life in the world's terms, of course might not understand this. But even so, they could agree at least that one cannot replace personal experience with the reading of fine books. And it was in this that Anna Ivanovna's weakness lay. (p. 548)

Von Burman's judgment concerning Anna and the community of Sisters reveals some shortcomings in his own knowledge of religious life. Even under normal conditions, the specific way of life and character of a newly created community, characteristic of it alone and depending on its tasks and goals, are established only gradually. Thus it has been in the past, is now, and will be in the future. The Moscow community of Dominican Sisters for all practical purposes was still in a state of initial organization during a time that was very difficult. Mistakes are always possible in the early stages of any such endeavor.

In the history of religious life there are several instances where the superior herself did not first progress along a "path in a religious community that was not short or easy." Saint Jane de Chantal, for example, did not go through a preparation in a convent, but had lived in the world prior to founding the Order of the Visitation. Judging a person's spiritual state from a distance, not being closely acquainted or in contact with him, and attributing to him a "role taken upon himself" is more than strange. Only a spiritual director would be able to pass judgment on that person's inner readiness for one or another work.

Von Burman does not even concede that perhaps this could have been the will of God and that the Lord had clearly, obviously shown its necessity.

He says in an undignified and absolutely unchristian tone, "to become the 'mother' it is not sufficient to be domineering by nature.... Moving the furniture around in the apartment, establishing new relations with one's beloved husband ... does not mean that one is elevated to the role of the head of the community, the spiritual mother of the Sisters."

Once again he speaks about Anna's love for her husband as though it were some kind of shortcoming. He forgets, and does not take into account, the fact that God, in calling a person to one or another kind of work, and all the more so in calling a person to a great work, will give that person the corresponding necessary grace and assistance.

Why does the author not even grant this, instead of attributing everything to Anna's dominance? And why is it "dominance," and not "firmness" – a trait needed in every work and all the more so in a great work?

At this difficult time, if Anna had not been an inspired person, ready for all sacrifices for the glory of God and salvation of souls, she would never have taken upon herself such a heavy cross – not a "role," as von Burman strangely calls it.

Anna's spiritual motto was "Christ did not come down from the cross – they took him down dead." This motto was literally fulfilled in her life. After spending twelve years in prison – six years in the Tobolsk prison, five of which were in solitary confinement, and six years in solitary confinement in the Yaroslavl political isolator – she died in Butyrka Prison Hospital on July 24, 1936.

If Father Alexei Zerchaninov, who spent two and a half years (August 3, 1898 through January 1901) in the Suzdal prison at Spasso-Efimovsk Monastery for clergy criminals, made a favorable impression among Petersburg Russian Catholics in 1907 and "won everyone over with the aura of martyrdom" – why then can the same not be said about Anna Abrikosova?

Words like "improvisation," "role," and "fantasy" written with respect to her are absolutely inappropriate. At that time, the entire life of the parish and the community was under the sword of Damocles. It is strange that von Burman apparently did not understand this at all. Most likely, he was far removed from the conditions of life of that time.[2]

He ought to apply to himself the words "Secular people might not understand" – because it is precisely he and Julia Danzas who judge matters and people on the basis of superficial impressions, "in a worldly way," not knowing the real essence of the matter, taking as their point of departure

---

[2] Translator's Note: The identity of Basil von Burman, OSB, remained unknown to Sister Philomena. Born in Warsaw in 1891, he fought with Denikin and Wrangel in the Civil War, then emigrated with his family to Croatia. His wife was killed by Tito's partisans during World War II; in 1945 he converted to Catholicism and in 1949 professed monastic vows at Niederaltaich Abbey in Bavaria. He later moved to the United States where he died in 1959; buried at Saint Procopius Abbey, Lisle, Illinois. His biography of Exarch Feodorov was posthumously published in Rome by Josyf Cardinal Slypyi in 1966.

their sparse, rather theoretical knowledge, without any real understanding of the spiritual life and its laws.

All around them many people were thirsting for a deep spiritual life in Christ and with Christ, and they could find no help. Inspired by Anna's cheerfulness, by her sensitivity and responsiveness, they began to feel drawn to her. So was she supposed to push them all away, remain indifferent, as he believes? It was, after all, for this apostolic work in Russia that Anna and Vladimir had received the blessing of the Most Holy Father Pius X in 1913.

It is completely untrue that the Latin clergy took a negative attitude toward the parish of Russian Catholics. Through the pastor of the church of the Holy Apostles Peter and Paul, the Russian Catholics were subject to Metropolitan Kluczyński. When the laity turned to the pastors of the Latin Rite Catholic churches[3] with questions about a deeper Christian life, those pastors responded, "Go to the Eastern Rite Catholics – they have an intensive religious life."

After the arrests in 1923 and 1924 of Anna, Father Nikolay Aleksandrov, the Sisters and many parishioners and after their sentencing to prisons, camps and administrative exile, two of the remaining Sisters and the few parishioners still at liberty gathered around Father Sergey Soloviev, and it was Father Mikhail Tsakul [Cakul], the pastor of Immaculate Conception Church, who gave Father Sergey one of the side altars for daily Mass, which the remaining Russian Catholics attended.

The impressions of the Moscow community of Dominican Sisters written by Julia Danzas are especially distressing. The book contains much about her.

So who is this Julia Nikolayevna Danzas? From childhood she was considered a "wonder child" because of the outstanding capabilities of her mind and memory. She finished high school at age thirteen, and by the time she was fifteen she was reading not only historians, but philosophers as well. At age sixteen she became interested in religion, in Christianity – but from its external aspect: the historical and cultural significance of Christianity in Europe and in Catholicism as the core of world history. In 1906, at age twenty-seven, under the influence of Schopenhauer and Nietzsche, she wrote Pretensions of Thought [Zaprosy mysli], a deeply pessimistic work that

[3] Holy Apostles Peter and Paul and Immaculate Conception.

had great success, but also a negative influence on young people, affirming thoughts about the hopelessness of life and suicide as the only rational exit.

In her youth Julia Danzas participated in Petersburg court life, "giving herself up to secular life with a passion" (p. 404). By birth she was a member of an ancient Byzantine royal family, which allowed her to become a lady-in-waiting for Empress Alexandra Feodorovna. All these purely natural advantages, which have an enchanting significance in people's eyes, also developed in her an enormous self-assuredness – Julia Danzas "in general spoke harshly, since she had become accustomed to the fact that in this society she was allowed everything."

Self-assuredness is a blatant manifestation of pride, which is the most blinding obstacle for the action of God's grace in a person's soul. Not in vain did Father Leonid, her spiritual director, write later from prison that in the task of saving this person for the Church it was important "that her natural pride be crushed into the dust" (p. 430).

We note that Julia Danzas's religious consciousness evolved very slowly, such that prior to 1915, when she was already thirty-six years old, she had still not become a Christian and was not able to accept the divinity of Jesus Christ and his redemptive sacrifice (p. 402). In 1915, on the Front during World War I, grace was finally able to enlighten her soul, and she came to understand the life-giving power and essence of Christianity, the mystery of Christ's redemptive sacrifice and sufferings in general. By 1918, when she was already thirty-nine years old, she was ready to accept Catholicism, but she was not able to do so until the autumn of 1920. Not long before this, in the summer of 1920, she had become acquainted with the exarch of the Russian Catholics, Father Leonid Feodorov, and upon his advice and that of Bishop Cieplak she chose the path of the Eastern Rite in order to help the exarch in his mission.

A desire to create a women's religious community arose in the parish of the Petersburg Russian Catholics. For this purpose, Father Leonid asked Anna to send Sister Maria Rose [Vera Khmeleva] to Petrograd for establishing such a community, and when Anna did not send her, it was construed as meaning "Apparently Anna Ivanovna was displeased by the fact that a parallel work was being undertaken in Petrograd" (p. 549).

How easily they came to negative conclusions! Anna could not have sent Sister Maria Rose because Sister Maria Rose was needed in the community as the directress of novices and postulants and there was no one who could have replaced her.

How was it possible to attribute this to being "displeased," when any work undertaken for the benefit of souls and the glory of God can only be a cause for joy! Why were such base, undignified feelings, so uncharacteristic of Anna, so easily supposed?

In June 1922 Julia Danzas came to Moscow to meet Anna, to take a look at the life of the community and to borrow from the experience of an already-existing regular community of Dominican Sisters. In her memoirs about the Moscow community written later, one immediately notices the serious criticism of Anna Abrikosova and the Sisters of the community – a strange hostility that caused her to perceive everything in a negative light.

"Prior to this, Julia Danzas had heard only positive comments," that "life there is holy, full of spiritual ardor."

> When he was in Moscow, Father Leonid always visited Anna Ivanovna. He praised the discipline, noting the quiet that reigned in the small residence, despite the presence of almost twenty Sisters. (p. 549)

But despite all the good that Julia Danzas had heard, it was just the very idea that Anna Abrikosova "wanted to take her into the community under her direction" that put her on guard. When entering a community, women are entering an Order, not some kind of personal direction. The Order of Saint Dominic is the order of Truth; it as an Apostolic Order. Its mottos are:

> *Veritas* – Truth
>
> *Contemplare et contemplata aliis tradere* – to contemplate and to hand on the fruits of contemplation
>
> *Veritatem facientes in caritate* – Proclaiming the truth in love – i.e., in love, to embody the Truth one has learned in one's practical life and carry it forth to others in works of mercy.
>
> *Laudare, benedicere, praedicere* – To praise, to bless, to preach

What is more amazing is that Anna, upon becoming acquainted with Julia Danzas and seeing in her a worthy, educated person, treated her with an open sincerity and wanted to have her in the community. With her natural gifts, Julia Danzas was completely suited to the spirit and tasks of the Order.

It is absolutely incomprehensible how Julia Danzas could have thought that Anna Abrikosova wanted to take her into the community "under her direction and subject her in Russia and abroad to the authority of the Abrikosov family," and not for the community of the Order of Saint Dominic. How was it possible to attribute to a person such absurd and base ideas and intentions?

Anna was a highly cultured and inspired person of noble soul, and she always stood above petty personal ideas of self-love and vanity. In all spheres of her life she was entirely guided by the highest spiritual principles, the good of souls and the Church.

It is completely understandable why this contact between Anna Abrikosova and Julia Danzas did not work out. They spoke the same language, but as though different languages, starting from opposing points of view and different spiritual states.

Julia Danzas was an exceptionally intellectual person, who had become a Catholic only two years earlier and still had no spiritual experience. She was still in many respects far from true Christianity and very self-assured; in her views she took as her point of departure the little theoretical knowledge she had in the spiritual sphere; she was not free from prejudices and antagonism, which are completely alien to the spirit of Christianity. She was a person in whom the "old man" still prevailed, with all his shortcomings, weaknesses and limitations.

All people who are outstanding in their intelligence and natural giftedness are always in danger of falling into self-assuredness and, in connection with this, into an inevitable blindness and faulty perception of many things.

Anna Abrikosova was not inferior to Julia Danzas in any respect – not in culture, or in her grand intellect, or in her education. Julia Danzas had received her higher education at the Sorbonne in France – Anna Abrikosova, at Cambridge University in England. Anna had become a Catholic in 1908, when she was twenty-seven years old, and in 1910 she and Vladimir had begun their apostolic work in Moscow. From 1908 to 1913 they had deepened their theological knowledge and their inner spiritual life. They had studied specifically Dominican literature and had especially fallen in love with Saint Thomas Aquinas, as well as Saint Dominic and the Dominican apostolic spirit of piety. They had been able to combine an understanding of modernity with supernatural principles, and in this they possessed a great keenness of observation and psychological analysis. These character traits fostered in them the formation of accomplished spiritual directors.

In 1913, in Rome, Anna and Vladimir had been accepted into the Third Order of Saint Dominic by the Procurator General, Father Henri Desqueyrous. Also in 1913, at a private audience with the Most Holy Father Pope Pius X, who took a lively interest in the work in Moscow, they had received his apostolic blessing on their further work in Russia. Already by that time Russian Catholics who had joined the Eastern Rite began to gather around the Abrikosovs, including young women who wanted to give themselves entirely to the service of God and others.

Thus, by 1917, when Vladimir was ordained a priest of the Eastern Rite, a new parish had already taken shape and a community of Dominican Sisters was growing quickly. By the time of Julia Danzas's meeting with Anna Abrikosova in 1922, there were approximately twenty women in the community.

The charm of Anna's bright and noble personality attracted to her the hearts of all those around her, even people who were not inclined toward Catholicism or religion. They trustingly felt themselves drawn to her. Anna directed the souls of not only the Sisters, but of many parishioners as well. Thus, she had already had over twelve years of spiritual experience, and in this respect she had an unquestionable advantage over Julia Danzas.

Von Burman himself explains why the contact between Anna Abrikosova and Julia Danzas came to naught.

> One person would not submit to the authority of Anna Abrikosova. Indeed that person could not have submitted to her, by virtue of her exceptional giftedness, and as a result of belonging to another world of traditions and understanding, to which the Moscow merchant spirit, even in its gentle, relaxed and cultured aspect, was by its nature alien and unacceptable. This person was the "woman with Napoleon's profile" – Julia Danzas, whom Anna Ivanovna would

> have liked to take into the community under her direction and subject her, in Russia and abroad, to the authority of the family of the Abrikosovs. This intention went unrealized, but it caused Julia Danzas to be on her guard and to take the position of an observer. (p. 532)

This explanation reveals the defective understanding of the spirit of Christianity shared by Julia Danzas and von Burman. It demonstrates a purely human, primitive understanding of things, an understanding that was not free from prejudices and bias.

For Julia Danzas, apparently, even the thought of entering a community under the direction of Anna Abrikosova was humiliating. But how then did she understand Christianity, or religious life – both of which required self-renunciation and humility?

It is fully possible to doubt the accuracy of Julia Danzas's transmittal of Anna's words. It very often happens that a self-assured and inimically disposed person who has not analyzed her own feelings and impressions unconsciously gives a different nuance to the words and actions of another. What has been transmitted as the words of Anna Ivanovna is contradictory to a grand mind that was clear and far from narrowness and prejudices.

Anna was a direct and open person, and she was fully right when she said that the Sisters in the community knew what the Church, grace and the spiritual life were. And not just the Sisters and parishioners, but even those outsiders who came to the community for lectures and conversations that were "for everyone."

It is hard to imagine the requirements with which Julia Danzas approached the Moscow community. Still not having any spiritual experience, she took as her point of departure the little natural, theoretical knowledge she had, guided by her own mind which, no matter how outstanding, was inevitably limited. Her impressions are superficial and the conclusions drawn from them are far from true. Indeed, owing to the self-assuredness that blinded her, she apparently did not even try to learn the truth about what she observed. For example, she acknowledged with approval the vocation of one of the Sisters with whom she came into brief contact:

> Among the completely uneducated women, Julia Danzas found

> several fine, humble, sincerely believing young women. Anna Davidyuk (Sister Lucia), the cook, made an especially dear impression on her. She was barely literate, but a fine, genuinely holy soul. For some reason they worked her to the bone and spoke peremptorily with her, as with a servant in times past. Julia Danzas managed to speak several times with Sister Lucia. She found in her "one of those pure souls with a real religious vocation." (pp. 555-556)

Here one can only wonder how Julia Danzas could have concluded that the Sisters were "completely uneducated," when in fact no fewer than ten Sisters had a higher education and the rest had finished high school. One of the Sisters even held a professorship at the university – Sister Catherine de Ricci (Selenkova). As for the "cook," Sister Lucia, whom Julia Danzas considered "barely literate," but a fine, genuinely holy soul, "with a real religious vocation," this Sister could hardly be called barely literate, as she had graduated from the finest Moscow gymnasium with a gold medal and by that time had already completed two years at the university. And of course she was not a cook, but along with the other Sisters she had been assigned to help the Sister-housekeeper. In the community she was among three of the so-called "church sisters" and served at the liturgy. While she was indeed a fine Sister, she in no way could be distinguished among the other Sisters, who also possessed the same fine qualities noted in her by Julia Danzas. Such is the worth of her independent opinion and impressions!

Perhaps Julia Danzas believed that all the Sisters ought to be erudite and have a higher education. If so, this only reveals her complete lack of understanding of the structure and spirit of religious communities, where there is first of all a constant striving toward greater perfection, work on oneself, a life lived not by natural, secular notions, but by faith, penetrated by the evangelical spirit of the three vows: obedience, chastity and poverty.

In all convents of all orders – men's and women's – brothers and sisters are engaged, some exclusively in mental work, others in physical, agricultural works, and works of mercy – but primarily, in a contemplative, prayerful life. Depending on the founding direction of the Order and its individual communities, something will predominate, but it will not preclude the others. A community needs different kinds of members, which creates the fullness of the harmony of religious life. And this is necessary.

At that time (summer of 1922) there were nine professed Sisters in the community, five novices and four postulants. Noticing that some of the Sisters broke the rule of absolute silence[4] with gestures that, most likely, were called for by a serious need to clarify something, Julia Danzas clearly exaggerated this, saying that "they were always conversing in sign language. I found these lengthy, wordless, gesticulated conversations amusing."[5] It could not have been so. The Sisters treated the fulfillment of the charter and rules with seriousness and diligence.

Furthermore, Julia Danzas of course absolutely failed to take into account the fact that neither novices nor those who had recently entered as postulants had yet fully entered into the regimen of religious life, their formation had not been completed, and inevitably they still had failings in some rules of conduct. No one enters a community as a perfected, prepared and exemplary religious, but once having entered, she begins to learn everything and gradually achieves everything. Once again, this speaks of a lack of understanding of religious life. Later she notes the "unpopularity of the Sisters of this community among the convicts in those prisons where I was with them..." (p. 604)

Popularity or unpopularity depends not only on virtues, the perfection of the person and his behaviors, but on many external factors as well: on the circumstances and the surrounding milieu; on the development, psychology, moral and spiritual state of the surrounding people. In this respect, popularity will not always be a good thing – and unpopularity, not always a bad thing. Popularity or unpopularity cannot be a measure for characterizing a person. One can certainly say that none of the Sisters ever even thought about popularity or her prestige, because the main thing in Christianity and especially in religious life are the words of Christ, binding on all – "Deny yourself, take up your cross, and follow me" – and not the quest for one's significance and popularity.

> Everyone froze in Anna Ivanovna's presence, and on their faces was reflected not only fear, but some kind of servility. Father Nikolay

---

[4] Absolute silence began after evening prayer and lasted through the end of morning prayer.

[5] I entered the community several months prior to the arrests, and I never saw such major violations of the rule.

> Aleksandrov would sit long hours in his office, receiving visitors. (pp. 556-557)

In Julia Danzas's words, Anna Ivanovna "bossed him around without ceremony" and he behaved in her presence like a "frightened schoolboy." The author writes absolutely absurd stuff, having nothing in common with what was really going on. Why was it that I, a Sister who had entered the community a little after Julia Danzas's visit, did not notice fear, much less servility on the part of the Sisters with respect to Anna Ivanovna? The Sisters deeply loved, honored and revered her. I knew that Mother Catherine was for many of the Sisters like their conscience. They kept no secrets from her. And children literally adored her. As for Father Nikolay, I can only suggest one thing – Julia Danzas most likely did not know that Father Nikolay had a speech defect – he stuttered, and she interpreted his stuttering in accordance with her disposition against Anna Ivanovna, as showing him to be like a "frightened schoolboy." We note that Julia Danzas did not even try to find out the true situation of things and, being prejudiced and non-objective, she did not verify her impressions and conclusions.

> However, it is necessary nevertheless to emphasize once more that the blame for all the internal problems here was not only Anna Ivanovna's inexperience and even her inability, about which she herself eloquently attested on pages of her letters, but also the extremely unfavorable influence of the surrounding milieu, in the midst of which the community thought, in the words of Anna Ivanovna, that "it was to grow spontaneously" under the protection and defense of Saint Dominic. (p. 557)

Speaking – and not for the first time – about Anna's lack of experience and ability, "about which she herself eloquently attested on pages of her letters," von Burman again shows his complete lack of understanding of the spiritual life and its rules. Anna was an open and direct woman. She wrote sincerely about the enormous difficulties that were cropping up[6] and she acknowledged her own weakness and inexperience. But what does this

[6] Given the exceptional nature of what was going on at that time, it would have been impossible to have had experience in these events.

say? It speaks about a fitting spiritual state, about her humility. She saw everything and herself in the light of God's truth. Humility is the first and necessary condition for the action of God's grace in a person's soul.

It is this main, principal aspect of the work that von Burman completely does not understand – and it constantly shows. It is as inaccessible to him as it was to Julia Danzas. They judge everything from a very superficial, "worldly," human point of view. It is impossible to understand the kind of inner troubles and unfavorable influences of the surrounding milieu he is talking about. The Sisters of the community had an intensive spiritual life with ardent zeal and it was not weakened by the external, unfavorable, difficult circumstances of their common life – rather, it grew even stronger.

Von Burman writes that

> Memoirs written by Peter Volkonsky from the words of Julia Danzas contain very valuable statements about the Moscow community. These words had been given to Metropolitan Andrey to read; he recognized their value and told Volkonsky it would be good if Julia Danzas would be willing to confirm in writing what she had told him. Julia Danzas gave him a written oath that she had described "the truth" exactly. (p. 724)

In a letter to Volkonsky, Metropolitan Andrey wrote: "In any event, Sister Danzas can rest assured since she has done something good and useful" (p. 724). In her letter to Metropolitan Andrey dated October 22, 1937, in other words fifteen years after her meeting with Anna Abrikosova, when she was already in Paris, Julia Danzas notes:

> I did not hide from him [Volkonsky] that I was doing this with the utmost difficulty, taking upon myself the role of an exposer, even though it be in a secret document. All the same, I made myself believe that it was my duty and that I ought to fulfill it.
>
> As a devoted daughter of the Church, I believe that I am serving the Church, speaking the truth, i.e., what I saw and felt in this matter, where so much still remains obscure. (p 724)

Julia Danzas wrote these impressions when she was already abroad, in 1934-1935, i.e., twelve years afterwards. She made herself believe that it was her duty and with the utmost difficulty she took upon herself the role of an exposer.

...

And thus this bent mirror, the impressions of Julia Danzas, an inexperienced novice in the Christian spiritual life (in 1920-1922), came to be regarded as a valuable statement about Anna Abrikosova and the Moscow community of Dominican Sisters. It is endlessly sad that even Metropolitan Andrey Sheptytsky, such a worthy, great person of righteous life, recognized this piece of writing, in von Burman's words, "as valuable," and found it necessary only that Julia Danzas confirm in writing under oath the truth of what she had said.

...

Why did they not pay any attention to the numerous positive remarks of people who knew the Abrikosovs and the community of Dominican Sisters well? And if it was not possible at that time, under the external circumstances, to be in contact with these people and to record their remarks, then how was it that no one in any way verified the impressions of a single person, who was clearly not objective, and then allowed those impressions to be entered into a "historical document"? [...] Metropolitan Andrey did not personally know Julia Danzas – he knew of her only from Volkonsky's words and recommendation.

...

It is endlessly sad that these impressions which are so far from the truth are regarded as a valuable statement about the Moscow community of Dominican Sisters headed by Anna Abrikosova, that Metropolitan Andrey considered their writing as a "good and useful work." (p. 724)

It is impossible in any way to consider something a "good and useful work" when it has represented worthy people, who have given themselves and all that they had entirely for the service of God and the Church in the work of the unification of the Churches – in the loose talk of superficial impressions in a negative light, casting a shadow on worthy people who have proven with their own sacrificial lives, suffering and death their devoted fidelity to the Church.

Of course, if Anna Abrikosova had known how Julia Danzas – and from her words, Peter Volkonsky and Basil von Burman – would characterize her, she would not have been embittered at all – she would have treated this as just another shadow from that Cross which she had consciously taken upon herself.

The Abrikosovs had a different understanding of their mission in Russia than Father Leonid Feodorov; their understanding arose in parallel with his, when there as yet had been no contact between them. In his first two brief visits from abroad in 1910 and 1911, they made only an initial acquaintance, followed by very brief contact, but with positive impressions on both sides. The work in Moscow and in St. Petersburg proceeded independently. From 1912 to 1917 there was absolutely no contact with Father Leonid, and it was only from 1917 through 1923 that Father Leonid began to be more often in Moscow and he usually dropped in on the Abrikosovs.

The main work of the Russian Catholics in St. Petersburg was the preservation of a pure Slavic rite, the legalization of their parish, and the on-going creation of similar parishes. The main work in Moscow was the creation of a Russian Catholic bastion-foundation (parish and community) and laying the groundwork for recognition that the Churches needed to be unified.

To adhere to a strictly Eastern Slavic rite, excluding all the beautiful practices of the Western rite, as was done in St. Petersburg, was not possible, because, in belonging to the Dominican Order they [the Moscow Catholics] were obliged to adopt the spirit and practice of the Order with which they were connected and to which they had subjected themselves.

Despite all the negative statements and all the attacks on Anna Abrikosova and the community that came from Julia Danzas and others, apparently under the influence of her "strong personality," von Burman nevertheless found it impossible not to speak of the obvious good that the Abrikosovs and the Moscow community accomplished:

Exarch Leonid: "The only person who is completely devoted to me is Father Vladimir." Thus he briefly, but clearly, with these words expressed the spiritual loneliness in which he languished at his post.

It is difficult even to imagine what the Exarch would have been able to undertake in the conditions of those times and in the absence of all means for setting up a parish in Moscow, if the Abrikosovs had not given all that they could for this work, and if they had not given their very selves to him. If not them, who could the exarch have sent to Moscow? It would only be a joke to suggest Zerchaninov and Deibner or Trofim Semiatsky [...] or even more serious candidates, such as, for example, Diodor Kolpinsky and Gleb Verkhovsky [...] it is impossible to get around this sad side of things in silence, in order to recognize the help that Father Vladimir rendered the exarch just by the fact that he could rely on him entirely. In the sense of the strictness of morals, the home of the Abrikosovs was truly irreproachable.

Only thanks to the apostolic work of the Abrikosovs did the Russian Catholics come together, increase in number, and enter the parish that had been formed.

In their home in the evenings they regularly hosted discussions and papers on various religious themes for Catholics and non-Catholics, and their guests acquired new and necessary knowledge about the Church, Truth, God – with the successful development of their own spiritual life. (p. 539)

Patriarch Tikhon permitted and encouraged meetings in the Abrikosovs' home with leading members of the Orthodox clergy, at which lectures were given and questions concerning the unification of the Churches were discussed. And thanks to this, there was created a necessary positive contact as a preparation for furthering this holy work. Exarch Leonid was the soul of these meetings. (p. 543)

In the last two nights a whole slew of arrests took place in Moscow, taking in up to seventy professors and literary figures. Kuzmin-Karavayev was arrested at the same time as Father Vladimir. They were held in prison for about a week along with representatives of the intelligentsia, including several members of the "meetings on unity."

In the course of the last three years Father Vladimir had been arrested twice, and then on June 17, 1922, he was arrested for the third time. He was sentenced to the "supreme penalty," but his execution by firing squad was commuted to immediate expulsion from the country. Kuzmin-Karavayev and a hundred other leading representatives of the Russian intelligentsia met the same fate. (pp. 544-545)

Almost on the eve of his departure abroad, Anna Ivanovna wrote to Princess Volkonskaya: "I am alone in the full sense of the word – with half-dressed children, Sisters torn in all directions, with the young, wonderful, holy, but so young priest, Father Nikolay, who himself needs support; with bewildered parishioners, and myself awaiting arrest, since during the search they took all our rules and regulations [...] We have to live on pure acts of faith, hope and love."

As sacrificial as such a life was, full of religious asceticism, everything was done under extreme need, enveloping everyone in a difficult struggle for existence, but mainly, it was done in the name of a higher idea, which they sincerely wanted to serve. (p. 547)

The life of the parish and community continued to go along normally, as before. Anna Ivanovna, Father Nikolay and the Sisters experienced constantly God's continual help, the action of His grace and fidelity of His words: "... for you, O Lord, have not forsaken those who seek you" (Ps. 9:10) and "We know that in everything God works for good with those who love Him, who are called according to His purpose." (Romans 8:28)

In anticipation of the events that would come upon them Anna Ivanovna gradually came to the resolution of what had to be done

> and how to be prepared for what was inevitable. Correctly or not, at the basis of everything she placed the conviction that "Christ now wants in Russia only individual victims who walk toward complete sacrifice, like the Sisters (of her community). So it seems to me that now is not a time for any kind of precautions, but a time only for chivalry and holiness – and mainly, for sacrifice and humility.
>
> Obedience to the point of death on the cross and humility – these are the virtues that I preach to the sisters. Holy Communion and the rosary – these are the two means of victory – nothing else is needed. An ardent spiritual life, a pure faith and an iron will – i.e., a love that demands nothing, but yields everything." (pp. 588-589, citing a letter dated February 11, 1923)
>
> What was to be done? This question was, without any doubt, very serious, even tragic. One cannot lose sight of the fact that she was only forty years old and that she loved her husband dearly. Nevertheless her decision was clear and firm: "I cannot leave the Sisters, the children and the parish. I am, in the fullest sense of the word, their mother and their only support."
>
> Having thus spoken, Anna Ivanovna did not turn back from what she had decided. Father Vladimir invited her to go abroad. She resolutely responded: "My departure from Moscow is absolutely unthinkable. I cannot leave them under the present political situation." (p. 589)
>
> No, Anna Ivanovna did not waver, she firmly stood at her post in this very difficult moment when, in her words, at any minute destruction awaited them. (p. 590)

Anna's understanding of her situation and of that of her community essentially coincided with the notion that Exarch Leonid expressed to Julia Danzas during their last meeting in the Solovetsky camp in a former church that had been converted into a museum, namely, that the key to the rebirth of the Russian church lay in its suffering:

> He spoke for a long time about this mysterious predestination [of the Russian church]. … As yet there were few who understood that the messianic role of Russia lay precisely in her suffering. … [T]he whole history of the Russian church had been formed so frightfully, so absurdly, that we have here a kind of mystery of redemption. Perhaps the contribution of the Russian Church to the treasury of the Universal Church lies precisely in the fact that only through suffering, and not through victory, does she show her membership in the Mystical Body of Christ.
>
> I have not forgotten these words spoken by him on Solovetsky – after many years they are remembered and repeated, like the testament of the exarch: "I will not stop repeating that we are sacrifices [in reparation] for the schism of the East. We ought to bear our cross with patience." (pp. 660-661)

All who were devoted to the work of Uniatism, to Eastern Rite Catholicism in many places in the country, as well as in both Petrograd and Moscow, who endured so many difficulties and obstacles, who endured no small sacrifices in a complete giving of themselves, of all they had and of their lives for this great and holy work – they all possessed a grand courage, unflagging zeal, a heroic readiness for all sacrifices. Each participated in this grand work to the extent of his consciousness, his external and internal capabilities and possibilities.

And at the same time, all these worthy people had within themselves so many shortcomings and weaknesses. And you will unwittingly say, "What poor, poor people! How limited and how superficial are their consciousness and their ability to understand, how easily they judge only from the human point of view and not, as is befitting a Christian, from a spiritual point of view, as reborn 'children of God.' How unconsciously they give in to their own shortcomings, thus interfering in the grand, holy work and in their own personal purification and enlightenment of soul."

God – the Lord of all and the Judge of everyone – will look upon everything and He will reward each in accordance with the sincerity, the zeal and the purity of the heart's intention.

I so regret that my rebuttal to Deacon von Burman's statements about the Dominican Sisters and the Abrikosovs will probably remain just a voice crying in the wilderness, never reaching the Dominican Center of Study of Russia in Lille, France, where the private archive of Peter Volkonsky is kept, along with that "historical document," the impressions of Julia Danzas.

How many people were enlivened in spirit, having entered onto the bright path of a deep spiritual life, how many were fortified in their living faith and growth in union with God and in an ever greater desire to serve Him and others!

How many people are indebted to the Abrikosovs!

My whole life, I have given thanks to God that in His incomprehensible mercy He gave me the good fortune, at the last minute, one might say, to become acquainted with the parish of Russian Catholics in Moscow and to enter the community. I have never regretted the trials and difficulties that have filled my whole life – the exiles, the prisons, the camps. The Lord wondrously saved me from being sucked into a swamp and enduring the stagnation of spiritual lethargy, from a narrow, blind, mindless, unconscious life and opened up to me the limitless expanses of a spiritual life in ever-greater knowledge of Him and participation in His divine plans, for which alone man was created.

Although it is more than fifty years since God called her to her eternal reward, the image of Anna Ivanovna Abrikosova – noble, bright, inspired, full of peace and spiritual strength – has remained my whole life in my soul and in the souls of all who came into contact with her, as a holy example of sacrificial love and total surrender to God.

It was a great honor to come into contact with such a person as Mother Catherine and to share with her and with the Sisters their sufferings for the faith and the Church.

Appendix 3: Remembering Father Sergey Soloviev

By Sister Catherine of Siena, OP (Nora Rubashova).

IT was the beginning of 1926 – a small room on the premises of Lenin Library. Two men were living here – Sergey Soloviev and Vladimir Nilender. It was amazing that they were able to fit in such a small room. It was here that I first met Sergey Soloviev. He was forty years old, or perhaps forty-one. I was seventeen years old. He was tall, rather thin, with dark brown hair; his eyes were a bright blue, with long eyelashes. I heard that in his childhood he was called "Little Lord Fauntleroy." Thus I remember him. I also remember his laughter – he laughed often, loud and sadly. You could sense that there was some kind of nervousness that he was restraining with difficulty. The more I got to know him, the more I saw the sharpness of his mind, his peculiar sharp-wittedness, the depth of his thinking, his exceptional friendliness toward people, his childlike simplicity and his amazing inability to adjust to all worldly affairs. By this time his worldview had been defined and established.

He had traveled a long and difficult path of searching in coming to his worldview. He was religious from childhood, but in the years 1913 to 1916 he was fully converted to God. He became a priest in 1916, I think – I'm not exactly sure of the date. After 1917 he set out on an even more painful quest for the fullness of truth, for the true church. His gravitation toward Catholicism went on for a long time; he officially converted in 1923. When we met in 1926 he was a staunch Catholic priest of the Eastern rite. Over the course of five years we saw each other every day and sometimes even twice a day – we were great friends even though he was twenty-four years older than I. He knew so well how to approach each person.

Father Sergey said Mass in the church of the Immaculate Conception on Malaya Gruzinskaya Street, a large Gothic-style church. The small group of Russian Catholics who remained at liberty after the arrests in 1923 and 1924 were given the side altar of Our Lady of Ostra Brama for their Slavonic liturgy.

Father Sergey said Mass each day at this altar, and on the eve of the major feasts he observed the all-night vigil. Rarely would one ever see so beautiful a liturgy. The church was large, tall and unheated. Father Sergey's lips became bloodied from touching them every day to the freezing cold metal of the chalice.

He earned his living with literary works: he translated Aeschylus, Sophocles, Shakespeare, Mickiewicz – he had begun a translation of Dante's Divine Comedy but this was not completed because of his arrest in 1931. In addition to his translations, he also taught at the Literature Institute. The pay was irregular, with long delays, and I remember that he was always in need, hungry, poorly dressed and poorly shod, in torn boots with soles coming loose. He sent almost his entire salary to his two daughters, Natasha and Olenka, who lived with their mother halfway between Tambov and Voronezh. Now and then the daughters would come to visit him; I saw them a few times on Plyushchy, where he later lived in a little room on the fifth floor in a building without amenities.

With respect to material, economic matters he was as helpless as a child. I remember him asking someone to help him wash his hair, and one of his friends heated up some water on the kerosene stove and poured it over his head while he knelt there. He easily and simply accepted the slightest sign of attention, an insignificant favor. He was as joyful as a child if one of us friends would give him some shoes, boots or a shirt.

When Mass in Slavonic was no longer permitted in the church, Father Sergey continued to say Mass in his friends' apartments. He also gave papers in their apartments: I remember his works on Saint Sergius of Radonezh, Serafim of Sarov, the unification of the Churches and other theological themes. He had an excellent command of language, both in conversation and in scholarly works; his thinking was always original and deep, his speech was artistically gifted.

On February 15, 1931, Father Sergey and his few friends were arrested. I saw him only once in prison, and he was already completely ill. His tender, easily wounded, undefended psyche was not up to the kind of trials meted out. He fell psychologically ill – there were some short-lived improvements.[1] I never had the opportunity to see him again.[2]

He died at the end of December 1941 in a special psychiatric hospital in Kazan of illness and exhaustion.[3]

---

[1] Editor's Note: August 18, 1931, Sergey Soloviev was sentenced to ten years in corrective labor camps, commuted to exile to Kazakhstan. October 7, 1931, he was sent to forced treatment in a psychiatric hospital run by the Ministry of Internal Affairs. October 23, 1931, he was released from the hospital and entrusted to the care of his relatives.

[2] Editor's Note: Nora Nikolayevna Rubashova was arrested in the case against Soloviev and other Catholics and on August 18, 1931, was sentenced to five years in corrective labor camps.

[3] Editor's Note: According to documents in the investigatory case file, he died March 2, 1942.

Appendix 4: Poetry

Manuscript provided by Father Georgy Friedman, OP. Translated by Sister Maria Gemma Marek, OP. All but the last poem are by Vera Gorodets (Sister Stephania, OP). The last is by Natalia Borozdina.

The Paths of the Soul

The paths of the soul, like souls, vary,
But the goal for each – like God – is one,
We all traverse through temptations,
But are preserved by one dream alone…

Where do earthly roads lead?
The end of things is concealed in fog.
Yet I know, I know – on the threshold –
Of pearly tears – lies the crown…

Let the darkness envelop. Summer will come
And bright days will dawn;
The blazing hot sun warms our life
And shows us the way to go.

The paths of the soul, like souls, vary,
But the goal for each – like God – is one,
We all traverse through temptations,
But are preserved by one dream alone.

Moscow, before 1917

To A.I. Abrikosova

A radiant peace hangs above the earth,
A multicolored expanse on the ground;
The contours of the mountains
Are outlined with a golden-purple border.

We make our way through the green valley
All ahead – a fragrant path;
But we continue on to reach the desert
To set out on the red-yellow sand.

We go to build on the threshold
A white-marbled temple for daydreaming
And, as knights returning from sweet battle,
There we'll lay our unbroken shield!

Let the simooms[1] whirl above us
And burn with a scorching-hot fire;
Let the desert meet us with lions –
We will reach the red-yellow sand.

Moscow, 1920

[1] Translator's note: *Simoom* – hot, dry, dust-laden Asian or African desert wind

Aux Soeurs[2]

Upon the altar of Christ and God
You sacrificed the bloom of your young life,
Toward the heights of the heavenly bridal chamber
By the narrow path you ascended ...

In earthly valleys the forces of evil
Threw down their black standard,
Nocturnal temptations – grief and darkness –
Encircled your shining path.

But the light of eternal Love
Illuminated by the vision of Christ
Burned with an inextinguishable flame
And called you onward to the end.

In the narrow gorge of Roncesvalles[3]
Like knights, you battled
And sowed with the blood of strife
Perennial flowers of truth.

O, how many times in the toil of battle
Did your courageous spirit grow weary;
Suddenly the terrestrial boundaries shifted,
And earth whispered that the light had been quenched.

O how many times did bodily languor
Lure you toward creation's shores –
Blushing with a fiery rose,
Blocking your way to the snows.

Pertinacious hands seized you,
To throw you maliciously into disgrace;

---

[2] To Our Sisters

[3] Translator's note: Battle of Roncesvalles in 778 in Northern Spain.

But the power of faith, like a chain,
Kept you on the mountain heights!

May no one on earth know
How costly the wounding thorns,
Strewn down by the demons
Along your sacrificial path.

Let it be said that you have faded,
That your clear eyes have dimmed;
For the blossoms of life have fallen from love,
And for love has the carpet been trampled.

So, dear Sisters, courageously
Continue your lofty ascent;
For the cause of faith, God's cause –
Pour out your bloody travail!

Now is the hour of final anguish,
The terrible evening hour is nigh;
For crucifixion – and resurrection
And the victorious angels' cry.

Stavropol, 1932

At the Sixth Lagpunkt

Peacefully, pensively the lake slumbers
Under a canopy of green shrubbery;
A white night stretches over the North,
A limpid, yet severe shroud…

All is still. Weary people
Are asleep. Their brief rest is uneasy.
Hark! A prolonged whistle sounds –
Heralding a train bound for my hometown.

I remember, at the dacha, in a faraway time
How I loved to hear our night train;
Speeding towards some secret distant place,
As if repeating: "Come – fly away with me!"

All is quiet, as at our dacha in the pines,
The air breathed the fragrance of flowers.
Visions whirled about, carrying me,
Beckoning me to a world of sweet dreams.

On the train of life I sped recklessly…
Suddenly we were arrested and sent on our way,
The roads crossed, stones rained down,
And someone whispered to me: "Here you shall not pass."

And now I am in captivity. Recent years
Here in the North I spend,
Where nights are white with a strange melancholy,
And, nevertheless, towards the goal I *shall* pass!

Abez, 1951

To Nora

No, do not cry. After all, the strong-hearted
Do not take anything back.
Let your heart think that all within has been extinguished,
That it is totally in aridity.

Underneath the dead ashes often lies
A concealed, powerful flame;
Flaring up in tempest and wind,
Driving away our doleful slumber.

Suddenly life splatters with a hot stream
And flashes a thousand colors.
Like a wayfarer who, traversing the mountain the intense heat of day,
Forgets the cool of the forests.

Under the heavy blows there we forgot
That our way had been freely chosen;
That in suffering we drained the chalice of love,
And that we journey along the way of perfection.

Let the will be compressed like a steel spring,
And faith burn with a life-giving fire.
Our sacrificial way will not seem protracted,
When we unite our faith with our will.

Abez, 1952

Custodio sum[4]

When on the thorny path of life
The agonizing hour of temptation arrives
And you are attacked by a host of vulgar enemies –
Do not fear them – I am protecting you.

When evil prevails absolutely everywhere
And the basilisk[5] continues to stare you down
And a gloomy darkness creeps into your soul –
Do not fear them – I am protecting you.

When the sacred foundations of love and faith are destroyed
And one class rises up against another,
When blood and tears are mingled and
poured out into the world again –
Do not be afraid, no – I am protecting you.

When your heart is stung with evil slander
By others, like wasps, over and over again –
And you grow weary of your earthly existence –
Do not be afraid, no – I am protecting you.

When you bear the agonizing cross
And it seems that the light of love has been extinguished,
And a cry is heard: "crucify them, crucify them!"
Do not be afraid, no – I am protecting you.

O, preserve your wise hope,
When the hopeful hour arrives.
Do not forget in the bitterness of suffering:
Always, in everything – I am protecting you.

---

[4] I am the watchman; I stand guard.

[5] Translator's note: Basilisk – a legendary reptile with fatal breath and glance.

Who is the Sentinel of eternal protection
Who, with His whole heart took all suffering upon Himself –
Who is not frightened by deception,
Nor sorrow, nor the world, nor the pain of the cross?!

Abez, 1952

***

Neither the impending gray fog,
Nor ice floes in the northern seas,
Nor the green deceptions of the shores,
Can provoke fear in the heart.

For the free, deep soul
No obstacles stand in the way of its flight.
Soaring over high boundaries,
It looks toward the light in the East.

There, there –where the mountain peaks
Are illuminated with crimson beams,
Where only the stately eagle soars
With strong, beating wings.

There, there – where the world with its strife
Appears as a meager anthill,
Where you breathe in another realm,
And burn with a blazing fire!

Where the hidden meaning of all things
And the connection of the journey to its end
Are opened to the mind, as in a dream,
And reveal the eternal wisdom in everything.

Abez, 1954

Stanzas for Easter

The radiant joy of Sunday
Inspires our hearts;
The triumphant path to salvation
Is open to all from earth to heaven.

Faith in the Resurrection is not in vain
And earthly suffering lasts only a moment,
Over the lasting earthly battle
An image of glory and joy appears.

The Resurrection is the glory of Christ
And victory over death and evil;
Our earthly bodies perish
And we are resurrected with love in Him.

Over the entire world from end to end
Let Paschal hymns resound;
And, like brothers, embracing one another,
We shall love more strongly and deeply.

On Sunday let us forget discord –
Unity is given by faith;
And he who previously sowed violence and grief
Shall render deeds of love.

Let him open his heart to the light –
The magnificent grace of Sunday –
And, as warmed by the spring sun –
Everything is suddenly covered with flowers.

The Resurrection is the glory of Christ
And victory over death and evil;
Our earthly bodies perish
And we are resurrected with love in Him.

Abez, 1954

The Assumption

The gentle joy of the Assumption –
Is truly a celestial melody;
You are a sublime, incorruptible Mother –
Prepared to be reunited with –

Your Son, who raised you from the earth
To an eternal blessed destiny;
To be adorned with a brilliant golden crown
And be clothed with regal glory.

Our Mother, your Beloved Son,
Your God forever and ever,
The angels – led by the spirit –
Sang a chorus without words.

An anthem of loving admiration
Of your radiant beauty,
And your marvelous ascension
Into joyous, eternal peace.

An anthem of your compassion
Toward men – orphans below
And of your ardent desire
For every tear of the world

To be revealed in the chalice before you,
So that the gifts of your Son
With a lavish Mother's hand
Might be poured out from the heights to earth below.

You comforted in sorrow
Your poor, doleful children;
From a sweet distance
We waited for tidings of grace.

The gentle joy of the Assumption –
Is the light of the silvery moon,
Our sublime, incorruptible Mother,
Shines with celestial beauty.

(No Date)

To Nora Nikolayevna (Sister Catherine) Rubashova

I am fond of the story of a pure maiden,
Who laid down, in service to Christ
Her dawn, the flower of fragrant youth,
Together with her wisdom and love.

Saint Catherine of Siena, during her entire life
Was given to Christ's Church;
Unwaveringly, with fidelity,
She gave herself as an oblation.

With her undivided, pure heart
She loved Her Blessed Holy Bridegroom,
She dedicated all her efforts to the little ones, her neighbors,
And was devoted to the sick and the afflicted.

She received as a reward from Christ
The pain of His Sacred Wounds during her lifetime,
In the prime of her years she did not descend to a dark grave
But went down to Holy Cana.

In Holy Baptism, and now bearing her name,
You took up her cross and carried it
Along the way of afflictions, slavery and patience,
And discovered the blessed way to her.

And on that day, when in the churches of Christ
The memory of her luminous deeds is honored,
In the midst of your relentless tribulations
May the rays of her love descend upon you.

Let those rays fortify you with the light of faith
And give you sweet repose.
In everything, following her heroic example,
Be proud of your venerable Saint.

Natalia Kornilyevna Borozdina
Abez, April 30, 1954
(Feast of Saint Catherine of Siena)

Appendix 5: Brief Biographies of the Abrikosova Dominicans

BIOGRAPHIES of other Russian Catholics and persons mentioned in this book who suffered persecution during the period 1918 through 1954 have been included in the martyrology compiled by Irina Osipova and Father Bronisław Czaplicki, *Kniga pamiati: Martirolog Katolicheskoi Tserkvi v SSSR* [Book of Remembrance: A Martyrology of the Catholic Church in the USSR] (Moscow, 2000), and translations are available online at https://biographies.library.nd.edu.

Anna Ivanovna Abrikosova (Mother Catherine, OP)

Born December 22, 1881 [OS], into a merchant family in Moscow. Her mother died in childbirth and her father soon thereafter died of galloping consumption. She was raised with her four brothers in an atmosphere of kindness and love in the family of her uncle Nikolay Alekseevich Abrikosov – who by that time already had five children of his own. In 1903 she graduated from Girton College of Cambridge University. She was known by her classmates as "completely serious."

In 1903 she returned to Russia and married Vladimir Vladimirovich Abrikosov [a cousin]. From 1905 to 1910 they traveled in Europe and on December 20, 1908, she was received into the Catholic Church in Paris. In 1910 they returned to Moscow and in 1913, in Rome, she was accepted into the Third Order of Saint Dominic as Sister Catherine, in honor of Saint Catherine of Siena. She and her husband affiliated themselves with the Eastern Rite, and her husband was ordained a priest of the Eastern Rite in 1917. Soon thereafter she founded a women's community of Third Order Sisters of Saint Dominic.

Mother Catherine became the soul not only of the Sisters' community, but of the parish community as well. In the spring of 1923, after her husband, Father Vladimir, had been expelled from Russia, and foreseeing her own imminent arrest, she wrote to him in Rome: "In Russia Christ now wants only those who walk toward the complete sacrifice of themselves, like the Sisters. So it seems to me that this is not a time for taking any kind of precautions – only a time for chivalry and holiness – and above all, for sacrifice and humility. . . . Obedience even to death on the cross and humility – these are the two virtues I teach the Sisters."

During the night of November 12/13, 1923, she and nine other Sisters were arrested in connection with the case against Russian Catholics. During the investigation and while in the prisons she conducted herself with steadfast dignity, evoking respect and giving an example not only to her Sisters but also to the other arrested women, who were prepared to defend her. She continued on the path of spiritual perfection even in prison. In the indictment she was identified as the "leader of a counter-revolutionary Moscow organization with connections to the Supreme Monarchist Council abroad." May 19, 1924 – sentenced under Articles 61 and 66 of the Criminal Code of the RSFSR to ten years in prison. Before her departure, on the threshold of her cell, she met her convicted Sisters and in her last words to them, recorded by one of the Sisters, she said: "Most likely each of you, having fallen in love with God and now following Him, has asked more than once in your heart that the Lord give you the opportunity to share in His sufferings. That moment has arrived. Your wish to suffer for His sake has now been fulfilled." She was sent to the political isolator prison in Yekaterinburg – then in Tobolsk, then Yaroslavl, and in 1932 she was brought back to the hospital in Butyrka Prison for surgery. She was released early from prison on account of her health, but forbidden to live in the twelve major cities or the borderland regions. She settled in Kostroma. When she came to Moscow for medical appointments, she attended Mass and went to confession at Saint Louis des Français Church. In 1933 she secretly met with young women interested in religious questions at the apartment of a Catholic friend, Camilla Kruczelnicka. August 5, 1933 – arrested in Kostroma and brought to Butyrka Prison for further investigation. February 19, 1934 – sentenced under Articles 58-10 and 58-11 of the Criminal Code of the RSFSR to eight years in corrective labor camps. Sent to the Yaroslavl political isolator. June 1936 – transferred to the Butyrka Prison Hospital, where she died July 23. Her body was cremated the following day.[1*]

Aleksandra Vasilyevna Balasheva
(Sister Catherine of Siena, OP)

Born in 1878 in Barnaul, Altay kray. Completed courses at the women's high school and then worked as an instructor. She resided in Moscow; converted to Catholicism and joined the community of Dominican Sisters led by Anna Abrikosova. She took the name Catherine of Siena in religious life. In 1920 she worked at an institute and gave

1 * See *www.en.catholicmartyrs.org* for information about the cause of canonization of the Servant of God, Mother Catherine Abrikosova.

private music lessons. November 13, 1923, she was arrested with a group of Russian Catholics. May 19, 1924, she was released from custody so that she could care for the ailing Sister Catherine Galkina. Until 1927 she was engaged in sending money and packages to the Sisters of the Abrikosova community who had been sent to the Solovetsky Special Purpose Camp and Siberia. She was arrested in July 1927. September 2, 1927, at age 49, she was sentenced under Article 58-5 of the Criminal Code of the RSFSR to three years in the corrective labor camps. She was sent to the Solovetsky Special Purpose Camp. October 28, 1928, her sentence was reduced to a year, at the end of which she was released from the camp. She returned to Moscow, where, at the beginning of 1929, she was again arrested, this time charged with the "organization of assistance to Father Leonid Feodorov, the exiled exarch of Russian Catholics." July 12, 1929, she was sentenced to three years' exile in Siberia. She was sent to the village of Kargasok, Narym region, from where she was released February 7, 1933, but forbidden from living in the twelve major cities, the Urals or the borderlands. Before the end of her exile, wishing to return to the community of Dominican Sisters, she sent her belongings to the Sisters in Maloyaroslavets, but the Sister Superior sent them back. She remained in Siberia. In March 1936 she was in the village of Svetolobovo, in Krasnoyarsk region. In 1939, at age 61, she was freed from exile and wanted to join the Sisters of the Abrikosova community who were living in Maloyaroslavets, but the Sister Superior refused to accept her. Her fate thereafter is unknown.

Anna Kirillovna Davidyuk (Sister Lucia da Narni, OP)

Born into a peasant family in 1900 in Mishlitsa, Kobryn district, Grodno province. Until 1915 the family lived in Kobryn, where Anna completed the 4-year pre-gymnasium. In 1915 her family moved to Moscow; in 1918 she finished gymnasium and for two years studied at Shanyavsk University. In 1919 she completed the courses for pre-school education and began to work in a kindergarten at Three Mountains Beer Brewery. She converted to Catholicism and entered the Abrikosova community of Dominican Sisters where she took the name Sister Lucia da Narni. March 10, 1924 – arrested in Moscow in connection with the case against Russian Catholics; imprisoned in Butyrka Prison. May 19, 1924 – sentenced under Article 68 of the Criminal Code of the RSFSR to three years' exile. Sent to Tobolsk, where she worked in a kindergarten; December 1924 – transferred to the village of Samarovo [now Khanty-Mansiysk], Tobolsk region. June 1925 – transferred to Obdorsk [now Salekhard], where she spent her novitiate and earned a living by drawing pictures for sale. June 1926 – returned to Samarovo, whence she was released May 9, 1927, but restricted from living in the six major cities or the borderland regions for a period of three years. She settled in Romny, Poltava region, where in July 1930 she was again arrested, this time charged with "systematic counter-revolutionary activity in the village with the goal of undermining the economic power of the USSR" October 16, 1930 – sentenced under Article 54-10, Part 2, of the Criminal Code of the Ukrainian SSR to three years in corrective labor camps. Sent to Siblag (outside Novosibirsk); worked in a brick factory, then as a dishwasher in a dining hall. September 1932 – released early from the camp but restricted from living in the twelve major cities or the borderland regions. Settled in Orel – for a long time was unable to find work or food. She eventually found work as a childcare worker in the Rospistkan shop. She enrolled in the medical institute and began to work as a nurse in a tuberculosis dispensary. In 1935 she was again arrested – charged with "having connections with the international bourgeoisie." Sentenced to three years in the corrective labor camps and sent to Karlag, where she worked as the head of a medical station in the central camp in Dolinskoye, Karaganda region (Kazakhstan). 1939 – released from the camp but restricted from living in the twelve major cities and the borderland regions. She lived in Maloyaroslavets, moving later to Kaluga; worked as a nurse. November 30, 1948 – arrested in connection with the case against Russian Catholics and accused of "active espionage activity on behalf of the Vatican." August 17, 1949 – sentenced under Articles 58-1(a), 58-10 and 58-11 of the Criminal Code of the RSFSR to ten years in the corrective labor camps. Sent to Taishetlag, whence she was released in 1955. Returned to Maloyaroslavets where she lived with Sister Rosa Maria Vasileni-Pozharskaya, OP. In 1956 they emigrated to Lithuania. Settled in the small town of Maishiagala outside Vilnius, where she worked as a nurse in the local hospital. Died November 9, 1978.

Sophia Vladislavovna Eismont (Sister Philomena, OP)

Born into a family of the nobility in Vilnius in 1900. Lived in Moscow; finished high school and enrolled in the piano department at the conservatory but did not complete it. In the summer of 1923 she adopted the Eastern Rite and entered the Abrikosova community of Dominican Sisters. March 8, 1924 – arrested in the case against Russian Catholics. May 19, 1924 – sentenced under Article 61 of the Criminal Code of the RSFSR to three years' exile. Sent to Obdorsk (on the Ob River, at the Arctic Circle), Narym region, where she worked as a typist in an office. May 9, 1927 – released, but prohibited from living in the six largest cities or the borderland regions for a period of three years. She settled in Krasnodar and earned her living giving private music lessons. July 22, 1929 – made her final vows as Sister Philomena, OP, in the presence of Father Pietro Alagiagian, SJ. In the autumn of 1930, she moved to Odessa, then to Smolensk. From 1931 she lived in Moscow; worked as a typist in a bank. In March 1933 she went to Ryazan, where, on August 15, she was arrested and sent back to Moscow as part of the investigation in the second case against Anna Abrikosova and other Russian Catholics. February 19, 1934 – sentenced under Articles 58-10 and 58-11 of the Criminal Code of the RSFSR to eight years in corrective labor camps. Sent to Bamlag (Urulga Station) where, on February 2, 1935, she was arrested and sent to Ukht-Pechlag. In 1938 she was transferred to Vorkutlag; released June 23, 1942, but prohibited from living in the six largest cities or the borderland regions for a period of three years. Lived in Kuibyshev region [now Samara]; in 1943 she moved to Uralsk; in March 1947, to Maloyaroslavets. From April 1947 she was living in Kaluga, where, on November 30, 1948, she was again arrested and drawn into the investigation in the case against Russian Catholics. August 17, 1949 – sentenced under Articles 58-1(a), 58-10 and 58-11 of the Criminal Code of the RSFSR to ten years in corrective labor camps. Sent to Taishetlag; later transferred to Angarlag; released November 3, 1954, and exiled to Kazakhstan. May 26, 1956 – early release; went to the little village of Maishiagala outside Vilnius to live with the Dominican Sisters. She later moved to Vilnius to live with Dominican Sisters Antonina Kuznetsova, Teresa Kugel and others. February 23, 1993 – died in Vilnius.

Tatiana Jakovlevna Galkina (Sister Catherine de Ricci, OP)

Lived in Moscow. Converted to Catholicism and entered the Abrikosova community of Dominican Sisters where she took the name Sister Catherine de Ricci. In 1924 she was drawn into the investigation of a group of Russian Catholics, but was not arrested or convicted because of a serious illness. She died in Moscow in February 1926 (exact date unknown).

Vera Lvovna Gorodets (Sister Stephania, OP)

Born in Kiev in 1893. Completed post-secondary education. Lived in Moscow and gave private lessons. She converted to Catholicism and entered the Abrikosova community of Dominican Sisters where she took the name Sister Stephania. March 10, 1924 – arrested in Moscow in connection with the case against Russian Catholics and imprisoned in Butyrka Prison. May 19, 1924 – sentenced under Article 68 of the Criminal Code of the RSFSR to three years' exile. Lived in a village outside Tobolsk; released May 9, 1927, but restricted from living in the six major cities and the borderland regions. Settled in Romny, Poltava region; in 1928 she moved to Kostroma; in 1930, to Odessa; in 1932, to Krasnodar; and in 1933, to Stavropol where in that same year she was arrested and drawn into an investigation concerning a group of Catholics. She was released for "lack of facts constituting a crime." In 1934 she was living in Tambov where, in 1935, she was again arrested, this time in connection with a case against Catholic clergy. After a closed judicial proceeding in Voronezh on November 16, 1935, she was found not guilty and released November 27. She then lived in Maloyaroslavets, which was occupied by the Germans during the war; in September 1942, after the city had been liberated from the Germans, she was again arrested. She was sentenced to five years' exile and sent to the village of Novo-Shulba, Semipalatinsk region [Kazakhstan], until she was released in September 1947. She returned to Maloyaroslavets and in the summer of 1948 moved to Kaluga. November 30, 1948 – arrested in Kaluga in connection with a case against Catholics. She was accused of "active espionage activity on behalf of the Vatican." August 17, 1949 – sentenced under Articles 58-1(a), 58-10 and 58-11 of the Criminal Code of the RSFSR to ten years in corrective labor camps. Sent to Vorkutlag (Abez, Kozhvinsk region, Komi Autonomous SSR); in 1954 she was transferred to a home for disabled convicts in Ukhta (Komi ASSR), and then released in 1956. She went to Moscow and lived with Sister Catherine Rubashova, OP. She dedicated herself entirely to her spiritual life. Died May 25, 1974, at age 81. Buried in Khovanskoye Cemetery in Moscow.

Catherine Ivanovna Gotovtseva (Sister Joanna, OP)

Born into a lower middle class family in 1883. She graduated from the Mathematics and Physics Department of the University of Moscow and completed four years of medical school. Converted to Catholicism and entered the Abrikosova community of Dominican Sisters, where she took the name Sister Joanna. March 8, 1924 – arrested in Moscow in connection with the case against Russian Catholics. May 19, 1924 – sentenced under Article 68 of the Criminal Code of the RSFSR to three years' exile in the Urals. Sent to Tobolsk, where she worked as a schoolteacher; transferred to the village of Demyanskoye in 1926. Released from exile May 9, 1927, but restricted from living in the six largest cities and the borderland regions for a period of three years. She lived at first in a Cossack village outside Krasnodar, then in Krasnodar itself, where she worked temporarily as a statistician, then gave private lessons in math and physics. July 22, 1929, Father Pietro Alagiagian, SJ, accepted her final vows. In 1931 she prepared Ruvin Propishchin, who was studying for his exams in physics, for his conversion to Catholicism and stood as his godmother at his baptism. October 5, 1933 – arrested and drawn into the investigation in the second case against Anna Ivanovna Abrikosova and others. February 19, 1934 – sentenced under Articles 58-10 and 58-11 of the Criminal Code of the RSFSR to five years in corrective labor camps. Sent to Urulga Station, Bamlag, where in 1938 she was arrested and sent to a punitive isolator. She died July 14, 1938, at age fifty-five.

Sophia Aleksandrovna Ivanova, OP

Born into the family of a province secretary in 1885. Completed higher education. Converted to Catholicism and joined the Abrikosova community of Dominican Sisters. March 8, 1924 – arrested in Moscow in connection with the case against Russian Catholics and imprisoned in Butyrka Prison. May 19, 1924 – sentenced under Article 61 of the Criminal Code of the RSFSR to five years' exile. Sent to Siberia. Fate thereafter unknown.

Galina Fadeyevna Jętkiewicz
(Sister Rose of the Heart of Mary, OP)

Born into a family of the nobility in Vitebsk province in 1896. Completed the natural (science?) department of Moscow University for Women [nka Moscow State Pedagogical University] with a major in pedagogy. Lived in Moscow and worked as a high school teacher. Entered the Abrikosova community of Dominican Sisters where she took the name Sister Rose of the Heart of Mary. In November 1921, her family emigrated to Poland, but she chose not to join them. She translated and distributed theological works. November 26, 1923 – arrested in Moscow in connection with the case against Russian Catholics. May 19, 1924 – sentenced under Article 61 of the Criminal Code of the RSFSR to five years' confinement in prison. Sent to the Irkutsk isolator. In June 1929 she was sentenced to three years' exile. Sent to the village of Kolpashevo, Narym region, whence she was released April 30, 1932, but restricted from living in the six major cities or the borderland regions for a period of three years. From August 1932 she lived in Rybinsk; in 1934, she was living in Tambov, where, on February 1, 1935, she was arrested in connection with a case against Catholic clergy. She was acquitted after a closed judicial proceeding November 16-19, 1935, in Voronezh. November 27 she was released from prison. October 1936 she was living in Maloyaroslavets. In the autumn of 1942 she went to Novo-Shulba, Semipalatinsk region, to help the ailing Sister Stephania Gorodets, who had been exiled there. She died February 11, 1944, in Novo-Shulba.[2]

Vera Aleksandrovna Khmeleva
(Sister Maria Rose of Lima, OP)

Born into a family of the nobility in Vologoda province in 1891. Graduated from Moscow State University. Lived in Moscow and worked in a museum. She converted to Catholicism and entered the Abrikosova community of Dominican Sisters, taking the name Sister Maria Rose of Lima. She became the mistress of postulants and novices. November 13, 1923 – arrested in Moscow in the case against Russian Catholics. May 19, 1924 – sentenced under Article 61 of the Criminal Code of the RSRSR to three years' exile. Sent to Muzhi, Tobolsk region, where, in 1926, she broke her religious vows and married. She had a daughter born in exile, and soon thereafter her husband tragically died. May 9, 1927 – released from exile, but forbidden to live in the six major cities or the borderland regions for a period of three years. In 1929 the residence restrictions were lifted. She settled in Moscow; on the night of October 8/9, 1933, she was arrested in the second case against Anna Abrikosova and other Russian Catholics. January 10, 1934

---

2 See *www.en.catholicmartyrs.org* for information about the cause of canonization of the Servant of God, Sister. Rose of the Heart of Mary.

– sentenced under Articles 58-10 and 58-11 of the Criminal Code of the RSFSR to three years' exile. From January 1934 she lived in Gorkov region; she was released early (April 1934) with no residence restrictions. Returned to Moscow; in 1944 went to Kazakhstan; returned to Moscow in 1956 where she died in 1965 (exact date of death unknown).

Louisa (Lyudwiga) Koch, OPL

Lived in Moscow. Joined the Third Order Dominicans. Attended the illegal Masses said by Father Sergey Soloviev in parishioners' apartments. In February 1931 she was drawn into the investigation in the case against Father Soloviev and others, but she was not convicted. It was in her apartment that Anna Abrikosova stayed in Moscow when she came from Kostroma for medical appointments and met with Dominican Sisters who had been released from prison. In 1933 she was arrested in connection with the second case against Anna Abrikosova and others. Convicted (?). Fate thereafter unknown.

Maria Grigoryevna Komarovskaya (Sister Magdalina, OP)

Born into a family of the nobility in Mogilev in 1898. She did not complete higher education. Lived in Moscow and worked as a high school teacher. She entered the Abrikosova community of Dominican Sisters, where she took the name Sister Magdalina. November 13, 1923 – arrested in Moscow in connection with the case against Russian Catholics. May 19, 1924 – sentenced under Article 61 of the Criminal Code of the RSFSR to three years' exile. Exiled to the village of Samarovo, Tobolsk region; in June 1925 she was transferred to Obdorsk, where she worked as a laundress; then in June 1926 she was returned to Samarovo. May 9, 1927 – released but restricted from living in the six major cities or the borderland regions for a period of three years. She lived in Romny, Poltava region. In 1928 she moved to Smolensk; in 1929, to Saratov; then in July 1930 she returned to Smolensk, where, on September 10, 1930, she organized the funeral of Father Chryzogon Przemocki, who had died in prison. April 10, 1931 – arrested. October 28, 1931 – sentenced to exile with restriction on living in the six major cities or the borderland regions for a period of three years. She lived in Saratov, then later in Krasnodar, where in 1934 she was again arrested. She was brought into the investigation in the case against Anna Abrikosova and others. Transported to Moscow and imprisoned in Butyrka Prison. She died January 29, 1934, at the age of 35, while under investigation in Butyrka Prison.

Raisa Ivanovna Krylevskaya (Sister Margaret of Hungary, OP)

Born into the family of an Orthodox deacon in Vladimir in 1896. Graduated from the church school. Served as a nurse during World War I. Converted from Orthodoxy to Catholicism, for which her father placed her under house arrest and deprived her of food, demanding that she return to Orthodoxy. She refused and was kicked out of the house. She became acquainted with Anna Abrikosova and became a member of a parish of Russian Catholics. She joined the Abrikosova community of Dominican Sisters and took the name Sister Margaret of Hungary. January 30, 1924 – arrested in connection with the case against Russian Catholics. May 19, 1924 – sentenced under Article 61 of the Criminal Code of the RSFSR to three years' exile. Sent to Tobolsk region; released May 9, 1927, but restricted from living in the six major cities or the borderland regions. She remained in Tobolsk in order to help with parcels sent to Anna Abrikosova, who was in the Tobolsk political isolator. In 1930, after Anna Abrikosova had been transferred to the Yaroslavl political isolator, Sister Margaret moved to Kostroma where, on the night of October 8/9, 1933, she was arrested. Transported to Moscow and imprisoned in Butyrka Prison for questioning in the second case against Anna Abrikosova and others. February 19, 1934 – sentenced under Articles 58-10 and 58-11 of the Criminal Code of the RSFSR to ten years in corrective labor camps. Sent to the camps in Komi Autonomous SSR; released from the camp in October 1943, but exiled to Kazakhstan. Released from exile in the spring of 1947. She went to Maloyaroslavets but was unable to find work. A month later she moved to Kaluga. November 30, 1948 – arrested in Kaluga and charged with "espionage activity on behalf of the Vatican." August 17, 1949 – at age 53 – sentenced under Articles 58-1(a), 58-10 and 58-11 of the Criminal Code of the RSFSR to ten years in corrective labor camps. Sent to Vorkutlag (village of Abez); transferred in 1954 to Karlag. October 10, 1955 – given an early release as an invalid.

She thereafter lived in Kaluga, where she died in 1964 (exact date unknown).

Minna Rakhmielovna Kugel
(Sister Teresa of the Child Jesus, OP)

Born in 1912 in Orekhove-Zueve, Moscow province. She finished school in 1929 in Yaroslavl and returned to her parents in Kostroma, where she became acquainted with two Dominican Sisters – Sister Stephania Gorodets and Sister Margaret Krylevskaya. In 1931 she became a Catholic and in 1932 went to Krasnodar where she joined the Dominican Sisters and took the name Sister Teresa. October 6, 1933 – arrested in Krasnodar. Transported to Moscow and imprisoned in Butyrka Prison for interrogation in the second case against Anna Abrikosova and others. February 19, 1934 – sentenced to three years in corrective labor camps. Sent to Bamlag; released November 16, 1935. From December 1935 she lived in Bryansk; in October 1937 she moved to Maloyaroslavets, which was occupied by the Germans during the war. On August 21, 1942, after Maloyaroslavets had been liberated by the Red Army, Sister Teresa was arrested and charged with collaborating with the Germans. October 31, 1942 – sentenced to five years in corrective labor camps as a "socially dangerous element." Sent to Temlag; released March 25, 1947. She then lived in Maloyaroslavets; in the autumn of 1948 she moved to Kaluga. April 3, 1949 – arrested on charges of "espionage activity on behalf of the Vatican." She refused to sign the indictment. July 2, 1949 – deemed psychologically incompetent and September 17 sent for coercive treatment at a special hospital of the Ministry of Internal Affairs in Kazan; October 15, 1952, transferred to a regular psychiatric hospital. After her release in 1953 she lived in Vilnius and worked at first as a cleaning woman/custodian at the market, then as a nurse in the railroad hospital. She undertook the revival of the religious community, having arranged for official invitations to Dominican Sisters who had been released from homes for invalids. She died December 2, 1977, in Vilnius after an operation.

Valentina Vasilyevna Kuznetsova (Sister Antonina, OP)

Born into a family of peasant Protestants in St. Petersburg in 1897. Completed high school. Lived in Moscow and converted to Catholicism. She joined the Abrikosova community of Dominican Sisters, where she took the name Sister Antonina. March 8, 1924 – arrested in connection with the case against Russian Catholics. May 19, 1924 – sentenced under Article 68 of the Criminal Code of the RSFSR to three years' exile. Exiled to the village of Inkino, Narym region; released May 9, 1927, but restricted from living in the six major cities and the borderland regions for a period of three years. She lived in Kostroma; in 1930 she moved to Odessa, then to Krasnodar, and later to Stavropol. In 1934 she was living in Tambov where, on February 1, 1935, she was arrested in connection with a case against Catholic clergy. At a closed judicial proceeding in Voronezh November 16-19, 1935, she was found not guilty and released. Then she lived in Maloyaroslavets, where in 1941 she was again arrested and charged this time with "the organization of an anti-Soviet group of Catholic Dominicans" and sentenced to three years in corrective labor camps. Sent to Siblag (outside Novosibirsk); released in 1945. Returned to Maloyaroslavets, then in the autumn of 1948 moved to Kaluga. April 3, 1949 – arrested in connection with a case against Catholics, charged with "espionage activity on behalf of the Vatican." October 29, 1949 – at age 51 – sentenced under Articles 58-1(a), 58-10 and 58-11 of the Criminal Code of the RSFSR to fifteen years in corrective labor camps. Sent to Angarlag; given an early release June 14, 1956. She settled in with her sister in the village of Lesnoi, Kaliningrad region, then in 1958 she moved to Vilnius and lived with the Dominican Sisters. She died October 9, 1989, in Vilnius.

Catherine Antonovna Malinovskaya, OPL

Born into a merchant's family in 1876. Completed higher education, lived in Moscow and taught foreign languages. In 1921 she converted to Catholicism; she joined the Abrikosova community of Dominican Sisters, and after its disruption [1924] she joined the Soloviev community of Russian Catholics. Father Sergey Soloviev said secret Masses in her apartment; she also kept his correspondence and manuscripts and religious literature there. February 15, 1931 – arrested in Moscow in connection with the case against Father Soloviev and others. August 18, 1931 – sentenced under Articles 58-6, 58-10 and 58-11 of the Criminal Code of the RSFSR to three years' exile in Eastern Siberia. July 8, 1932 – exile was cancelled. Later she was again arrested and exiled to Siberia, where she died in exile from tuberculosis (exact date and place of death unknown).

Anatolia Iwanowna Nowicka (Sister Josafata, OPL)

Born into a lower middle class family in Belorussia in 1891. Finished school in Smolensk and obtained higher education in St. Petersburg. Lived in Petrograd, was employed as an office worker. In 1922, in Moscow, she adopted the Eastern Rite and joined the Abrikosov community of Russian Catholics. 1924 – arrested in Moscow in the case against "a counter-revolutionary organization, 'the Christian Student Union'," but after a month and a half she was released. In 1926 she joined the Third Order of Saint Dominic, taking the name Josafata, and energetically assisted convicted priests and laity; she traveled to visit her husband [Father] Donat Nowicki, who was in the Solovetsky Special Purpose Camp [where he was secretly ordained a priest of the Russian Catholic Rite]. Upon her return reported her impressions in detail to Bishop Pius Neveu. February 15, 1931 – arrested in the case against Russian Catholics in Leningrad (Soloviev and others). August 18, 1931 – sentenced under Articles 58-6, 58-10 and 58-11 of the Criminal Code of the RSFSR to three years of corrective labor. Sent to the Yaroslavl political isolator, later transferred to Kotlas camp. 1932 – early release from the camp, sent to Moscow and imprisoned in Butyrka prison. September 15, 1932 – sent to Poland as part of a prisoner exchange. Died in Poland, April 15, 1975 – at age eighty-four.

Elena Agafonovna Plavskaya, OPL

Born in 1887 in Kostroma. Completed high school. Lived in Moscow and worked in an institution. Converted to Catholicism and entered the Third Order of Saint Dominic. In November 1933 – arrested in Moscow in the second case against Anna Abrikosova and Russian Catholics. February 19, 1934 – sentenced under Articles 58-10 and 58-11 of the Criminal Code of the RSFSR to five years' corrective labor. Sent to Bamlag, from where she was released November 27, 1937, and sent for three years to Kazakhstan. Fate thereafter unknown.

February 8, 1936, the head of Bamlag reported to Moscow that they had intercepted a letter from Dominican Sister Elena Plavskaya and other Sisters that was to have been sent secretly by the released Asakiani to the Superior General of the Order of Saint

Dominic. We present an excerpt from that letter: "In spirit we are strong – no camp, no organ of the NKVD can tear the faithful daughters and sons of the One Catholic Church from the true path. Even here we try to recruit the same kind of zealously inclined advocates of the Catholic Church."

Nora Nikolayevna Rubashova (Sister Catherine of Siena, OP)

Born into a merchant family in Moscow in 1909. Lived in Moscow, enrolled in the historical-philology department at Moscow State University but was unable to complete her degree on account of her arrest. In April 1926 – became a Catholic and later became a nun, taking the name Sister Catherine of Siena. She was the spiritual daughter of Father Sergey Soloviev and attended the clandestine Masses he celebrated in parishioners' apartments. February 15, 1931 – arrested in the case against Russian Catholics (Soloviev and others). In the indictment the investigator noted in particular that she was a "Tertian [Third Order religious], a fanatic, an active member of a community closely linked with [Bishop] Neveu and [Father] Soloviev, and was engaged in counter-revolutionary agitation." August 18, 1931 – sentenced under Articles 58-6, 58-10 and 58-11 of the Criminal Code of the RSFSR to five years in corrective labor camps. Sent to the Mariinsk section of Siblag; released in 1936 from Siblag and exiled to Michurinsk; worked in a botanical garden. Summer of 1936 – after her release she went to Maloyaroslavets where she joined the Dominican Sisters of the Abrikosova community. During the war she and the Sisters found themselves under the German occupation. In May 1944 she went to Novo-Shulba outside of Semipalatinsk (Kazakhstan) to help Sister Stephania Gorodets, an older sister in the community who had been exiled there; she worked in a school there. In 1947, she and Sister Stephania returned to Maloyaroslavets, and in the summer of 1948 they moved to Kaluga. November 30, 1948 – arrested in the case against Russian Catholics; October 29, 1949 – sentenced under Articles 58-1(a), 58-10 and 58-11 of the Criminal Code of the RSFSR to fifteen years in corrective labor camps. Sent to Vorkutlag (Abez village); in 1954 – transferred to Karlag; released in 1956. Returned to Moscow and went to work at the Historical Library, where she worked until she went on pension; she later sometimes worked there for short periods. She attended Saint Louis des Français Church. Later parishioners from the old community of Russian Catholics would gather around her and Sister Stephania. The Sisters' apartment became a place of meetings and the spiritual center of a new community, which soon included young people, university students. Father Evgeny Geinrikhs, OP, and Father Georgy Friedman, OP, who came to Moscow from Leningrad, began to celebrate clandestine Masses there. May 12, 1987 – at age 78, and only four years before the fall of the Communist regime – she died and was buried in Khovanskoye Cemetery.

Tamara Arkadyevna Sapozhnikova, OPL

Born into a lower middle class family in Podolsk in 1886. Received a post-secondary education. Became a Catholic and later joined the Third Order of Saint Dominic. She entered the Abrikosov community, where she served as treasurer. November 26, 1923 – arrested in Moscow in the case against Russian Catholics. She was kept in solitary confinement and as Anatolia Nowicka, OPL, later recalled, "by means of uninterrupted interrogations and pressure the investigation tried to drive her to insanity." May 19, 1924 – sentenced under Articles 61 and 66 of the Criminal Code of the RSFSR to ten years in prison. Sent to Solovetsky Special Purpose Camp; at first she was on Kond Island, then in the summer of 1925 she was transferred to the central island; and later to Anzer Island where, in 1932, she was drawn into the investigation of a group of Catholic clergy. At her interrogation she stated: "I am a staunch Catholic. To whom did I go to confession? I categorically refuse to answer that question and no amount of persecution on your part will force me to do so." Fate thereafter unknown.

Valentina Arkadyevna Sapozhnikova, OPL

Born into a lower middle class family in Podolsk in 1887. Received a post-secondary education, graduating with a double major from Moscow State University. She lived in Moscow and taught at an institute. In 1912 she converted to Catholicism and joined the Third Order of Saint Dominic as an individual tertiary. She attended Mass at Nativity of the Most Holy Virgin Mary parish at the Abrikosovs' apartment. In 1924 she joined the Soloviev community of Russian Catholics and attended the illegal Masses that Father Sergey celebrated in parishioners' apartments and prepared several Orthodox for their conversion to Catholicism. February 15, 1931 – arrested in the case against Russian Catholics (Soloviev and others). She was recognized by the investigation as the "ideological inspiration of the community." August 18, 1931 – sentenced under Articles 58-6, 58-10 and 58-11 of the Criminal Code of the RSFSR to five years of corrective labor. Sent to Siblag; released from Siblag in August 1936, but restricted from living in the twelve major cities and the borderland regions. She settled in Podolsk, where she died in 1943 (exact date of death unknown).

Anastasia Vasilyevna Selenkova (Sister Catherine de Ricci, OP)

Born into the family of an estate owner in Khriperovo, Rzhev district, Tver province, in 1893. She graduated from the Philological Department of Moscow State University and remained there to work as a specialist in Old Russian literature. She converted to Catholicism, and from 1915 was under police surveillance. She lived in Moscow; joined the Abrikosova community of Dominican Sisters and took the name Sister Catherine de

Ricci; she later directed a men's group of Dominican novices in the Abrikosov community. November 14, 1923 – arrested in Moscow in the case against Russian Catholics. May 19, 1924 – sentenced under Article 61 of the Criminal Code of the RSFSR to ten years in prison. Sent to Orel Prison; in 1927, transferred to Suzdal Prison; in July 1930, to the Yaroslavl political isolator. Released in 1932, restricted from residing in the six largest cities and the borderland regions for a period of three years. She lived in Saratov and worked as an economist in a factory; from 1935 she was with her brother in Leningrad. On the night of October 2/3, 1935, she was again arrested. February 7, 1936 – sentenced to five years of corrective labor. Sent to the Kotursk section of Karlag (Dolinskoye, Karaganda region), where she died during the war (exact date of death unknown).

Father Donat Nowicki later recalled: "Father Francis Andruszkiewicz told me of the significant role that Anastasia Vasilyevna played in his life, when he, having undergone extraordinarily severe GPU interrogation (22 days of uninterrupted interrogation), was psychologically out of his mind and could not recover for a long time. He also told of the deep spiritual influence she had on the political convicts in the Yaroslavl isolator."

Anna Spiridonovna Serebriannikova (Sister Imelda, OP)

Born into a peasant family in Saratov in 1890. Did not complete high school; worked as a village shool teacher. Converted to Catholicism and joined the Abrikosova community of Dominican Sisters under the name Sister Imelda; she was the Sisters' choir director. November 26, 1923 – arrested in Moscow in the case against Russian Catholics. May 19, 1924 – sentenced under Article 61 of the Criminal Code of the RSFSR to eight years in prison. Sent to Solovetsky Special Purpose Camp. She was on Kond Island until 1925; in the summer she was transferred to Central Island and worked there as a nurse in the camp hospital. In 1931 she was released from the camp, restricted from living in the six largest cities and the borderland regions. Fate thereafter unknown.

Maria Filippovna Sokolowska (Sister Catherine de Ricci, OP)

Born in 1902 (1900?) in Bolshie Nemeritsy, Proskurov district, Podolsk province. She completed the four-year village school. In 1920 she was living in Petrograd; then she moved to Moscow where she worked as a maid for various families. From her youngest years she had a calling to religious life but because of complicated life circumstances she was not able to actualize this vocation for many years. In 1946 she arrived in Maloyaroslavets where she joined the Abrikosova community of Dominican Sisters and received the name Sister Catherine de Ricci. In the autumn of 1948 she moved to Kaluga where, on April 3, 1949, she was arrested and charged with "espionage activity on behalf of the Vatican." October 10, 1949 – sentenced under Articles 58-1(a), 58-10 and

58-11 of the Criminal Code of the RSFSR to ten years in corrective labor camps. Sent to Vorkutlag (Abez settlement); 1954 – transferred to the home for disabled convicts in Ukhta, whence she was released in July 1956. At the end of August she arrived in Vilnius. Until 1974 she lived in a small room with a blind woman; then she moved in with the Dominican Sisters of the Abrikosova community. She died in Vilnius March 28, 1985.

Olga Aleksandrovna Spechinskaya (Sister Margaret Mary, OP)

Born into a family of the nobility in 1891. She had a high school education. Lived in Moscow, converted to Catholicism and joined the Abrikosova community of Russian Catholics. September 13, 1923 – arrested in Moscow in the case against Russian Catholics and held in Butyrka Prison. May 19, 1924 – sentenced under Article 61 of the Criminal Code of the RSFSR to three years exile to Siberia. Sent to Kolpashevo, Tomsk region; in 1925, transferred to Inkino. Became a nun under the name Sister Margaret Mary. May 9, 1927 – released from exile but restricted from living in the six largest cities and the border regions. Lived in Kostroma; in the summer of 1930 she moved to Odessa, where, in 1932, she was again arrested. Sentenced to three years' corrective labor and sent to Bamlag; later transferred to Siblag (Mariinsk), from where she had an early release in 1934. She lived in Moscow and in Bryansk – where, in 1937, she was once again arrested and sentenced to five (?) years of corrective labor. At the end of 1937 or the beginning of 1938 she died on the prison convoy to the labor camp. Date and place of death unknown.

Tatiana Kuzminichna Tomilova (Sister Agnia, OP)

Born into the family of a businessman in 1900. Finished high school. Lived in Moscow and worked as a kindergarten teacher. Converted to Catholicism and joined the Abrikosova community of Russian Catholics, taking the name Sister Agnia. January 30, 1924 – arrested in the case against Russian Catholics and imprisoned in Butyrka Prison. May 19, 1924 – sentenced under Article 61 of the Criminal Code of the RSFSR to three years' exile. Sent to Kolpashevo, Narym region; released May 9, 1927. Left for the Crimea, where she broke her religious vows and married. Fate thereafter unknown.

Nadezhda Yefimovna Tsvetkova (Sister Teresa, OP)

Born into a peasant family in Smolensk province in 1901. Had a high school education specializing in pre-school education. Lived in Moscow and gave private lessons. Converted to Catholicism and entered the Abrikosova community of Dominican Sisters, taking the name Sister Teresa. November 13, 1923 – arrested in the case against Russian Catholics. May 19, 1924 – sentenced under Article 61 of the Criminal Code of the RSFSR to three years' exile. Sent to Chernoye, Tobolsk region. Released May 9, 1927, but prohibited from living in the six largest cities or the borderland regions for a period of three years. She settled with her parents in Smolensk, where she broke her religious vows and married. Fate thereafter unknown.

Vera Yefimovna Tsvetkova (Sister Veronica, OP)

Born into a peasant family in Smolensk province in 1903 (1905?). Had a high school education. Lived in Moscow and worked as a teacher in a music school. Converted to Catholicism and entered the Abrikosova community of Dominican Sisters, taking the name Sister Veronica. March 8, 1924 – arrested in Moscow in the case against Russian Catholics. May 19, 1924 – sentenced under Article 68 of the Criminal Code of the RSFSR to three years' exile. Sent to Chernoye, Tobolsk region. May 9, 1927 – released, but prohibited from living in the six largest cities or the borderland regions for a period of three years. Returned to Moscow, enrolled in the Economics Institute. From 1932 she lived in Smolensk. August 22, 1933 – arrested in Sychevka, Smolensk region, where she was spending the holidays at her parents' home. Sent to Moscow and imprisoned in Butyrka; drawn into the second case against Anna Abrikosova and other Russian Catholics. January 10, 1934 – sentenced under Articles 58-10 and 58-11 of the Criminal Code of the RSFSR to three years in corrective labor camp; sent to Bamlag; released September 19, 1935. In 1956 Vera Aleksandrovna Khmeleva stated at an interrogation that Sister Veronica ended up on occupied territory during the war (exact date and place of death unknown).

Nadezhda Andreevna Tsybina (Sister Osanna, OP)

Born into a peasant family in 1891. Had a high school education. Lived in Moscow and worked as a school teacher. Converted to Catholicism and entered the Abrikosova community of Dominican Sisters, taking the name Sister Osanna. After 1920, she gave private lessons. March 8, 1924 – arrested in Moscow in the case against Russian Catholics. May 19, 1924 – sentenced under Article 61 of the Criminal Code of the RSFSR to three years' exile. Sent to Altayevo, Narym region; in 1925, transferred to Kolpashevo; released May 9, 1927, but prohibited from living in the six largest cities of the borderland regions for a period of three years. She settled in Saratov where she broke her religious vows and married. She had two sons. Fate thereafter unknown.

Anna Iosifovna Tyshman, OPL

Born in Poland in 1871. In 1900 she joined the Third Order of Saint Dominic. Lived in Moscow and was the housekeeper for the pastor of Immaculate Conception of the Most Holy Virgin Mary Church. February 18, 1931 – arrested in Moscow in a case against Catholic clergy and laity of the Moscow churches. Charged with being "an out-and-out Polish nationalist and fanatically religious, and over the course of several years having had an illegal connection with the Polish and Latvian [diplomatic] missions and a number of Polish spies, whose espionage activity she had fostered." November 18, 1931 – sentenced under Articles 58-6, 58-10 and 58-11 of the Criminal Code of the RSFSR to three years' exile to Kazakhstan. Fate thereafter unknown.

Elena Vasilyevna Vakhevich (Sister Agnes, OP)

Born into a merchant family in Moscow in 1882. She was a friend of Anna Ivanovna Abrikosova from their years in the lycee. She completed higher education, converted to Catholicism and entered the Abrikosova community of Dominican Sisters, where she took the name Sister Agnes. She organized an illegal school for parish children in her own apartment. March 10, 1924, she was arrested in Moscow along with a group of Russian Catholics. May 19, 1924 – sentenced under Article 61 of the Criminal Code of the RSFSR to five years in prison. Sent to the Irkutsk political isolator. February 28, 1929 – internally exiled in eastern Siberia for three years. From March 1929 she was in a village outside Kirensk in Irkutsk region, from where she was released, but prohibited from living in the six major cities and the borderland regions for a period of three years. From 1931 she lived in Smolensk, where she gave private lessons. On the night of October 8/9, 1933, she was arrested and drawn into the investigation in the second case against Anna Abrikosova and others. February 19, 1934 – sentenced under Articles 58-10 and 58-11 of the Criminal Code of the RSFSR to eight years in the corrective labor camps. In April 1934 she was at the 13th Section of Bamlag (at Birobidzhan Station on the Ussuriisk Railroad), where she died of typhoid in the autumn of 1935 or early 1936 (exact date of death unknown).

Elizabeth Vasilyevna Vakhevich (Sister Dominica, OP)

Born into a merchant family in Moscow in 1885. She did not complete higher education. Converted to Catholicism and entered the Abrikosova community of Dominican Sisters, where she took the name Sister Dominica. She taught in the illegal school of the Russian Catholic parish. March 10, 1924, she was arrested in Moscow along with a group of Russian Catholics. Imprisoned in Butyrka Prison. May 19, 1924, sentenced under Article 61 of the Criminal Code of the RSFSR to five years in prison. Sent to Orel Prison; November 25, 1925, sent to the Suzdal political isolator, from which she was released in February 1928 and internally exiled to Siberia. From 1928 she was in the village of Kutima, western Siberia, from where she was released in 1931, but prohibited from living in the six major cities and the borderland regions. She lived in Smolensk; then in early 1933 she moved to Voronezh, and on August 18 she was arrested and sent to Smolensk Prison for interrogation in the investigation of a group of Russian Catholics.

March 12, 1934, sentenced to eight years in corrective labor camps. At first she was in the Smolensk Prison, but in March 1936 she was sent to Karlag (village of Dolinskoye, Karaganda region). In August 1936 she received news of her sister Elena's death in the infirmary of the 13th Section of Bamlag (Birobidzhan Station on the Ussuriisk Railroad). Later she was transferred to Bamlag, from where she was released in early 1941. She went to Maloyaroslavets in order to be reunited with the Dominican community – but at the beginning of 1941 she was sent by the Sister Superior of the community to Bryansk, where she disappeared during the military activities on territory occupied by the Germans. Fate thereafter unknown.

Nina Iosifovna Vasileni-Pozharskaya (Sister Rosa Maria, OP)

Born into a peasant family in 1891 in the village of Matushi, Porozov county, Grodno province. Educated at home. Lived in Moscow, worked as a dressmaker. Converted to Catholicism and joined the Abrikosova community of Dominican Sisters, where she took the name Sister Rosa Maria. March 8, 1924, she was arrested in Moscow along with a group of Russian Catholics. She was charged under Article 68 of the Criminal Code of the RSFSR. April 24, 1924, she was presented with the indictment, in which the investigator recommended five years' exile to Siberia or Kazakhstan. May 18, 1924, sentenced under Article 68 of the Criminal Code of the RSFSR to three years' exile in Siberia. She was exiled to a village outside Tobolsk, where she earned a living as a seamstress. May 9, 1927, she was released but restricted from living in the six major cities or the borderland regions for a period of three years. She lived in Romny, Poltava district, where, on October 16, 1930, she was again arrested. She was accused of "converting Orthodox to Catholicism, arousing an atmosphere of Polish nationalism, the collection of donations for the support of exiled priests and systematic counter-revolutionary agitation in the village with the goal of undermining the economic power of the USSR" September 28, 1931, sentenced under Article 58-10, part 2, of the Criminal Code of the RSFSR to three years in the corrective labor camps. Sent to Siblag (a camp outside Novosibirsk), where she worked in a brick factory, and then later as a dishwasher in a dining hall. In September 1932 she was released early from the camp, but restricted from living in the three capital cities and the borderland regions. She settled in Orel – for a long time she was unable to find work and nearly starved to death, but she found work doing embroidery in the shop "Rospistkan." April 29, 1933, she was drawn into the investigation of a group of Russian Catholics. February 19, 1934, sentenced under Articles 58-10 and 58-11 of the Criminal Code of the RSFSR to three years in the corrective labor camps, but in the summer she was released early from prison. She returned to Orel. In 1935 she was again arrested on charges of "connections with international bourgeoisie." In the spring of 1936 she was sentenced to three years in the corrective labor camps. She was sent to Karlag (village of

Dolinskoye, Karaganda region, Kazakhstan), where she arrived in July. She worked at a distant camp outpost in a tailor shop, where she often went hungry because her cellmates stole her bread. When she began to show signs of worsening tuberculosis she was sent to the camp hospital. She survived in the camp only thanks to the help of her friend, Sister Lucia Davidyuk, who was the head of the clinic and sent her food. In 1939 she was released from the camp; returned to Maloyaroslavets, lived with Sister Lucia, and worked in the embroidery shop. During the war she and the other Sisters came under the German occupation; after the return of the Red Army she returned to Maloyaroslavets; later she was expelled. In 1955 she was living in Maloyaroslavets, but in 1956 she and Sister Lucia emigrated to Lithuania. They settled in the little town of Maishiagala outside Vilnius – she kept house and died there (exact date of death unknown).

Olga Volokhina (Sr. Maria Cecilia, OP)

Born in 1880. Completed Moscow University for Women. Lived in Moscow, worked as a librarian. Converted to Catholicism and entered the order of Dominicans where she was known as Sr. Maria Cecilia. January 30, 1924 – arrested in Moscow in connection with a case against Russian Catholics. Convicted (?). Fate thereafter unknown.

Anna Ivanovna Zolkina (Sister Hyacinth, OP)

Born into a peasant family in 1901. In the beginning of the 1920s she was a student in the Physics and Mathematics Department of Moscow University and an unofficial collaborator of the Polish Red Cross. She converted to Catholicism. In 1923 she joined the Abrikosova community of Dominican Sisters and took the name Sister Giatsinta (Hyacinth). November 23, 1923 – arrested in connection with the case against Russian Catholics. May 18, 1924 – sentenced under Article 66 of the Criminal Code of the RSFSR to three years' exile. She was released so that she could care for the ailing Sister Catherine Galkina; she kept the library of the Abrikosova community. In 1926 she became acquainted with Bishop Pius Neveu and thanks to him she was able to constantly help the convicted Abrikosova Dominican Sisters who had been sent to the Solovetsky Special Purpose Camp or exiled to Siberia. She worked with Father Sergey Soloviev; she kept his manuscripts and correspondence; and she attended illegal Masses that Father Sergey celebrated in parishioners' apartments. February 6, 1931 – arrested in Moscow in connection with the case again Father Sergey Soloviev and others. August 18, 1931 – sentenced under Articles 58-6, 58-10 and 58-11 of the Criminal Code of the RSFSR to three years in corrective labor camps. Sent to the Mariinsk section of Siblag, whence she was released in July 1934, but restricted from living in the six major cities and the borderland regions. She lived in Bryansk region and worked as a caretaker in an orphanage. In June 1941 she and all the orphans were evacuated to Yelets where, at the end of 1941, she was again arrested and sentenced to five years in corrective labor camps. Sent to the camps. Fate thereafter unknown.

From the recollections of Anatolia Nowicka: "At the interrogation of Sister Hyacinth there were ten young students of the GPU School for Investigators under the supervision of the main investigator. They took an active role in the course of the interrogation; they mocked religion and they badgered Sister for an answer to the question as to how she, a young woman, could live without a man, and whether she "was sleeping with Bishop Neveu." After this question, she – a completely healthy person – suffered a serious attack of hysteria. Thus was repeated one of the usual, despicable methods of the GPU: to create by means of threats and actions against the psyche and the body of the imprisoned person a heinous provocation against serious clergy who were respected by everyone."

Monica Antonovna Zvidrin, OP

Born in 1900 in St. Petersburg; lived there and belonged to Saint Casimir parish. October 9, 1929 – arrested in connection with the case against Bishop Teofil Matulianis and others. She was accused of "organizing assistance to priests sent to Solovetsky [Camp]." September 8, 1930 – sentenced to five years in corrective labor camps. Sent to Belbaltlag, whence she was released in 1935 but restricted from living in the six major cities and the borderland regions for a period of three years. She lived in Bryansk, then in September 1937 she moved to Maloyaroslavets where she entered the Abrikosova community of Dominican Sisters. In 1941, during the war, they came under the German occupation; after the liberation of Maloyaroslavets by the Red Army, in September 1942, Sister Monica was arrested and sentenced to five years' exile. She was sent to Kazakhstan, whence she was released in 1946. She returned to Maloyaroslavets, and in the autumn of 1948 moved to Kaluga. April 3, 1949 – arrested in connection with the case against Russian Catholics. August 17, 1949 – sentenced under Articles 58-10 and 58-11 of the Criminal Code of the RSFSR to ten years in corrective labor camps. Sent to Vorkutlag (village of Abez), and in 1954 she was transferred to a facility for disabled convicts; released in 1955. From July 1956 she lived in Vilnius where she died July 1, 1972.

RECOMMENDED READING

Applebaum, Anne. *Gulag: A History*. New York: Doubleday, 1993.

Braun, Leopold. *In Lubianka's Shadow: The Memoirs of an American Priest in Stalin's Moscow, 1934-1945*. Ed. G.M. Hamburg. Notre Dame, Ind.: Univ. of Notre Dame, 2006.

Dunn, Dennis J. *The Catholic Church and the Soviet Government, 1939-1949*. East European Monograph, No. XXX. East European Quarterly. Boulder, Colorado, 1977.

__________. *The Catholic Church and Russia: Popes, Patriarchs, Tsars and Commissars*. Burlington, Vt.: Ashgate, 2004.

Hoffman, Deborah. *The Littlest Enemies: Children in the Shadow of the Gulag*. Bloomington, Ind.: Slavica Publishers, 2008.

Mailleux, S.J., Paul. *Exarch Leonid Feodorov: Bridgebuilder Between Rome and Moscow*. New York: P.J. Kenedy & Sons, 1964.

McCullagh. *Bolshevik Persecution of Christianity*. New York: E.P. Dutton and Company, 1924.

Nichols, Aidan, O.P. "Ekaterina Sienskaya Abrikosova (1892-1936): A Dominican Uniate Foundress in the Old Russia," 72 848 (1991) *New Blackfriars*, 164-172.

Osipova, Irina. *Hide Me Within Thy Wounds: The Persecution of the Catholic Church in the USSR*. Trans. Malcolm Gilbert. Fargo, North Dakota, 2003.

Parfentiev, Pavel. "Servant of God, Maria Catherine Sienskaia (Anna Ivanovna Abrikosova)." Trans. Joseph Lake. www.en.catholicmartyrs.org

Rossi, Jacques. *The Gulag Handbook: An Encyclopedia Dictionary of Soviet Penitentiary Institutions and Terms Related to the Forced Labor Camps*. Trans. William A. Burhans. New York, 1989.

Sister Mary of the Sacred Heart, OP. *To Courageously Know and Follow*

After Truth: The Life and Work of Mother Catherine Abrikosova. Summit, NJ: DNS Publications, 2013.

Snyder, Timothy. *Bloodlands: Europe Between Hitler and Stalin.* New York: Basic Books, 2010.

Solzhenitsyn, Alexander. *The Gulag Archipelago – 1918-1956.* Trans. Thomas P. Whitney. New York, 1973.

Solzhenitsyn, Alexander. *One Day in the Life of Ivan Denisovich.* Trans. H.T. Willetts. New York, 1991.

Tzouliadis, Tim. *The Forsaken: An American Tragedy in Stalin's Russia.* New York: Penguin, 2008.

Viola, Lynne. *The Unknown Gulag: The Lost World of Stalin's Special Settlements.* Oxford, 2007.

Zugger, Christopher Lawrence. *The Forgotten: Catholics of the Soviet Empire from Lenin through Stalin.* Syracuse: Syracuse University Press, 2001.

UNIVERSITY of NOTRE DAME

Book of Remembrance

Biographies of Catholic Clergy and Laity Repressed in the Soviet Union (USSR) from 1918 to 1953

Search biographies by keyword

Book of Remembrance: A Martyrology of the Catholic Church in the USSR, 1918-1953

Compiled by
Irina Osipova and
Fr. Bronisław Czaplicki
Published by the Apostolic
Administration for Catholics of
North European Russia, 2000,
With funding provided by
Renovabis

Now available on line
www.biographies.nd.edu

Hesburgh Libraries
University of Notre Dame

Working from State archives that became available after the collapse of the Soviet Union, Irina Osipova of the Memorial Society and Father Bronisław Czaplicki of the Catholic Martyrology Commission compiled brief biographies of close to 1,900 Latin and Eastern Rite Catholics who were persecuted under the Soviet regime. The collection includes both clergy and laity, some of whom are already known in the West, but most of whom were known only to family, friends and other parishioners. Some paid the ultimate price for their witness to the faith; some survived; but of many, the last words written are "fate thereafter unknown."

An essay by Father Czaplicki on the "History of the Persecutions" provides new insights into this tragic period of the history of the Church; the work also includes a bibliography.

The work was translated by Geraldine Kelley and the website was developed by Jaron Kennel, Andy Wetherill, Bozena Karol and Pamela Brzezinski under the guidance of Natasha Lyandres, Russian and East European Curator and Head of Rare Books and Special Collections at the University of Notre Dame.

The search features in the electronic version make this website an invaluable resource for specialists and non-specialists interested in the fate of Catholics under the Soviet regime.

Index of Additional Biographies

Brief biographies of many other Latin and Eastern Rite Catholics mentioned in this collection were among the 1,900 included in *Kniga pamiati: Martirolog Katholicheskoi Tserkvi v SSSR* (Moscow, 2000) [Book of Remembrance: A Martyrology of the Catholic Church in the USSR], compiled by Irina Osipova and Bronisław Czaplicki. The biographies of the persons listed below can be viewed at https://biographies.library.nd.edu.

Podlivakhina, Kapitolina
Polibina, Lyudmila
Polotebneva, Sofia
Posseypol, Anna
Pozen, Catherine
Preobrazhenskaya, Catherine
Prilezhayev, Sergey
Prokopiv, Fr. Vladimir
Prudovskaya, Iraida
Prussak, Anna
Remov, Abp. Bartholemew
Rossiyskaya, Maria
Rozhina, Elena (Sr. Evgenia)
Ryabinina, Lidia
Sapfirskaya, Vera
Sazonova, Sofia
Sharova, Margarita
Shimanovskaya, Aleksandra
Shorcheva, Lyubov
Skalski, Fr. Teofil
Smirnova, Rozalia
Solovey, Lyudviga
Soloviev, Fr. Sergey
Sorochinskaya, Tamara
Tire, Olga
Tolstoy, Fr. Nikolay
Tsakul, Fr. Mikhail
Vasilyev, Fr. Alexander
Vladimirov, Sergey
Werth, Vera
Wolf, Fr. Jacob
Zenkevich, Ksenia
Zerchaninov, Fr. Aleksey
Zhukovskaya, Emilia